Computing Concepts
with Java Essentials

Third Edition

Advanced Placement*
Computer Science Study Guide

FRANCES P. TREES

Drew University

CAY HORSTMANN

San Jose State University

JOHN WILEY & SONS, INC.

* *AP and Advanced Placement are registered trademarks of the College Entrance Examination Board, which was not involved in the production of and does not endorse this product.*

ACQUISITIONS EDITOR	Paul Crockett
MARKETING MANAGER	Katherine Hepburn
PROJECT MANAGER	Cindy Johnson
EDITORIAL ASSISTANT	Simon Durkin
COVER DESIGN	Susan Cyr / Harry Nolan

This book was set in Times New Roman and printed and bound by Victor Graphics, Inc. The cover was printed by Victor Graphics, Inc.

This book is printed on acid-free paper.

The paper in this book was manufactured by a mill whose forest management programs include sustained-yield harvesting of its timberlands. Sustained-yield harvesting principles ensure that the numbers of trees cut each year does not exceed the amount of new growth.

* AP and Advanced Placement are registered trademarks of the College Entrance Examination Board, which was not involved in the production of and does not endorse this product.

ISBN 0-471-44939-3

Printed in the United States of America

10 9 8 7 6 5 4 3 2 1

PREFACE

This Study Guide is designed to assist high school students preparing for the AP Computer Science Examination. It is organized and designed to accompany *Computing Concepts with Java Essentials, 3rd. ed.,* and *Big Java,* both by Cay Horstmann and published by John Wiley & Sons, Inc.

To the Student

Advanced Placement Computer Science is a college level course. As a student in an AP course, you are expected to understand college level material and to read college level textbooks. Because these texts may be used in multiple college courses, they contain material that is not tested on the AP Computer Science (CS) Examinations. This guide identifies and stresses the content that is tested on the AP CS Exams. This does not imply that you should skip the additional material in the text. Your teacher may include the additional material in your course and hold you responsible for that material. Some of the material that is not tested on the exam is extremely useful and may be included in your course. By following this guide, you will be able to focus on the topics included in the AP CS 2003-2004 Topic Outline and the elements of the AP Java subset that will be tested on the exam. Because the guide is designed for students taking either the A or the AB Computer Science exam, topics covered on the AB Exam are marked "AB only." If you are participating in an AP CS A course, this should not discourage you from reading these sections; it merely indicates that those topics will be tested on the AB exam and not the A Exam.

Features of the Study Guide

This guide is organized to help students recognize and master those topics that will be tested on both the A and AB examinations. Where applicable, each chapter includes:

Topic Summary
This section parallels the material in the textbook, adding additional examples and explanation of topics presented in the text. Students will find special emphasis here on topics that are likely to be tested.

Expanded Coverage of Topics not Found in the Text
Any topics in the AP CS Topic Outline or the AP Java subsets that are not covered in the text are presented in this section. In addition, Appendix A includes two additional textbook chapters that expand the coverage of data structures and algorithms needed for the AP exam.

Topics That are Useful but not Tested

This section alerts students to sections of the textbook that present useful features of the Java language. Although these sections are not required for the AP exam, they address features of Java programs that students are likely to encounter, or that they will need to progress in their programming ability.

Things to Remember When Taking the Exam

Each chapter restates important concepts and provides specific suggestions for avoiding common errors.

Key Words

Vocabulary used in the chapter is listed alphabetically here for student review and reference. Each key word is accompanied by the page number(s) where it is defined and/or discussed in the text.

Connecting the Detailed Topic Outline with the Text

This listing links the topics presented in the guide to the pages in the text where the same topics are covered.

Practice Questions (Multiple Choice and Free Response)

A large number of practice questions, modeled after those on the AP exam, are included in each chapter. The questions use the multiple-choice and free-response formats that students will encounter on the exam. Answers to the practice questions are provided in Appendix D.

AB Examination Topics

Any sections (and practice questions) that cover topics that will not be tested on the Computer Science A exam are clearly marked "AB only." Students who are preparing for the AB exam should be sure to complete these sections.

Web Resources

The AP Computer Science Topic Outline and Quick Reference Guides that students may use during the AP exam are available from the College Board's Web site at http://www.collegeboard.com/ap/students/compsci/. The Quick Reference Guides list the classes, interfaces, and methods contained in the Java subset covered by the AP exam. The AP Computer Science Topic Outline and the AP testable Java subsets may be revised from time to time, so you are encouraged to check for the most current version of these documents in the AP Computer Science Course Description on the College Board site.

Web sites associated with this guide and with *Computing Concepts with Java Essentials, 3rd. ed.,* and *Big Java* are another important resource for users of this guide. Cay Horstmann's site, http://www.horstmann.com, contains an expansion of Chapter 19, Help with Common Compilers, that provides installation tips and getting started instructions for the most commonly used Java compilers and environments. You will also find source code for programs in the text(s) and Appendix A, solutions to selected exercises in the text(s), frequently asked questions, a programming style guide, and more.

Many of these same items are also available from the Wiley Web site at http://www.wiley.com/college/horstmann, plus instructor resources not available to students.

Acknowledgments

It has been a sincere pleasure working with Cay Horstmann, master computer scientist and teacher, in the creation of this guide. I will always value this experience.

Many thanks to Paul Crockett for providing the opportunity for me to be involved in this project and to Cindy Johnson and her staff at Publishing Services for their hard work, support, and patience throughout. I am extremely grateful to Joe Kmoch, *Washington High School*, whose review offered many valuable comments and suggestions. I also am grateful to Judy Hromcik, *Arlington High School*, and David Levine, *St. Bonaventure University*, for their suggestions and encouragement.

My energy and enthusiasm for AP Computer Science is constantly renewed by the many AP CS teachers that I work with at AP CS workshops and, of course, by my AP CS students, some of whom are now AP CS teachers!

Finally, thanks to Eli for his patience, encouragement and support.

This work is dedicated to my mother.
F.T.

CONTENTS IN BRIEF

[*] Parenthesis indicates the corresponding chapter in *Computing Concepts with Java Essentials, 3rd ed.*, and *Big Java*.

CONTENTS

Appendices

CHAPTER 1

Introduction

TOPIC OUTLINE

■ Topic Summary

1.1   What is Advanced Placement?

The Advanced Placement (AP) Program is a joint educational undertaking of the College Board, secondary schools, and colleges. This program provides a means by which secondary schools and colleges collaborate to develop college-level course descriptions and exams which are accessible to high school students. By participating in an AP course and taking the AP Exam, you have an opportunity to earn college credit, placement in higher-level courses, or both. You will gain confidence and develop skills that will be indispensable in college.

The AP Program currently offers 35 courses.
- Art History
- Biology
- Calculus AB and Calculus BC

- Chemistry
- Computer Science A and Computer Science AB
- Economics: Macro and Economics: Micro
- English Language & Composition and English Literature & Composition
- Environmental Science
- European History
- French Language and French Literature
- German Language
- Government & Politics: Comparative and Government & Politics: US
- Human Geography
- International English Language
- Latin Literature and Latin Vergil
- Music Theory
- Physics B, Physics C: Electricity and Magnetism, and Physics C: Mechanics
- Psychology
- Spanish Language and Spanish Literature
- Statistics
- Studio Art Drawing, 2D Design, and 3D Design
- US History
- World History

Each offering is the responsibility of a development committee appointed by the College Board. The committee members include both high school AP teachers and college professors from the respective academic discipline. Committee members are appointed to three-year overlapping terms and represent a variety of types of secondary schools and colleges from various areas of the country.

1.1.1 Computer Science as an AP Subject

Although AP Exams were first offered in the early 1950s, the first Advanced Placement Computer Science (AP CS) Exam was not administered until 1984. The early 1980s were a time of significant change in the computer industry, with many companies manufacturing personal computers (PCs). PCs became more accessible and affordable; computer science departments flourished in universities; the number of college students interested in computer science increased rapidly. In response to this, the College Board added computer science to its list of Advanced Placement offerings. In 1984, a total of 4,263 students took the first AP CS Exam. In 2002, the number of AP CS Exams administered was close to 23,500.

Since 1984, Advanced Placement Computer Science has undergone many changes. These changes parallel the changes that have taken place in the computer science curriculum in colleges and universities. The most recent is the change in the implementation language from C++ to Java. Beginning in May 2004, the delivery language used on the AP CS Exams will be Java.

1.2 Who Takes AP Courses?

In 2001, over 1,400,000 AP Exams were taken by 844,741 students worldwide. In 2002, more than 1,500,000 AP Exams were taken in more than 80 different countries. A variety of initiatives have been undertaken to make the AP Program accessible to all. The federal AP Incentive Program provides monies in the form of grants to encourage low-income students to participate in AP. Some states use their own resources to provide support by encouraging or requiring AP courses in high schools and assisting with students' AP examination fees.

There is no risk in taking an AP Exam and there are numerous benefits. In addition to experiencing the academic demands of a college-level course, students who succeed on multiple AP Exams could earn enough credits to enter college with sophomore standing. Any credits earned can free valuable course time so more electives can be taken or a dual major pursued. It is up to the specific college to grant placement or credit.

1.2. Who takes AP Computer Science?

The intent of AP CS is to parallel the goals of the introductory sequence of courses for computer science majors in colleges. It is not expected that all students taking the AP CS Exam will major in computer science. In fact, AP CS can benefit students majoring in just about any area that involves problem solving and analysis.

Although AP CS is intended to be an introductory course, some secondary schools offer pre-AP courses that serve as prerequisites for AP CS. Students enrolling in AP CS should have skills in problem solving, writing, and algebra. The required prerequisite courses are usually designed to sharpen these skills and are taught in a variety of implementation languages.

1.3 What is the Difference between AP Computer Science A and AB?

Advanced Placement Computer Science is intended to be an introductory course in computer science. The content of AP Computer Science A parallels that of most first-semester college courses. The content of the AB course more closely corresponds to the first two semesters of college computer science. Additional topics covered in AP CS AB include formal analysis of algorithms, advanced data structures and algorithms, and a more detailed design of classes and their relationships and responsibilities.

AP CS A covers less material but should not be considered an easier exam. Offering two separate AP CS Exams allows secondary schools to choose the appropriate course offering based on the school's environment and resources. Many schools do not have the time, resources, and/or enrollment to offer both AP CS A and AP CS AB. Others have an extended computer science curriculum offering multiple computer courses and including both AP CS courses.

1.3.1 AP CS Course Organization

There are two essential parts to any computer science course: lecture and lab. In the lecture portion, the course material is presented. In the lab portion of the course, you apply what you have learned to solving problems on the computer. Lab time is handled by different schools in different ways. Time on the computer does not have to be part of class time but is an essential element of successful completion of the course. You should spend as much time as possible working on AP CS lab assignments. The more experience you have, the more knowledge you will absorb.

1.4 Which Elements of Computer Science Are on the AP Exam?

The elements of computer science that will be tested on the AP CS Exams include basic programming concepts (branches and loops, method calls), object-oriented programming (classes, interfaces, inheritance), data structures, and algorithms. The focus of the exams is not the Java programming language. Java is a very large language and cannot be mastered in the AP course. The exam will focus on the elements of computer science.

The tested materials are well defined in College Board documents. These resources are: the AP CS Topic Outline, the AP CS Java Subsets, the Quick References for the Java AP subset of classes, and the current case study documents. Before taking the exam, you should be familiar with the material contained in these documents.

1.4.1 Format of the AP CS Exam

The AP CS Exam is divided into two parts. Part 1 contains 40 multiple-choice questions which must be answered in 1 hour and 15 minutes. Part 2 contains 4 free-response questions with a time limit of 1 hour and 45 minutes. The two parts of the exam are weighted equally when determining the final AP score. The following documents are provided for use during both sections of the exam:

- Quick Reference for A Exam *or* Quick Reference for AB Exam
- Case Study Materials
  - Source code for visible classes
  - Index for the source code of the visible classes
  - Summary of class documentation for black box classes

1.5 Strategies for Taking the AP CS Exam

You first should decide which AP CS Exam you are prepared to take, A or AB. If you are enrolled in an AP CS A course and you are following that curriculum then there really is no decision and you should sign up for the A exam. However, if you are enrolled in AP CS AB, or if you are enrolled in AP CS A and doing additional work on the AB topics, you need to make a decision. The A exam is not necessarily easier then the AB exam but it does cover significantly less material. In order to feel comfortable with the AB exam, you need to be very, very comfortable with designing classes, and understand and be able to apply advanced data structures and algorithms.

You will be given supplemental materials that you may use during both parts of the exam. These materials are available to you throughout the entire year. Do not wait until the exam to become familiar with them. On exam day, briefly scan over these documents so that you are familiar with the official resources that you will be able to reference.

1.5.1 Strategies for Part 1

The first part of the exam contains 40 multiple-choice questions. Usually the questions are in a somewhat increasing order of difficulty but questions that are not difficult for one person may seem difficult to another.

- Read each question carefully. If you do not know the answer, circle the question, skip it for the moment and go on. Come back to that question later if you have time.
- Do not haphazardly guess on the multiple-choice questions. There is a deduction of one-quarter of a point for each wrong answer. Omitted questions do not add or subtract points from the total. If you can eliminate two of the possible choices, then your odds of choosing the correct answer are better.
- Review all possible answers before choosing one.
- If there is code in the question, read the entire question before reading the code.
- There may be several questions dealing with one code segment or problem specification. If you do not know the answer to the first question in a series, do not assume the following questions in the series are more difficult. Read them all.

1.5.1   Strategies for Part 2

The second part of the exam contains four free-response questions. Each of these four questions is weighted equally. Usually the questions are in a somewhat increasing order of difficulty but, as with the multiple-choice questions, what is difficult for one person may not be difficult for another. If the first question seems difficult, go on to another.

- Don't panic if the question seems extremely long. Read the question introduction and the comments in the code. Many times the comments outline an algorithm that solves the problem.
- Read the question carefully before you begin to write your answer. Read the question again after you answer the question to make sure that you satisfied the problem specifications.
- Most of the free-response questions have more than one part. If you do not know how to answer the first part, do not give up on the entire problem. Read all parts of the problem. Sometimes the last part of the problem is the easiest part to answer. Each part is graded independently from other parts.
- In a multiple-part free-response question, part (b) or part (c) may indicate that you may use a call to a method you wrote in part (a): "Assume that this method works as intended regardless of what you wrote for part (a)." This is usually a hint that the call to the method from part (a) will be useful. You may be able to answer this part of the question even if you skipped the previous parts.
- Do not worry about the efficiency of your algorithm unless explicitly told to do so.
- Do not include "extra" code in a solution.
  - Do not add `System.out.println` statements unless required by the problem.
  - Do not write code to check preconditions. Assume preconditions are satisfied.
- Though not an absolute rule, stay within the AP Java subsets when writing code.
- If you are told to justify your answer, you need to provide an explanation. Points will be deducted if you do not include a justification.
- Strive for clarity in your code.
  - Indent properly.
  - Use meaningful variables names.
  - Use braces where needed and for clarity.
- Comment only when absolutely necessary.
- The first solution on your paper is the solution that will be graded. If you rewrite a solution to a problem, be sure to cross out the unwanted solution. Do not waste time erasing.

- If you are running out of time, write as much code as you have time to write. Do not write comments on how you would solve the problem if you had time. No credit is given for comments!
- The exam answer booklet provides plenty of blank space for all of your answers. You should not run out of room. But, if you do, continue your work on a blank page in the back of the booklet. Clearly label the page with the problem number and indicate in the original space provided where the exam reader should find your answer. If there are no blank pages and you use additional paper, your paper has to be appropriately labeled. Your exam proctor should provide you with information on how to do this. Do not just include an unlabeled piece of paper in your answer booklet.
- Be neat! Real people have to read your answers!

1.5.3 *Materials You Should Bring to the Exam*

- Several #2 pencils.
- Erasers: Bring erasers that erase! Incorrect multiple choice answers need to be completely erased.
- A watch: If the start time and end time are not clearly stated on the board, take note of these on your exam booklet. Look at your watch frequently.
- Your social security number for identification purposes.
- A photo I.D. if you are taking the exam at a school other than your high school.

1.5.4 *Last-Minute Reminders*

- Get a good night's sleep.
- Eat a good breakfast.
- Try to relax!
- Enjoy the exam. You worked very hard all year to prepare for this day!

1.6   How Are the Exams Graded?

The score on the multiple-choice part is equal to the number of questions answered correctly minus one-quarter of the number of incorrect answers. This part of the exam is graded by computer.

The free-response questions are graded by a group of experienced AP computer science teachers and university computer science professors. Each of the four questions is scored on a 9-point scale. A grading rubric is developed at the reading and used to insure that the student solutions are graded in a consistent manner.

The multiple-choice section and the free-response section are weighted equally when determining the composite score. A corresponding AP Grade (1–5) is then assigned.

Meaning of AP Grades

AP Grade	Possible Interpretation
5	Extremely Well Qualified
4	Well Qualified
3	Qualified
2	Possibly Qualified
1	No Recommendation

1.6.1   Special Recognition for Doing Well

The College Board recognizes excellent student performance on AP Exams through the AP Scholar Awards. In 2002, over 13,000 students were designated AP Scholars. This distinction is based on the student's average AP Exam grades (from that year and previous years) and the AP grade requirement for the specific award. There are 10 different AP Scholar distinctions including Scholar, Scholar with Honors, State Scholar, and International Scholar. You may cite the AP Scholar Awards among your achievements on college applications.

The Siemens Foundation recognizes America's most promising science and mathematics students by awarding monetary scholarships to 24 students, two females and two males in each of the six College Board regions. These awards are presented to the students who have earned the highest number of AP scores on the following AP Exams: Biology, Calculus BC, Chemistry, Computer Science AB, Environmental Science, Physics C (Physics C: Mechanics and Physics C: Electricity and Magnetism each count as half), and Statistics.

1.7   How Should this Guide be Used to Prepare for the AP CS Exam?

This study guide is intended to be used in combination with *Computing Concepts with Java Essentials,* 3rd ed., or with *Big Java* (both written by Cay Horstmann and published by John Wiley & Sons, Inc.). Because these texts are college-level texts, they include material that is not tested on the AP CS Exam.

This study guide will lead you through the chapters of the text, focusing on the topics that will be tested on the AP CS Exams. The elements of each chapter are:
- Topic summary
- Expanded coverage of material that is not found in the text
- Topics that are useful but not tested (if applicable)
- Things to remember when taking the AP Exam (if applicable)
- Key words (with references to the text)
- Connecting the topic outline to the text
- Practice questions

1.8   Where Can I Get More Information?

You can access general information about the Advanced Placement Program at:
http://www.collegeboard.com/ap/students/index.html

Information about the AP Scholar Awards can be found at:
http://www.collegeboard.com/ap/students/benefits/awards.html

Siemens Foundation Award information can be found at:
http://www.siemens-foundation.org/apawards/awards.htm

Specific information about AP Computer Science can be found at:
http://www.collegeboard.com/ap/students/compsci/

1.8.1   Where Can I Get the Text Ancillaries?

The student companion site for *Computing Concepts with Java Essentials,* 3rd ed., is:
http://www.wiley.com/college/horstmann

Cay Horstmann's site for *Computing Concepts with Java Essentials,* 3rd ed. is:
http://www.horstmann.com/ccj.html

1.9   Are There Other Suggestions for Success in AP CS?

- The AP Computer Science Examinations will include questions based on the current AP CS case study. Chapter 18 of this guide describes why and how the case study is used in AP CS courses and on the AP CS Exam. Begin reading the case study documents early in the year so that the materials will be familiar to you *before* the day of the exam.
- Keep good notes of your teacher's lectures.
- Keep your graded programming assignments and review your teacher's comments on the assignments. Don't just look at the grade on the paper and throw it away!
- Do not be afraid to ask for help on your assignments or to seek alternate solutions to problems.
- Volunteer to help your classmates debug their programs. Looking at someone else's code is not as easy as looking at your own code and may help you when exam time comes around.

CHAPTER 2

Hardware and Software

■ Topic Summary

2.1   Hardware Components

For the AP CS Exam, you are expected to have a working knowledge of major hardware components, system software, and responsible uses of computers. This chapter will review some commonly used vocabulary that may be included in multiple-choice questions.

2.1.1   *The Anatomy of a Computer*

The basic hardware components in a computer include

- the Central Processing Unit (CPU)
- primary memory
- secondary memory
- peripheral devices

The Central Processing Unit (CPU) is the "brain" of the computer. The CPU processes individual commands or statements of a program. The CPU consists of a chip or a small number of chips. Each chip contains transistors that send and receive electrical signals that control program execution, data transfer, and arithmetic operations. Processors execute machine instructions and processors from different companies (e.g., Intel Pentium, Sun SPARC, PowerPC G4) have different sets of machine instructions.

Primary, or main, memory stores software and data while it is being used. Primary storage, or Random Access Memory (RAM), loses its data when the power is turned off.

Secondary memory stores data in a permanent way. It is much cheaper and slower than primary memory. Some secondary storage devices popular today are the hard disk, the compact disk (CD), the digital video disc or digital versatile disc (DVD), the floppy disk (diskette), and the USB keychain memory device.

Input/Output (I/O) devices enable us to communicate with the computer. Input devices such as the keyboard or the mouse are used to input data and programs. Monitors and printers are used to display information. Other computer peripherals include speakers, digital cameras, scanners, light pens, and barcode readers.

2.2   System Software

A compiler translates a program written in a high-level language into machine code. An interpreter is similar to a compiler but translates and executes a small segment (perhaps one statement) at a time. Usually, a Java program is entered into the computer through an editor. It is then submitted to the compiler. The editor and compiler may be part of an integrated development environment (IDE). The compiler checks the program and reports any syntax or grammar errors such as missing semicolons. If the program is free of compilation errors, the compiler translates the Java program code into Java bytecode. The bytecode is written for the Java Virtual Machine (JVM). A JVM has been written for every major operating system. The JVM is like a simulated CPU that lives on top of an operating system. The JVM is the reason that the same Java program will run on different operating systems such as Windows XP, UNIX, Linux, or Mac OS X. The JVM, or Java interpreter, reads the bytecode and executes the program.

The operating system manages the computer resources. Typical services provided by an operating system include deciding the priority in which programs are to run, loading the programs into memory, managing files, and printing. It is the operating system that makes the computer user-friendly (easy to use). *Random Fact 9.1* of your text discusses operating system tasks in detail.

2.3   Types of Systems

Many of us own single-user systems. A single-user system is a self-contained unit. Many computer labs are permanently connected to a local network. These computers are connected together so that information can be shared among them. The Internet is a world-wide network.

2.4   A Simple Program

Section 1.8 of your text introduces the traditional "Hello World!" program. This section explains the basic syntax of a trivial Java program. A string is printed to the screen using `System.out.println`. You should enter and compile this simple program using the guidelines in Sections 1.8 and 1.10 in your text. By doing so, you will become familiar with the environment in which you will be programming.

2.4.1   Escape Sequences

Some characters have a special meaning in Java and cannot be used alone as characters in a string. Two such characters are the backslash (\ ) and the double quotes ("). The backslash is used as an escape character and the double quotes character either begins or ends a string literal. Java provides escape sequences that enable us to include these characters as characters in a string.

Example 2.1

```
System.out.println("C:\\My Documents\\Hello.java");
System.out.println("He said: \"Hello!\"");
System.out.println("One\nTwo\nThree");
```

will print

> C:\My Documents\Hello.java
> He said: "Hello!"
> One
> Two
> Three

2.4.2   Java Comments

The two types of comments that you may see on the AP CS Exam are the single line comment

```
// This is a comment
```

and the multi-line comment.

```
/*
This is a comment
This is another comment
*/
```

These comments are discussed in *Advanced Topic 1.1* of your text.

2.5   Errors

Our first attempt in writing, compiling, and executing a program is not always perfect. Many of our errors can be classified as syntax errors. A syntax error is a violation of the rules of the programming language. The compiler will detect syntax errors. Missing semicolons and missing or unmatched braces and parentheses are examples of syntax errors. We may also have an error that causes a result other than the result that we originally intended. This is called a run-time or logic error. A logic error causes a program to take an action that the programmer did not intend. You must test your programs for logic errors.

■ Expanded Coverage of Material That Is Not Found in the Text

- Included in the AP CS Topic Outline is "Responsible Use of Computer Systems." This topic is one that you deal with every time you access information on your computer.
    - The Association for Computing Machinery (ACM) has a Code of Ethics and Professional Conduct that every member of ACM is expected to uphold. This Code of Ethics is accessible on-line at <u>http://www.acm.org/ constitution/code.html</u> and best summarizes the issues related to this topic in the AP CS curriculum. The General Moral Imperatives expected to be upheld include:
        - ◆ Contribute to society and human well-being.
        - ◆ Avoid harm to others.
        - ◆ Be honest and trustworthy.
        - ◆ Be fair and take action not to discriminate.
        - ◆ Honor property rights including copyrights and patents.
        - ◆ Give proper credit for intellectual property.
        - ◆ Respect the privacy of others.
        - ◆ Honor confidentiality.

Also included in this on-line document are Professional Imperatives and Leadership Imperatives.

-
    - The Computer Ethics Institute has written "The Ten Commandments of Computer Ethics" which can be accessed at <u>http://www.brook.edu/ dybdocroot/its/cei/overview/Ten_Commandments_of_Computer_Ethics.htm</u>.
    - The Computer Professionals for Social Responsibility is a public-interest group of computer scientists and others concerned about the impact of technology on society. General information about papers and projects can be accessed at <u>http://www.cpsr.org/cpsr/about-cpsr.html</u>.

■ Topics That Are Useful But Not Tested

- Becoming familiar with your computer system and the Java compiler is the first important step toward a successful programming experience. Sections 1.7, 1.8, and 1.10 of your text guide you through writing, compiling, and executing your first Java program.
- *Productivity Hint 1.1* discusses developing a strategy for keeping backup copies of your work before a disaster strikes. (The key word is *before*.)
- Escape sequences are useful for including international characters in a string. *Advanced Topic 1.2* discusses the Unicode encoding scheme.

■ Things to Remember When Taking the AP Exam

- Although points are not deducted for missing semicolons on the free-response part of the AP CS Exam, try to remember to write clear, correct code in answering all questions.
- Time is limited during the AP CS Exam. Do not spend time writing comments in your free-response answers unless your solution needs to be explained or you are specifically instructed to include comments.

■ Key Words

You should understand the terms below. The AP CS Exam questions may include references to these terms. The citation in parentheses next to each term identifies the page number where it is defined and/or discussed in *Computing Concepts with Java Essentials*, 3rd ed., and *Big Java*.

backup (16)
case sensitivity (17)
chip (3)
class (18)
comments (20)
compiler (10)
computer program (2)
Central Processing Unit
   (CPU) (3)
editor (26)
escape sequences (23)
file (14)
integrated circuit (3)

Integrated Development
   Environment (IDE) (14)
Input/Output (I/O) devices
   (6)
Java interpreter (27)
Java Virtual Machine (JVM)
   (8)
library packages (13)
logic error (24)
`main` (20)
method (19)
network (5)
peripheral (6)

primary storage (4)
Random Access Memory
   (RAM) (4)
removable storage device (5)
run-time error (24)
secondary storage (4)
statement (20)
string (21)
syntax error (24)
transistors (3)
variable (10)

■ Connecting the Detailed Topic Outline to the Text

The citations in parentheses identify where information in the outline can be located in *Computing Concepts with Java Essentials*, 3rd ed., and *Big Java*.

- Hardware Components
  - The Anatomy of a Computer (3–8)
- System Software (8–11, 386–388)
- Types of Systems (5, 388)
- A Simple Program (17–21)
  - Escape Sequences (23)
  - Java Comments (22)
- Errors (24–26)

■ Practice Questions

Multiple Choice

1. Every Java program contains a class with

    a. a `main` method
    b. a `System.out.println` statement
    c. a compiler
    d. a string
    e. comments

2. A syntax error is a violation of programming language rules. Syntax errors are detected by

    a. the operating system
    b. the compiler
    c. the Java Virtual Machine
    d. the Java interpreter
    e. the CPU

3. What output is produced by the following code segment?

    ```
    System.out.println("\"One\"");
    System.out.print(2 + "Two");
    System.out.println(" \"Three\""+3);
    ```

    a. *"One"*
        2Two "Three"3

    b. *One*
        2Two
        Three3

    c. *"One"*
        2"Two" "Three"3

    d. *"One"*
        2"Two"
        "Three"3

    e. Nothing is printed. There is a syntax error.

4. Consider the following output.

```
*
**
***
```

Which of the following code segments prints the design above?

I.
```java
System.out.println("*");
System.out.println("**");
System.out.println("***");
```

II.
```java
System.out.print("*\n");
System.out.print("**\n");
System.out.print("***\n");
```

III.
```java
System.out.println("*\n**\n***\n");
```

   a. I only
   b. II only
   c. III only
   d. I and III only
   e. I, II, and III

5. Which of the following is not a legal string?

   a. `"//"`
   b. `"\n\""`
   c. `"\"\\"`
   d. `"\n\n"`
   e. `"\""\\"`

Free Response Questions

1a. You are to complete the program below so that the following sentence is printed to the screen:

The secret to success is in C:\Temp\Success.txt.

```java
public class Basics
{
    public static void main(String[] args]
    {
        // Code goes here
    }
}
```

1b. Revise the program from part a so that each word of the sentence is written on a separate line.

> *The*
> *secret*
> *to*
> *success*
> *is*
> *in*
> *C:\Temp\Success.txt.*

CHAPTER 3

An Introduction to Objects and Classes

■ Topic Summary

3.1 Using and Constructing Objects

Object-orientation is an important approach in software development and design that supports the development of programs that are easy to understand, can be adapted to different situations, and can be reused in multiple contexts. *Objects* and *classes* are the central concepts of object-oriented programming and are a primary focus of the AP Computer Science courses.

You can think of a *class* as a factory for objects or a blueprint from which an object is created. Many objects can be created using the same blueprint. An *object* is an instance of a class that you can manipulate in your program. Each object has *behavior* and *state*. In order to manipulate an object, the object needs to be constructed or created by using the `new` operator.

If a `Student` constructor is defined to accept a student's first name, last name, and identification number, a `Student` object might be constructed with

```
new Student("John", "Smith", "111111");
```

To construct an object, you use the `new` operator, the name of the class, and a list of parameters that are required by the class. The `new` operator allocates memory to hold an object. A call to

```
new Student("John", "Smith", "111111");
```

constructs the `Student` object below.

```
          Student
   ┌──────────────────────────┐
   │  fName = [  "John"   ]    │
   │  lName = [  "Smith"  ]    │
   │     id = [ "111111"  ]    │
   │  sumOfGrades = [  0.0  ]  │
   │ numberOfGrades = [  0  ]  │
   └──────────────────────────┘
```

Constructors do not always require information. Consider the call:

```
new Student();
```

This is a call to a constructor that requires no parameters (information passed to the constructor). This call will construct a `Student` object with default values where "" denotes an empty string.

```
          Student
   ┌──────────────────────────┐
   │  fName = [    ""    ]     │
   │  lName = [    ""    ]     │
   │     id = [    ""    ]     │
   │  sumOfGrades = [  0.0  ]  │
   │ numberOfGrades = [  0  ]  │
   └──────────────────────────┘
```

The instance fields `sumOfGrades` and `numberOfGrades` will change in the lifetime of the object and are not part of the information passed to the constructor. We will see how these fields get values a little later.

3.2   Object Variables

In order to do anything with the object that we created, we must store a reference to the object in an object variable.

```
Student artStudent = new Student("John", "Smith", "111111");
```

or

```
Student csStudent = new Student();
```

The object variables `artStudent` and `csStudent` are references to `Student` objects. There can be many instances of a class. Each object (or instance) has its own memory that contains specific information about it. An object variable stores the object's location. Every variable has a type that identifies the kind of information it can contain. `artStudent` contains a reference to a `Student` object; once declared as a reference to a `Student` object, it cannot reference a `double`, a `Rectangle` object, or any other type of object.

```
Student csStudent = new Student();       // This is OK.
Rectangle cerealBox = new Rectangle();   // This is OK.

Student csStudent = new Rectangle();     // WRONG!
Student csStudent = 4.35;                // WRONG!
```

You can choose any appropriate variable names for object variables. Rules for naming variables are discussed in Section 2.2 of your text. Object variables must be initialized before you access them. In the declaration,

```
Student bioStudent;
```

`bioStudent` is not initialized. The new operator creates a new object and returns its location.

```
Student bioStudent;
bioStudent = new Student();   // Now initialized
```

You can have multiple references to the same object.

```
Student chemStudent = bioStudent;
```

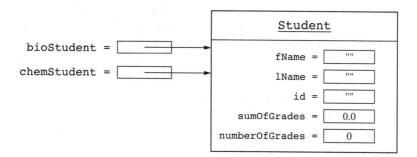

3.2.1   Importing Classses

Java classes are grouped into packages. `System` and `String` classes are in the `java.lang` package. All classes from the `java.lang` package are automatically imported to all Java programs. These classes are considered to be fundamental necessities to most Java programs. We do not need to explicitly import `java.lang`. All Java programs can be thought of as having the following `import` statement.

```
import java.lang.*;
```

The asterisk means that all classes of the `java.lang` package will be imported.

To use classes from other packages, we need to explicitly include an `import` statement or fully qualify the class name. For example, the `Rectangle` class is contained in the `java.awt` package. In order to include a `Rectangle` object in our program, we need to import the `java.awt.Rectangle` class.

```
import java.awt.Rectangle;
```

or use the fully qualified name for the `Rectangle` class:

```
java.awt.Rectangle box = new java.awt.Rectangle();
```

The package name is `java.awt`. The class name is `Rectangle`.

3.3   Defining a Class

Most classes contain attributes (data) and behaviors (methods). Section 2.3 of your text looks at the very simple `Greeter` class. This class has one behavior (method) and no attributes (data). The definition of this simple class is shown in your text. `Greeter` contains one method, `sayHello`.

Example 3.1

```
1      public String sayHello()
2      {
3          String message = "Hello, World!";
4          return message;
5      }
```

Line 1 is the method header. `public` is the access modifier and controls which other methods can call this method. `String` is the return type of the method. The tag `void` would be used here in its place if no value is returned. The method name is `sayHello`. The parameters of a method would be included within parentheses after the method name. The method `sayHello` has no parameters.
Line 2 indicates the beginning of the method body.
Lines 3 and 4 contain the body of the method.
Line 3 stores the address of the `String` object `Hello, World!` in the `String` reference variable `message`.
Line 4 returns this reference to the calling method.
Line 5 indicates the end of the method body.

Example 3.2

```
1      public void sayHello()
2      {
3          System.out.println("Hello, World!");
4      }
```

In this example, line 1 has the tag `void`. No value is returned. *Hello, World!* is printed to the screen.

3.4   Testing a Class

In order to test your class, you can use an interactive development environment such as BlueJ or you can write a simple test class. This is discussed in Section 2.4 of your text. If you choose to write a test class, a good organizational technique is to name the test class with the name of the class you are testing followed by the word "Test". For example, a test class for the `Greeter` class will have the name `GreeterTest`. A test class for the `Student` class will have the name `StudentTest`. The `StudentTest` class will be in a separate file named `StudentTest.java`.

3.5   Instance Fields

An object of a class has its own set of instance fields (variables) that define its state (data). These instance fields are usually hidden from the programmer who uses the class (the client program). This process of hiding the data and providing methods for data access is called *encapsulation*. Think of this as a "black box" where the operations are visible and the data and implementation are hidden. *Information hiding* refers to the idea that the client, or user, of a class does not need to know about the inner workings of the class in order to use it. A typical real-life analogy would be that you do not need to understand the inner circuitry of a radio in order to use the radio. To remain true to the meaning of object-oriented programming, our data (or instance fields) should be declared `private`. Access to this data should be allowed only through the methods defined in the class. Declaring instance fields as `private` does not permit access from methods outside the class. In the AP Java subset, all instance fields are declared as `private`. Example 3.3 shows an incomplete definition of our `Student` class. The attributes (data) are declared as `private`. The `public` method `getID` returns the value of the private instance variable `id`.

Example 3.3

```
public class Student
{
    // More code here

    public String getID()
    {
        return id;
    }

    // More code here

    private String fName;
    private String lName;
    private String id;
    private double sumOfGrades;
    private int numberOfGrades;
}
```

A client program (or test class) containing the statements

```
Student artStudent = new Student("John", "Smith", "111111");
System.out.println("The student ID is: " + artStudent.getID());
```

would print *The student ID is 111111*. The expression `artStudent.getID()` calls the `getID` method of the `artStudent` object. The `id` of `artStudent` is returned to the calling method.

The `System.out.println` statement illustrates string concatenation, an operation that uses the + operator to combine two strings, or a string and a numerical value, to create a new string. For example, `"dog"` + `"house"` prints `"doghouse"`. String concatenation is commonly used in `System.out.println` statements. Notice that the `System.out.println` method call has one `String` parameter.

3.6   Constructors

Constructors contain instructions to initialize objects. A constructor has the same name as the class and does not have a return type. The syntax for a constructor is:

```
accessSpecifier  ClassName  (parameterType  parameterName,  ...)
{
    constructor  implementation
}
```

The `Student` constructor specifies how a `Student` object should be initialized.

Example 3.4

```
public Student(String first, String last, String idNumber)
{
    fName = first;
    lName = last;
    id = idNumber;
    sumOfGrades = 0.0;
    numberOfGrades = 0;
}
```

Private instance variables are initialized.

3.7   Designing the Public Interface of a Class

The `Student` class in Example 3.4 contains five private instance variables. When implementing the `Student` class, we need to think about what attributes a student has. To begin, a student has a first and last name, and an ID number. We will include methods that will retrieve this information for the client program (test class). The methods that return the first name, last name, and ID number will have a `String` return type because these instance variables are of type `String`. The student will also be accumulating test grades throughout the term. We will also include a method `addGrade` that allows the user to add a grade for a student. This method will increment `numberOfGrades` and add the grade to the `sumOfGrades`. The method `addGrade` will have a `void` return type because no value will be returned. We can then have a method `getGpa` that returns the average of the student grades (an easy calculation—if we assume that each grade has equal weight!).

The process of determining the key features of our class is called *abstraction*. Abstraction permits us to hide complex details and focus only on the level of detail that is necessary for our application.

We will include two constructors in the `Student` class. In addition to the constructor in Example 3.4, we will add a constructor that has no parameters. This constructor will initialize the private instance variables with default values.

3.7.1   Overloading

Since our additional constructor will have no parameters, the statement

```
Student csStudent = new Student();
```

initializes the private instance fields to default values that will be assigned in the constructor implementation.

When the same name is used for more than one method or constructor, we say the name is *overloaded*. Constructors are commonly overloaded. Methods can also be overloaded provided that their signatures are different. The signature of a method is determined from the number, types, and order of its parameters. For overloading purposes, the return type of the method does not matter and is not included when referring to the method signature.

3.8   Commenting the Public Interface

When you define classes, you should include documentation of your methods and constructors. Section 2.8 of your text explains how to use the `javadoc` utility and implement `javadoc` comments. In the examples presented in this guide, we use `javadoc` comments. Because `javadoc` comments are not part of the AP CS subset, however, the practice questions will not use `javadoc` comments. The AP CS Java subset uses `/* */`, and `//` comments.

3.9   Specifying the Implementation of a Class

Now that we have some idea of the public interface for the `Student` class, let's look at the implementation.

Example 3.5

```
/**
    A Student has a first name, a last name, and an ID number.
    When a student grade is entered, it is added to sumOfGrades and
    the numberOfGrades is incremented by 1.
*/
public class Student
{
```

```java
/**
   Constructs a Student with the given information.
   @param first is the student's first name
   @param last is the student's last name
   @param idNumber is the student identification number
*/
public Student(String first, String last, String idNumber)
{
   fName = first;
   lName = last;
   id = idNumber;
   sumOfGrades = 0.0;
   numberOfGrades = 0;
}

/**
   Constructs a Student with default values.
*/
public Student()
{
   fName = "";
   lName = "";
   id = "";
   sumOfGrades = 0.0;
   numberOfGrades = 0;
}

/**
   Gets the first name of the Student.
   @return the first name of the Student
*/
public String getFirstName()
{
   return fName;
}

/**
   Gets the last name of the Student.
   @return the last name of the Student
*/
public String getLastName()
{
   return lName;
}

/**
   Gets the ID number of the Student.
   @return the id of the Student
*/
public String getID()
{
   return id;
```

```
    }

    /**
        Modifies sumOfGrades and numberOfGrades to include new
        grade.
        @param grade is new grade to add to student record
    */
    public void addGrade(double grade)
    {
        sumOfGrades = sumOfGrades + grade;
        numberOfGrades = numberOfGrades + 1;
    }

    /**
        Gets the GPA of the Student.
        The number of grades is greater than 0.
        @return the grade point average of the Student
    */
    public double getGPA()
    {
        return sumOfGrades / numberOfGrades;
    }

    private String fName;
    private String lName;
    private String id;
    private double sumOfGrades;
    private int numberOfGrades;
}
```

Example 3.5 contains two constructors. A constructor with no parameters is called a default constructor. This type of constructor initializes the private instance fields to default values.

HOWTO 2.1 lists seven helpful steps to follow when designing and implementing a class.

3.10   Variable Types

The `Student` class demonstrates the use of two types of variables: instance fields (`fName`, `lName`, `id`, `sumOfGrades`, `numberOfGrades`) and parameter variables (`grade`). The implementation of the `BankAccount` class in Section 2.9 of your text is another example of a simple class. The `BankAccount` class demonstrates the use of three types of variables: instance fields (`balance`), local variables (`newBalance`), and parameter variables (`initialBalance` and `amount`). Instance fields and parameter and local variables have two major differences:

- Life span: Instance fields belong to an object and live as long as some client method refers to the object. Parameter variables and local variables belong to a method. They die (go out of scope) when the method is over.
- Initialization: You must initialize all local variables. If you do not initialize local variables, the compiler complains. Parameter variables are initialized with the values that are supplied in the method call. All instance fields should be initialized but if

they are not, those instance fields that are numbers are initialized to 0 and those instance fields that are object references are initialized to a special `null` value. The AP subsets do not include the rules for default initialization (with `0`, `false`, or `null`).

3.11   Explicit and Implicit Method Parameters

In Example 3.5, the `addGrade` method changes the value of the private instance fields, `sumOfGrades` and `numberOfGrades`, of a `Student` object:

```
public void addGrade(double grade)
{
    sumOfGrades = sumOfGrades + grade;    // adds grade to
                                          // sumOfGrades
    numberOfGrades = numberOfGrades + 1;  // increments
                                          // numberOfGrades by 1
}
```

Each `Student` object has its own instance fields. Calls to `addGrade` could be

```
artStudent.addGrade(90);
artStudent.addGrade(96);
```
or
```
csStudent.addGrade(85.5);
```

The object whose `sumOfGrades` and `numberOfGrades` will be set is determined by the method call. The statement

```
sumOfGrades = sumOfGrades + grade;
```

will add `grade` to the current object's `sumOfGrades`. The implicit parameter of a method is the object on which the method is invoked. The `this` reference denotes this implicit parameter.

```
sumOfGrades = sumOfGrades + grade;
```

is equivalent to

```
this.sumOfGrades = sumOfGrades + grade;
```

When an instance field is used in the implementation of a method, the compiler automatically applies the `this` parameter. The explicit parameter in `addGrade` is `grade` because it is explicitly named in the method definition.

■ Topics That Are Useful But Not Tested

- If you are not using an integrated development environment, you can invoke the editor, the compiler, the linker, and the program to test manually by using command line editing. This is explained in *Productivity Hint 2.1.*
- The `javadoc` utility produces HTML files created from the documentation in your code. Most of the comments included in your text use `javadoc` comments. This utility is explained in *Productivity Hint 2.2.* Your IDE may provide a tool that will produce the HTML files from your `javadoc` comments.

■ Things to Remember When Taking the AP Exam

- Initialize all objects before you access them.
- Do not try to reset an object by calling a constructor. You cannot invoke a constructor on an existing object. This is explained in *Common Error 2.2* of your text.
- Although instance fields are initialized with default values if you do not initialize them, the AP Exam will not test these rules. You will be expected to implement constructors that initialize the instance variables.
- When calling methods from a test class (client program), include the implicit parameter in the call.

```
artStudent.getID();   // This is OK.
getID();   // WRONG! You need to supply an object reference.
```

- Do not name parameter variables of methods with the same variable name as your instance fields. A parameter variable with the same name as an instance variable leads to complications when referencing the instance variable in the method.
- Remember to include a `return` statement if your method is to return a value.
- Do not attempt to access `private` data or methods from outside the class. If you need to use the value of an instance field, look for an accessor method that returns the value of the instance field. If there isn't one, then there probably is no need for you to access that private value outside the class.

■ Key Words

You should understand the terms below. The AP CS Exam questions may include references to these terms. The citation in parentheses next to each term identifies the page number where it is defined and/or discussed in *Computing Concepts with Java Essentials*, 3rd ed., and *Big Java.*

abstraction (53)	import (41)	overloading (53)
access specifier (42)	instance fields (47)	package (39)
class (35)	interface (34)	parameter (43)
concatenation (48)	method (34)	private (47)
constructor (49)	method body (42)	public (47)
encapsulation (47)	`new` (36)	`return` (44)
explicit parameter (68)	object (34)	return type (42)
implementation (32)	object reference (38)	`this` (68)
implicit parameter (68)	object variable (37)	type (37)

■ Connecting the Detailed Topic Outline to the Text

The citations in parentheses identify where information in the outline can be located in *Computing Concepts with Java Essentials*, 3rd ed., and *Big Java*.

- Using and Constructing Objects (34–36)
- Object Variables (37–38)
  - Importing Classes (41)
- Defining a Class (42–44)
- Testing a Class (44–46)
- Instance Fields (47–49)
- Constructors (49–51)
- Designing the Public Interface of a Class (51 - 53)
  - Overloading (53)
- Commenting the Public Interface (54 - 56)
- Specifying the Implementation of a Class (58 - 62)
- Variable Types (66)
- Explicit and Implicit Method Parameters (67–68)

■ Practice Questions

Multiple Choice

1. Which of the following statements about *classes* is true?

   a. Classes are examples of objects.
   b. Classes are factories or blueprints for objects.
   c. Every class belongs to an object.
   d. The interface of a class is hidden from the user.
   e. The `new` operator is used to construct a new class.

2. Constructors are always invoked by

    a. a `println` statement
    b. a `return` statement
    c. the `new` operator
    d. an = sign
    e. overloading

3. An object location is stored in

    a. an object variable
    b. a class
    c. an instance field
    d. a `String`
    e. another object

4. An object stores its state in

    a. reference variables
    b. instance fields
    c. `double` variables
    d. a constructor
    e. a `String`

5. Consider the following three method headers.

    I.   `double findAnswer(String a, int b)`
    II. `int findAnswer(String a, int b)`
    III. `double findAnswer(int b, String a)`

    Which of the following statements is true about their method signatures?

    a. I and II have the same method signature and this signature is different from the method signature of III.
    b. II and III have the same method signature and this signature is different from the method signature of I.
    c. I and III have the same method signature and this signature is different from the method signature of II.
    d. I, II, and III all have the same method signature.
    e. I, II, and III all have different method signatures.

6. Suppose the `Car` class has the following instance field declarations.

    ```
    private double mileage   // mileage on odometer
    private double mpg   // miles per gallon
    private double tankSize   // size of gas tank in gallons
    ```

What is true about the initialization of the instance fields? **(not tested on the AP Exam)**

a. The instance fields must be initialized in the constructor. If they are not, there will be a compile-time error.

b. The instance fields must be initialized in the constructor. If they are not, the program will compile but there will be a run-time error when the `Car` object constructor is called.

c. The instance fields should be initialized in the constructor. If they are not, they will automatically be initialized to `null`.

d. The instance fields should be initialized in the constructor. If they are not, they will automatically be initialized to `0`.

e. The instance fields should be initialized to `null` by passing values to the constructor as parameters.

7. The implicit parameter of a method in a class is denoted by

a. a `double`
b. a `String`
c. `null`
d. `this`
e. the empty string

8. If two methods have the same name and different signatures, the method name is

a. overloaded
b. encapsulated
c. implemented
d. an implicit reference
e. illegal

9. Which of the following statements about objects and classes is **not** true?

a. Object locations are stored in object variables.
b. All object variables must be initialized before you use them.
c. An object reference describes the location of an object.
d. Multiple object variables can contain references to the same object.
e. Every class has a particular type that identifies what kind of information it can hold.

10. Consider the `BankAccount` class whose incomplete definition is shown below.

```
// A bank account has a balance that can be changed by
// deposits and withdrawals.
public class BankAccount
{
    // Constructs a bank account with a given balance.
    public BankAccount(double initialBalance)
    {
        balance = initialBalance;
    }

    // Deposits money into the bank account.
```

```
public void deposit(double amount)
{
   double newBalance = balance + amount;
   balance = newBalance;
}

// Gets the current balance of the bank account.
public double getBalance()
{
   return balance;
}

   private double balance;
}
```

Suppose the following statements were executed.

```
BankAccount b1 = new BankAccount(500);
BankAccount b2 = new BankAccount(500);

b1.deposit(b2.getBalance());
b2.deposit(b1.getBalance());
```

What are the balances of b1 and b2 after the code is executed?

a. b1 has balance = 500, b2 has balance = 500.
b. b1 has balance = 1000, b2 has balance = 500.
c. b1 has balance = 500, b2 has balance = 1000.
d. b1 has balance = 1000, b2 has balance = 1000.
e. b1 has balance = 1000, b2 has balance = 1500.

Free Response Questions

1. An Employee object has a first name (a String), a last name (a String), and a salary (a double). An incomplete class definition is given below.

```
public class Employee
{
   // Constructs default Employee.
   public Employee()
   {
      fName = "";
      lName = "";
      salary = 45000;
   }

   // Other constructor(s) here

   // Returns employee's salary.
   public double getSalary()
```

```
    {
        return salary;
    }

    // Employee salary increased by byPercent percent.
    public void raiseSalary(double byPercent)
    {
        // Code goes here
    }

    private String fName;
    private String lName;
    private double salary;
}
```

a. Write a constructor for the `Employee` class that has three parameters: `firstName` (a `String`), `lastName` (a `String`), and `moneyEarned` (a `double`). The private instance variables should be initialized to the values of the parameters.

b. Write a method `raiseSalary` for the `Employee` class. The method `raiseSalary` will raise the employee's salary by a given percentage passed as a parameter to the method. For example:

```
Employee worker1 = new Employee("John", "Smith", 50000);
    // John Smith has salary = $50,000.

worker1.raiseSalary(20);
    // John Smith now has salary = $60,000.
```

Use the method header below to write `raiseSalary`.

```
public void raiseSalary(double byPercent)
```

2. A `Book` class is to be implemented with the following properties. A `Book` object has a title (a `String`), an author (a `String`), and a price (a `double`). An incomplete definition for the `Book` class is shown below.

```
public class Book
{
    // Constructor goes here

    // Returns price of book.
    public double getPrice()
    {
        return price;
    }

    // Decreases book price.
    public void giveDiscount(double byPercent)
    {
        // Code goes here
```

```
        }
    private String title;
    private String author;
    private double price;
}
```

a.   Write a constructor for the `Book` class that has three parameters: a title (a `String`), an author (a `String`), and a price (a `double`).

b.   Write the method `giveDiscount` that modifies the `price` of the book by decreasing the price of the book by a given percentage. Use the method header below to write `giveDiscount`.

```
    public void giveDiscount(double byPercent)
```

Sample Usage:

```
    Book myFavoriteBook = new Book("The Cat in the Hat Comes Back",
        "Dr. Seuss", 10.00);
    myFavoriteBook.giveDiscount(15);
        // newPrice = 8.5

    System.out.println("The new price of the book is " +
        myFavoriteBook.getPrice());
        // Output would be The new price of the book is 8.5.
```

CHAPTER 4

Fundamental Data Types

■ Topic Summary

4.1 Number Types

Most Java programs require us to work with expressions and to define variables. Each expression and each variable has a type. These types can be primitive data types or objects. The primitive number data types that you are responsible for are `int` and `double`. The objects that are tested on the AP CS Exam are strings, arrays (which we will cover in Chapter 11), and objects instantiated from existing classes (like the `BankAccount` class or the `Car` class from Chapter 2 of your text).

Chapter 3 of your text introduces the `Purse` class. The `Purse` class defines variables of type `int`. Integer numbers have no fractional part. Both `double` and `int` are somewhat restrictive in that they cannot represent very large integer or floating-point numbers. Section 3.1 of your text gives details on the exact ranges of these types. You do not need to memorize the exact upper and lower limits for `int` and `double` numbers but you do need to know that there are restrictions. The `double` type also has a precision problem. Although you will probably not have to worry about this in writing answers to the free-response questions on the AP Exam, you do need to understand that possible precision errors may exist. This is discussed in detail in *Advanced Topic 3.1* of your text.

Let's look at some declarations of primitive number types and objects:

Example 4.1

```
int numberOfCoins;
double taxRate;
Purse yourPurse;
Purse myMoney = new Purse();
```

The `int` variable `numberOfCoins` and the `double` variable `taxRate` are defined but not initialized. The declaration of `yourPurse` defines an object variable that may reference a `Purse` object. However, the object variable `yourPurse` is uninitialized. The object variable `myMoney` actually initializes a `Purse` object and calls the `Purse` default constructor. The statements

```
System.out.println(yourPurse.getTotal());
System.out.println(numberOfCoins);
System.out.println(taxRate);
```

would all cause the compiler to complain because the primitive data types and the object variable `yourPurse` are not initialized. That is, the local variables `numberOfCoins` and `taxRate` have not been assigned values and the object hasn't been created with `new`.

The call `new Purse()` creates a new object and returns its location. The declaration of `myMoney` allocates the variable `myMoney` and initializes it with that location. The compiler does not complain about the statement

```
System.out.println(myMoney.getTotal());
```

because `myMoney` is a reference to a `Purse` object that has been constructed with the `new` operator.

4.2   Assignment

The assignment operator sets the variable on the left-hand side of the = operator to the value of the expression on the right-hand side of the = operator. Java also permits the combining of basic arithmetic operators with assignment by providing us with special assignment operators. For example, the arithmetic operation + can be combined with assignment to give us the += operator. The statement

```
total += count;
``` is equivalent to ```total = total + count;
```

and will add the value of `count` to the value of `total` and assign this sum to `total`. The other combined arithmetic/assignment operators are -=, *=, /=, and %=.

In addition, Java provides an *increment* operator (++) and a *decrement* operator (--). The statement

```
count++;
``` has the same effect as ```count = count + 1;
```

and

count--; has the same effect as count = count - 1;

Example 4.2

```
1     int numberOfCoins = 10;    // numberOfCoins = 10
2     int moreCoins = 12;    // numberOfCoins = 10
                             // moreCoins = 12
3     numberOfCoins = numberOfCoins + 1;   // numberOfCoins = 11
4     numberOfCoins++;    // numberOfCoins = 12
5     numberOfCoins += moreCoins;    // numberOfCoins = 24
6     numberOfCoins--;    // numberOfCoins = 23
```

Lines 1 and 2 assign integer constants to int variables.
Line 3 increments the int variable numberOfCoins by 1 and assigns this new value to numberOfCoins.
Line 4 increments numberOfCoins by 1.
Line 5 adds the value of moreCoins to the value of numberOfCoins and assigns this new value to numberOfCoins.
Line 6 decrements the value of numberOfCoins by 1.

Java is a strongly typed language. We must take care that the type of the value on the right-hand side of the = sign is compatible with the type of the variable on the left-hand side of the = sign. We cannot make the following assignment because Purse and 10 are not compatible types.

```
Purse myPurse = new Purse();
myPurse = 10;    // WRONG
```

An int can be assigned to a double.

```
int numberOfCoins = 7;
double taxRate = numberOfCoins;
System.out.println(taxRate);    // Prints 7.0
```

A double cannot be assigned to an int.

```
double taxRate = 7;    // This is OK.
int numberOfCoins = taxRate;    // WRONG
      // This is an error (loss of precision).
System.out.println(taxRate);
```

4.3   Constants

Sometimes it is convenient to use *constants* in our programs. A constant is used when a value of a variable remains the same throughout the life of the variable. Some examples might include:

- MAXSEATS   // the maximum number of seats on an airplane
- TAX_RATE   // sales tax rate
- NICKEL_VALUE   // the value of a nickel

In Java, we declare constants as `final` variables. Once a `final` variable has been given a value, that value cannot be changed. Constants are usually given variable names that are all uppercase letters. `final` variables declared within a method can be used only within that method. Method `getTotal` in Section 3.3 of your text illustrates this usage.

Example 4.2

```
public double getTotal()
{
final double NICKEL_VALUE = 0.05;
final double DIME_VALUE = 0.1;
final double QUARTER_VALUE = 0.25;
return nickels * NICKEL_VALUE
    + dimes * DIME_VALUE + quarters * QUARTER_VALUE;
}
```

`NICKEL_VALUE`, `DIME_VALUE`, and `QUARTER_VALUE` are only accessible from within the method `getTotal`.

It may be more useful to have these constants accessible throughout the class definition, in which case the `final` variables should be declared as `static` and either `public` or `private`. If your constant will be called only by methods within your class, then you should declare it as `private`. If you wish to allow the client programs access to your constants, then you would declare them as `public`.

Example 4.3

```
public class Purse
{
   public double getTotal()
   {
      return nickels * NICKEL_VALUE
            + dimes * DIME_VALUE + quarters * QUARTER_VALUE;
   }

// Other methods and declarations

   private static final double NICKEL_VALUE = 0.05;
   private static final double DIME_VALUE = 0.1;
   private static final double QUARTER_VALUE = 0.25;
}
```

4.4   Arithmetic and Mathematical Functions

Most applications require us to write expressions that contain arithmetic operations. Computers will do exactly what we tell them to do, so take care in writing complicated algebraic expressions. Use parentheses just as you do in algebra. The order of operations shown in Table 4.1 lists operators with the highest priority at the top. If two operations on the same level are contained in one expression, these operations are evaluated from left to right, just as they would be in an algebraic expression. Sometimes splitting a complicated expression into smaller parts and combining these parts to obtain the final result enhances readability and decreases errors. This is discussed in *Quality Tip 3.4* in your text.

Table 4.1
Operator Precedence

Operator Order of Precedence
++ --
* / %
+ -
= *= /= %= += -=

All of the operators listed above except for the modulus operator (%) can be applied to `double` and `int` values. The modulus operator applies only to integers and gives the remainder of integer division. You must be careful when dividing and using the modulus operator in arithmetic expressions, especially if you are combining doubles and integers.

Table 4.2
Arithmetic Expressions

Expression	*Operand*	*Operand*	*Result*	*Result Type*
4 + 5	int	int	9	int
14 / 5	int	int	2	int
4 / 5	int	int	0	int
14 / 5.0	int	double	2.8	double
14.0 / 5	double	int	2.8	double
14 % 5	int	int	4	int
4 % 5	int	int	4	int

Java provides a library of math functions that can help us with solutions to complicated applications. The AP CS subsets include only those math functions listed in Table 4.3.

Table 4.3
class java.lang.Math

Method	Method Summary
`static int abs(int x)`	Returns the absolute value of the integer x.
`static double abs(double x)`	Returns the absolute value of the double x.
`static double pow(double base,` `        double exponent)`	Returns the value of base raised to the power exponent
`static double sqrt(double x)`	Returns the correctly rounded positive square root of a double number x.

4.4.1   Calling Static Methods

The functions from `java.util.Math` are `static` functions. You can see this by the word `static` before the return type in the method header.

```
static double sqrt(double x)
```

This indicates that the method does not operate on an object. To invoke the square root function, we write

```
Math.sqrt(x)
```

Because of the Java convention of naming variables, methods, and classes, we can tell that the call above is a static method. `Math` begins with a capital letter which designates this as a class and not an object. *Quality Tip 3.1* and Section 3.5 of your text discuss the convention of naming variables, classes, and methods.

4.4.2   Type Conversion

We have mentioned that Java is a strongly typed language. This means that the compiler will complain if we try to assign incompatible types.

```
int a = 4;
double b = 2.1;
int c = a + b;    // Compiler complains about loss of precision.
```

If we intentionally want to discard the fractional part of this result, we need to *cast* the result to an `int` before the assignment can be made.

```
int a = 4;
double b = 2.1;
int c = (int)(a + b);    // Compiler no longer complains.
```

You do need to realize that this results in a loss of precision. The behavior resulting from casting to an `int` is sometimes referred to as "truncation towards 0" behavior, because the rounding truncates (cuts off) the decimal part of the double number, the result being an integer that is closer to zero than the original double number.

Table 4.4

Truncation towards 0 Behavior

Expression	Result
int num = (int)(3.4);	3
int num = (int)(3.7);	3
int num = (int)(-3.4);	-3
int num = (int)(-3.7);	-3

You can use this behavior to round floating-point numbers to integer values. The expression

```
(int)(x + 0.5)
```

rounds positive double numbers to integers and the expression

```
(int)(x - 0.5)
```

rounds negative double numbers to integers.

Table 4.5

Rounding Numbers

Statements	Rounding Result
double x = 4.2 int xRounded = (int)(x + 0.5)	4
double x = 4.8 int xRounded = (int)(x + 0.5)	5
double x = -4.2 int xRounded = (int)(x - 0.5)	-4
double x = -4.7 int xRounded = (int)(x - 0.5)	-5

Of course, `java.lang.Math` provides a method `round` that returns the closest integer to its argument. The Java `round` method will not be tested on the AP Exams.

You also need to be aware that roundoff errors occur when binary digits are lost in the internal representation of a floating-point number. This error is explained in detail in *Common Error 3.3* of your text. Binary Numbers are explained in *Advanced Topic 3.4* of your text. You should be able to represent numbers in different bases. Three common bases are binary (base 2), octal (base 8), and hexadecimal (base 16).

Here is a method for converting the decimal number 100 to a binary number (base 2):

100/2 = 50 remainder 0

50/2 = 25 remainder 0

25/2 = 12 remainder 1

12/2 = 6 remainder 0

6/2 = 3 remainder 0
3/2 = 1 remainder 1
1/2 = 0 remainder 1

If you read the remainders from bottom to top you have the binary representation of the decimal number. 1100100 is the binary representation of the decimal number 100. Binary numbers contain only the digits 0 and 1.

Similarly, to convert the decimal number 100 to an octal number (base 8):

100/8 = 12 remainder 4
12/8 = 1 remainder 4
1/8 = 0 remainder 1

If you read the remainders from bottom to top you have the octal representation of the decimal number. 144_8 is the octal representation of the decimal number 100. Octal numbers contain only the digits 0, 1, 2, 3, 4, 5, 6, and 7.

To convert the decimal number 100 to a hexadecimal number (base 16):

100/16 = 6 remainder 4
6/16 = 0 remainder 6

If you read the remainders from bottom to top you have the hexadecimal representation of the decimal number. 64_{16} is the hexadecimal representation of the decimal number 100. Hexadecimal numbers contain the digits 0–9 plus A, B, C, D, E, and F where A has the value of 10, B has the value 11, C = 12, D = 13, E = 14, and F = 15.

To convert the decimal number 27 to a hexadecimal number (base 16):

27/16 = 1 remainder 11
1/16 = 0 remainder 1

$1B_{16}$ is the hexadecimal representation of the decimal number 27.

You can reverse the algorithm to convert back to base 10. To convert the binary number 1100100 to a decimal (base 10) number, multiply each remainder by the corresponding power of 2:

$$(0)(2^0) + (0)(2^1) + (1)(2^2) + (0)(2^3) + (0)(2^4) + (1)(2^5) + (1)(2^6) = 100 \text{ base } 10.$$

To converting the octal number 144_8 to a decimal, multiply by the power of 8:

$$(4)(8^0) + (4)(8^1) + (1)(8^2) = 100 \text{ base } 10.$$

To convert the hexadecimal number 64_{16} to a decimal, multiply by the power of 16:

$$(4)(16^0) + (6)(16^1) = 100 \text{ base } 10.$$

4.5   Strings

Strings are one of the most commonly used data types. A `String` is a sequence of characters enclosed within double quotes. A `String` is an object. We have already discussed `String` concatenation. The + operator concatenates two strings. If one expression to the left or right of the + is a `String` then the other is automatically converted to a `String` and the two parts are concatenated. For example,

```
String s = "The number of ";
s += "Dalmatians is: ";   // two strings concatenated
```

s is now the string: *The number of Dalmatians is:*

```
s += 101;   // 101 is automatically converted
System.out.println(s);
```

The number of Dalmatians is: 101 is printed.

Although the `String` class has many methods, you are responsible for those listed in Table 4.6.

Table 4.6

class java.lang.String implements java.lang.Comparable

Method	Method Summary
int compareTo(Object other)	Compares two strings lexicographically. Returns value < 0 if this `String` is less than `other` Returns value = 0 if this `String` is equal to `other` Returns value > 0 if this `String` is greater than `other`
boolean equals(Object other)	Compares this `String` to specified object. The result is `true` if and only if `other` is not `null` and is a `String` object that represents the same sequence of characters as this object.
int length()	Returns the length of the `String`.
String substring(int from, int to)	Returns a new string that is a substring of this one beginning at `from` and ending at `to - 1`.
String substring(int from)	Returns a new string that is a substring of this one beginning at `from` and ending at `length - 1`.
int indexOf(String str)	If `str` occurs as a substring within this object, then the index of the first character of the first such substring is returned; if it does not occur as a substring, `-1` is returned.

Example 4.4 demonstrates these `String` methods.

Example 4.4

```
1    public class StringTest
2    {
3        public static void main(String[] args)
4        {
```

```
5              String greeting = "Hello";
6              String bookName = "Computing Concepts with Java Essentials";
7              System.out.println(greeting);
8              System.out.println(bookName);
9
10             String subBook = bookName.substring(10,18);
11             System.out.println(subBook);
12
13             System.out.println(greeting.length());
14             System.out.println(greeting.substring(3));
15
16             int position = bookName.indexOf("with");
17             System.out.println(position);
18
19             greeting = greeting + " there!";
20             System.out.println(greeting);
21         }
22     }
```

Lines 5 and 6 create `String` objects and assign values to these `String` objects.

Line 7 prints *Hello*

Line 8 prints *Computing Concepts with Java Essentials*

Line 10 creates a new `String` containing the characters in positions 10 to 17 inclusive. The first character in a string is in position 0.

Line 11 prints *Concepts*

Line 13 prints *5*

Line 14 prints *lo*

   This prints the substring from position 3 to the end of the string.

Line 16 assigns to the integer variable `position` the index of the first occurrence of *with* in the `String` *Computing Concepts with Java Essentials*

Line 17 prints *19*

Line 19 creates a new `String` with the value obtained from concatenating *Hello* with *there!* Strings are immutable objects. This means that a `String` object is never changed. A new `String` object is created when an assignment such as the one in line 19 is executed.

Line 20 prints *Hello there!*

The `String` methods `compareTo` and `equals` will be discussed in Chapter 5.

4.6   Comparing Primitive Types and Objects

Number variables hold values. Object variables hold references. A copy of an object reference is another reference to the same object.

```
int aNum = 5;
int anotherNum = aNum;
```

aNum = [5]

anotherNum = [5]

```
Car myBeemer = new Car(20);    // mpg
Car yourNewVehicle = myBeemer;
```

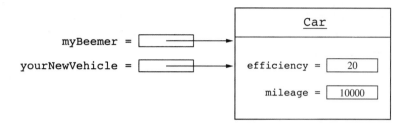

Changing information for myBeemer will be reflected in yourNewVehicle. Both variables refer to the same object. Whether or not yourNewVehicle gets 20 miles to the gallon, since yourNewVehicle references the same object as myBeemer, that's what you'll get! And when you *drive* yourNewVehicle, myBeemer's mileage goes up! This may not necessarily be your intended result.

Figures 12 and 13 in Chapter 3 of your text illustrate the difference between primitive types and object references.

■ Expanded Coverage of Material That Is Not Found in the Text

The String method indexOf is part of the AP CS language subset.

```
int indexOf(String s)
```

If s occurs as a substring within this object, then the index of the first character of the first such substring is returned; if it does not occur as a substring, -1 is returned.

```
String greeting = "Hello";
System.out.println(greeting.indexOf("e"));    // prints 1
System.out.println(greeting.indexOf("x"));    // prints -1
```

■ Topics That Are Useful But Not Tested

- java.lang.Math has many useful functions that will not be tested on the AP CS Exam. These functions are listed in Section 3.4, Table 1 of your text.
- toUpperCase and toLowerCase methods of the String class discussed in Section 3.7 of your text can be very useful.
- If a String contains the digits of a number, you can use the Integer.parseInt or Double.parseDouble method to obtain the number value. This is discussed in Section 3.7 of your text.
- It is often important to output information in a specific format. You may want a currency output or you may wish to have a certain number of decimal places printed. You can achieve proper formatting with the NumberFormat class in the java.text package. This is explained in *Advanced Topic 3.5* of your text.

- Strings are composed of individual characters. Characters are values of the `char` type. The `char` type is discussed in Section 3.9 of your text.
- Sometimes it is convenient to have values input by the person using the program. Section 3.8 discusses reading input using the `JOptionPane.showInputDialog` method and *Advanced Topic 3.6* discusses console input. On the AP CS Exam, if input by the user is required, you will see something similar to:

```
double x = call to a method that reads a floating-point number;
```

or

```
double x = IO.readDouble();    // read user input
```

■ Things to Remember When Taking the AP Exam

- Remember to declare all variables before you use them.
- Initialize variables that need to be initialized.
- Do not use *magic* numbers in your code. Magic numbers are constants that appear in your code with no explanation. They explained in *Quality Tip 3.2* of your text.
- Use parentheses as you would in algebra. If in doubt about the need for parentheses in an expression, use them.
- Remember that integer divided by integer equals integer. Sometimes casting to a `double` is required to obtain a correct result.
- Remember that the first character of a `String` is in position 0.
- The `indexOf` method of the `String` class returns `-1` if the string being searched for is not found.
- The last character of a `String s` is in position `s.length() - 1`.
- When you assign one object variable to another object variable, both object variables reference the same object.

■ Key Words

You should understand the terms below. The AP CS Exam questions may include references to these terms. The citation in parentheses next to each term identifies the page number where it is defined and/or discussed in *Computing Concepts with Java Essentials*, 3rd ed., and *Big Java*.

assignment (84)	increment operator (86)	precision (81)
binary numbers (105)	`int` (79)	roundoff error (104)
concatenation (107)	integer (79)	static method (99)
constant (88)	`Math.sqrt` (95)	`String` (107)
decrement operator (86)	`Math.pow` (95)	String length (107)
`final` (89)	`Math.abs` (95)	substring (108)
immutable (108)		

■ Connecting the Detailed Topic Outline to the Text

The citations in parentheses identify where information in the outline can be located in *Computing Concepts with Java Essentials*, 3rd ed., and *Big Java*.

- Number Types (79–82)
- Assignment (84–86)
- Constants (88–90)
- Arithmetic and Mathematical Functions (92–95)
  - Calling Static Methods (99)
  - Type Conversion (100–106)
- Strings (107–109)
- Comparing Primitive Types and Objects (119–120)

■ Practice Questions

Multiple Choice

1. Consider the following declarations.

   ```
   int a = some integer value
   int b = some integer value
   int c = some integer value
   ```

   Which of the following statements will correctly calculate the average of a, b, and c?

   ```
   a. int average = (a + b + c) / 3
   b. double average = a + b + c / 3
   c. double average = (a + b + c) / 3.0
   d. double average = (double)((a + b + c) / 3)
   e. double average = (a + b + c) / 3
   ```

2. The expression

   ```
   5 + 6 * 3 % 2 - 1
   ```

   evaluates to

   a. 0
   b. 1
   c. 4
   d. 10
   e. 13

3. Given the following declarations:

```
int m = 18;
int n = 4;
```

What is the value of the following expression?

```
m / n + m % n
```

a. 0
b. 2
c. 6
d. 6.5
e. 10.5

Questions 4 and 5 refer to the following segment of code.

```
String bookName = "Computing Concepts with Java Essentials";
String newWord = bookName.substring(10,18)
        + bookName.substring(6,8)
        + bookName.substring(0,9);
```

4. After the code is executed, what is the `String` that `newWord` references?

a. `" ConcepttiComputin"`
b. `"Concepts ingComputing "`
c. `"Concepts in Computing"`
d. `"ConceptsinComputing"`
e. An error message is generated

5. The statement

```
System.out.println(bookName.indexOf("cat"));
```

prints

a. *-1*
b. *0*
c. *null*
d. *1*
e. An error message is generated

Questions 6, 7, and 8 refer to the following incomplete definition of the `Purse` class.

```
public class Purse
{
    // constructor-initializes nickels, dimes, and quarters to 0
    public Purse()
```

```
        // adds nickels to the purse
        public void addNickels(int count)

        // adds dimes to the purse
        public void addDimes(int count)

        // adds quarters to the purse
        public void addQuarters(int count)

        // returns total value of all the coins in the purse
        public double getTotal()

        // takes count dimes from the purse
        public void subtractDimes(int count)

        private static final double NICKEL_VALUE = 0.05;
        private static final double DIME_VALUE = 0.1;
        private static final double QUARTER_VALUE = 0.25;
        private int nickels;   // number of nickels in purse
        private int dimes;   // number of dimes in purse
        private int quarters;   // number of quarters in purse
    }
```

6. The code for method `subtractDimes` should be

   a.
   ```
   {
       dimes = dimes - DIME_VALUE * count;
   }
   ```

   b.
   ```
   {
       dimes = dimes - count;
   }
   ```

   c.
   ```
   {
       double amount = dimes - count;
       return amount;
   }
   ```

   d.
   ```
   {
       int amount = dimes - 1;
       return amount;
   }
   ```

   e.
   ```
   {
       int amount = dimes - DIME_VALUE * count;
       return amount;
   }
   ```

7. A client program is to print the total value of the coins in `myPurse`. Which of the following code segments will complete the intended task?

I.
```
double totalMoney = myPurse.getTotal();
System.out.println(totalMoney);
```

II.
```
double totalMoney = nickels * NICKEL_VALUE + dimes
        * DIME_VALUE + quarters * QUARTER_VALUE;
System.out.println(totalMoney);
```

III.
```
double totalMoney = nickels * 0.05 + dimes * 0.10 + quarters
        * 0.25;
System.out.println(totalMoney);
```

   a. I only
   b. II only
   c. III only
   d. I and III only
   e. II and III only

8. Consider the following code segment.

```
Purse p = new Purse();
Purse q = p;
p.addNickels(5);
q.addNickels(3);
double c = p.getTotal();
double d = q.getTotal();
```

   After this code is executed, what are the values of c and d?

   a. c = 5   d = 3
   b. c = 0.25   d = 0.15
   c. c = 0.25   d = 0.25
   d. c = 0.15   d = 0.15
   e. c = 0.4   d = 0.4

9. Which of the following statements about objects and classes is true?

   a. A `final` variable in a class must be declared as `private`.
   b. Multiple object references cannot contain references to the same object.
   c. A client program can create only one object of a class.
   d. A `static` method is a method that operates on an object that has been instantiated.
   e. Every object belongs to a class.

10. Consider the following code segment.

```
1    int numberOfCoins = 5;
2    double taxRate = 4;
```

```
3    double number = 3.0;
4    Purse yourPurse;
5    Purse myMoney = new Purse();
6    taxRate = numberOfCoins;
7    numberOfCoins = number;
```

Which of the following statements is true?

a. A compile-time error occurs in line 2 because 4 is an `int` and not a `double`.
b. A compile-time error occurs in line 4 because an object is not being created with `new`.
c. An error occurs in line 6 because `numberOfCoins` and `taxRate` are not compatible types.
d. An error occurs in line 7 because a `double` cannot be assigned to an `int`.
e. The program will compile without errors.

Free Response Questions

1. Consider the `Car` class, whose incomplete definition is shown below.

```
public class Car
{
    // Constructs a car with given values
    public Car(double milesPerGal, double miles,
          double gasTankHolds, double gasTankHas)
    {
        mpg = milesPerGal    // miles per gallon
        mileage = miles;    // total mileage of car
        tankCapacity = gasTankHolds;    // amount of gas tank holds
        gasInTank = gasTankHas    // amount of gas in the gas tank
    }

    // Updates mileage and gasInTank
    // to reflect numMiles being driven.
    // There is enough gas in tank to make trip.
    public void drive(double numMiles)
    {
        // Code goes here
    }

    // Returns amount of gas consumed by car in numMiles miles
    public double findGasUsed(double numMiles)
    {
        // Code goes here
    }

    // Returns the total mileage on car
    public double getMileage()
    {
        return mileage;
    }
```

```
        // Returns the amount of gas in tank
        public double getGasInTank()
        {
            return gasInTank;
        }

        private double mpg;
        private double mileage;
        private double tankCapacity;
        private double gasInTank;
    }
```

a. Write the method `findGasUsed`. This method should calculate and return the amount of gas used in driving `numMiles` miles. Assume that you have enough gas to make the requested trip!

Call to findGasUsed	*mpg*	*Value returned*
findGasUsed (100)	20	5.0
findGasUsed (25.2)	25	1.008
findGasUsed (10)	25	0.4

Use the method header below.

```
    // Calculates and returns gas used in driving numMiles miles.
    public double findGasUsed(double numMiles)
```

b. Write the method `drive`. The method `drive` is given the number of miles the car has traveled as a parameter. Certain `private` instance variables need to be updated as a result of this action. You may include a call to `findGasUsed` from part a. Assume that this function works as specified regardless of what you wrote for part a. Use the method header below to write your method `drive`.

```
    // There is enough gas in tank to make the trip.
    public void drive(double numMiles)
```

2. A `Purse`, whose definition is shown below, is used to keep track of a number of coins.

```
    // A purse computes the total value of a collection of coins.
    public class Purse
    {
        public Purse()    // constructor
        {
            nickels = 0;
            dimes = 0;
            quarters = 0;
        }

        // Add nickels to the purse.
        // count is the number of nickels to add
        public void addNickels(int count)
```

```java
{
    nickels += count;
}

// Add dimes to the purse.
// count is the number of dimes to add
public void addDimes(int count)
{
    dimes += count;
}

// Add quarters to the purse.
// count is the number of quarters to add
public void addQuarters(int count)
{
    quarters += count;
}

// Get the total value of the coins in the purse.
// Returns the sum of all coin values
public double getTotal()
{
    return nickels * NICKEL_VALUE + dimes * DIME_VALUE
            + quarters * QUARTER_VALUE;
}

// Returns the total value of the coins in the purse in
// pennies.
public int totalInPennies()
{
    // Code goes here
}

// Returns the number of whole dollars in the purse.
public int getDollars()
{
    // Code goes here
}

// Returns the number of cents in the purse.
public int getCents()
{
    // Code goes here
}

private static final double NICKEL_VALUE = 0.05;
private static final double DIME_VALUE = 0.1;
private static final double QUARTER_VALUE = 0.25;
private static final int PENNIES_PER_DOLLAR = 100;

private int nickels;   // number of nickels in the purse
private int dimes;    // number of dimes in the purse
```

```
        private int quarters;   // number of quarters in the purse
    }
```

a. Write the method `totalInPennies` that returns the total value of the coins in the purse in pennies. In writing your solution, you may include calls to other methods defined in this class.

Total value of coins in Purse	Value returned
2.14	214
0.30	30
2.00	200

Use the method header below.

```
    public int totalInPennies()
```

b. Write the method `getDollars` that returns the number of whole dollars in the `Purse`, as an integer. In writing your solution, you may include calls to `totalInPennies` from part a. Assume `totalInPennies` works as intended. Examples of calls to `getDollars` appear below.

Total value of coins in Purse	Value returned
2.14	2
0.30	0
2.00	2

Use the method header below.

```
    public int getDollars()
```

c. Write the method `getCents` that returns the number of cents in the `Purse`, as an integer. In writing your solution, you may include calls to other class methods defined in this class. Examples of calls to `getCents` appear below.

Total value of coins in Purse	Value returned
2.14	14
0.30	30
2.00	0

CHAPTER 5

Decisions

■ Topic Summary

5.1   The if Statement

The if statement is used to control the flow of a program based on a condition. Examples 5.1, 5.2, and 5.3 are the general forms used most often in AP CS.

Example 5.1

```
if (condition)
    statement1;
```

If *condition* evaluates to true, *statement1* is executed; otherwise it is not.

Example 5.2

```
if (condition)
    statement1;
else
    statement2;
```

If *condition* evaluates to true, *statement1* is executed; otherwise *statement2* is executed.

Example 5.3

```
if (condition1)
    statement1;
else if (condition2)
    statement2;
else
    statement3;
```

If *condition1* evaluates to `true`, *statement1* is executed; otherwise *condition2* is checked. If *condition2* evaluates to `true` then *statement2* is executed; otherwise *statement3* is executed. Example 5.3 could be extended to include more conditions.

Each *statement* in Examples 5.1, 5.2, and 5.3 can be replaced by a block statement as described in Section 5.1 of your text.

```
if (condition)
{
    statement1;
}
else
{
    statement2;
}
```

It is a good idea to always use a block statement format with `if` statements. This makes your code less confusing—especially if you have nested `if` statements (one `if` statement inside another).

5.2   Comparing Values

An `if` statement performs a test. Many of these tests compare values with relational operators. There are six relational operators:

Table 5.1
Relational Operators

Relational Operator	Meaning
>	Greater than
>=	Greater than or equal to
<	Less than
<=	Less than or equal to
==	Equal to
!=	Not equal to

Relational operators involving integer expressions work as one would expect but you should be very careful when comparing doubles. We talked about limited precision and roundoff errors in Chapter 4. Because of these roundoff errors, doubles should never be compared with ==. Section 5.2.2 discusses this in detail.

We also should not use == to compare strings. Strings are objects. If you compare two `String` variables with the == operator, you are testing whether they reference the same object. The Java `String` class provides methods to compare strings. These methods are `equals` and `compareTo` and are summarized in Table 5.2.

Table 5.2
class java.lang.String implements java.lang.Comparable

Method	Method Summary
`int compareTo(Object other)`	Compares two strings lexicographically. Returns value < 0 if this string is less than `other` Returns value = 0 if this string is equal to `other` Returns value > 0 if this string is greater than `other`
`boolean equals(Object other)`	Compares this string to object `other`. The result is `true` if and only if `other` is not `null` and is a `String` object that represents the same sequence of characters as this object and is the same length.

Example 5.4

```
1     String string1 = "cat";
2     String string2 = "dog";
3     String string3 = "animal";

4     String firstInOrder = string1;
5     if (string2.compareTo(firstInOrder) < 0)
6         firstInOrder = string2;
7     if (string3.compareTo(firstInOrder) < 0)
8         firstInOrder = string3;
9     System.out.println(firstInOrder);
```

Lines 1–3 create `String` objects and assign values to these `String` objects.
Line 4 `firstInOrder` references "cat".
Line 5 compares "dog" with "cat". The Boolean expression (`string2.compareTo(firstInOrder) < 0`) evaluates to `false` because "dog" is not alphabetically before (<) "cat".
Line 6 is not executed.
Line 7 compares "animal" with "cat". The Boolean expression (`string3.compareTo(firstInOrder) < 0`) evaluates to `true` because "animal" is alphabetically before (<) "cat".
Line 8 `firstInOrder` now references "animal".
Line 9 prints *animal*.

Example 5.5

```
1     String string3 = "animal";
2     String string4 = "animal house";
```

```
3      if (string3 == string4.substring(0,6))     // evaluates to false
4          System.out.println("EQUAL");
5      else
6          System.out.println("NOT EQUAL");

7      if (string3.equals(string4.substring(0,6)))    // evaluates to true
8          System.out.println("EQUAL");
9      else
10         System.out.println("NOT EQUAL");
```

The Boolean expression in line 3 evaluates to `false` because `string3` and `string4.substring(0,6)` are not referencing the same `String` object. Line 7 evaluates to `true` because both `String` variables are referring to the same literal string "animal".

Because Java treats strings differently than other objects, the result can be somewhat confusing. *Common Error 5.1* in your text explains this in detail. It is very important to remember that the `==` operator should not be used with strings or with other objects to test whether two objects have the same contents.

If you use `==` when comparing objects, you are asking whether two object variables reference the same object. If your intention is to check whether the objects are equal in value, you need to call an `equals` method. This method is provided for Java `String` objects. With your own classes, you will need to write the `equals` method. It is not automatically provided for you. The `equals` method can be defined using any criterion that is appropriate for the class. It is always a good idea to check the class methods to be sure `equals` is included for any class whose objects you want to compare. Chapter 11 of your text covers `equals` in more detail. The implementation of `equals` is not in the AP subsets.

It is important to remember that when concatenating two strings, a new `String` object is created. For example,

```
String stringA = "Super";
String stringB = "man";
```

creates references to `String` objects.

```
stringA =  [ "Super" ]

stringB =  [ "man" ]
```

The code segment

```
String stringC = stringA
stringA = stringA + stringB
```

creates a new `String` object and `stringA` now references that new object.

```
stringC = [ "Super" ]
stringB = [  "man"  ]
stringA = ["Superman"]
```

5.2.1   The null Reference

Consider the declaration

```
Car myCar;
```

After this statement is executed, no object is allocated. This declaration does not create an object. The variable myCar is uninitialized. The declaration simply states that the variable myCar may reference a Car object. If you attempt to execute the statement

```
System.out.println(myCar.getMileage());
```

the compiler will complain that myCar has not been initialized.

However, sometimes you want to indicate that an object variable *does not* reference an actual object. Then you use the null reference:

```
Car myCar = null;   // I don't have a car right now
```

The null reference refers to no object.

If your program is organized in such a way that you sometimes initialize a variable with null, then you need to include a test before applying a method to such a variable:

```
if (myCar != null) mileage = myCar.getMileage();
```

A run-time error occurs when an attempt is made to invoke a method on a null reference. In this case, a NullPointerException will be thrown. Chapter 11 will cover NullPointer-Exceptions in more detail.

The declaration

```
String name;
```

indicates that the variable name may hold a reference to a String object. At this point name is uninitialized.

```
String name = "";
```

initializes name with a reference to an *empty* string—a string of length 0 that has no characters. However,

```
String name = null;
```

initializes name with null. It doesn't refer to any string at all!

Example 5.6

```
String a;    // a not initialized
String b = null;   // b initialized to null
String c = "";   // c initialized to the empty string
System.out.println(a);    // compile-time error
System.out.println(b);    // prints null
System.out.println(c);    // prints nothing
System.out.println(a.length());    // compile-time error
System.out.println(b.length());    // run-time error: throws
                                   // NullPointerException
System.out.println(c.length());    // prints 0
```

Note that *instance fields* are always initialized with some value. If you don't specifically initialize an instance field whose type is a class, then it is initialized with null. This is a common cause of programming errors. Consider this example,

```
public class Person
{
    ...
    private String name;
}
```

If the Person constructor does not set the name field to a specific string, then it is initialized with null. Calling a method on the name field causes a NullPointerException.

5.2.2 Dangling else

Because you can nest if statements (put one if statement inside another), the placement of braces becomes very important. Proper indentation will help you (and others) read your program more easily, but indentation does not control the flow of your program.

Example 5.7

```
int x = 9;
if (x < 4)
   if (x < 7)
       System.out.println("Hello there!");
else
   System.out.println("Have a great day!");
System.out.println("See you soon!");
```

Example 5.7 prints *See you soon!* Because the else is paired with the *nearest* if. The indentation in Example 5.7 is very confusing and misleading. The example is rewritten with proper indentation in Example 5.8.

Example 5.8

```
int x = 9;
if (x < 4)
   if (x < 7)
       System.out.println("Hello there!");
   else
```

```
        System.out.println("Have a great day!");
    System.out.println("See you soon!");
```

If the intention of Example 5.7 was to print:

> *Have a great day!*
> *See you soon!*

then braces must be used to clarify the pairing of the `else`. Example 5.9 illustrates this.

Example 5.9

```
int x = 9;
if (x < 4)
{
    if (x < 7)
        System.out.println("Hello there!");
}
else
    System.out.println("Have a great day!");
System.out.println("See you soon!");
```

It is always a good idea to design test cases before you begin to write your code. In this way you can think through your algorithm and plan for all possible conditions that need to be tested. *Quality Tip 5.3* in your text discusses test cases in more detail.

5.3   Using Boolean Expressions

Java has another primitive type, `boolean`. A Boolean variable has a value of `true` or `false`. These values do not convert into numbers. You can perform complicated tests by combining Boolean expressions using the logical operators.

Table 5.3

Logical Operators

Logical Operator	Meaning
!	not
&&	and
||	or

When working with Boolean expressions, it is sometimes helpful to review a truth table.

Table 5.4
Truth Table for Logical Operators

A	B	A && B	A || B	!A
true	true	true	true	false
true	false	false	true	false
false	true	false	true	true
false	false	false	false	true

If a legal grade is defined as a grade between 0 and 100 inclusive, an expression that checks whether a grade is legal (0–100) would be:

```
if (0 <= grade && grade <= 100)
```

not

```
if (0 <= grade <= 100)    // WRONG
```

The expression that checks whether a grade is NOT a legal grade is:

```
if (!(0 <= grade && grade <= 100))
```
or
```
if (0 > grade || grade > 100)
```

Negating a Boolean expression can be very confusing. Many errors in programming and on the AP CS Exam are due to writing incorrect Boolean expressions. De Morgan's Laws can be used to simplify complicated Boolean expressions. You can safely expect that the AP Exam will include questions that test your understanding of complex Boolean expressions!

`!(A && B)` is the same as `(!A || !B)`
`!(A || B)` is the same as `(!A && !B)`

5.3.1 Short Circuit Evaluation

The `&&` operator is used to combine two Boolean expressions. If the first expression evaluates to `false`, the second expression is not evaluated. If the first expression evaluates to `true`, then the second expression is evaluated. If it is `true`, the entire expression evaluates to `true`; otherwise it evaluates to `false`. This is called *short-circuit evaluation*. For example, suppose the statement

```
if ((n != 0) && (a / n < minSoFar))
```

is executed when n has the value 0. Since the first Boolean expression evaluates to `false`, the second Boolean expression will not be evaluated so there will be no division-by-zero error. If the first expression evaluates to `true` (n != 0), then the entire Boolean expression will be evaluated.

Short-circuit evaluation is discussed in *Advanced Topic 5.3 (Lazy Evaluation of Boolean Operators)* in your text.

5.3.2 Using Boolean Variables

A Boolean variable can be used in a test.

> `if (found)` is equivalent to `if (found == true)`

The first method is simpler and easier to read. This is explained in Section 5.4.5 of your text. With the inclusion of relational operators, we have an expanded table of operator precedence.

Table 5.5

Expanded Operator Order of Precedence

Operator Order of Precedence					
`++`	`--`				
`*`	`/`	`%`			
`+`	`-`				
`<`	`<=`	`>`	`>=`		
`==`	`!=`				
`&&`					
`||`					
`=`	`*=`	`/=`	`%=`	`+=`	`-=`

■ Topics That Are Useful But Not Tested

- A sequence of statements that has several alternatives can sometimes be written using a `switch` statement instead of multiple `if` statements. This is explained in *Advanced Topic 5.2* of your text.

■ Things to Remember When Taking the AP Exam

- In Java we check if x is between two values by writing `if (0 < x && x < 100)`. Do not write `if (0 < x < 100)`.
- Do not use `==` with strings. Use the `String` method `equals` to check whether two `String` variables have the same value.
- Do not use `==` with objects if you want to test whether two objects have the same contents. Use the object's `equals` method for this.
- Remember that the `null` reference is not the same as an empty `String`.
- Remember that a local variable that holds `null` is not the same as an uninitialized local variable.
- When comparing strings lexicographically, use the `String` method `compareTo`. Do not use < or > with strings.
- Be careful of a dangling `else` when nesting `if` statements. Remember that the `else` is paired with the *nearest* `if`.

- Do not compare doubles with the == operator. Use a method similar to that explained in Section 5.2.2 in your text.
- Do not confuse == with =. The == operator checks equality. The = is used for assignment.
- Know De Morgan's Laws. They may help you in writing complex Boolean expressions.
- Indent the body of if/else statements. Proper indentation makes your program easier to read.
- Remember that indentation does not control the flow of the program. Use braces to create a block statement when necessary for flow, and also to improve legibility.

■ Key Words

You should understand the terms below. The AP CS Exam questions may include references to these terms. The citations in parentheses next to each term identify the page numbers where it is defined and/or discussed in *Computing Concepts with Java Essentials*, 3rd ed., and *Big Java*.

and (213)	if (186)	null (106)
Boolean (210)	if/else (187)	or (213)
condition (188)	indentation (190)	relational operators (191)
dangling else (208)	lexicographic (194)	short circuit evaluation (214)
De Morgan's Laws (214)	logical operator (211)	side effects (196)
equals (194)	nesting (190)	statement (188)
expressions (189)		

■ Connecting the Detailed Topic Outline to the Text

The citations in parentheses identify where information in the outline can be located in *Computing Concepts with Java Essentials*, 3rd ed., and *Big Java*.

- The if Statement (186–190)
- Comparing Values (191–195)
  - The null reference (196)
  - Dangling else (208)
- Using Boolean Expressions (210–215)
  - Short Circuit Evaluation (214)
  - Using Boolean Variables (214–215)

■ Practice Questions

Multiple Choice

1. Consider the following code segment.

```
x = 6;
y = 19;
z = 2;
if (x > y)
    if (z > x)
        z++;
else
    z -= 5;
y += x;
```

After this code is executed, the values of x, y, and z are:

a. x = 6, y = 25, z = -3
b. x = 6, y = 19, z = 2
c. x = 6, y = 25, z = 3
d. x = 6, y = 25, z = 2
e. x = 6, y = 19, z = 3

2. Assume the following declarations have been made.

```
String fName = "Robert";
String lName = "Roberts";
```

Which of the following code segments returns `true`?

```
I.   return (fName == lName.substring(0, fName.length()));
II.  return (fName.equals(lName.substring(0, fName.length())));
III. return (fName.equals(lName.substring(0, lName.length())));
```

a. I only
b. II only
c. III only
d. I and II only
e. II and III only

3. Consider the following code segment.

```
int x = some integer value
double a = x;
double c = Math.pow(Math.sqrt(a), 2);
return (a == c);
```

Which of the following statements about the code segment is true?

a. A compile-time error occurs because x is not a double.
b. A compile-time error occurs because a method call cannot be a parameter to a method.
c. A run-time error occurs.
d. `true` is returned.
e. `true` or `false` may be returned, depending on roundoff errors.

4. Consider the following segment of code.

```
String word = "compute";
int len = word.length();
int num = 3;
String foo = word.substring(len % num, num);
String hoo = word.substring(num + 1);
if (foo.compareTo(hoo) < 0)
{
    hoo += foo;
}
else
{
    foo += hoo;
}
```

After this code is executed, what are the values of `foo` and `hoo`?

a. foo = "om", hoo = "uteom"
b. foo = "ute", hoo = "omute"
c. foo = "ute", hoo = "uteom"
d. foo = "m", hoo = "utem"
e. foo = "ute", hoo = "mute"

5. In a simplified game of craps you roll 2 dice. If you get a 7 or an 11 on the *first* roll, you win; otherwise the game continues. Given the following declarations,

```
int diceSum;
int numRolls;
```

where `diceSum` holds the sum of the two dice rolled and `numRolls` holds the number of times the dice were rolled. Which of the following code segments is a correct test for the *first* roll of the dice in the game of craps? Assume `diceSum` and `numRolls` are assigned their values before this code is executed.

I.
```
if (numRolls == 1 && diceSum == 7 || diceSum == 11)
    System.out.println("WIN");
else
    // Game continues
```

II.
```
if (numRolls == 1 && (diceSum == 7 || diceSum == 11))
    System.out.println("WIN");
else
    // Game continues
```

III.
```
if (numRolls != 1 || (diceSum != 7 && diceSum != 11))
    // Game continues
else
    System.out.println("WIN");
```

a. I only
b. II only
c. III only
d. II and III only
e. I and III only

6. Consider the following code segment.

```
int sum = 200;
int n = 0;
if ((n != 0) && (sum / n > 90))
    return sum += sum;
else
    return sum;
```

What is the result when this code is executed?

a. A run-time error occurs when evaluating sum / n.
b. A compile-time error occurs when evaluating sum / n.
c. 0 is returned.
d. 200 is returned.
e. 400 is returned.

7. Consider the following code segment.

```
String string1 = "Hello";
String string2 = "World";
string2 = string1;
string1 += "There!";
```

After the code is executed, what are the values of string1 and string2?

a. string1 = "Hello", string2 = "World"
b. string1 = "HelloWorld", string2 = "World"
c. string1 = "HelloThere!", string2 = "HelloThere!"
d. string1 = "HelloThere!", string2 = "World"
e. string1 = "HelloThere!", string2 = "Hello"

Questions 8 and 9 refer to the `Point` class partially defined below.

```java
public class Point
{
    private int x;    // x-coordinate of point
    private int y;    // y-coordinate of point

    // Constructor
    Point(int x1, int y1)
    {
        x = x1;
        y = y1;
    }

    // Sets new Point coordinates
    public void setPoint(int num1, int num2)
    {
        x = num1;
        y = num2;
    }

    // Returns x-coordinate of Point
    public int getX()
    {
        return x;
    }

    // Returns y-coordinate of Point
    public int getY()
    {
        return y;
    }
}
```

8. A client program needs to check to see whether two `Points` have the same x- and y-coordinates. Which of the following code segments will test that equality?

I.   `if (p1.x == p2.x && p1.y == p2.y)`
          statement;

II.   `if (p1.equals(p2))`
          statement;

III.   `if (p1.getX() == p2.getX() && p1.getY() == p2.getY())`
          statement;

    a. I only
    b. II only
    c. III only
    d. I and II only
    e. II and III only

9. If the following code segment is executed,

```
Point p1 = new Point(1, 5);
Point p2 = new Point(2, 3);
p2 = p1;
p1.setPoint(2, 8);
p2.setPoint(4, 6);
```

what points are represented by p1 and p2?

    a. p1(1, 5)   p2(2, 3)
    b. p1(2, 8)   p2(4, 6)
    c. p1(2, 8)   p2(2, 8)
    d. p1(4, 6)   p2(4, 6)
    e. p1(4, 6)   p2(2, 8)

10. The Boolean expression !(!A && !B) is equivalent to

    a. (!A && !B)
    b. (!A || !B)
    c. (A || B)
    d. !(A || B)
    e. (!A || B)

Free Response Questions

1. Consider the Car class, whose incomplete definition is shown below.

```
public class Car
{
    // Constructor
    public Car(double miles, double milesOnCar,
            double gasTankHolds, double gasTankHas)
    {
        mpg = miles;    // miles per gallon car gets
        mileage = milesOnCar;    // total mileage on car
        tankCapacity = gasTankHolds;   // amount tank holds
        gasInTank = gasTankHas;    // gas now in tank
    }

    // Updates mileage and gasInTank.
    // to reflect numMiles being driven.
    public void drive(double numMiles)
    {
        // Code goes here
    }

    // If tank is less than half full, fills tank and updates
    // gasInTank.
    public void fillTank()
```

```
    {
        //  Code goes here
    }

    // Returns amount of gas consumed by car in numMiles miles.
    public double gasUsed(double numMiles) {...}

    // Returns the current mileage on the car.
    public double getMileage() {...}

    // Returns the amount of gas in the gas tank.
    public double getGasInTank(){...}

    private double mpg;
    private double mileage;
    private double tankCapacity;
    private double gasInTank;
}
```

a.   Write the method `fillTank` that will fill the gas tank of the car if it is less than half full. If the car has half of a tank of gas or more, `fillTank` does nothing. Use the function header below to write `fillTank`.

```
    public void fillTank()
```

b.   Write the method `drive`. `drive` is given the intended number of miles the car is to travel. However, the gas tank in the car contains a finite amount of gas. If the car has enough gas to travel the specified number of miles, the appropriate private instance variables should be updated. If the car does not have enough gas to make the requested trip, the car should travel until it runs out of gas. The appropriate private variables should be updated.

Assume that a client program constructs a `Car` with the following statement.

```
    Car myMini = new Car(25, 600, 20, 20);
```

Examples of calls to `drive` are listed in the table below.

Before call to *drive*			After call to *drive*	
gasInTank	mileage	Call to *drive*	gasInTank	mileage
20	600	myMini.drive(100)	16	700
20	600	myMini.drive (0)	20	600
20	600	myMini.drive(1000)	0	1100

Use the following method header to write your function. You may include calls to other member functions when writing `drive`.

```
    public void drive(double numMiles)
```

2. Consider the `Point` class partially defined below.

```
public class Point
{
    private int x;    // x-coordinate of point
    private int y;    // y-coordinate of point

    // Constructor
    Point(int x1, int y1)
    {
        x = x1;
        y = y1;
    }

    // Sets new Point coordinates
    public void setPoint(int num1, int num2)
    {
        x = num1;
        y = num2;
    }

    // Returns x-coordinate of Point
    public int getX()
    {
        return x;
    }

    // Returns y-coordinate of Point
    public int getY()
    {
        return y;
    }

    // Returns the distance this point is from the point (0,0).
    public double getDistanceFromOrigin()
    {
        // Code goes here
    }

    // Returns true if p2 has the same x- and y-coordinates as this
    // Point, false otherwise.
    public boolean equals(Point p2)
    {
        // Code goes here
    }
}
```

a. Write the method `getDistanceFromOrigin` with the following header.

```
public double getDistanceFromOrigin()
```

that will return the distance between the `Point` and the origin (0,0).

b. A *client* program is to include a function `findFarPoint` that accepts three points as parameters and returns the `Point` that is the farthest away from the origin (0,0). Write your function using the header.

```
public static Point findFarPoint(Point p1, Point p2, Point p3)
```

You may include calls to `getDistanceFromOrigin` in your solution. Assume `getDistanceFromOrigin` works as intended regardless of what you wrote for part a. Assume that no two points are the same distance from the point (0,0).

c. **(not tested on the AP Exam)** Write the `equals` method for the `Point` class. The method `equals` will return `true` if two points have the same x- and y-coordinates; it will return `false` otherwise.

CHAPTER **6**

Iteration

TOPIC OUTLINE

■ Topic Summary

6.1   `while` **Loops**

Many applications require us to execute statements (or blocks of statements) multiple times. For example, averaging grades for all of the students in a particular course, printing a calendar of twelve months, processing a payroll for many employees, and any number of other applications involve doing the same task more than once. One way to implement this type of algorithm is to use a `while` loop. The general form of a `while` loop is

```
while (condition)
{
    statement;
}
```

Example 6.1 uses a `while` loop to sum the positive integers less than 10.

Example 6.1
```
int sum = 0;
int x = 1;   // Initializes loop control variable x.
while (x < 10)   // Checks end condition.
{
    sum += x;
```

```
    x++;    // Loop control variable updated.
}
// At the termination of the loop, x has value 10.
```

The three important pieces of a loop are initializing the loop control variable, testing for the end condition, and advancing the value of the loop control variable so that its value approaches the end condition. If you don't change the variable value within the loop, you create an endless loop.

Example 6.2

```
int sum = 0;
int i = 1;
while (i < 10)    // Infinite loop
{
    sum += i;    // WRONG! i is not incremented.
}
```

Example 6.2 will add i to sum repeatedly but, because the value of i starts at 1 and never changes, i is always less than 10. The end condition of the loop is never satisfied. This is called an *infinite loop*. *Common Error 6.1* discusses infinite loop errors.

Example 6.3 is designed to accept non-negative integers (points scored in basketball games) and return the sum of those points. The user must enter a negative value to end input.

Example 6.3

```
public static int getSum()
{
    int total = 0;
    int points;
    System.out.println("Enter game points, enter a negative number
            to quit.");
    points = number input by user;
    while (points >= 0)
    {
        total += points;
        System.out.println("Enter game points, enter a negative
                number to quit.");
        points = number input by user;
    }
    return total;
}
```

An alternate method for accomplishing this same task using a type of infinite while loop implementation is called a *loop and a half* and is discussed in *Advanced Topic 6.4* in your text.

6.2   `for` Loops

Another method for iterative control is a `for` loop. If you know exactly how many times a block is to be executed, a `for` loop is often the best choice. The general form of a `for` loop is

```
for (initialization; test; update)
{
    statement;
}
```

Examples 6.4 and 6.5 add the integers 1 to 10 inclusive. The order in which the integers are added is different but the result is the same.

Example 6.4

```
sum = 0;
for (int i = 1; i <= 10; i++)
{
    sum += i;
}
// At the termination of this loop, i has value 11.
```

Example 6.5

```
sum = 0;
for (int i = 10; i >= 1; i--)
{
    sum += i;
}
// At the termination of this loop, i has value 0.
```

The loop control variable, i, is initialized. The loop continues while the test is true. The variable i is updated (incremented or decremented) by 1 each time the loop executes. Example 6.6 gives the equivalent while loop for Example 6.5

Example 6.6

```
sum = 0;
int i = 10;
while (i >= 1)
{
    sum += i;
    i = i - 1;
}
```

The initialization, the test, and the update in the for header should be related (see Example 6.7). The code to update the loop control variable should occur in the for header only, not in the body of the loop (see Example 6.8).

Example 6.7

```
int j = 1;
int k = 8;
for (int i = 0; j <= 10; k = k + 2)      // BAD STYLE!
                                         // Variables are not related.
{
    j += 2;
    i = i + 1;
```

```
        System.out.println(i + " " + j + " " + k);
    }
```

Example 6.8

```
    for (int i = 0; i <= 10; i++)
    {
        sum += i;
        i = i + 1;    // WRONG! Update should occur only in for header.
    }
```

It is common to see the loop control variable declared in the header as it is initialized.

```
    for (int i = 1; i <= 10; i++)
    {
        Statement;
    }
```

A variable declared in this manner cannot be accessed outside the loop. We say that the *scope* of the variable extends to the end of the loop. This is explained in *Advanced Topic 6.2* in your text.

A `for` loop should be used when a statement, or group of statements, is to be executed a *known* number of times. *Quality Tip 6.1* discusses this. Use a `for` loop for its intended purpose only.

6.3   Nested Loops

Loops can be nested (one loop inside another loop). One typical application of a nested loop is printing a table with rows and columns.

Example 6.9

```
        final int MAXROW = 5;
        final int MAXCOL = 4;
        for (int row = 1; row <= MAXROW; row++)
        {
            for (int col = 1; col <= MAXCOL; col++)
            {
                System.out.print("*");
            }
        System.out.println();
        }
```

This program prints:

```
    ****
    ****
    ****
    ****
    ****
```

6.4   Off-by-1 Errors

It is common to have off-by-1 errors when writing `while` loops and `for` loops. Consider the following problem.

Problem

Count the number of times the letter "a" occurs in the word "mathematics".

Solution Outline

- Loop through each letter of "mathematics".
- Each time an "a" is encountered, increment a counter.

Examples 6.10 and 6.11 illustrate two correct solutions.

Example 6.10

```
String word = "mathematics";
int count = 0;
String lookFor = "a";

for (int i = 0; i < word.length(); i++)
{
   if (word.substring(i, i + 1).equals(lookFor))
   {
      count++;
   }
}
```

Example 6.11

```
String word = "mathematics";
int count = 0;
String lookFor = "a";

int j = 0;   // Init to 0
while (j < word.length())   // Note: < not <=
{
   String temp = word.substring(j, j + 1);
   if (lookFor.indexOf(temp) != -1)
   {
      count++;
   }
   j++;   // Increment outside if
}
```

Possible Off-by-1 Errors

- The loop variable should start at 0, not 1, because the index of the first letter in a `String` is 0.
- The loop test should be `<` `word.length()` not `<=` `word.length()` because the last letter in a `String` has index `length() - 1`.
- The variable used as the counter should be initialized to 0, not 1.

Off-by-1 errors are discussed in *HOWTO 6.1* in your text.

6.5   Random Numbers and Simulations

Random number generators are useful in programs that simulate events. The Java library's `Random` class implements a *random number generator*. This random number generator can produce random integers and random floating-point (double) numbers.

The AP testable subset includes the `java.util.Random` methods listed in Table 6.1.

Table 6.1
class java.util.Random

Method	Method Summary
`int nextInt(n)`	Returns a random integer in the range from 0 to n - 1 inclusive.
`double nextDouble()`	Returns a random floating-point number between 0 (inclusive) and 1 (exclusive).

Example 6.12 demonstrates basic calls to the methods of the `Random` class.

Example 6.12

```
Random generator = new Random();
   // Constructs the number generator.

int randInt = generator.nextInt(10);
   // Generates a random integer from 0-9 inclusive.

double randDouble = generator.nextDouble();
   // Generates a random double from 0(inclusive) to 1(exclusive).
```

When writing programs that include random numbers, keep in mind that two `Random` objects created within the same millisecond will have the same sequence of random numbers. For example, if the following declarations are executed in the same millisecond,

```
Random generator1 = new Random();
Random generator2 = new Random();
```

`generator1` and `generator2` will generate the same sequence of random numbers.

It is a better idea to share a single random number generator in the entire program. We rarely want to generate identical sequences of random numbers!

Example 6.13 uses the `Random` class to simulate rolling two 6-sided dice until doubles are rolled (the same number appears on both dice). The variable `count` counts the number of rolls it takes to roll doubles.

Example 6.13

```
Random die = new Random();
int count = 1;
while (die.nextInt(6) != die.nextInt(6))
{
```

```
        count++;
    }
    // count is the number of rolls it takes to roll doubles.
    System.out.println("Doubles were rolled on roll #" + count);
```

6.6   Loop Invariants (AB only)

A loop invariant is a statement that is true before a loop executes, at the start of each iteration of the loop, and after the loop terminates. Loop invariants can be used to help explain algorithms that are not completely obvious. They are also statements that can be used for proving the correctness of loops. Correctness proofs, though not part of the AP CS subset, are discussed in *Random Fact 6.2* of your text.

Example 6.14

This segment of code is intended to count the number of letters in `word` that are vowels (a, e, i, o, or u).

```
String vowel = "aeiou";
String word = some String;
int count = 0;
// loop invariant: count = number of vowels in word.substring(0, i)
for (int i = 0; i < word.length(); i++)
{
    if (vowel.indexOf(word.substring(i, i + 1) >= 0)
        count++;
}
```

The `for` loop visits each letter of `word`. If the letter is a vowel, `indexOf` returns a value between 0 and 4 and `count` is incremented. After each execution of the loop, `count` is the number of vowels in the substring looked at so far. The loop invariant is true before the loop executes, after each iteration of the loop, and after the loop terminates. After the loop terminates, `count` is the number of vowels (a, e, i, o, u) in `word`.

A more detailed example of a loop invariant is discussed in *Advanced Topic 6.8* in your text.

■ Topics That Are Useful But Not Tested

- It is often useful to read test data from a *file* instead of typing it for each execution of a program. You can then create a test data file once and reuse it. Reading data from a file is discussed in *Productivity Hint 6.1* in your text.
- Sometimes an input line may contain several items of input data. The `StringTokenizer` class can be used to break the input line into separate strings. This is discussed in Section 6.4.2 of your text.
- It is sometimes useful to traverse the characters in a string using the `charAt` method of the `String` class. This method uses the primitive type `char` which is not tested on the AP CS Exams.

- Sometimes you may want to execute the body of a loop at least once and perform the loop test at the end of the loop. A do loop serves this purpose and is explained in *Advanced Topic 6.1* in your text.

■ Things to Remember When Taking the AP Exam

- When implementing a while loop be sure to initialize the loop control variable before the loop begins and to advance the variable's value inside the loop.
- Be careful not to put a semicolon after a for loop header or a while statement.

```
for (i = 1; i < 10; i++);    // WRONG!

while (i < 10);   // WRONG!
```

- Be sure to use braces where needed for the body of a loop. If in doubt, use the braces.
- Check the initialization and the test condition in your loops. It is common to have an off-by-1 error when writing loops.
- Be careful when implementing tables with nested loops. The outer loop controls the rows of the table and the inner loop controls the columns.
- **(AB only)** Know the definition of a loop invariant. You may be asked to choose the correct loop invariant on a multiple-choice question.

■ Key Words

You should understand the terms below. The AP CS Exam questions may include references to these terms. The citations in parentheses next to each term identify the page numbers where it is defined and/or discussed in *Computing Concepts with Java Essentials*, 3rd ed., and *Big Java*.

file (253)	nested loops (244)	simulation (262)
for loops (236)	random number	variable scope (241)
infinite loops (231)	generator (262)	while (228)
loop invariants (267)	random numbers (262)	
(AB only)		

■ Connecting the Detailed Topic Outline to the Text

The citations in parentheses identify where information in the outline can be located in *Computing Concepts with Java Essentials*, 3rd ed., and *Big Java*.

- while Loops (228–232)
- for Loops (236–244)
- Nested Loops (244–245)
- Off-by-1 Errors (232–233)

■ Practice Questions

Multiple Choice

1. Consider the following segment of code.

```
String word = "mathematics";
String vowels = "aeiou";
String tempWord = "";
String newWord = "";

for (int i = 0; i < word.length(); i++)
{
   tempWord = word.substring(i, i + 1);
   if (vowels.indexOf(tempWord) >= 0)
   {
      newWord += tempWord;
   }
}
```

After the loop is terminated, what is the value of `newWord`?

   a. "mathematics"
   b. "mthmtcs"
   c. "aeai"
   d. "aei"
   e. the empty string

2. Consider the `Die` class as defined below.

```
public class Die
{
   // Constructs an s-sided die.
   public Die(int s) {...}

   // Simulates a throw of the die, returning a random integer from
   // 1 to s (the number of sides) inclusive.
   public int cast() {...}

   // Private stuff goes here
}
```

The following declaration is made.

```
Die d1 = new Die(6);
```

Which segment of code returns the number of rolls it takes to roll double 1s (both dice have the value 1)?

I.
```
count = 1;
while (!(d1.cast() == 1 && d1.cast() == 1))
{
    count++;
}
return count;    // Double 1s rolled on roll #count.
```

II.
```
count = 1;
while (true)
{
    if (d1.cast() == 1 && d1.cast() == 1)
    {
        return count;
    }
    count++;    // Double 1s rolled on roll #count.
}
```

III.
```
count = 1;
while (d1.cast() != 1 || d1.cast() != 1)
{
    count++;
}
return count;    // Double 1s rolled on roll #count.
```

a. I
b. II
c. III
d. II and III only
e. I, II, and III

3. Consider the following code segment.

```
for (int i = 0; i < 5; i++)
{
    for (int j = 0; j < 5; j++)
        System.out.print(i * j % 5);
    System.out.println();
}
```
What is the output produced?

a. *01234*
    12340
    23401
    34012
    40123

b. *12345*
    12345
    12345
    12345
    12345

c. *00000*
    01234
    23401
    34012
    40123

d. *00000*
    01234
    02413
    03142
    04321

e. *00000*
    00000
    00011
    00112
    00123

4. The following triangle design is to be printed.

    4
    33
    222
    1111

Which of the following code segments correctly prints this design?

I.

```
for (int i = 4; i >= 1; i--)
{
    for (int j = 4 - i + 1; j >= 1; j--)
        System.out.print(i);
    System.out.println();
}
```

II.

```
for (int i = 1; i <= 4; i++)
{
    for (int j = 1; j <= i; j++)
        System.out.print(4 - i + 1);
    System.out.println();
}
```

```
III.    for (int i = 1; i <= 4; i++)
        {
            for (int j = 4; j >= 4 - i + 1; j--)
                System.out.print(4 - i + 1);
            System.out.println();
        }
```

a.   I only
b.   II only
c.   III only
d.   I and II only
e.   I, II, and III

5.   Consider the following code segment.

```
int n = some integer value;
int a = 0 ;
while (n > 0)
{
    a += n % 10;
    n /= 10;
}
System.out.println("answer is :" + a);
```

Which of the following statements best describes the result of executing this code?

a.   *0* is printed.
b.   The number of digits in `n` is printed.
c.   The sum of the digits in `n` is printed.
d.   The original value of `n` is printed.
e.   An endless loop results.

6.   Consider the code segment below.

```
String word = "computer";
String tempWord = "";
for (int i = word.length() - 1; i >= 0; i--)
{
    tempWord = word.substring(i, i + 1) + tempWord;
}
System.out.println(tempWord);
```

What will be printed when the code is executed?

a.   *computer*
b.   *retupmoc*
c.   *erteutpumpomco*
d.   Nothing will be printed. `tempWord` is an empty `String`.
e.   An error message.

7. Consider the following code segment in which `IO.readInt()` is a call to a method that reads an integer.

```
String tempSequence = "";
int x = IO.readInt();
int y = IO.readInt();
while (y >= x)
{
    tempSequence += x;
    x = y;
    y = IO.readInt();
}
tempSequence += x;
System.out.println(tempSequence);
```

What is the output if the series of integers being input is: 1 1 2 3 5 4 7 8?

a. *1 1 2 3*
b. *1 2 3 5*
c. *1 1 2 3 5*
d. *1 2 3 5 4 7 8*
e. *1 1 2 3 5 4 7 8*

8. Consider the following code segment where `IO.readWord()` is a call to a method that reads a `String`.

```
String word = IO.readWord();
for (int i = 0; i < word.length() - 1; i++)
{
    if (word.substring(i, i + 1).equals(word.substring(
        i + 1, i + 2)))
    {
        return true;
    }
}
return false;
```

Which of the following describes its results?

a. Returns true if any letter in `word` is repeated, false otherwise.
b. Returns true if the first and second letters are the same, false otherwise.
c. Returns true if any two consecutive letters are the same, false otherwise.
d. Always returns true.
e. Always returns false.

9. Given the following declarations:

```
String vowel = "aeiou";
String word = some String value;
int count = 0;
```

Which of the following segments of code accurately counts the number of letters in `word` that are vowels (a, e, i, o, or u)?

I.
```java
for (int j = 0; j < vowel.length(); j++)
{
    String temp = vowel.substring(j, j + 1);
    if (word.indexOf(temp) != -1)
    {
        count++;
    }
}
```

II.
```java
for (int j = 0; j < word.length(); j++)
{
    String temp = word.substring(j, j + 1);
    if (vowel.indexOf(temp) != -1)
    {
        count++;
    }
}
```

III.
```java
for (int i = 0; i < word.length(); i++)
{
    for (int k = 0; k < vowel.length(); k++)
    {
        if (word.substring(i,i + 1).equals(vowel.substring(
            k, k + 1)))
        {
            count++;
        }
    }
}
```

   a. I only
   b. II only
   c. III only
   d. I and III only
   e. II and III only

10. Consider the following code segment.

```java
int p = 1;
int i = 1;
int n = some positive integer value;
// loop invariant
while (i <= n)
{
    p = p * i;
    i++;
}
```

Which of the following statements is a correct loop invariant?

a. $i < n$
b. $0 < i < n$
c. $p = i!$
d. $p = (i - 1)!$
e. $p = n^i$

11. Consider the following code segment.

```
for (int i = 0; i < 5; i++)
    for (int j = i; j < 5; j++)
        System.out.print("*");
```

How many stars will be printed?

a. 5
b. 10
c. 15
d. 20
e. 25

12. Consider the following code segment.

```
int count = 0;
for (int x = 0; x < 3; x++)
    for (int y = x; y < 3; y++)
        for (int z = y; z < 3; z++)
            count++;
```

What is the value of `count` after the code segment is executed?

a. 81
b. 27
c. 10
d. 9
e. 6

13. Each segment of code below correctly calculates the sum of the integers from 1 to n inclusive and stores this value in the integer variable sum.

I.
```
int sum = 0;
for (int i = 1; i <= n; i++)
    sum += i;
```

II.
```
int sum = 0;
int i = n;
while (i > 0)
{
    sum += i;
    i--;
}
```

III.
```
int sum = (n + 1) * n / 2;
```

For large values of n, which of the following statements is true about the execution efficiency of the above code segments?

 a. I is more efficient than II and III because it sums the numbers in increasing numeric order.
 b. II is more efficient than I and III because it sums the numbers beginning with the largest value.
 c. III is more efficient than I and II because there are fewer operations.
 d. I and II are more efficient than III because they are easier to understand.
 e. I, II, and III always operate with the same execution efficiency.

Questions 14 and 15 refer to the following code segment.

```
int n = some integer value;
int x = 0;

while (n > 0)
{
    n = n / 2;
    x++;
}
```

14. If *n* refers to the original integer value, which of the following statements is always true after the loop is terminated?

 a. $2^{x-1} = n$
 b. $2^x \geq n$
 c. $2^x \leq n$
 d. $2 \cdot x = n$
 e. $2 \cdot n = x$

15. If *n* has the value of 32 before the loop is executed, how many times is the statement

```
x++;
```

executed?

 a. 2
 b. 5
 c. 6
 d. 8
 e. 16

Free Response Questions

1. Consider the `Investment` class, whose incomplete definition is shown below.

```
public class Investment
{
    // Constructs an Investment object from a starting balance and
```

```
   // interest rate.
   public Investment(double aBalance, double aRate)
   {
      balance = aBalance;
      rate = aRate;
      years = 0;
   }

   // Interest is calculated and added to balance at the end of
   // each year for y years.
   public void waitForYears(int y)
   {
      // Code goes here
   }

   // Returns the current investment balance.
   public double getBalance() {...}

   // Returns the number of years this investment has accumulated
   // interest.
   public int getYears() {...}

   // Calculates the amount of interest earned in y years
   // compounded n times per year at an annual interest rate, rate.
   // balance is updated.
   public void compoundTheInterest(int y, int n)

   // Other methods here

   private double balance;
   private double rate;
   private int years;
}
```

a. Write the method `waitForYears` for the `Investment` class that will calculate the amount of interest earned in a given number of years. Interest is accumulated and the balance is updated at the end of each year. The table below contains sample data values and appropriate updates.

Starting Balance	Interest Rate	Years (y)	Ending Balance
100.00	5%	10	162.88
500.00	4%	20	1095.56
1000.00	5%	10	1628.89

Implement the method `waitForYears` using the following header.

```
   public void waitForYears(int y)
```

b. Write the method `compoundTheInterest` for the `Investment` class that will calculate the amount of interest earned in y years compounded n times per year at an annual interest rate of r%.

The method `compoundTheInterest` will update the balance appropriately. For example, if your original balance is $100.00 and you invest your money in a bank with an annual interest rate of 5% compounded quarterly (4 times a year) and you leave your money in the bank for 1 year, the interest and the ongoing balance is calculated as described below.

If your original balance is $100.00, then

  After the first quarter your balance is 100 + (100)(.05/4) = $101.25.
  After the second quarter your balance is 101.25 + (101.25)(.05/4) = $106.52.
  After the third quarter your balance is 106.52 + (106.52)(.05/4) = $107.85.
  After the fourth quarter, your balance is 107.85 + (107.85)(.05/4) = $109.20.
Your balance at the end of the year is $109.20.

The private instance variable, `balance`, should be updated appropriately. The table below contains sample data values and appropriate updates.

Starting Balance	Interest Rate	Years (y)	Times Per Year (n)	Ending Balance
100.00	5%	10	12	164.70
500.00	4%	20	4	1108.35
1000.00	5%	10	4	1643.62

Use the method header below to write `compoundTheInterest`.

```
// Balance is compounded n times annually for y years.
public void compoundTheInterest(int y, int n)
```

2. A modified game of roulette is played as follows. A player has a purse that contains coins. The player bets one coin (chosen randomly from the purse) on a number on the roulette wheel. This modified roulette wheel is shown below.

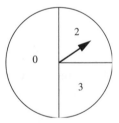

The spinner spins. If the spinner lands on "0", the player gets nothing back. If the spinner lands on "2", the player gets the wagered coin back and an additional coin of equal value. If the spinner lands on "3", the player gets 3 coins of the same value as the coin that was bet.

In this particular version of roulette, you either win big or you lose big because the spinning continues until you double the money in your purse or you have no coins left in your purse! The classes used are:
  • The `Spinner` class, used to "spin" the roulette wheel
  • The `Coin` class, which defines a coin
  • The `Purse` class that holds the coins
  • The `Game` class that simulates the roulette game

Incomplete definitions of these classes are below.

```java
// The Spinner class is used to simulate the spin.
public class Spinner
{
    // Constructs a spinner with s choices.
    public Spinner(int s) {...}

    // Returns an integer from 0 to the number of choices - 1
    // inclusive.
    public int spin() {...}

    // Private stuff here
}
```

```java
public class Coin
{
    // Constructs a coin.
    // aValue the monetary value of the coin
    // aName the name of the coin
    public Coin(double aValue, String aName) {...}

    // Returns the coin value.
    public double getValue() {...}

    // Returns the coin name.
    public String getName() {...}

    // Other methods and private stuff here
}
```

```java
public class Purse
{
    // Constructs an empty purse.
    public Purse() {...}

    // Adds a coin to the purse.
    public void add(Coin aCoin) {...}

    // Removes a coin from the purse.
    public Coin removeCoin() {...}

    // Returns the total value of the coins in the purse.
    public double getTotal() {...}

    // Returns the number of coins in the purse.
    public int coinCount() {...}

    // Other methods and private stuff goes here
}
```

```
public class Game
{
    // Game constructor
    // Creates the roulette wheel by constructing the
    // appropriate Spinner.
    public Game(Purse myPurse)
    {
        // Code goes here
    }

    // Simulates a spin returning a 0, 2, or 3 as defined by the
    // roulette wheel pictured in the problem.
    public int spinTheWheel()
    {
        // Code goes here
    }

    // Simulates the game of roulette as follows:

    // Until the purse total is twice its original value
    // or there are no coins left in the purse,
    // removes a coin from the purse, and
    // updates the number of coins in purse according to the
    // winnings.

    // Returns the total value in the purse.
    public double playRoulette(Purse myPurse)
    {
        // Code goes here
    }

    private Spinner myWheel;
}
```

a.   Write the Game constructor. This constructor should construct a Spinner that will be able to appropriately simulate the wheel shown in the problem description above. Notice that all outcomes on the wheel do not have equal probabilities.

b.   Write the method spinTheWheel that will call spin to generate a random number and then return the appropriate number on the roulette wheel. Notice that all outcomes on the wheel do not have equal probabilities. Use the header below when writing spinTheWheel.

```
public int spinTheWheel()
```

c.   Write the method playRoulette that will bet (remove a coin from the purse), spin the roulette wheel, and accumulate appropriate winnings by adding coins to the purse until the player either wins big (doubles the original purse value) or loses big (has no coins left in the purse). Write playRoulette using the method header below.

```
public double playRoulette(Purse myPurse)
```

CHAPTER **7**

Designing Classes

■ Topic Summary

7.1   Choosing Classes

Object-oriented programming is a major focus of AP Computer Science. The center of this programming paradigm in Java is a class. Both the AP CS A and AB Exams may test your ability to design and implement a class. The AP CS AB Exam may also test your ability to decompose a problem into classes and to define the relationships and responsibilities of those classes. A class should represent a single concept from the problem description. Some examples of classes that we have studied so far include `Rectangle`, `Coin`, `Purse`, and `Car`. The properties of these classes were relatively easy to understand. The names of these classes are nouns that clearly identify the class. When you choose a class to implement, it should represent a single concept and should be named with a noun that easily identifies the class.

One particular category of classes is called an *actor* class. This class does work for you, as the `Random` class did. We also have *utility* classes, such as `Math`, that have no objects. These types of classes are explained in Section 7.1 of your text. The AP subsets do not require you to classify classes as actor or utility classes.

7.2   Cohesion and Coupling

A class should represent one concept. All of the class responsibilities (interface features) should be closely related to the concept that the class represents. If they are, we say the class is *cohesive* or has a high degree of cohesion. Some classes need other classes so that the class can do its job. A Purse class needs the Coin class because a purse contains coins. A roulette Game class needs the Spinner class to create and spin the roulette wheel. If many classes in a program depend on each other, we say that there is a high degree of *coupling*. It is a good programming practice to have high cohesion and low coupling. If a high degree of coupling exists, then modifying one class may affect many other classes. Figure 2 in Section 7.2 of your text illustrates high and low class coupling. When designing a class, you should be able to list the class's responsibilities and collaborators (the classes that it uses or depends on). Doing so will help you see the amount of cohesion and coupling in your class design.

Let's look at an example of class responsibilities and collaborators.

Consider the New York (or any state) lottery game. Each evening the lottery is televised and we observe the following. There is a *container* that holds the numbered *balls* such that no two balls have the same number. There is a *popper* that "pops" a random ball. It is this popped ball's number that is one of the lottery number choices.

Classes:
- Container has a collection of Balls. If asked for a Ball, the Container will return the Ball that is requested.
    - Responsibilities
        - hold Objects (Balls);
        - return an Object (Ball);
    - Collaborators (other classes the Container needs or uses)
        - Ball
- Ball has a number on it. It can return its number to whoever wants to know it.
    - Responsibilities
        - return its number
    - Collaborators (other classes the Ball needs or uses)
        - none
- Popper will ask the Container how many Balls it has and then will ask the Random class for a random number generator to generate a random number in the range of the numbers on the Balls. The Popper will then ask the Container to remove a particular Ball.
    - Responsibilities
        - ask Container for the number of Balls
        - ask Random for number
        - ask Container for Object (Ball)
    - Collaborators (other classes the Popper needs or uses)
        - Random
        - Container
- Random (Java library class)
    - Responsibilities
        - return a random number

- Collaborators
  - none

We see that there is some degree of coupling in this example because classes collaborate with other classes. We also see that the `Ball`'s cohesion allows it to be used in other games: billards (add a color to the "ball"), croquet, Scrabble (add a letter to the "ball" and view it as a "tile"), and any game that has a game "piece" with a number on it.

7.3   Accessor and Mutator Methods

Classes define the behavior of its objects by supplying methods. These methods either change the state of the object or they do not. Methods that change the state of an object are called *mutator* methods or *modifiers* and usually have a `void` return type. Examples of modifiers include `deposit` and `withdraw` in the `BankAccount` class. Both of these methods change the state of the `BankAccount` object by modifying its `balance`. The methods `drive` and `fillTank` in the `Car` class change the state of a `Car` object by modifying its `mileage` and `gasInTank`. Accessor methods do not change the state of the object. The method `getBalance` returns the balance of a `BankAccount` object without changing the state of the object. The method `getMileage` returns the total mileage of a `Car` object without changing the state of the object.

A class with no modifiers is an immutable class. The `String` class is immutable. After a string has been constructed, its contents cannot change. The methods of the `String` class do not change the state of the `String` object.

7.4   Parameter Passing

In Java, a method can never change parameters of a primitive type. A method can change the state of an object reference but it cannot replace the reference with another. Example 7.1 demonstrates these very important concepts.

Example 7.1

```
public class Point
{
   Point(int x1, int y1)
   {
      x = x1;
      y = y1;
   }

   public void setPoint(int xCoordinate, int yCoordinate)
   {
      x = xCoordinate;
      y = yCoordinate;
   }

   public int getX()
   {
      return x;
   }
```

```java
    public int getY()
    {
        return y;
    }

    public String toString()
    {
        String s = "(" + x + "," + y + ")";
        return s;
    }
    private int x;
    private int y;
}
```

```java
public class ParamsTest
{
    public static void main(String[] args)
    {
        // Trying to change primitive parameters
        int a = 10;
        int b = 11;
        System.out.println("Before call to change:");
        System.out.println("a = " + a + " b = " + b);
            // a = 10 b = 11
        change(a, b);
        System.out.println("After call to change:");
        System.out.println("a = " + a + " b = " + b);
            // a = 10 b = 11
        System.out.println();

        // Trying to change object references
        Point p1 = new Point(1, 2);
        Point p2 = new Point(3, 4);
        System.out.println("Before call to changePoints:");
        System.out.println("p1 = " + p1);    // p1 = (1, 2)
        System.out.println("p2 = " + p2);    // p2 = (3, 4)
        changePoints(p1, p2);
        System.out.println("After call to changePoints:");
        System.out.println("p1 = " + p1);    // p1 = (1, 2)
        System.out.println("p2 = " + p2);    // p2 = (3, 4)
        System.out.println();

        // Changing the state of an object
        System.out.println("Before call to changeState:");
        System.out.println("p1 = " + p1);    // p1 = (1, 2)
        System.out.println("p2 = " + p2);    // p2 = (3, 4)
        changeState(p1, p2);
        System.out.println("After call to changeState:");
        System.out.println("p1 = " + p1);    // p1 = (3, 4)
        System.out.println("p2 = " + p2);    // p2 = (3, 4)
        System.out.println();
```

```
    }

    public static void change(int x, int y)
    {
        x = 123;
        y = 789;
    }

    public static void changePoints(Point first, Point
            second)
    {
        Point anotherPoint = new Point(9, 9);
        first = anotherPoint;
        second = first;
    }

    public static void changeState(Point first, Point
            second)
    {
        first.setPoint(second.getX(), second.getY());
    }
}
```

Output of ParamsTest

```
Before call to change:
a = 10 b = 11
After call to change:
a = 10 b = 11

Before call to changePoints:
p1 = (1, 2)
p2 = (3, 4)
After call to changePoints:
p1 = (1, 2)
p2 = (3, 4)

Before call to changeState:
p1 = (1, 2)
p2 = (3, 4)
After call to changeState:
p1 = (3, 4)
p2 = (3, 4)
```

Example 7.1 shows that all parameters are copied into the parameter variables when a method starts. You may see this described as "primitive parameters are passed by value". With objects, the object *reference* is passed by value, not the object.

7.5   Side Effects

Every method should be designed to do one task. If a method modifies some value other than its implicit parameter, it has a side effect. A side effect of a method is any externally observable behavior outside the implicit parameter (object). You should minimize side effects. Do not add `System.out.println` statements to indicate that a method has been completed. *Quality Tip 7.2* discusses side effects and classifies method behavior. Unwanted side effects may result in a deduction of points on the free-response portion of the AP CS Exam.

7.6   Preconditions and Postconditions

Preconditions and postconditions are statements that document the intended behavior of the method. They should appear in the method documentation. A *precondition* is a statement that describes the requirements that must be met in order for the method to complete its intended task correctly. If the precondition is not met, no promise about the method's behavior is made. It is the responsibility of the calling method to satisfy the precondition. If the precondition is not satisfied, how should the method behave? One way of handling a violation of the precondition is to throw an *exception* to indicate that the method was called inappropriately. Exceptions are introduced in Section 7.5 of your text and discussed more thoroughly in Chapter 14. We will look at exceptions in more detail in Chapter 12 of this guide. Throwing exceptions is included in the AB testable subset only.

A *postcondition* is a promise that the value returned by the method is computed correctly or that the object is in a certain state. A postcondition's promise is valid only if the precondition is satisfied. Example 7.2 contains information about a `Product` class. The class contains the name and the number of available products with this name. The method `buyProduct` shows a pre- and postcondition and throws an appropriate exception when the precondition is not met.

Example 7.2

```
/**
    Product contains information about products in a store
    Class invariant: getNumAvailable() >= 0
*/
public class Product
{
    /**
        Constructs a product with given name and number
        available
        Precondition: nm is the name of a product, number
        >= 0
    */
    public Product(String nm, int number)
    {
        numAvailable = number;
        name = nm;
    }

    /**
        Postcondition: returns number of product available
```

```
      @return number of product available
   */
   public int getNumAvailable()
   {
      return numAvailable;
   }

   /**
      Precondition: n >= numAvailable
      Postcondition: numAvailable is updated accounting for the
      number of items bought
   */
   public void buyProduct(int numWanted)
   {
      if (numWanted > numAvailable)
         throw new IllegalArgumentException();
      numAvailable -= numWanted;
   }

   //  Other methods here

   private int numAvailable;
   private String name;
   //  Other private stuff
}
```

Note that the comment

```
   /**
      Postcondition: returns number of product available
      @return number of product available
   */
```

is redundant. Since `javadoc` comments are not required in AP CS, you may see the postcondition explicitly written as in the first line of the comment above. If using `javadoc` comments, this postcondition can be stated as the `@return` comment.

If you supply a method that only works correctly under certain conditions, be sure to use preconditions to document this fact. If you supply a method that is guaranteed to have a certain effect, use postconditions to document this fact. When you are using other classes in your programs, be sure to read the pre- and postconditions carefully. Remember that the calling method is responsible for satisfying the preconditions.

Reading and understanding pre- and postconditions is important. Many times an algorithm for solving a free-response question is given in the documentation.

7.6.1   Class Invariants (AB Only)

In addition to pre- and postconditions, a *class invariant* was also included in Example 7.3. A class invariant is a statement that is true about an object after every constructor and that is preserved by every modifier provided that the preconditions were met. Class invariants are discussed in *Advanced Topic 7.2* in your text.

7.7 Static Methods

Up to now, the methods we have included in our classes have been instance methods. These methods belong to the object and operate on the object that is instantiated. A static method belongs to the *class*, not to an object, and is sometimes referred to as a *class* method. A static method has no implicit parameter. Static methods are always invoked through a class never, an object (i.e., `Class.methodName()`, not `obj.methodName()`). In the `Car` class shown in Example 7.3, the class variable `numCarsMade` keeps a count of the number of `Car` objects that have been instantiated. Each time a `Car` object is created, `numCarsMade` is incremented by 1. The class method `getCarsMade` returns that number to the calling method.

7.8 Static Fields

The class variable, `numCarsMade`, is a static field of the `Car` class. The initialization of `numCarsMade` is done only once, when the `Car` constructor is called the first time. The statement

```
System.out.println(Car.getCarsMade());
```

will print the value of `numCarsMade` which is the number of `Car` objects constructed.

Example 7.3

```java
public class Car
{
    /**
        Default constructor initializes instance variables
    */
    public Car()
    {
        // Private instance variables initialized here
        numCarsMade++;    // Number of cars manufactured so far
    }

    // Other public methods here

    /**
        @return number of cars manufactured so far
    */
    public static int getCarsMade()
    {
        return numCarsMade;
    }

    // Counts cars instantiated
    private static int numCarsMade = 0;
```

```
        // Initializes static field
}
```

The statement `System.out.println(Car.getCarsMade());` will print the value of `numCarsMade` which is the number of `Car` objects constructed.

7.9   Scope

The word *scope* is used to describe the part of a program in which a variable is accessible. We have already discussed instance variables, local variables of methods, parameter variables, and variables declared in the initialization of `for` loops. The issue of variable scope is an important reason to choose variable names wisely. It is bad programming technique to give instance variables the same names as the parameter or local variables. If you do, the scope issues become complicated.

7.9.1   Scope of Local Variables

The scope of a local variable extends from the point of its declaration to the end of the block that encloses it. If a variable is declared in the loop initialization, it is accessible only within the loop. If a variable is declared at the start of a method, it is accessible in that method. Parameter variables in a method header are accessible only within that method. If you try to give two local variables with overlapping scopes the same name, the compiler will complain. You can have local variables with the same name if their scopes do not overlap. To avoid all of this confusion, use different names for different variables and never change the values of parameter variables.

7.9.2   Scope of Class Members

Within a method of a class, you can access all other methods and all fields of that class by their simple names (without an object name prefix). If you are using a method outside the object, you must qualify it by prefixing the method name with the object name (for an instance method) or by the class name (for a class method). Whenever you see an instance method call without an implicit parameter (object name prefix), the method is called on the `this` parameter. Several examples of referencing variables with different scopes are given in Sections 7.8.2 and 7.8.3 of your text.

7.10   Initializing Variables

The methods for initializing variables depend on the type of variable. The initialization of different variable types is summarized below:

- Local variables belong to an individual method. A local variable can be accessed only from within that method and must be initialized before you use it. Failure to initialize will cause the compiler to complain.
- Parameter variables also belong to an individual method. Parameter variables are initialized with the values that are supplied by the calling method.
- Instance fields belong to an object and can be used by all methods of its class. Instance fields should be initialized in the constructor of the class. If instance fields are not initialized explicitly, default values are assigned. Numbers are initialized to 0, objects to `null`, and `boolean` values to `false`. Even though these default values are assigned to instance fields, it is good programming practice to initialize instance

variables in the constructors. The AP CS Exam will expect you to implement constructors that initialize all instance variables.

- Static fields are initialized when the class is loaded. This should be done by an explicit initializer. However, if no initialization is done explicitly, default values are assigned. Numbers are initialized to 0, objects to null, and boolean values to false.
- Static constants are initialized with a value.

The AP Exam will not test default initializations. You should initialize instance variables in constructors and you should include explicit initializers for static fields.

7.11 Packages

A package is a set of related classes. Several common packages that we use in Java are listed in Table 1 of Section 7.9 in your text. If you are using classes that belong to any of these packages (except java.lang), you must import the package. The import directive allows you to refer to the class of the package without fully qualifying the class name with the package prefix each time you use it.

Example 7.4

```
import java.awt.Rectangle
//  Other stuff here

Rectangle = new Rectangle(5, 10, 15, 20);
```

is much easier to read and understand than

```
java.awt.Rectangle = new java.awt.Rectangle(5, 10, 15, 20);
```

You are expected to have a basic understanding of packages and a reading knowledge of import statements. *Common Error 7.3* discusses Java naming conventions that can help you avoid confusion when looking at names with many connecting dots!

You will not be required to create packages on the AP Exam.

■ Topics That Are Useful But Not Tested

- You can sometimes avoid duplication of code when writing multiple constructors for a class by calling one constructor from another. An example of this is given in *Advanced Topic 7.4* of your text.
- Overlapping scopes (Section 7.8.3) and shadowing (*Common Error 7.2*) will not be tested but reading these sections in your text will give you a more thorough understanding of variable scope.
- More information on creating packages and choosing package names is given in Section 7.9 of your text. This section also explains how classes are located by the compiler.

■ Things to Remember When Taking the AP Exam

- Do not put extraneous `System.out.println` statements in free-response answers to indicate that the method is done or to print the answer before returning its value. This is a side effect and will result in a deduction of points on free-response questions.
- Do not print error messages inside of methods unless specifically instructed to do so. This is a side effect.
- On the AP Exam, you do not need to check that the precondition of the method is satisfied unless explicitly told to do so. A method should not be called unless its precondition is satisfied.
- Do not try to modify parameters of a primitive type. A Java method can never modify numbers that are passed to it.
- Do not try to replace an object reference parameter with another reference. You can change the state of an object reference parameter but you cannot replace the object reference with another.
- Do not use parameter variables as temporary variables. Do not change the contents of parameter variables. This is discussed in *Quality Tip 7.3* of your text.
- Carefully read the pre- and postconditions given in problems, especially in the free response questions. Many times an algorithm for solving the problem is given in the problem documentation. Read the documentation carefully!
- Unless specifically asked to write pre- and postconditions on the AP Exam, do not spend time doing this.

■ Key Words

You should understand the terms below. The AP CS Exam questions may include references to these terms. The citations in parentheses next to each term identify the page numbers where it is defined and/or discussed in *Computing Concepts with Java Essentials*, 3rd ed., and *Big Java*.

assessor method (287)	mutator method (287)	scope (304)
class invariant (296)	package (310)	side effect (287)
cohesion (283)	postcondition (295)	static method (297)
coupling (285)	precondition (293)	static field (299)
`import` (312)		

■ Connecting the Detailed Topic Outline to the Text

The citations in parentheses identify where information in the outline can be located in *Computing Concepts with Java Essentials*, 3rd ed., and *Big Java*.

- Choosing Classes (282)
- Cohesion and Coupling (283)
- Accessor and Mutator Methods (286)

- Parameter Passing (290)
- Side Effects (287)
- Preconditions and Postconditions (293)
  - Class Invariants **(AB only)** (296)
- Static Methods (297)
- Static Fields (299)
- Scope (304)
  - Scope of Local Variables (304)
  - Scope of Class Methods (306)
- Initializing Variables (301, 66)
- Packages (310)

■ Practice Questions

Multiple Choice

1. A class is being designed to represent an athlete. Which of the following public methods would not be a good choice for a cohesive public interface for this class?

   a. `getName()`
   b. `getSport()`
   c. `getFavoriteSong()`
   d. `setPointsPerGame()`
   e. `getTotalGamesPlayed()`

2. Which of the following statements is true about designing programs involving multiple classes?

   a. It is a good practice to have high degree of cohesion and a high degree of coupling.
   b. It is a good practice to have low degree of cohesion and a low degree of coupling.
   c. It is a good practice to have high degree of cohesion and a low degree of coupling.
   d. It is a good practice to have low degree of cohesion and a high degree of coupling.
   e. It is a good practice to have neither class cohesion or coupling with a program involving multiple classes.

3. An immutable class in Java is

   a. a class that has no private methods.
   b. a class that has no accessor methods.
   c. a class that has no instance fields.
   d. a class that has no modifier methods.
   e. a class that has only modifier methods.

4. Consider the problem of modeling a `Point` class. A `Point` object represents a point in the rectangular coordinate system. A `Point` object has an *x*-coordinate and a *y*-coordinate. Which of the following methods would not be a good choice for a cohesive public interface for this class?

a. `getX();`
b. `setY();`
c. `distancefromOrigin();`
d. `distanceFrom(Point a);`
e. `perimeter(Point a, Point b, Point c);`

5. **(AB)** A method `giveChange` accepts two parameters: `cost` and `tendered`, where `cost` is a `double` representing the price of an item and `tendered` is a `double` representing the amount tendered by the purchaser. The method has the following header, precondition, and postcondition:

```
// Precondition: Money tendered >= cost and cost > 0
// Postcondition: Returns the amount of change
public static double giveChange(double tendered, double cost)
```

To ensure that the precondition is met, which of the following code segments is the best choice for the method body?

a.
```
if (tendered < cost || cost <= 0)
{
    System.out.println("WRONG! Your values to this
        function are not correct!");
    return 0;
}
else return (tendered - cost)
```

b.
```
if (tendered < cost || cost <= 0)
{
    System.out.println("WRONG! Your values to this
        function are not correct!");
    return 0;
}
else return (cost - tendered)
```

c.
```
if (tendered < cost || cost <= 0)
{
    cost = tendered;
}
else return 0;
```

d.
```
if (tendered < cost || cost <= 0)
{
    throw new IllegalArgumentException();
}
else return (tendered - cost);
```

```
e.  if (tendered < cost || cost <= 0)
    {
        throw new IllegalArgumentException();
    }
    else
    {
        tendered = tendered - cost;
    }
```

(Note: Using `javadoc` comments, the postcondition in Question 5 would be replaced by the `@return` comment. Since the AP subset does not include `javadoc` comments, this type of postcondition may appear on the AP Exam.)

6. Which statement below is true about preconditions?

    a. It is the method's responsibility to check that its precondition is satisfied.
    b. A precondition describes what is returned by the method.
    c. A precondition describes the parameters and their restrictions in order for the method to function as intended.
    d. A precondition describes how a method is implemented.
    e. If a precondition is not satisfied, the compiler will automatically throw an exception.

Questions 7 and 8 refer to the `Student` class whose incomplete definition is below.

```
public class Student
{
    public Student()
    {
        fName = "";
        lName = "";
        id = "";
        gpa = 0.0;
    }

    public Student(String first, String last,
            String idNumber, double gradePointAvg)
    {
        fName = first;
        lName = last;
        id = idNumber;
        gpa = gradePointAvg;
    }

    public double getGPA()
    {
        return gpa;
    }

    public void setGPA(double newGPA)
    {
        gpa = newGPA;
```

```
        }

        private String fName;
        private String lName;
        private String id;
        private double gpa;
    }
```

7. Consider a client program of the `Student` class that includes the following methods.

```
    public static void change1(Student stdt1, Student stdt2)
    {
        stdt1 = stdt2;
    }

    public static void change2(Student stdt1, Student stdt2)
    {
        stdt1.setGPA(stdt2.getGPA());
    }
```

After the code segment below is executed,

```
    Student student1 = new Student();
    Student student2 = new Student("Joe", "Smith", "111",
            3.86);
    Student student3 = new Student("Marie", "Jones", "222",
            3.52);
    change1(student1, student2);
    change2(student3, student1);
```

What are the gpas of `student1`, `student2`, and `student3`?

   a. `student1.gpa = 0.0, student2.gpa = 3.86, student3.gpa = 0.0`
   b. `student1.gpa = 0.0, student2.gpa = 3.86, student3.gpa = 3.52`
   c. `student1.gpa = 3.86, student2.gpa = 3.86, student3.gpa = 3.86`
   d. `student1.gpa = 3.52, student2.gpa = 3.52, student3.gpa = 3.52`
   e. `student1.gpa = 3.52, student2.gpa = 3.86, student3.gpa = 3.52`

8. For the `Student` class defined above, which of the following statements is true regarding constructors, accessor methods, and mutator methods?

   a. The `Student` class has 1 constructor and 3 accessor methods.
   b. The `Student` class has 1 constructor and 3 mutator methods.
   c. The `Student` class has 2 constructors and 2 accessor methods.
   d. The `Student` class has 2 constructors and 2 mutator methods.
   e. The `Student` class has 2 constructors, 1 accessor method, and 1 mutator method.

9. Consider the following program description: A user inserts coins into a vending machine to purchase candy. Which is the best choice of classes to be implemented for this program?

I. A `VendingMachine` class that defines private instance variables to hold coin values and product items.

II. A `VendingMachine` class that defines private instance variables to hold product information and uses coins from a `Coin` class.

III. A `VendingMachine` class that uses coins from a `Coin` class and products from a `Product` class.

    a. Method I is the best choice because there is a high degree of cohesion with this method.
    b. Method II is the best choice because products are a part of the vending machine's structure but coins are not.
    c. Method III is the best choice because the different vending machines can be implemented using different products and the products and coins can be used in other applications.
    d. None of the above methods. The coins and products should be part of a utility class because they are used by the `VendingMachine` class and they will not be instantiated.
    e. All methods are equally good.

10. Consider the following code segment.

```java
public class TriangleTest
{
    public static void main(String[] args)
    {
        printTriangle(5);
        // scopeCheck1
    }

    public static void printTriangle(int maxStars)
    {
        int count = 0;
        for (int r = 1; r <= maxStars; r++)
        {
            for (int c = 1; c <= r; c++)
            {
                System.out.print("*");
                count++;
                // scopeCheck2
            }
            System.out.println();
        }
        // scopeCheck3
    }
}
```

Which of the following statements is true about variable scope?

    a. At **scopeCheck1**, variables `maxStars`, r, c, and `count` are accessible.
    b. At **scopeCheck1**, only variables r, c, and `count` are accessible.
    c. At **scopeCheck2**, variables `maxStars`, r, c, and `count` are accessible.

d.   At **scopeCheck2**, only variables `maxStars`, `c` and `count` are accessible.

e.   At **scopeCheck3**, variables `maxStars`, `r`, `c`, and `count` are accessible.

Free Response Questions

1.   Consider the problem of modeling book information for a small book store. A book has these attributes:

- The book title
- The author's name
- An identification number that is unique to each book title. The identification numbers are positive integers assigned in increasing numerical order as the `Book` objects are created.
- The price of the book (a floating-point number).

When a new `Book` object is created, it must be assigned an identification number that will be the next consecutive identification number available. The new book is created with a title, an author's name, and a price. The only operations valid for a `Book` object are:

- Retrieve the identification number for the book.
- Retrieve the author's name.
- Set the price of the book (in the event that the price of the book is to be changed). The price of the book will always be a positive number.
- Retrieve the price of the book.

The class described above will be called `Book`.

a.   Write the public interface for the `Book` class as it would appear in a `Book.java` file. In writing this, you should write the headers for the constructor and the public methods. You must:

- Choose appropriate variable and method names.
- Provide the preconditions and postconditions where necessary.
- Provide appropriate data representation for the specifications above.
- Be consistent with information-hiding principles.

DO NOT WRITE THE IMPLEMENTATIONS OF THE METHODS.

Use the following class declaration to write your interface.

```
public class Book
{
    // Your interface goes here
}
```

b.   Write the declarations for the private instance fields and private class fields that will be needed in the `Book` class.

c.   Implement the `Book` class constructor. (**AB Students**: If appropriate, include exception handling to ensure that the precondition is satisfied.)

d. Describe two alternative actions that the programmer of a method can take if a precondition of the method is not satisfied. Give an advantage and/or disadvantage for each alternative.

2. Get Lean Fitness (GLF) is a company dedicated to improving the fitness level of its clients. GLF has several weight reduction plans. Each plan is an instance of a class `WeightCalculator`. That class has the following public interface.

```
public class WeightCalculator
{
    //  Constructor(s) here

    // Precondition: gender is sex of person,
    // howTall is height of person
    // Postcondition: Returns the ideal weight for a person
    // with height howTall.
    public int getIdealWeight(String gender, int howTall) {...}

    // Precondition: howTall is height of person,
    // gender is sex of person
    // Postcondition: Returns recommended calorie intake for a
    // person with the given height and sex.
    public int getCalorieIntake(int howTall, String gender) {...}

    //  Private implementation here
}
```

The company keeps a record on each client. This client record includes the person's name, height, initial weight, and sex (all attributes of the client). The client record also includes the client's suggested daily calorie intake.

Consider the problem of modeling the client information for Get Lean Fitness in a class called `Client`.
- When a new `Client` object is created, it is created with the name, sex, height, and weight of the client.

The operations available on a `Client` object are:
- Retrieve the client's name.
- Retrieve the client's height.
- Retrieve the client's weight.
- Set the client's calorie intake per day.
- Retrieve the client's calorie intake per day.

a. Write the public interface for the `Client` class (except for the `setCalories` method) as it would appear in the `Client.java` file. The `setCalories` method will be described in part c. In writing the interface, you should write the headers for the constructor and the public methods. You should:
- Choose appropriate variable and method names;
- Provide the preconditions and postconditions where necessary.
- Provide appropriate data representation for the specifications above.
- Be consistent with information-hiding principles.

DO NOT WRITE THE IMPLEMENTATIONS OF THE METHODS.

Use the following class declaration to write your interface.

```
public class Client
{
    //  Your interface goes here
}
```

b.   Write the declarations for the private instance fields that will be needed in the `Client` class.

c.   A client's ideal weight is based on sex and height and is found by giving the required information to the appropriate method of a `WeightCalculator`. Implement the `Client` method that sets the suggested number of calories to be consumed per day. An instance of the `WeightCalculator` is a parameter of the client's `setCalories` method. The algorithm used to determine daily calorie intake is as follows.
   - If the client's weight is less than or equal to the client's ideal weight, the calorie intake per day is the value that is returned by the `WeightCalculator`'s `getCalorieIntake` method.
   - If the client's weight is more that the client's ideal weight, the calorie intake per day is the value that is returned by the `WeightCalculator`'s `getCalorieIntake` method minus the constant 500.

CHAPTER **8**

Testing and Debugging

TOPIC OUTLINE

■ Topic Summary

8.1   Unit Tests

Most computer programs have errors when they are first written. We have discussed compile-time errors, run-time errors, and logic errors, and the *Common Error* sections that appear throughout your text discuss some of the more common programming errors and how to avoid them. Your goal should be to minimize the likelihood and impact of errors. Even though you take precautions and attempt to program defensively, sometimes your programs will not function exactly as expected. When this happens, you will need to use debugging strategies to locate the errors.

The most important testing technique is the *unit test*. This is the process of compiling and testing a class in isolation. In the BlueJ environment, an object can be created, its attributes can be inspected, and each of its methods can be tested individually by choosing them from a list of methods for that object. In other environments, it is an easy task to write a test class (test harness) that supplies values to the individual methods for testing. These values can be supplied by user input, by file input, random generation of values, or by variable assignment.

Generating the appropriate test data is an important debugging skill. You should test your programs using positive test cases, boundary test cases, and negative test cases. Positive test cases (or typical values) are the values you would expect the user to supply. Boundary test cases are values that lie on the boundary of acceptable input. You should test a value on the boundary, one that is one unit below the boundary and one that is one unit above the boundary to ensure that you are not off-by-1 with your calculations. Negative test cases (or degenerate values) are values that the program should reject. Test these values and decide on a method of handling illegal input.

You want to make sure that each part of your program is executed at least once by one of your test cases. This ensures that all branches in all conditional statements are executed during your tests.

After all individual classes have been thoroughly tested, you should begin the process of integration testing, in which the classes are put together in a program and tested.

After a program is completed, it is a good idea to keep the test cases in the event that modifications are made to the program. You can then retest your new version with the old test cases to see if the functionality is the same. One way to easily keep test case data is to create a text file from which the data is read by using text file input. This is discussed in Chapter 15 of your text. Reading from text files is not tested on the AP CS Exam.

8.2   Test Case Evaluation

After you have selected test data and decided on the input method, you need to determine whether the output produced by the program is correct. One way to verify the output is to calculate the values by hand. Other methods for checking output are discussed in Section 8.2 of your text.

8.3   Program Traces and Assertions

A program trace is a procedure in which output messages are added to a program to show its path of execution. For a proper trace, messages should be added at each method entry and exit point. More messages can be added to give additional information. Of course, your program will be more difficult to read because of the additional message statements and the output may be confusing; these statements should be removed when testing is complete. That means, if you revise the program at a later time, the procedure of adding and deleting message statements has to be repeated.

It is possible to create a `Debug` class to generate trace messages that you can turn on and off at your discretion. In this way, you can determine if and when you want to print your debugging messages, and you do not have to constantly add and delete these extra statements. This `Debug` class would be a utility class whose methods are `static`. There would be no need to create instances of this class. The College Board case study uses this technique to provide debugging statements throughout the Java Marine Biology Simulation case study.

You can also hand-trace the program. To do so, develop a set of test data. Calculate the correct results by hand so that you know what results to expect. Then simply use the test data and simulate a computer. Trace the execution of the program to see what the program will do. In order to be successful with this, you must keep track of variables (both primitive and reference) and their states.

Programs often contain implicit assumptions. An assertion is an assumption that you believe to be true. Java version 1.4 includes assertions as part of the language. The use of `assert` as an assertion test is detailed in Section 8.4 of your text. Although you are responsible for understanding assertions, the use of `assert` is not tested on the AP CS Exam.

For the AB Exam, you should understand that a loop invariant provides an assertion about the loop, insures that the assertion remains true at the start of each iteration of the loop, and is true at the termination of the loop. A class invariant provides an assertion about the class that is true after every constructor and is preserved by the modifiers.

8.4 The Debugger

The debugging method that is most popular among professional programmers is the use of a debugger. Most modern development environments contain a special program called a debugger that allows you to follow the execution of a program in order to locate errors. Adding breakpoints to your programs, inspecting variables, and stepping through the program execution are a few tools included in most debuggers. The debugger and a debugging session are discussed in Sections 8.5 and 8.6 of your text. The use of a debugger is not tested on the AP Exam. For less complicated programs, the use of testing techniques is sufficient and is easier than mastering the use of a debugger.

HOWTO 8.1 lists strategies that you can use to recognize program errors and their causes.

■ Topics That Are Useful But Not Tested

- Regression testing, black-box testing, and white-box testing are classifications given to particular testing procedures. Although we have discussed these methods, we did not refer to them by any particular classification. These testing methods are described in Section 8.3 of your text. The AP CS Exam will not require you to know this vocabulary but the concept of testing programs is included in the AP CS Topic Outline.
- The use of `assert` as a way to monitor pre- and postconditions is discussed in Section 8.4 of your text.
- Section 8.6 describes a sample debugging session. Following this session might help you familiarize yourself with the debugger available in your integrated development environment.

■ Things to Remember When Taking the AP Exam

- Understand the differences among compile-time errors, run-time errors, and logic errors.
- If asked to choose test data for a situation, remember to include typical, boundary, and degenerate test cases.

■ Key Words

You should understand the terms below. The AP CS Exam questions may include references to these terms. The citations in parentheses next to each term identify the page numbers where it is defined and/or discussed in *Computing Concepts with Java Essentials*, 3rd ed., and *Big Java*.

assertion (344)
boundary test cases (337)
debugger (345)

negative test cases (337)
positive test cases (336)
program trace (342)

typical test cases (336)
unit test (330)

■ Connecting the Detailed Topic Outline to the Text

The citations in parentheses identify where information in the outline can be located in *Computing Concepts with Java Essentials*, 3rd ed., and *Big Java*.

- Unit Tests (330)
- Test Case Evaluation (337)
- Program Traces and Assertions (342–344)
- The Debugger (345–348)

■ Practice Questions

Multiple Choice

1. Which of the following statements about debugging is true?

   a. All classes that are needed for the program should be written. Integration of these classes should be tested first. If there is a problem, the debugging procedure should be initiated.
   b. Each class should be written and tested separately before integrating the classes in a program.
   c. Message output statements should be included at the entry and exit points of all methods when they are initially written. This will make the program easier to read.
   d. To accurately trace a program, input statements should be included at the entry and exit points of all methods when you initially write them.
   e. Adding assertions to methods will allow the inspection of variable values during program execution.

2. Which of the following errors is **not** classified as a compile-time error?

   a. Division by 0
   b. Missing semicolon
   c. Misspelled variable name
   d. Uninitialized local variable
   e. Mismatched parentheses

3. Assume that a class provides the following instance methods for easily reading integers from a file. The object variable `input` represents the file and the file is open and ready for reading.

```
// Returns true if the end-of-file was read on the previous read,
// false otherwise
public boolean eof()

// Returns the next integer in file
public int readInt()
```

Consider the following code segment that is intended to find the average of the integer values read from `input`.

```
int n, count = 0, sum = 0;
while (!input.eof())    // testing for end-of-file
{
   n = input.readInt();   // read integer from file
   if (!input.eof())
   {
      sum += n;
      count++;
   }
}
double avg = sum / count;
System.out.println("The average is: " + avg);
```

I.   A logic error may occur because the variable n is not initialized.
II. A run-time error will occur if the file is empty.
III. A logic error may occur because the average returned is not always the correct value.

Which statements above correctly describe the errors in this code segment?

    a. I only
    b. II only
    c. III only
    d. II and III only
    e. I, II, and III

Questions 4–7 refer to the following problem.

The method `weeklyPay` is to return the amount of pay an employee will receive for one week's work. The parameters for `weeklyPay` are the hours worked during the week and the hourly pay. The weekly pay is based on the following standards. If the employee worked 40 hours or less during the week, he receives his regular hourly rate times the number of hours he worked. For every hour over 40 hours, the employee receives time and a half (1.5 times his regular hourly pay). The following information and method header is given.

```
final int MAX_HOURS_IN_WEEK = 168;   // 7 * 24
// Precondition: 0 <= hoursWorked and
// hoursWorked <= MAX_HOURS_IN_WEEK, 0 < hourlyPay
public static double weeklyPay(double hoursWorked,
     double hourlyPay)
```

4. Which is the best set of test values for the variable `hoursWorked`?

    a. 0, 40, 168
    b. 5, 10, 20, 30, 40, 170
    c. −1, 0, 1, 39, 40, 41, 167, 168, 169
    d. −10, 20, 30, 40, 50, 200
    e. −20, −10, 10, 20, 30, 40, 100, 200

5. Which of the following method calls would test illegal input?

I.   `weeklyPay(0, 0)`
II. `weeklyPay(168, 169)`
III. `weeklyPay(0, 200)`

    a. I only
    b. II only
    c. III only
    d. I and II only
    e. I and III only

6. Which of the method calls would be good choices to test boundary conditions or branches of conditionals in the `weeklyPay` method?

I.   `weeklyPay(0, 10)`
II. `weeklyPay(168, 20)`
III. `weeklyPay(40, 40)`

    a. I only
    b. II only
    c. III only
    d. I and II only
    e. I, II, and III

7. If all preconditions are satisfied, what assertion can you make after the call

```
myPay = weeklyPay(hours, rate);
```

is executed?

    a. `hours >= 0` and `rate >=0`
    b. `myPay > 0`
    c. `myPay >= 0`
    d. `rate >= 0`
    e. No assertion can be made.

8. Consider the following incomplete implementation of the `BankAccount` class.

```
public class BankAccount
  {
```

```
// Constructs a bank account with a given balance.
public BankAccount(double initialBalance)
{
   balance = initialBalance;
}
// Return the current balance.
public double getBalance()
{
   return balance;
}

// Precondition: amount >= 0
// Deposits amount in account. Updates balance.
public void deposit(double amount)
{
   balance += amount;
   // Assertion : ???????
}

   private double balance;
}
```

Which of the following statements should replace ??????? as an assertion after the statement

```
balance += amount;
```

in the `deposit` method is executed?

   a.   amount < 0
   b.   balance > 0
   c.   amount <= balance
   d.   amount < balance
   e.   amount >= balance

9. Values for testing a method can come from all of the following except

   a.   user input
   b.   file input
   c.   generating random numbers
   d.   non-initialized local variables
   e.   variable assignment

10. Which of the following statements is **not** true about program testing?

   a.   Once a method has passed all of the test cases, the cases should be discarded because they are of no more use.
   b.   A method of checking the accuracy of a program is to test a set of input values and then compute the results by hand using the same input values.
   c.   A method of testing revisions in a program is to test against past failures.
   d.   A method of checking the accuracy of a program is to use values for which you know the answers.

e. A method of testing a program is to use test cases that ensure that each statement of your program has been executed at least once.

Free Response Questions

1. Consider the `BankAccount` class incompletely defined below.

```
public class BankAccount
{
   // Constructs a bank account with a given balance.
   public BankAccount(double initialBalance)
   {
      balance = initialBalance;
   }

   // Returns the current balance.
   public double getBalance()
   {
      return balance;
   }

   // Precondition goes here
   public void withdraw(double amount)
   {
      // Code goes here
   }

   private double balance;
}
```

a. Write the public method `withdraw` that has one parameter of type `double`. The method `withdraw` will modify the private instance variable `balance` by removing the specified amount of money (passed as a parameter to the method) from the account. (**AB students** may throw an exception if the precondition is not met.) Use the header below to write `withdraw`.

```
public void withdraw(double amount)
```

b. Write the precondition for `withdraw`.

c. Assume that a `BankAccount` object was constructed with the following statement.

```
BankAccount myAccount = new BankAccount(500);
```

Describe the test data that you would use to test your `withdraw` method and list these test values.

CHAPTER **9**

Interfaces and Polymorphism

■ Topic Summary

9.1   Developing Reusable Solutions

A Java interface declares methods that classes are expected to implement. It encapsulates a set of associated behaviors that can be used by dissimilar classes. Interfaces contain no instance fields and cannot be instantiated. A class realizes (implements) an interface by promising to provide the implementation for all of the methods in the interface. An interface can be implemented by many classes and a class can implement multiple interfaces. Consider the following trivial but illustrative example. A `Flier` is one that flies.

Figure 9.1

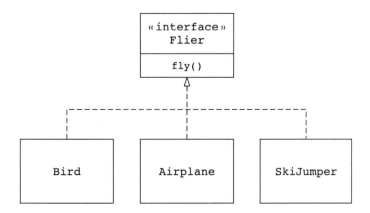

Figure 9.1 is a UML diagram. Although UML diagrams will not be tested on the AP CS Exam, you will see them throughout your text as they are commonly used to illustrate relationships among classes.

It is clear that the three classes `Bird`, `Airplane`, and `SkiJumper` are three dissimilar classes. Each of these classes defines the method `fly` in a very different way. The interface for this trivial descriptive example would be

```
public interface Flier
{
    void fly();
}
```

Notice that the `public` visibility modifier is not included. The methods declared in an interface are public by default. The classes that realize this interface might include the following code implementation for the `fly` method.

Example 9.1

```
public class Bird implements Flier
{
    public void fly()
    {
        System.out.println("Using my wings to fly");
    }
}
```

```
public class Airplane implements Flier
{
    public void fly()
    {
        System.out.println("Using my jet engines to fly");
    }
}
```

```
public class SkiJumper implements Flier
{
    public void fly()
    {
        System.out.println("Using skis to take me into the air");
    }
}
```

An athlete is one that competes. A `SkiJumper` is an `Athlete`. An athlete trains for hours to perfect performance in a particular sport. Most of us would agree that neither a `Bird` nor an `Airplane` is an `Athlete`. Therefore, if `Athlete` were an interface, a `SkiJumper` might implement `Athlete` as well as `Flier`.

Figure 9.2

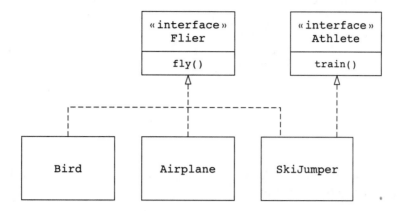

Example 9.2

```
public interface Athlete
{
   void train(double hours);
}
```

```
public class SkiJumper implements Flier, Athlete
{
   // Constructor
   public SkiJumper(String fName, String lName)
   {
      firstName = fName;
      lastName = lName;
      numberOfJumps = 0;
      hoursTraining = 0;
   }

   public void fly()
   {
      System.out.println("Using skis to take " + firstName + " "
            + lastName + " into the air.");
      numberOfJumps++;
   }

   public void train(double hours)
   {
      System.out.println("I am on the slopes " + hours + " hours
            today.");
      hoursTraining += hours;
   }

   public double getHoursTrained()
   {
      return hoursTraining;
   }
```

```
        public int getJumps()
        {
            return numberOfJumps;
        }
        private String firstName;
        private String lastName;
        private double hoursTraining;
        private int numberOfJumps;
    }
```

Now that you have an intuitive understanding of an interface and how it works, look at two examples that might be a bit more useful.

Section 9.1 in your text defines the `Measurable` interface. The `Measurable` interface is realized by `Coin` and `BankAccount`, two dissimilar classes. The only method declared in this interface is `getMeasure`. This method simply returns a `double`. In the text example, either a coin's value or a bank account's balance is returned. The `DataSet` class in Section 9.1 becomes usable in different circumstances by implementing a method `add` whose parameter realizes the `Measurable` interface. Interfaces are not instantiated. The variable `x` refers to a class object that realizes `Measurable`.

```
        public void add(Measurable x)
```

This method will add `Coin` values or `BankAccount` balances (or any other object instantiated by a class that realizes `Measurable`) and will keep track of the largest `Coin` value or `BankAccount` balance in the private instance field `maximum`.

Example 9.3

```
1    public class DataSet
2    {
3    // More code here

4        public void add(Measurable x)
5        {
6            sum = sum + x.getMeasure();
7            if (count == 0 || maximum.getMeasure() < x.getMeasure())
8                maximum = x;
9            count++;
10       }

11       public Measurable getMaximum()
12       {
13           return maximum;
14       }

15       // Other variables here
16       private Measurable maximum;
17       private int count;
18   }
```

Line 4: The parameter x is of any type that realizes the Measurable interface. If the declaration were

```
DataSet bankData = new DataSet()
```

the call to this method might be

```
bankData.add(new BankAccount(100))
```

If the declaration were

```
DataSet coinData = new DataSet()
```

the call to this method might be

```
coinData.add(new Coin(0.25, "quarter"))
```

Line 6: Adds values as defined in the getMeasure method of the individual class. If x were instantiated from the BankAccount class, we would be adding balances. If x were instantiated from the Coin class, we would be adding Coin values.

Lines 7–8: Checks for a new largest object based on the comparison of double values and resets present value of maximum if necessary. Notice that maximum is a type that realizes the Measurable interface. For the BankAccount class, maximum will store a BankAccount object. For the Coin class, maximum will store a Coin object.

Line 13: getMaximum will return the object with the largest measure.

Line 16: The private instance field is of type Measurable. This field can refer to any class that realizes the Measurable interface.

Our third example of an interface is one that we have already used with the String class.

```
class java.lang.String implements java.lang.Comparable
```

The Comparable interface has one method declared, compareTo. The String class implements this method so that it compares two strings lexicographically.

Table 9.1

`class java.lang.String implements java.lang.Comparable`

Method	Method Summary
int compareTo(Object other)	Compares two strings lexicographically. Returns value < 0 if this String is less than other. Returns value = 0 if this String is equal to other. Returns value > 0 if this String is greater than other.

Table 9.2

`interface java.lang.Comparable`

Method	Method Summary
`int compareTo(Object other)`	Returns a value < 0 if `this` is less than `other`. Returns a value = 0 if `this` is equal to `other`. Returns a value > 0 if `this` is greater than `other`.

We might want a `Student` class to allow for the ordering of students, perhaps by the student GPA, or the student ID number. If a `Student` class realized `Comparable`, we would add our preferred definition of `compareTo` to the `Student` class implementation. The `Comparable` interface can be implemented by the `Coin` class, the `Car` class, and any class that may want to provide an ordering for objects instantiated from the class. `Coin` objects may be compared based on their value. `Car` objects may be compared based on their mileage or their price.

A `Car` class might implement `compareTo` in the following way.

```
public int compareTo(Object obj)
{
   Car temp = (Car)obj;
   if (mileage < temp.mileage)
      return -1;
   if (mileage > temp.mileage)
      return 1;
   return 0;
}
```

The `Coin` class defined below,

```
public class Coin
{
   public Coin(double aValue, String aName) {...}

   public double getValue() {...}

   public String getName() {...}

   private double value;
   private String name;
}
```

would implement `compareTo` in the following way:

```
public int compareTo(Object obj)
{
   Coin tempMoney = (Coin)obj;
   if (value < tempMoney.value)
      return -1;
   else if (value > tempMoney.value)
      return 1;
   else
```

```
        return 0;
    }
```

The methods in an interface are *abstract*. They are not implemented in the interface. All methods in an interface are public by default. An interface can have constants but not instance variables. An interface should not grow. Many classes realize an interface. If the interface is modified, all classes that realize the interface will be affected.

9.2   Converting Between Types

In Example 9.3, the call to the method add could be

```
    bankData.add(new BankAccount(100));
```

or

```
    coinData.add(new Coin(0.25, "quarter"));
```

Any object whose class realizes Measurable can be passed as a parameter to add. This type conversion from the class to the interface is legal. Section 9.2 of your text explains this example in detail.

When converting from an interface type to a class type, you must cast to the appropriate class type. The example that is explained in your text casts Measureble to Coin.

```
    Measurable max = coinData.getMaximum();
    String name = ((Coin)max).getName();   // Notice parentheses!
```

Parentheses are necessary because of the order of precedence of the operators in this statement. In Java, the access class feature (.) has higher precedence than the (cast). Without parentheses we would have

```
    (Coin)max.getName()
```

max is of type Measurable and getName is not defined for Measurable. Without the parenteses, a compile-time error will result. It is a common error to forget needed parentheses! Table 9.3 contains a summary of operator precedence.

Table 9.3

Operator Order of Precedence	Description	Associativity
.	Access class feature	Left to Right
[ ]	Array Subscript	Left to Right
( )	Method call	Left to Right
++ --	Increment, decrement	Right to Left
!	Boolean not	Right to Left
+ (unary) - (unary)	Unary operators	Right to Left
(*TypeName*)	Cast	Right to Left
new	Object allocation	Right to Left
* / %	Arithmetic operators	Left to Right
+ -	Arithmetic operators	Left to Right
< <= > >=	Relational operators	Left to Right
== !=	Equals, not equals	Left to Right
&&	And	Left to Right
||	Or	Left to Right
= *= /= %= += -=	Assignment with operator	Right to Left

9.2.1   *Constants in Interfaces*

An interface can also declare constants. Since all variables declared in an interface are `public static final`, those keywords can be omitted when defining the constants.

9.3   Polymorphism

Polymorphism means having many shapes or many forms. Since the interface name is used to declare an object reference variable, it can refer to any object that is instantiated from a class that realizes the interface. In the declaration

```
Flier skyReacher;   // skyReacher is an object variable.
                    // The interface CANNOT be instantiated.
```

`skyReacher` can refer to objects of different types.

```
skyReacher = new Airplane();
```

or

```
skyReacher = new Bird();
```

or

```
skyReacher = new SkiJumper("Joe", "Smith");
```

The actual type of the object `skyReacher` is determined at run-time.

Consider the statement

```
skyReacher.fly();
```

The actual type of the object determines the method to be called. This principle is called *polymorphism*. The program has to run before the object to which `skyReacher` refers is determined. The virtual machine selects the appropriate method, not the compiler. This is referred to as late, or *dynamic*, binding.

Example 9.4

```
Flier skyReacher;
skyReacher = new SkiJumper("Joe", "Smith");
skyReacher.fly();
```

This segment of code will bind `skyReacher` to a `SkiJumper` object and the method call to `fly` will print *Using skis to take Joe Smith into the air.*

Early binding takes place at compile time. This type of binding occurs with method overloading. Your text explains this difference in Section 9.3.

■ Topics That Are Useful But Not Tested

- The `instanceof` operator tests whether an object belongs to a particular type. This is explained in Section 9.2 of your text.
- The use of a "strategy" interface for improving reusability is explained in Section 9.4 of your text.
- An inner class is a class that is declared inside another class. They are commonly used for tactical classes that are not visible elsewhere in the program. Inner classes are explained in Section 9.4 of your text.
- UML diagrams are useful for illustrating class relationships and dependencies. The UML notation for showing dependency and interface realization is explained in Section 9.1 of your text.
- Timer events are useful for programming animations and are explained in Section 9.5 of your text.

■ Things to Remember When Taking the AP Exam

- Early binding (overloading) of methods occurs if the *compiler* selects a method from several possible candidates, as it does with overloaded methods. Late binding (polymorphism) occurs if the method selection takes place when the program runs. This concept may be tested in multiple-choice questions.
- All methods in an interface are public. The methods in the interface are not declared as public because they are public by default. When implementing the methods of the interface in a class, remember to include the keyword `public`.
- An interface does not have any instance variables.

- You can convert from a class type to an interface type if the class realizes the interface, but you need a cast to convert from an interface type to a class type.
- For both the A and the AB Exams, you should be able to read the definitions of interfaces. For the AB exam, you should be able to define your own interfaces.
- An interface does not have constructors and cannot be instantiated, but you can assign an object created from a class that implements the interface. For example,
  - `Flier f = new Flier();   // WRONG!`
  - `Flier f = new Airplane();   // OK`

■ Key Words

You should understand the terms below. The AP CS Exam questions may include references to these terms. The citations in parentheses next to each term identify the page numbers where it is defined and/or discussed in *Computing Concepts with Java Essentials*, 3rd ed., and *Big Java*.

abstract (365)
cast (370)
constants (372)
early binding (373)

implements (366)
interface (365)
late (dynamic) binding (373)

polymorphism (372)
realize (implement) an
  interface (366)

■ Connecting the Detailed Topic Outline to the Text

The citations in parentheses identify where information in the outline can be located in *Computing Concepts with Java Essentials*, 3rd ed., and *Big Java*.

- Developing Reusable Solutions (364–368)
- Converting Between Types (370)
  - Constants in Interfaces (372)
- Polymorphism (372–373)

■ Practice Questions

Multiple Choice

1. Which of the following choices might serve as an interface for the other choices listed?
   a. `Piano`
   b. `Drum`
   c. `Guitar`
   d. `Instrument`
   e. `FrenchHorn`

Questions 2–5 refer to the `Flier` interface and the `Airplane` and `SkiJumper` classes whose incomplete definitions are given below.

```java
public interface Flier
{
   void fly();
}

public interface Athlete
{
   void train(double hours);
}

public class Airplane implements Flier
{
   public void fly()
   {
      System.out.println("Using my jet engines to fly");
   }
}

public class SkiJumper implements Flier, Athlete
{
   // Constructor
   public SkiJumper(String fName, String lName)
   {
      firstName = fName;
      lastName = lName;
      numberOfJumps = 0;
      hoursTraining = 0;
   }

   public void fly()
   {
      System.out.println("Using skis to take " + firstName + " "
            + lastName + " into the air.");
      numberOfJumps++;
   }

   public void train(double hours)
   {
      System.out.println("I am on the slopes for " + hours + "
            hours per day.");
   }

   public double getHoursTrained()
   {
      return hoursTraining;
   }

   public int getJumps()
   {
      return numberOfJumps;
   }
```

```
        private String firstName;
        private String lastName;
        private double hoursTraining;
        private int numberOfJumps;
    }
```

2. Which of the following code segments causes a compile-time error?

   a. `Airplane boeing707 = new Airplane();`

   b. `Flier boeing707 = new Flier();`

   c. `Flier boeing707 = new Airplane();`

   d. `Airplane boeing707 = new Airplane();`
      `Flier airTraveler = boeing707;`

   e. `Airplane boeing707 = new Airplane();`
      `Flier airTraveler;`
      `airTraveler = (Airplane)boeing707;`

3. Consider the following code segment.

```
1       Airplane skyRider = new Airplane();
2       Flier skyRider2 = skyRider;
3       Athlete skyRider3 = (Athlete)skyRider2;
4       Airplane skyRider4 = (Airplane)skyRider2;
5       Flier skyRider5 = skyRider4;
```

   Which statement above will cause a run-time error and throw an exception?

   a. Statement 1
   b. Statement 2
   c. Statement 3
   d. Statement 4
   e. Statement 5

Questions 4 and 5 refer to the following declarations.

```
        Airplane c = new Airplane();
        Flier f = new Airplane();
        Athlete a = new SkiJumper("Ann", "Smith");
        SkiJumper s = new SkiJumper("John", "Doe");
```

4. Which of the following statements is **not** legal?

   a. `c.fly();`
   b. `f.fly();`
   c. `a.train(3);`

   d. `s.train(3);`
   e. `a.fly();`

5. Which of the following statements needs a cast?

I. `f = c;`
II. `a = s;`
III. `s = a;`

    a. I only
    b. II only
    c. III only
    d. I and II only
    e. I and III only

6. Suppose a class `C` realizes an interface `I` by implementing all of the methods of `I` and no further methods. Then which of the following *must* be true?

    a. All instance variables of `C` are public.
    b. All methods of `C` are abstract.
    c. All methods of `C` are public.
    d. All constants of `C` are public.
    e. All instance variables of `C` are private.

7. Which of the following statements is true about casting?

    a. You must cast to convert from an interface type to a class type.
    b. You must cast to convert from a class type to an interface type.
    c. You cannot cast to convert an interface type to a class type.
    d. You cannot cast from a class type to an interface type.
    e. Both a and b above are true.

8. Which of the following statements is true about dynamic binding?

    a. Dynamic binding occurs during compile time.
    b. Dynamic binding occurs when the appropriate overloaded method is selected.
    c. Dynamic binding is another name for early binding.
    d. In dynamic binding, the virtual machine selects the appropriate method.
    e. Dynamic binding occurs only when an interface declares `public static final` constants.

9. Which of the following statements about interfaces is **not** true?

    a. An interface can specify constants that will be inherited by all classes that realize the interface.
    b. An interface can specify variables that will be inherited by all classes that realize the interface.

   c.   An interface can specify methods that will be inherited by all classes that realize the interface.

   d.   An interface name can be used anywhere a type can be used.

   e.   The interface contains declarations but not implementations.

10. Suppose `foo` is an object of class `C`, and `C` realizes the interface type `I`. Which of the following statements must be true?

   a.   `foo` was constructed with the constructor of `I`.

   b.   `C` assigns values to all constants declared in the interface `I`.

   c.   `C` supplies an implementation for all methods of the interface `I`.

   d.   `foo` is declared as

```
I foo = new C();
```

   e.   All methods of `I` are declared as `private`.

Free Response Questions

1. The `SkiJumper` class is to realize the `Comparable` interface. The present definition of `SkiJumper` is defined below.

```
public class SkiJumper implements Flier, Athlete
{
    // Constructs a default ski jumper.
    public SkiJumper(String fName, String lName)
    {
        firstName = fName;
        lastName = lName;
        numberOfJumps = 0;
        hoursTraining = 0;
    }

    // Simulates a ski jumper flying.
    public void fly()
    {
        System.out.println("Using skis to take " + firstName +
            " " + lastName + " into the air.");
        numberOfJumps++;
    }

    // Adds hours to total training time.
    // hours is the number of hours to add
    public void train(double hours)
    {
        System.out.println("I am on the slopes " + hours +
            " hours today.");
        hoursTraining += hours;
    }

    // Returns hours of training.
    public double getHoursTrained()
```

```
   {
      return hoursTraining;
   }

   // Returns total jumps made.
   public int getJumps()
   {
      return numberOfJumps;
   }
   private String firstName;
   private String lastName;
   private double hoursTraining;
   private int numberOfJumps;
}
```

a.   Adjust the class header so that the `Comparable` interface is realized by `SkiJumper`.

b.   Implement the necessary methods so that the `Comparable` interface is realized by the `SkiJumper` class. `SkiJumper` objects are compared by the number of jumps completed.

2.   Modify the `Purse` class defined below to realize the `Comparable` interface. Purses are compared by the total value of money contained in the purse.

```
public class Purse implements Comparable
{
   // Constructs an empty purse.
   public Purse()
   {
      nickels = 0;
      dimes = 0;
      quarters = 0;
   }

   // Adds nickels to the purse.
   // count is the number of nickels to add
   public void addNickels(int count)
   {
      nickels += count;
   }

   // Adds dimes to the purse.
   // count is the number of dimes to add
   public void addDimes(int count)
   {
      dimes += count;
   }

   // Adds quarters to the purse.
   // count is the number of quarters to add
   public void addQuarters(int count)
   {
      quarters += count;
```

```java
   }

   // Get the total value of the coins in the purse.
   // Returns the sum of all coin values.
   public double getTotal()
   {
      return nickels * NICKEL_VALUE
            + dimes * DIME_VALUE + quarters * QUARTER_VALUE;
   }

   private static final double NICKEL_VALUE = 0.05;
   private static final double DIME_VALUE = 0.1;
   private static final double QUARTER_VALUE = 0.25;

   private int nickels;
   private int dimes;
   private int quarters;
}
```

CHAPTER **10**

Inheritance

■ Topic Summary

10.1 Introduction to Inheritance

Inheritance extends classes that already exist. By extending existing classes, you can create new, more specific classes *and* take advantage of using code that is already written. Chapter 11 of your text revisits the `BankAccount` class to illustrate the key concepts of inheritance. We will revisit our `SkiJumper` class and redefine `Athlete` to illustrate these same concepts and to provide you with another example. In this example, `Athlete` will now be a class, not an interface. All methods in the `Athlete` interface now are implemented in the `Athlete` class.

We will make some basic assumptions:
- All athletes have a name and a sport in which they participate.
- An athlete keeps track of the number of hours of training done.
- All athletes train for the sport in which they participate.
- An athlete participates in only one sport.
- Athletes participating in different sports train in different ways.

Figure 10.1

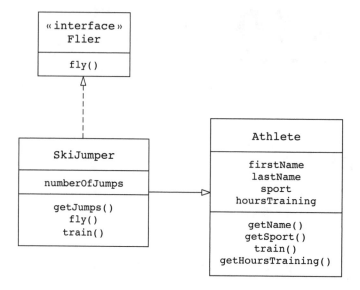

Figure 10.1 shows our `SkiJumper` class *implementing* the `Flier` interface and *extending* the `Athlete` class. `SkiJumper` is a *subclass* of `Athlete`. `Athlete` is a *superclass* of `SkiJumper`. `SkiJumper` *inherits* the instance fields `firstName`, `lastName`, `sport`, and `hoursTraining` and defines an additional instance field, `numberOfJumps` that is specific to `SkiJumper` and not particularly applicable to other athletes. `SkiJumper` will implement the methods `fly` (as promised when realizing the `Flier` interface) and `getJumps`. `SkiJumper` will also *override* the method `train` by implementing the `train` method in a particular way that differs from the training routine of other athletes. Inheriting from `Athlete` differs from realizing `Flier`. `Flier` is an interface and cannot be instantiated. `Flier` does not have state or behavior. `Athlete` is a class. `Athlete` defines state and behavior and can be instantiated. Example 10.1 adds code to our visual interpretation.

Example 10.1

```
/**
    Describes any class whose objects can fly.
*/
public interface Flier
{
    void fly();
}
```

```
/**
    Defines an athlete.
*/
public class Athlete
{
    /**
        Constructs an athlete; hoursTraining is initialized to 0.
        @param fName first name of athlete
        @param lName last name of athlete
        @param sportPlayed sport in which athlete participates
```

```
*/
public Athlete(String fName, String lName,
      String sportPlayed)
{
   firstName = fName;
   lastName = lName;
   sport = sportPlayed;
   hoursTraining = 0;
}

/**
   Updates hoursTraining.
   @param hours number of hours athlete trained
*/
public void train(double hours)
{
   System.out.println("Athlete training for " +
         hours + " hours.");
   hoursTraining += hours;
}

/**
   Gets athlete name.
   @return name of athlete
*/
public String getName()
{
   return (firstName + " " + lastName);
}

/**
   Gets sport of athlete.
   @return sport participated in
*/
public String getSport()
{
   return sport;
}

/**
   Gets hoursTrained by athlete.
   @return hoursTraining
*/
public double getHoursTraining()
{
   return hoursTraining;
}

private String firstName;
private String lastName;
private String sport;
```

```java
        private double hoursTraining;
}
```

```java
public class SkiJumper extends Athlete implements Flier
{
    /**
        Constructs a SkiJumper object.
        Sport is ski jumping.
        Number of jumps is initialized to 0.
        @param first the first name
        @param last the last name
    */
    public SkiJumper(String first, String last)
    {
        super(first, last, "Ski Jumping");
        numberOfJumps = 0;
    }

    /**
        Increments numberOfJumps, simulates flying.
    */
    public void fly()
    {
        System.out.println("Using skis to take " + getName() +
                " into the air.");
        numberOfJumps++;
    }

    /**
        Simulates training.
        @param hours hours of training
    */
    public void train(double hours)
    {
        System.out.println("I am on the slopes " + hours + " hours
                today.");
        super.train(hours);
    }

    /**
        Gets the current numberOfJumps of the SkiJumper.
        @return current numberOfJumps
    */
    public int getJumps()
    {
        return numberOfJumps;
    }
```

```
    private int numberOfJumps;
}
```

10.2   Inheritance Hierarchies

When the hierarchy in Section 10.1 was designed, the features and behaviors common to all athletes were collected in the `Athlete` superclass. All athletes have a first name, a last name, and a sport. It is therefore useful to include public methods that can return the name and sport of the athlete. All athletes train and it may useful to return the number of hours of training for any athlete. Figure 10.2 adds a `Runner` to our hierarchy and Example 10.2 implements the `Runner`. A `Runner` races. A `Runner` keeps track of the number of races run and the number of miles raced. A `Runner` does not fly.

Figure 10.2

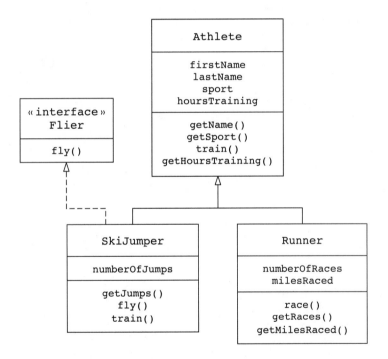

Example 10.2

```
public class Runner extends Athlete
{
    /**
        Constructs a Runner with a specified name.
        Sport is running.
        Number of races is initialized to 0.
        Miles raced is initialized to 0.
        @param first the first name
        @param last the last name
    */
    public Runner(String first, String last)
```

```
   {
       super(first, last, "Running");     // Call to super must be
                                          // first executable
                                          // statement in
                                          // constructor.
       numberOfRaces = 0;
       milesRaced = 0;
   }

   /**
       Increments number of races and updates miles raced.
       Simulates running a race.
   */
   public void race(double raceLength)
   {
       System.out.println(getName() + " is racing in a "
               + raceLength + " mile race.");
       numberOfRaces++;
       milesRaced += raceLength;
   }

   /**
       Gets the current number of races run by the runner.
       @return current numberOfRaces
   */
   public int getRaces()
   {
       return numberOfRaces;
   }

   /**
       Gets the current miles raced by the runner.
       @return current milesRaced
   */
   public double getMilesRaced()
   {
       return milesRaced;
   }

   private int numberOfRaces;
   private double milesRaced;
}
```

Notice that the `Runner` does not override `train`. The runner trains as a generic athlete trains but, in addition to hours of training, a `Runner` keeps track of hours racing and number of races run. The behavior and state of a `Runner` differ from those of the `SkiJumper`.

10.3   Inheriting Instance Fields and Methods

The methods `getName`, `getSport`, and `getHoursTraining` are inherited by the `SkiJumper` and the `Runner`.

The subclass `SkiJumper` of the `Athlete` class specifies the additional `getJumps` method and the `Runner` specifies the additional methods `race`, `getRaces`, and `getMilesRaced`.

The instance fields `firstName`, `lastName`, `sport`, and `hoursTraining` are inherited by `SkiJumper` and `Runner`. The subclass `SkiJumper` of the `Athlete` class specifies the additional instance field `numberOfJumps` and the `Runner` specifies the additional instance fields `numberOfRaces` and `milesRaced`.

Although the subclass inherits the private instance fields of the superclass, the subclass has no access to the private fields of the superclass. *Private* means that only the class in which the instance field or method is defined has access. In our examples, we update the private instance field `hoursTraining` of the superclass when the `Runner` trains and when the `SkiJumper` trains. This is done by invoking the public method `train` of the superclass thus preserving encapsulation. Each subclass does this is a different way.

- The `Runner` subclass does not have a `train` method defined. The `train` method that is invoked by `Runner` is the `train` method inherited from `Athlete`. `Athlete`'s `train` method updates `Athlete`'s own private instance variable `hoursTraining` that is inherited by the `Runner`.
- The `SkiJumper` implements a method `train` with the same signature as the method `train` of its superclass, `Athlete`. The `SkiJumper`'s `train` method overrides the `Athlete`'s `train` method. In order to update the inherited private instance field `hoursTraining`, the `SkiJumper`'s `train` method invokes the superclass `train` method with the call `super.train(...)`. The `super` keyword is used to call a method of the superclass that is overridden by a subclass.

Subclasses should not override instance fields. Subclasses can inherit instance fields and define new instance fields but should not override existing instance fields. The consequences of overriding instance fields are explained in Section 11.3 and *Common Error 11.2* in your text.

10.4   Subclass Construction

The constructor for `Athlete` has three `String` parameters, a first name, a last name, and a sport. The `Athlete` constructor initializes the appropriate instance fields with the values of these parameters and initializes `hoursTraining` to 0.

When the `Runner` or `SkiJumper` constructor is called, two `String` parameters are passed, the first and last names of the athlete. For example,

```
Runner racer1 = new Runner("Joe", "Thomas");
SkiJumper jumper = new SkiJumper("Jane", "Smith");
```

The `Runner` constructor invokes the `Athlete` constructor passing these two parameters and the `String` "Running" (the sport name) to the superclass constructor.

```
public Runner(String first, String last)
    {
        super(first, last, "Running");   // Call to super must be
                                         // first executable
                                         // statement in
                                         // constructor.

        numberOfRaces = 0;
        milesRaced = 0;
    }
```

The `SkiJumper` constructor invokes the `Athlete` constructor passing these two parameters and the `String` `"Ski Jumping"` (the sport name) to the superclass constructor.

```
public SkiJumper(String first, String last)
    {
        super(first, last, "Ski Jumping");
        numberOfJumps = 0;
    }
```

The call to the superclass constructor ensures that all inherited instance fields are properly initialized. When the superclass constructor is called from the subclass, it must be the first statement in the subclass constructor. If the subclass constructor does not include the call to the superclass constructor, the default constructor for the superclass will automatically be called. However, if there is no default constructor (as with `Athlete`), an error will be reported.

The instance fields that are not inherited are initialized in the subclass constructor.

10.5   Converting from Subclasses to Superclasses

If we wanted to have the ability to compare ski jumpers based on the number of jumps completed, the `SkiJumper` class would realize the `Comparable` interface

```
public class SkiJumper extends Athlete implements Flier,
        Comparable
```

and implement the `compareTo` method.

```
public int compareTo(Object other)
    {
        SkiJumper temp = (SkiJumper)other;
        if (numberOfJumps < temp.getJumps()) return -1;
        if (getJumps() > temp.getJumps()) return 1;
        return 0;
    }
```

Figure 10.3

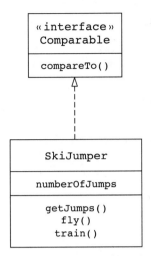

Since we want to compare the number of jumps of two `SkiJumper`s, we cast the `Object` parameter to a `SkiJumper`.

Suppose the following declarations were made.

```
SkiJumper jumper1 = new SkiJumper("John", "Miller");
SkiJumper jumper2 = new SkiJumper("Jane", "Dole");
Athlete jumper3 = new SkiJumper("Mark", "Morris");
Runner racer1 = new Runner("Mary", "Smith");
```

The following calls to `compareTo` are legal.

```
if (jumper1.compareTo(jumper2) > 0)
    // Code here

if (jumper2.compareTo(jumper1) > 0)
    // Code here

if (jumper1.compareTo(jumper3) > 0)
    // Code here
```

However, the statement

```
if (jumper3.compareTo(jumper1) > 0)    // WRONG!
    // Code here
```

will not compile. `jumper3` is an `Athlete` and `compareTo` is not defined in the `Athlete` class.

The statement

```
if (jumper1.compareTo(racer1) > 0)
    // Code here
```

will compile but will throw a `ClassCastException` at runtime because the `compareTo` method of the `SkiJumper` class tries to cast a `Runner` to a `SkiJumper` in the first statement.

The statements

```
jumper3.fly();
racer1.fly();
```

will cause a compile-time errors because `fly` is not defined for `Athlete` or for `Runner`.

The statement

```
jumper3.train(2);
```

is a legal statement because `train` is defined for `Athlete`. The `train` method of the `SkiJumper` class is invoked. Method calls are always determined by the type of the actual object (`SkiJumper`), not the type of the object reference (`Athlete`). This is an example of late (dynamic) binding.

The assignment

```
jumper3 = jumper1    // OK because SkiJumper is a subclass of
                     // Athlete
```

is legal. An object of a subclass can be assigned to an object of its superclass.

The assignment

```
jumper1 = (SkiJumper)jumper3    // OK, cast necessary
```

is legal. An object of a superclass can be assigned to an object of its subclass with proper casting.

Example 10.3 is a sample client program to test these concepts.

Example 10.3

```
public class InheritanceTest
{
   public static void main(String[] args)
   {
      SkiJumper jumper1 = new SkiJumper("John", "Miller");
      SkiJumper jumper2 = new SkiJumper("Jane", "Dole");
      Athlete jumper3 = new SkiJumper("Mark", "Morris");

      jumper1.fly();
      jumper1.fly();
      jumper2.fly();
      jumper2.fly();
      jumper2.fly();

      if (jumper1.compareTo(jumper2) > 0)
```

```
        {
            System.out.println(jumper1.getName() + " is better than "
                    + jumper2.getName() + ".");
        }
        else if (jumper1.compareTo(jumper2) < 0)
        {
            System.out.println(jumper2.getName() + " is better than "
                    + jumper1.getName() + ".");
        }
        else
        {
            System.out.println("The jumpers have completed an equal
                    number of jumps!");
        }
        jumper3.train(2);
    }
}
```

The results of program execution are:

> *Using skis to take John Miller into the air.*
> *Using skis to take John Miller into the air.*
> *Using skis to take Jane Dole into the air.*
> *Using skis to take Jane Dole into the air.*
> *Using skis to take Jane Dole into the air.*
> *Jane Dole is better than John Miller.*
> *I am on the slopes 2.0 hours today.*
> *Athlete training for 2.0 hours.*

10.6   Abstract Classes

An abstract method is a method whose implementation is not specified. An abstract class is a class that contains an abstract method. Abstract classes cannot be instantiated. Abstract classes can be used if you want to force programmers to define a method. Let's redefine our `Athlete` class one more time to demonstrate an `abstract` class. In the following example, `Athlete` is an abstract class which means it cannot be instantiated.

Example 10.4

```
public abstract class Athlete
{
    public Athlete(String fName, String lName, String sportPlayed)
    {
        firstName = fName;
        lastName = lName;
        sport = sportPlayed;
        hoursTraining = 0;
    }

    // Other methods here
    public abstract String getDietPlan();
```

```
        //  More code here

    }
```

Example 10.4 mandates that any subclass of `Athlete` must implement the method `getDietPlan`. If the subclass does not define this `abstract` method, the subclass cannot be instantiated and must be declared as `abstract` itself. `Runner` might define `getDietPlan` in the following way.

```
public String getDietPlan()
{
    return "25% protein, 65% carbohydrates, 10% fat";
}
```

An abstract class differs from an interface because an abstract class can have instance variables and concrete (implemented) methods that are inherited by subclasses. Although you cannot instantiate an abstract class, you can still have an object reference whose type is an abstract class. For example, the following assignment is legal.

```
Athlete jumper3 = new SkiJumper("Mark", "Morris");  // This is OK.
```

10.7 Access Control

Java has four levels of access to fields, methods, and classes.
- public
- private
- protected
- package

The AP CS Java subset does not include `protected` and package visibilities. The Java Marine Biology Simulation case study uses `protected` access control. Any questions about `protected` access control on the AP Exam will be limited to the case study questions.

The `protected` level of visibility allows for access by all subclasses and all classes in the same package. This method of access control is explained in *Advanced Topic 11.3* of your text. In our `Athlete` example, if we declared `hoursTraining` as `protected`, then the `Runner` and the `SkiJumper` would be able to access and update this instance field of `Athlete` directly. In our example, the `Athlete`'s `train` method is called to update this variable because it is private.

10.8 `Object`: The Cosmic Superclass

In Java, all classes inherit from the `Object` class. The methods of the `Object` class included in the AP CS subset are listed in Table 10.1.

Table 10.1

class java.lang.Object

Method	Method Summary
String toString()	Returns String representation of the object.
boolean equals(Object other)	Indicates whether the object other is "equal to" this one.

10.8.1 Overriding the toString Method

The toString method is automatically called by System.out.println. If our InheritanceTest client program invokes the statement

```
System.out.println(jumper1);
```

Object's toString method is called and a cryptic message about SkiJumper is printed to the screen. However, we may wish to print a meaningful message about SkiJumper that includes values of the instance variables. This will allow us to inspect the object for possible errors in our program. In order to do this, SkiJumper must override the Object toString method.

```
public String toString()
{
    return "SkiJumper numberOfJumps = " + numberOfJumps;
}
```

The statement

```
System.out.println(jumper1);
```

will now print *SkiJumper numberOfJumps = 2.*

It may be more useful to provide a toString that prints the values of all instance fields. A toString method for Athlete might be:

```
public String toString ()
{
    return ("class Athlete: \nname = " + firstName + " " + lastName
        + "\nsport = " + sport + "\nhoursTraining = " +
        hoursTraining);
}
```

and the more inclusive toString method for SkiJumper would be:

```
public String toString()
{
    String s = super.toString();
    return (s + "\nclass SkiJumper:\nnumberOfJumps = " +
        numberOfJumps);
}
```

The statement

```
System.out.println(jumper2);
```

would print

> *class Athlete:*
> *name = Jane Dole*
> *sport = Ski Jumping*
> *hoursTraining = 0.0*
> *class SkiJumper:*
> *numberOfJumps = 3*

You can include whatever meaningful information you need when you override `Object`'s `toString` method. It is a good programming habit to supply a `toString` method in the classes that you write.

10.8.2 Overriding the `equals` Method

If you wish to test whether two objects have equal states (have the same contents), you need to override `Object`'s `equals` method. An `equals` method for `Athlete` would be:

```
public boolean equals(Object other)
{
    Athlete temp = (Athlete)other;
    return ((firstName.equals(temp.firstName)) &&
            (lastName.equals(temp.lastName)) &&
            (sport.equals(temp.sport)) &&
            (hoursTraining == temp.hoursTraining));
}
```

The parameter `other` needs to be cast to `Athlete`. Since three of the instance fields are objects (`Strings`), they need to be compared using the `String equals` method. The `hoursTraining` instance field is a number. Numbers are compared using the == operator. Objects are compared using `equals`.

Although the implementation of the `equals` method is not part of the AP CS testable Java subset, you do need to understand the difference between object equality (`equals`) and identity (==).

■ Expanded Coverage of Material That Is Not Found in the Text

- The inheritance relationship between a subclass and its superclass is an *IS-A* relationship. The subclass is more specific than the superclass. For example,
  - A SkiJumper IS A Athlete
  - A Runner IS A Athlete

  Not all athletes are runners. Not all athletes are ski jumpers. A good check for subclass selection is to apply this IS-A phrase. Ask yourself if your IS-A statement is true. Chapter 16 of your text covers IS-A relationships in more detail.

- An object can be composed of other objects. For example, an `Athlete` has a first name, a last name, and a sport. All three of these instance fields are `String` objects. This situation is an example of a *HAS-A* relationship. *HAS-A* relationships are used when a class is composed of other types of object. This is often referred to as composition. For example,
  - A `SkiJumper` HAS-A name.
  - A `DeckOfPlayingCards` HAS-A `Card`.
  - An `Airplane` HAS-A `Engine`.

Chapter 16 of your text covers HAS-A relationships in more detail.

■ Topics That Are Useful But Not Tested

- `protected` features can be accessed by all subclasses and all classes in the same package. `protected` access is explained in *Advanced Topic 11.3* of your text.
- The `getClass().getName()` call can be used to print the class name in a `toString` method. This is explained in *Advanced Topic 11.4* of your text.
- The `getClass` method can also be used to test if two objects belong to the same class. This is explained in *Advanced Topic 11.5* of your text.

■ Things to Remember When Taking the AP Exam

- A subclass inherits the behavior and state of its superclass.
- Do not name an instance field of a subclass the same name as an instance field of its superclass. This "shadowing of instance fields" is explained in *Common Error 11.2* of your text.
- A subclass has no access to the private fields of its superclass.
- The call to a superclass constructor must be the first statement in the subclass constructor.
- An object of a subclass can be assigned to an object of its superclass.
- An object of a superclass can be assigned to an object of its subclass with the appropriate casting.
- An abstract class cannot be instantiated.
- The AP CS Java subset specifies that all classes are public and all instance variables are private. The AP CS Java subset does not use `protected` and package (default) visibility but you may see these access modifiers in the case study.
- For both the A and AB Exams you should be able to extend existing code using inheritance. For the AP CS A Exam, you should be able to modify subclass implementations. For the AP CS AB Exam, you should be able to design and implement subclasses.
- For the AP CS A Exam, you should understand the concepts of abstract classes. For the AP CS AB Exam, you should be able to design and implement abstract classes.
- Implementing the `equals` method is not part of the AP CS subsets, but you do need to understand the difference between object equality (`equals`) and identity (`==`).

■ Key Words

You should understand the terms below. The AP CS Exam questions may include references to these terms. The citations in parentheses next to each term identify the page numbers where it is defined and/or discussed in *Computing Concepts with Java Essentials*, 3rd ed., and *Big Java*.

abstract class (450)	inheritance (430)	super (439)
abstract method (449)	Object (430, 454)	subclass (430)
access control (451)	override (431)	superclass (430)
equals (459)	private (451)	toString (455)
extends (430)	public (451)	

■ Connecting the Detailed Topic Outline to the Text

The citations in parentheses identify where information in the outline can be located in *Computing Concepts with Java Essentials*, 3rd ed., and *Big Java*.

- Introduction to Inheritance (430–434)
- Inheritance Hierarchies (434–436)
- Inheriting Instance Fields and Methods (436–442)
- Subclass Construction (442)
- Converting from Subclasses to Superclasses (443–449)
- Abstract Classes (449–450)
- Access Control (451)
- Object: The Cosmic Superclass (454–462)
    - Overriding the toString Method (455–457)
    - Overriding the equals Method (459–460)

■ Practice Questions

Multiple Choice

1. A programmer notices that a method of a subclass has the same signature as a method in its superclass. Which of the following statements best characterizes this situation?

   a. The superclass method is overloaded.
   b. The superclass method shadows the subclass method.
   c. The subclass method overrides the superclass method.
   d. The superclass method overrides the subclass method.
   e. The program will not compile because methods of two classes in the same inheritance hierarchy cannot have the same name.

2. Which of the following statements is true about abstract classes?

   a. Instance fields declared in abstract classes are automatically `public`.
   b. Instance fields cannot be declared in abstract classes.
   c. A subclass that extends an abstract class must override instance variables declared in the abstract class.
   d. A subclass that extends an abstract class inherits the instance variables in the abstract class.
   e. The instance fields declared in an abstract class are automatically `static final`.

3. Which of the following statements is **not** true about subclass methods?

   a. A subclass can override methods in a superclass.
   b. A subclass can define new methods that are not in the superclass.
   c. A subclass can inherit methods in a superclass.
   d. A subclass can access private fields in a superclass.
   e. A subclass can access public methods of its superclass.

Questions 4, 5, and 6 refer to the `Employee`, `Manager`, and `Programmer` classes incompletely defined below.

```
public class Employee
{
    // Constructors and other methods here

    public void work()
    {
        System.out.println("Employee working.");
    }

    // Instance fields here
}
```

```
public class Manager extends Employee
{
    // Constructors and other methods here

    public void work()
    {
        System.out.println("Manager working.");
    }

    // Instance fields here
}
```

```
public class Programmer extends Employee
{
    // Constructors and other methods here
```

```
public void work()
{
    System.out.println("Programmer working.");
}

//  Instance fields here
}
```

4. Which of the following declarations will cause a compile-time error?

   a. Employee employA = new Employee();
   b. Employee employB = new Manager();
   c. Manager employC = new Manager();
   d. Manager employD = new Employee();
   e. Programmer employE = new Programmer();

5. Consider the following declarations.

   ```
   Employee employ1 = new Employee();
   Manager employ2 = new Manager();
   Employee employ3 = new Manager();
   ```

Which of the following assignments is legal?

I.   employ1 = employ2;
II. employ2 = (Manager)employ3;
III. employ1 = (Manager)employ2;

   a. I only
   b. II only
   c. III only
   d. I and II only
   e. I, II, and III

6. Consider the following declarations.

   ```
   Employee employ1 = new Employee();
   Manager employ2 = new Manager();
   Employee employ3 = new Manager();
   ```

What will be printed if the code segment below is executed?

   ```
   employ1 = (Manager)employ2;
   employ1.work();
   employ3.work();
   ```

   a. *Manager working.*
       Manager working.

b. *Employee working.*
Employee working.

c. *Employee working.*
Manager working.

d. *Manager working.*
Employee working.

e. Nothing is printed. A `ClassCastException` occurs.

7. You implement three classes: `Person`, `Student` and `Instructor`. A `Person` has a name and a year of birth. A `Student` has a major, and an `Instructor` has a salary. Which of the following would be the best design for this situation?

a. `Person` should be an interface. `Student` and `Instructor` should realize `Person`.
b. `Person` should be an abstract class that includes declarations for four abstract methods: `getName`, `getYearOfBirth`, `getMajor`, `getSalary`.
c. `Person` should be an abstract class that includes declarations for two abstract methods: `getName` and `getYearOfBirth`.
d. `Person` should be a superclass that includes implementations for four methods: `getName`, `getYearOfBirth`, `getMajor`, `getSalary`. `Student` and `Instructor` will be subclasses of `Person`.
e. `Person` should be a superclass that includes implementations for two methods: `getName`, `getYearOfBirth`. `Student` and `Instructor` will be subclasses of `Person`.

Questions 8 and 9 refer to the following scenario.

A Barbershop Quartet is a group of four singers: a lead, a tenor, a bass, and a baritone. These four singers harmonize to produce a purely American form of music developed in the 19th century. Consider the incomplete class definitions below.

```
public class BarberShopQuartet
{
    public BarberShopQuartet()
    {
        Tenor highSinger = new Tenor();
        Baritone bari = new Baritone();
        Lead melody = new Lead();
        Bass lowSinger = new Bass();
        System.out.println("Quartet created.");
    }
}
```

```
public class Singer
{
    public Singer()
    {
```

```
            System.out.println("Singing...");
        }
    }
```

```
    public class Tenor extends Singer
    {
        public Tenor()
        {
            System.out.println("Singing...the high notes");
        }
    }
```

```
    public class Baritone extends Singer
    {
        public Baritone()
        {
            System.out.println("Singing...harmonizing with the lead.");
        }
    }
```

```
    public class Lead extends Singer
    {
        public Lead()
        {
            System.out.println("Singing...the melody and providing the
                    emotion");
        }
    }
```

```
    public class Bass extends Singer
    {
        public Bass()
        {
            System.out.println("Singing...the very low notes");
        }
    }
```

8. What output would be produced if the following code was executed?

```
    BarberShopQuartet fourSingers = new BarberShopQuartet();
    System.out.println("This quartet is on stage!");
```

a. *Quartet created.*
    This quartet is on stage!

b. *This quartet is on stage!*

c. *Singing ... the high notes*
Singing ... harmonizing with the lead.
Singing ... the melody and providing the emotion
Singing ... the very low notes
This quartet is on stage!

d. *Singing ... the high notes*
Singing ... harmonizing with the lead.
Singing ... the melody and providing the emotion
Singing ... the very low notes
Quartet created.
This quartet is on stage!

e. *Singing ...*
Singing ... the high notes
Singing ...
Singing ... harmonizing with the lead.
Singing ...
Singing ... the melody and providing the emotion
Singing ...
Singing ... the very low notes
Quartet created.
This quartet is on stage!

9. Which of the following IS-A, HAS-A relationships is true?

a. A `BarberShopQuartet` is-a `Singer`.
b. A `Tenor` is-a `Singer`.
c. A `Baritone` has-a `BarbershopQuartet`.
d. A `Singer` has-a `BarberShopQuartet`.
e. A `Singer` has-a `Lead`.

10. Which of the following statements about inheritance is **not** true?

a. A class can be both a subclass and a superclass at the same time.
b. Every class is a subclass of the `Object` class.
c. Common features should be located as high in the inheritance hierarchy as possible.
d. The `toString` and `equals` methods are inherited by all classes.
e. The type of the reference, not the type of the object, is used to determine which version of an overridden method is invoked.

Free Response Questions

1. Consider the following detailed inheritance hierarchy diagram.

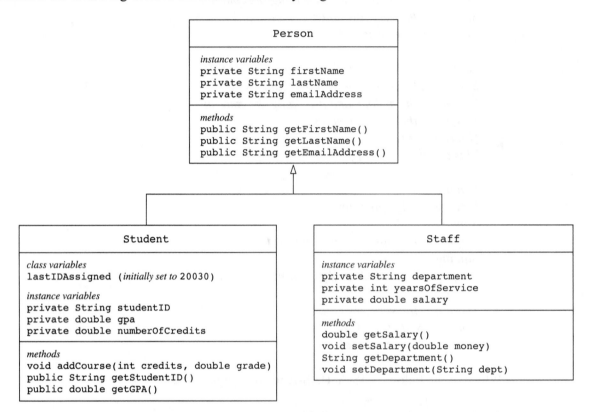

a. The `Person` constructor has two `String` parameters, a first name and a last name. The constructor initializes the email address to the first letter of the first name followed by the first five letters of the last name followed by @ccj.com. If the last name has fewer than five letters, the email address will be the first letter of the first name followed by the entire last name followed by @ccj.com. Examples:

Name	Email address
Jane Smith	JSmith@ccj.com
John Morris	JMorri@ccj.com
Mary Key	MKey@ccj.com

Implement the `Person` constructor.

b. Implement the `Student` class according to the following specifications. The `Student` is a subclass of `Person`. The `Student` constructor will be called with two `String` parameters, the first name and the last name of the student. When the `Student` is constructed, the inherited fields `firstName`, `lastName`, and `emailAddress` will be properly initialized, the `Student`'s `gpa` and `numberOfCredits` will be set to 0, and the `StudentID` will be set to the next available ID number as tracked by the class variable, `lastIDAssigned`. `lastIDAssigned` will be properly incremented each time a `Student` is constructed. The first `Student` constructed will have ID number 20031. Assume that the constructor written for part a of this problem works as intended.

c.   Override `Object`'s `toString` method for the `Person` class. The `toString` method should return the present state of the object. Assume that the constructors written for the previous parts of this problem work as intended.

d.   Override `Object`'s `toString` method for the `Student` class. The `toString` method should return the present state of the object. Assume that all methods and constructors written for the previous parts of this problem work as intended.

e.   Students need to be able to be sorted by their GPAs. Write the `Student` class header so that the `Student` class realizes the `Comparable` interface.

f.   Students are compared to each other by comparing GPAs. Implement the `compareTo` method for the `Student` class.

2.   Refer to the `Athlete` class and the `Runner` class below.

```
public class Athlete
{
   public Athlete(String fName, String lName, String sportPlayed)
   {
      firstName = fName;
      lastName = lName;
      sport = sportPlayed;
      hoursTraining = 0;
   }

   public void train(double hours)
   {
      System.out.println("Athlete training for " + hours + "
            hours.");
      hoursTraining += hours;
   }

   public String getName()
   {
      return (firstName + " " + lastName);
   }

   public String getSport()
   {
      return sport;
   }

   public double getHoursTraining()
   {
      return hoursTraining;
   }
```

```
        private String firstName;
        private String lastName;
        private String sport;
        private double hoursTraining;
    }
```

```
    public class Runner extends Athlete
    {
        public Runner(String first, String last)
        {
            super(first, last, "Running");
            numberOfRaces = 0;
            milesRaced = 0;
        }

        public void race(double raceLength)
        {
            System.out.println(getName() + " is racing in a "
                    + raceLength + " mile race.");
            numberOfRaces++;
            milesRaced += raceLength;
        }

        public int getRaces()
        {
            return numberOfRaces;
        }

        public double getMilesRaced()
        {
            return milesRaced;
        }

        private int numberOfRaces;
        private double milesRaced;
    }
```

A `Marathoner` is a long distance `Runner`. Write the `Marathoner` class according to the following specifications.

The `Marathoner` is a subclass of the `Runner` class. The `Marathoner`'s sport is "Running". However, in order for a race to "count" as a *race* for the `Marathoner`, the race must be at least 10 miles in length. If it is shorter than 10 miles, the race counts as a training run and the training time credited to `hoursTraining` is 8 1/2 minutes for each mile run. The `numberOfRaces` is not incremented, nor is the `milesRaced` increased if the race is shorter than 10 miles in length. The `Marathoner` class will override the `Runner`'s race method so that these specifications are met.

3. Sketch a class hierarchy for the following classes. (Think *is-a* and *has-a*.)

```
Person
Course
Lecture
Teacher
Lab
MathDepartmentChairperson
Student
Object
IndependentStudy
BiologyLab
Employee
Secretary
Nurse
ChemistryLab
```

CHAPTER **11**

Array Lists and Arrays

■ Topic Summary

11.1   Array Lists

It is very common for applications to require us to store a large amount of data and process that data in any number of ways. Up to now, we have dealt only with data that we were able to store in a single field as a primitive data type or as an object. We will now look at a way to store large amounts of data in a single collection that can be referred to with a single variable.

An array list is a sequence of objects that grows and shrinks as needed. This Java construct provides us with a means to easily deal with large amounts of data. The `ArrayList` class is part of the `java.util` package of the Java standard class library. It is this class that we will first investigate as a way to store a sequence of objects. There are many advantages to using array lists to store data, including

- Each element in the sequence can be accessed separately.
- We can explicitly overwrite an object at a specified position in the sequence, thus changing its value.
- We can inspect the object at a specified location in the sequence.
- We can add an object into a specified position of the sequence.
- We can add an object to the end of the sequence.
- We can remove an object from a specified location in the sequence.

Although the `ArrayList` class has many methods, only those listed in Table 11.1 are included in the AP Java subset to be tested on the AP CS Exam.

Table 11.1
class java.util.ArrayList

Method	Method Summary
`boolean add(Object x)`	Adds x to the end of the list and adjusts the size of the array list.
`void add(int index, Object x)`	Inserts x at position index, sliding elements at position index and higher to the right (adds 1 to their indices), and adjusts size.
`Object get(int index)`	Returns the element at index.
`Object remove(int index)`	Removes the element at position index, sliding elements at position index + 1 and higher to the left (subtracts 1 from their indices), and adjusts size.
`Object set(int index, Object x)`	Replaces the element at index with x and returns the element formerly at the specified position.
`int size()`	Returns the number of elements in this list.
`Iterator iterator() (AB only)`	Returns an iterator over the elements in this list in proper sequence.

We will examine these array list methods by looking at a simple example. It is important to remember that an array list contains *objects*. When we access elements from an array list, many times we must cast them to the appropriate type. As you read through the following array list example, think about the order in which the array list is being built.

Example 11.1

```
1      import java.util.ArrayList;
2      public class ArrayListTest
3      {
4         public static void main(String arg[])
5         {
6             ArrayList students = new ArrayList();
7             students.add("Mary");
8             students.add("James");
9             students.add("Kevin");

10            students.add(1, "Tanya");

11            String temp = (String)students.get(3);
12            System.out.println(temp);
13            students.remove(2);

14            students.set(1, "John");
15            System.out.println(students.size());
16        }
17    }
```

Line 1 The `Arraylist` class is contained in the `java.util` package.

Line 6 constructs an `ArrayList`. This `ArrayList` is empty.

Lines 7, 8, and 9 add `String` objects to the `ArrayList`, each at the end of the list.

At this point, `students` contains [Mary, James, Kevin].

Line 10 inserts "Tanya" into position 1 of `students`.

- The first position in an `ArrayList` has index 0.

At this point, `students` contains [Mary, Tanya, James, Kevin].

Line 11 accesses the object in position 3 and assigns this to the `String` variable `temp`.

- `temp` is a `String` so you must *cast* the `ArrayList` Object to a `String`.

Line 12 prints *Kevin*.

Line 13 removes "James" from `students`.

At this point, `students` contains [Mary, Tanya, Kevin].

Line 14 overwrites the object in position 1 thus changing "Tanya" to "John".

At this point, `students` contains [Mary, John, Kevin].

Line 15 prints *3*.

Although Example 11.1 deals with `String` objects, array lists can contain any type of objects. Section 13.1 of your text uses `Coin` objects to demonstrate these same methods.

You should be familiar with the simple array list algorithms that are discussed in Section 13.2 of your text. These algorithms include searching for a specific item in an array list, counting occurrences of some value in the list, and finding the minimum value or maximum value in the list. In many of these algorithms, an array list is traversed. We can do this with a simple `for` loop.

Example 11.2

```
for (int i = 0; i < students.size(); i++)
{
    String temp = (String)students.get(i);
    // Process temp.
    // Remember that an ArrayList contains Objects and
    // casting the Object may be necessary.
}
```

11.1.1 A Word about Efficiency

To add a student into a specific position in the array list requires one call to the `ArrayList` method `add`. From Example 11.1,

```
students.add(1, "Tanya");   // adds Tanya to position 1 of students
```

or, more generally

```
students.add(p, name);   // adds name to position p of students
```

The "hidden" implementation of this operation requires much more work than is visible to us with that one simple call! When the `add` method is called with two parameters, the elements in the `ArrayList` starting at position `p` (specified by first parameter) are each shifted "down" one position so that the new object can be inserted in the requested position. Of course, the "hidden" implementation takes care of making room for our addition and shifting the elements (adjusting the indices) correctly.

Figure 11.1

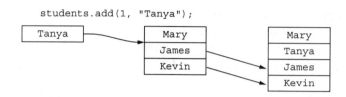

The `remove` method of the `ArrayList` class also requires more work than is evident to us. In Example 11.1, the call

```
students.remove(2);    // Removes the Object in position 2 of
                       // students.
```

or, more generally

```
students.remove(p);    // Removes the Object in position p of
                       // students.
```

removes the object is position p and shifts elements with indices greater than p "up" one.

Figure 11.2

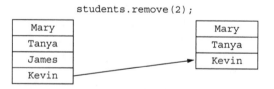

The "hidden" implementation again takes care of readjusting the `ArrayList size` and shifting the elements (adjusting the indices) correctly so we now must be careful not to index the out-of-bounds element by calling `students.get(3)`!

The `size`, `get`, and `set` methods operate in constant time. This means that the efficiency is not dependent on the size of the array list. These operations are very efficient. The `add` operation's hidden implementation shifts elements. Think about this. If we add an element to the end of the array list, no shifts are necessary. If we add an element to an array list in position 0, all of the elements in the array list need to be shifted! With the `remove` operation, removing the last element requires no shifting of elements. Removing an element in position 0 requires all of the elements in the array list to be shifted! We will look at a more formal analysis of algorithm efficiency in Chapter 15.

11.1.2   Wrapper Classes

One of the advantages of using array lists is that an array list grows dynamically. The size of the array list is not fixed. But array lists must contain objects. Numbers are not objects. In order to store doubles or integers in array lists you must use *wrapper* classes. These wrapper classes wrap numbers into objects. You can then store these objects in array lists.

The methods of the `Integer` wrapper class that are tested on the AP CS Exam are listed in Table 11.2.

Table 11.2
class java.lang.Integer implements java.lang.Comparable

Method	*Method Summary*
`Integer(int value)`	Constructs an object that represents the specified `int` value.
`int intValue()`	Returns the value of this `Integer` as an `int`.
`boolean equals(Object other)`	Compares this object to `other`. The result is `true` if and only if the argument is not `null` and is an `Integer` object that contains the same `int` value as this object.
`String toString()`	Returns a `String` object representing this `Integer`'s value.
`int compareTo(Object other)`	Compares this `Integer` object to `other`. If the object is an `Integer`, returns the value 0 if the argument is an `Integer` numerically equal to this `Integer`; a value less than 0 if `other` is an `Integer` numerically greater than this Integer; and a value greater than 0 if `other` is an `Integer` numerically less than this `Integer`. If the object is not an `Integer`, it throws a `ClassCastException` (because `Integer` objects are only comparable to other `Integer` objects).

Suppose we wish to write a program that generates some random number of random integers. These integers will be stored in an array list. The contents of the array list will be printed to the screen and the largest number in the array list will be found and printed to the screen. Let's look at a few methods that might help us accomplish these tasks.

Example 11.3   Filling the List

```
public static ArrayList generateRandomIntegers(ArrayList nums)
{
    final int UPLIMIT = some positive integer value;
    final int TOPNUM = some positive integer value;
    Random generator = new Random();
    int rnum;
    // Generates the number of numbers that nums will have.
    // 0 <= numberOfNums < UPLIMIT
    int numberOfNums = generator.nextInt(UPLIMIT);
    for (int i = 0; i < numberOfNums; i++)
    {
        rnum = generator.nextInt(TOPNUM);   // a random int,
                                            // 0 <= rnum < TOPNUM
        nums.add(new Integer(rnum));   // wrapped in Integer
    }
```

```
        return nums;
    }
```

Example 11.4   Printing the List

```
    public static void printArrayList(ArrayList nums)
    {
        for (int i = 0; i < nums.size(); i++)
        {
            System.out.print(nums.get(i) + " ");
        }
    System.out.println();
    }
```

Notice that `nums.get(i)` returns an `Object`. When included in the `System.out.println` statement, the `toString` method of the `Object` (in this case an `Integer`) returned by `get` is called. This results in the intended output of the integers.

Example 11.5   Finding the Largest Number in the List

```
    public static int findLargest(ArrayList nums)
    {
        Integer large = (Integer)nums.get(0);    // Initializes large to
                                                 // first element
        for (int i = 0; i < nums.size(); i++)
        {
            Integer tempLarge = (Integer)nums.get(i);
            if (tempLarge.compareTo(large) > 0)    // Compares each
                                                   // element to large
            {
                large = tempLarge;    // Reassigns to large if larger
                                      // value found
            }
        }
        return large.intValue();    // Returns the int value of large
    }
```

An alternate method for finding the largest value in an array list can be found in Section 13.2.3 of your text.

You are also responsible for the `Double` wrapper class. The `Double` wrapper class is very similar to the `Integer` wrapper class. The methods tested on the AP CS Exam are listed in Table 11.3.

Table 11.3
class java.lang.Double implements java.lang.Comparable

Method	Method Summary
Double(double value)	Constructs an object that represents the specified `double` value.
double doubleValue()	Returns the value of this `Double` as a `double`.
boolean equals(Object other)	Compares this object to `other`. The result is `true` if and only if the argument is not `null` and is a `Double` object that contains the same `double` value as this object.
String toString()	Returns a `String` object representing this `Double`'s value.
int compareTo(Object other)	Compares this `Double` object to `other`. If the object is a `Double`, returns the value 0 if the argument is a `Double` numerically equal to this `Double`; a value less than 0 if `other` is a `Double` numerically greater than this `Double`; and a value greater than 0 if `other` is a `Double` numerically less than this `Double`. If the object is not a `Double`, it throws a `ClassCastException` (because `Double` objects are only comparable to other `Double` objects).

11.2 Arrays

11.2.1 One-Dimensional Arrays

An *array* is a fixed-length sequence of values of the same type. One-dimensional arrays store linear sequences of primitive types or objects. When an array variable is declared, it must be given a length before adding elements to it.

Example 11.6

```
private static final int MAXELTS = 10;
int[] array1 = new int[MAXELTS];   // array1 is an array of 10
                                   // int values initialized to 0
for (int i = 0; i < MAXELTS; i++)
{
    array1[i] = i;   // array1 = {0 1 2 3 4 5 6 7 8 9}
}
System.out.println("Printing Array1");
for (int i = 0; i < array1.length; i++)
    // length is attribute of array1
    // notice that this is NOT a method call
{
    System.out.print(array1[i] + " ");   // 0 1 2 3 4 5 6 7 8 9
}
```

Arrays can also be instantiated using initializer lists.

Example 11.7

```
int[] array2 = {10, 20, 30, 40, 50, 60, 70, 80};
    // Initializer list
```

```
System.out.println("Printing Array2");
for (int i = 0; i < array2.length; i++)    // array2's length is 8
{
    System.out.print(array2[i] + " ");    // 10 20 30 40 50 60 70 80
}
```

When you declare an array of a certain size, its length is fixed. Well, what happens if you run out of room before you are done filling it? If this happens, you could create another array that is twice as large as the first, copy all of the elements from the first array to the second, and assign the reference of the first array to the second. Example 11.8 demonstrates this technique.

Example 11.8

```
int[] copyOfarray1 = new int[2 * array1.length];
    // copyOfarray1 is twice as big as array1

for (int i = 0; i < array1.length; i++)
{
    copyOfarray1[i] = array1[i];
        // Primitive types copied (ints)
        // and the rest of the elements of copyOfarray1 are
        // initialized to 0.
}

System.out.println("Printing Array3");
for (int i = 0; i < copyOfarray1.length; i++)
{
    System.out.print(copyOfarray1[i] + " ");
        // {0 1 2 3 4 5 6 7 8 9 0 0 0 0 0 0 0 0 0 0}
}
array1 = copyOfarray1;
```

As you can see in Example 11.8, the number of elements you actually have put into the array may be different from length. This will require you to keep track of the number of filled elements with another variable unless the array is filled and the number of filled elements doesn't change. Section 13.6 discusses partially-filled arrays.

Also remember to be careful when copying elements from one array (or array list) to another. If your array contains *objects*, you are dealing with references. If it is your intention to actually have a *copy* of the array or array list then be careful to create a new object for each object that you want to copy.

Example 11.9

```
1    final int MAXELTS = 3;
2    Coin[] coins = new Coin[MAXELTS];
3    coins[0] = new Coin(0.05, "nickel");
4    coins[1] = new Coin(0.10, "dime");
5    coins[2] = new Coin(0.01, "penny");

6    // Copies coins into money
```

```
7      Coin[] money = new Coin[MAXELTS];
8      for (int i = 0; i < coins.length; i++)
9      {
10        Coin temp = new Coin(coins[i].getValue(), coins[i].getName());
11        money[i] = temp;
12     }
```

Line 2 declares an array `coins` that will hold three `Coins`.
Lines 3–5 construct `Coins` and assign an array reference to each `Coin`.
Line 8–12 loop through the `coins` array.
Line 10 constructs a new `Coin` object that is a copy of each `Coin` object in `coins`.
Line 11 assigns a reference to this new `Coin` to the corresponding `money` array index.

11.2.1 Another Word about Efficiency

In inserting and removing elements from an array, we must implement the methods ourselves. To insert an element at the end of the array, we must make sure the array has room. No shifts are necessary. If we want to add an element to an array in position 0, we must first make sure we have room. All of the elements in the array need to be shifted before the element is added to position 0. You need to think about the order in which the shifting occurs. For example, if you want to add `newValue` to `arrayName` in position 0, the following code segment will NOT perform the intended task!

```
for (int i = 1; i < arrayName.length; i++)
    arrayName[i] = arrayName[i - 1];   // WRONG
arrayName[0] = newValue;
```

The `for` loop above will overwrite all of the elements of the array with whatever is in the original `arrayName[0]`. That is NOT the intended result!

```
for (int i = arrayName.length - 1; i > 0; i--)
    arrayName[i] = arrayName[i - 1];   // CORRECT
arrayName[0] = newValue;
```

will accomplish the intended task (assuming there is room in our array to add `newValue`).

When removing the last element of an array, no shifting of elements is necessary. However, removing an element in position 0 requires all of the elements in the array to be shifted! The number of filled elements is tracked by another variable. This value will need to be updated in the `insert` and `remove` operations. We will look at a more formal analysis of algorithms in Chapter 15.

11.2.2 Two-Dimensional Arrays (AB only)

Occasionally we want to store data in the form of a table consisting of rows and columns. Examples include airline or movie theater seating, survey results, or even a Tic-Tac-Toe game (really, any board game). To construct such a table variable (*matrix*) we need to specify the number of rows and columns that we have.

```
final int ROWS = 3;
final int COLUMNS = 4;
int[][] table = new int[ROWS][COLUMNS];
```

This declaration results in a table with 12 `ints`.

Figure 11.3

table[0][0]	table[0][1]	table[0][2]	table[0][3]
table[1][0]	table[1][1]	table[1][2]	table[1][3]
table[2][0]	table[2][1]	table[2][2]	table[2][3]

`table.length` = 3 is the number of rows.
`table[0].length` = 4 is the number of columns.

You can also use initializer lists to instantiate two-dimensional arrays.

```
int[][] table2 = {{1, 2, 3, 4}, {5, 6, 7, 8}, {9, 10, 11, 12}};
```

would result in the following 2-dimensional array being created.

Figure 11.4

1	2	3	4
5	6	7	8
9	10	11	12

Many of the problems involving two-dimensional arrays deal with visiting all of the elements in the table. We usually do this with the use of nested loops where the outer loop traverses the rows and the inner loop traverses the columns. Example 11.10 prints the contents of `table2` in the order above.

Example 11.10

```
1     int[][] table2 = {{1, 2, 3, 4}, {5, 6, 7, 8}, {9, 10, 11, 12}};
2     for (int row = 0; row < table2.length; row++)
3     {
4        for (int col = 0; col < table2[0].length; col++)
5        {
6           System.out.print(table2[row][col] + "\t");
7                 // \t tabs between columns
8        }
9        System.out.println();   // Advance to next line for next row.
10    }
```

Line 1 instantiates `table2` using initializer lists.
Line 2 loops through the rows of `table2`. Note that `table2.length` is the number of rows in `table2`.
Line 4 loops through the columns of `table2`. Note that `table2[0].length` is the number of columns.

Although Java allows for two-dimensional arrays where each row has a different number of columns (ragged arrays), this will not be tested on the AP CS Exam.

■ Expanded Coverage of Material That is Not Found in the Text

ArrayList Iterators (AB)

The AB Exam may also include questions on traversing an `ArrayList` using an `Iterator`. The Java `ArrayList` class implements the `Iterator` interface. An `ArrayList` iterator works very much like the `ListIterator` described for linked lists in Chapter 19 of your text. Consider the `for` loop we used to access our `ArrayList` entries in Example 11.2.

Example 11.2 (repeated here)

```
for (int i = 0; i < students.size(); i++)
{
    String temp = (String)students.get(i);
    // Process temp
}
```

This `for` loop can be replaced by the following code that implements the use of an `Iterator`. The methods of the `Iterator` interface that will be tested on the AP CS AB Exam are listed in Table 11.4.

Table 11.4
interface java.util.Iterator

Method	Method Summary
`boolean hasNext()`	Returns true if the iteration has more elements.
`Object next()`	Returns the next element in the iteration.
`void remove()`	Removes the last element returned by next.

Example 11.11

```
Iterator it = students.iterator();
while (it.hasNext())
{
    String temp = (String)it.next();
    // Process temp
}
```

or

```
for (Iterator it = students.iterator(); it2.hasNext();)
{
    String temp = (String)it.next();
```

```
      // Process temp
   }
```

The initial position of the `Iterator` is before the first element of the `ArrayList`. The `next` method advances the `Iterator`. The `remove` method removes and returns the object that was last referenced by the `next` method. Be careful not to call `remove` more than once after a call to `next` because the first `remove` removes the object that was last referenced by the `next` method. The second `remove` will try to remove an item that's no longer there! Example 11.12 demonstrates the movement of an `Iterator` in an `ArrayList`. It uses iterators to demonstrate the same operations that Example 11.1 demonstrated.

Example 11.12

```
import java.util.ArrayList;
import java.util.Iterator;    // Need to import class here.

public class IteratorTest
{
   public static void main(String arg[])
   {
      ArrayList students = new ArrayList();
      students.add("Mary");
      students.add("James");
      students.add("Kevin");
      students.add("Tanya");    // Mary, James, Kevin, Tanya (MJKT)
         // The symbol '1' indicates position of iterator
      Iterator it = students.iterator();    // 1MJKT
      it.next();    // M1JKT
      it.next();    // MJ1KT
      it.remove();    // M1KT
      // Another it.remove statement here would throw an
      // IllegalStateException.
      it = students.iterator();
      while (it.hasNext())
      {
         String temp = (String)it.next();
         System.out.println(temp);    // Mary, Kevin, Tanya
      }
   }
}
```

■ Topics That Are Useful But Not Tested

- Copying arrays can be done using the static `System.arraycopy` method. This is explained in Section 13.5 of your text.

■ Things to Remember When Taking the AP Exam

- Remember that the first element of both an array list and an array has index 0.
- The single most common loop error that occurs when dealing with arrays is an out-of-bounds error while the list is being traversed. The tests

```
while (index <= arrayName.length)    // WRONG
```

and

```
while (index <= arrayListName.size()    // WRONG
```

both try to access an out-of-bounds element. The test should be <, not <=. Remember that the last element in an array has index `arrayName.length - 1` and the last element in an `ArrayList` has index `arrayListName.size() - 1`. Think carefully about loop bounds and accessing array and `ArrayList` elements.
- Remember that an `ArrayList` stores objects. When accessing these objects to process, you will have to cast the object to the appropriate type.
- Do not confuse `.length` with `.size()`. Remember that `arrayName.length` is an instance variable that holds the length of an array (not necessarily the number of filled elements in the array) and `arrayListName.size()` is a method that returns the number of elements in an `ArrayList`.
- To access the sixth element of an array we write `arrayName[5]`. To access the sixth element of an `ArrayList`, we write `arrayListName.get(5)`.
- Using `equals` with array lists uses the default object `equals` and compares references, not contents. `equals` returns `true` if two `ArrayList` references are the same, `false` otherwise.
- When you use `equals` with arrays, you are also comparing references. `array1.equals(array2)` is asking if `array1` and `array2` reference the same array.
- **(AB only)** When visiting elements in a two-dimensional array, do not confuse rows and columns. This is a common mistake on the AP Exam.
- When shifting elements in an array, be careful not to overwrite values of other array elements. It is rare that this is an intended task! Think about the order in which the elements are being shifted.

■ Key Words

You should understand the terms below. The AP CS Exam questions may include references to these terms. The citations in parentheses next to each term identify the page numbers where it is defined and/or discussed in *Computing Concepts with Java Essentials*, 3rd ed., and *Big Java*.

array (530)	counting (526)	linear search (526)
array length (532)	`Double` (530)	matrix (544)
`ArrayList` (522)	index (522)	object (522)
bounds error (522)	`Integer` (530)	wrapper class (530)
cast (100)		

■ Connecting the Detailed Topic Outline to the Text

The citations in parentheses identify where information in the outline can be located in *Computing Concepts with Java Essentials*, 3rd ed., and *Big Java*.

- Array Lists (522–523)
  - A Word about Efficiency (754-757)
  - Wrapper Classes (530)
- Arrays (530–541)
  - One-Dimensional Arrays (530–541)
  - Another Word about Efficiency (754–757)
  - Two-Dimensional Arrays **(AB only)** (544–547)

■ Practice Questions

Multiple Choice

1. Consider the following declaration.

   ```
   int[] A = new int[10];
   ```

Which of the following choices describes the state of array A after this statement is executed?

   a. The elements `A[1]...A[10]` are not yet initialized and contain unknown `int` values.
   b. The elements `A[1]...A[10]` are initialized to 0.
   c. The elements `A[0]...A[9]` are not yet initialized and contain unknown `int` values.
   d. The elements `A[0]...A[9]` are initialized to 0.
   e. The elements `A[0]...A[10]` are initialized to 0.

Questions 2 and 3 refer to the `Coin` class whose incomplete definition is below.

   ```
   public class Coin
   {
      // Constructor
      public Coin(double aValue, String aName) {...}

      // Returns coin value.
      public double getValue() {...}

      //Returns coin name.
      public String getName() {...}

      // Returns true if this and other have same values,
      // false otherwise.
      public boolean equals(Object other)

      private double value;
   ```

```
      private String name;
}
```

2. Assume that the variable `money` has been initialized as follows.

```
    ArrayList money = new ArrayList();
```

and that 10 `Coin`s were added to `money`.

Which of the following statements or pair of statements would print the name of the sixth `Coin` in `money`?

   a.
```
String temp = (String)money[5].getName()
System.out.println(temp);
```

   b.
```
System.out.println (money[5].getName());
```

   c.
```
Coin temp = Coin(money.get(5));
System.out.println(temp);
```

   d.
```
Coin temp = (Coin)money.get(5);
System.out.println(temp.getName());
```

   e.
```
System.out.println(money.get(5).getName())
```

3. Assume that the variable `money` has been initialized as follows.

```
    ArrayList money = new ArrayList();
```

and that several `Coin`s were added to `money`. The following segment of code is intended to find the total value of the `Coin`s in `money`.

```
1     public double getTotal()
2     {
3        double total = 0;
4        int i = 0;
5        while (i < money.size())
6        {
7           Coin tempCoin = (Coin)money.get(i);
8           total += tempCoin.getValue();
9           i++;
10       }
11       return total;
12    }
```

Which of the following statements about this method is true?

   a. There will be a compile-time error because the cast is line 7 is incorrect.

   b. There will be an `indexOutOfBoundsException` thrown during runtime because line 7 will try to access an element not in bounds of `money`.

c. The method will compile and run but the total returned will be incorrect.

d. There will be a run-time error when money contains no Coins, otherwise the method works as intended.

e. This method will execute as intended.

4. Consider the method doTask defined below.

```java
public static int doTask(int[] a)
{
    int index = 0;
    int soFar = 1;
    int count = 1;
    for (int k = 1; k < a.length; k++)
    {
        if (a[k] == a[k - 1])
        {
            count++;
            if (count > soFar)
            {
                soFar = count;
                index = k;
            }
        }
        else
        {
            count = 1;
        }
    }
    return a[index];
}
```

When the following code segment is executed,

```java
int[] arr = {1, 2, 3, 3, 3, 3, 4, 2, 2, 2, 2, 2, 2, 2, 5, 6, 6, 6,
        6, 6, 6, 4, 7, 8};
System.out.println(doTask(arr));
```

What is printed to the screen?

a. *1*

b. *2*

c. *6*

d. *7*

e. *24*

5. Assume that the following declarations have been made.

```java
int[] A = {1, 2, 3, 4, 5, 6, 7, 8};
int[] B = {4, 5, 6, 7, 8};
```

Also assume that the method `printContents` is defined with the following header and works as specified in the comment.

```
// Prints the contents of array arr to the screen.
public static void printContents(int[] arr)
```

If the following segment of code is executed, what will be printed to the screen?

```
B = A;
B[3] = 0;
printContents(A);
printContents(B);
```

a.   *1 2 3 4 5 6 7 8*
     4 5 6 0 8

b.   *1 2 3 0 5 6 7 8*
     1 2 3 0 5 6 7 8

c.   *4 5 6 0 8*
     4 5 6 0 8

d.   *1 2 3 0 5 6 7 8*
     4 5 6 7 8

e.   *1 2 3 4 5 6 7 8*
     4 5 6 7 8

6.   Which of the following statements about arrays and array lists is **not** true?

   a.   A method can change the length of an array that is passed as a parameter.
   b.   A method can change the length of an `ArrayList` that is passed as a parameter.
   c.   A method can reverse the order of elements in its array parameter.
   d.   A method can reverse the order of elements in its `Arraylist` parameter.
   e.   A method can remove all of the elements in an `ArrayList`.

7.   Consider the following method `doTask`.

```
public static boolean doTask(int[] arr)
{
   boolean found = true;
   for (int i = 0; i < arr.length; i++)
   {
      found = found && (arr[i] % 2 == 1);
   }
   return found;
}
```

Which of the following statements is true about method `doTask`?

a. Method `doTask` returns `true` if all elements in its array parameter `arr` are even, `false` otherwise.
b. Method `doTask` returns `true` if all elements in its array parameter `arr` are odd, `false` otherwise.
c. Method `doTask` returns `true` if all elements in its array parameter `arr` are positive, `false` otherwise.
d. Method `doTask` returns `true` if all elements in its array parameter `arr` are equal to 1, `false` otherwise.
e. Method `doTask` will always return `true`.

8. Consider the following method definitions intended to find the smallest integer value in its `Arraylist` parameter.

I.
```
public static int findSmallest(ArrayList nums)
{
    Integer small = (Integer)nums.get(0);
    for (int i = 1; i < nums.size(); i++)
    {
        Integer tempSmall = (Integer)nums.get(i);
        if (tempSmall.compareTo(small) < 0)
        {
            small = tempSmall;
        }
    }
    return small.intValue();
}
```

II.
```
public static int findSmallest(ArrayList nums)
{
    Integer small = (Integer)nums.get(0);
    for (int i = 1; i < nums.size(); i++)
    {
        Integer tempSmall = (Integer)nums.get(i);
        if (tempSmall.intValue() < small.intValue())
        {
            small = tempSmall;
        }
    }
    return small.intValue();
}
```

III.
```
public static int findSmallest(ArrayList nums)
{
    int small = ((Integer)nums.get(0)).intValue();
    for (int i = 1; i < nums.size(); i++)
    {
        int tempSmall = ((Integer)nums.get(i)).intValue();
        if (tempSmall < small)
        {
```

```
            small = tempSmall;
        }
    }
    return small;
}
```

Which of the method definitions above will work as intended?

    a. I only
    b. II only
    c. I and II only
    d. II and III only
    e. I, II, and III

9. Consider the following method definitions intended to determine whether the two ArrayList parameters of Student are equal (have the same number of elements in the same order). Assume the equals method for Student works as intended.

I.
```
    public static boolean isTheSame(ArrayList A, ArrayList B)
    {
        if (A.size() != B.size())
            return false;
        return (A == B);
    }
```

II.
```
    public static boolean isTheSame(ArrayList A, ArrayList B)
    {
        if (A.size() != B.size())
            return false;
        for (int i = 0; i < A.size(); i++)
        {
            if (!((Student)A.get(i)).equals((Student)B.get(i)))
            {
                return(false);
            }
        }
        return true;
    }
```

III.
```
    public static boolean isTheSame(ArrayList A, ArrayList B)
    {
        if (A.size() != B.size())
            return false;
        return (A.equals(B))
    }
```

Which of the method definitions above will work as intended?

    a. I only
    b. II only

    c. I and II only

    d. II and III only

    e. I, II, and III

Questions 10 and 11 refer to the `Dog` and `Cat` class definitions below.

```
public class Cat
{
    // Constructor
    public Cat (String name)
    {
        catName = name;
    }

    public void print()
    {
        System.out.println("Cat:" + catName);
    }

    // Other useful method definitions

    private String catName;
}
```

```
public class Dog
{

    // Constructor
    public Dog(String name)
    {
        dogName = name;
    }

    public void print()
    {
        System.out.println("Dog: " + dogName);
    }

    // Other useful method definitions

    private String dogName;
}
```

10. The following test program is executed. Assume the method `IO.readWord()` returns a `String` input by the user.

```
1       import java.util.ArrayList;
2       public class CatsAndDogsTest
3       {
4           public static void main(String[] args)
5           {
```

```
6              ArrayList cats = new ArrayList();

7              for (int i = 0; i < 3; i++)
8              {
9                  System.out.print("Enter cat name: ");
10                 String aName = IO.readWord();
11                 cats.add(new Cat(aName));
12             }

13             System.out.print("Enter dog name: ");
14             String anotherName = IO.readWord();
15             cats.add(new Dog(anotherName));

16             for (int i = 0; i < cats.size(); i++)
17             {
18                 ((Cat)cats.get(i)).print();
19             }
20         }
21     }
```

Which of the statements below is true about the program compilation/execution?

    a.   There is a compile-time error in line 15. A `Dog` can't be added to `cats`.
    b.   There is a run-time error in line 15. A `Dog` can't be added to `cats`.
    c.   There is a compile-time error in line 18. An incorrect cast is attempted.
    d.   There is a run-time error in line 18. A `ClassCastException` is thrown.
    e.   The program works as intended. The names of three cats and one dog are printed to the screen.

11. Consider the following code segment.

```
1      Object obj = new Cat("Casper");
2      obj.print();
3      ((Cat)obj).print();
```

Which of the statements below is true about the program compilation/execution?

    a.   There is a compile-time error in line 1. This type of cast is illegal.
    b.   There is a compile-time error is line 2. The method `print` is undefined for `obj`.
    c.   There is a compile-time error in line 3. This type of cast is illegal.
    d.   There is a run-time error in line 3. This type of cast is illegal and an exception is thrown.
    e.   The program segment works as intended. There is no compile-time error and no run-time error.

12. Consider the following statements concerning operations with an array. Insertions and deletions are done so that the original order of the array elements is not changed.

I.   Inserting an element at position 0 of an array.
II. Inserting an element at the end of an array.

III. Removing an element from the beginning of an array.
IV. Removing an element from the end of an array.

Which of the following statements about the efficiency of these operations is true?

    a. If the array is large, I and II are more efficient than III and IV.
    b. If the array is large, I and III are more efficient than II and IV.
    c. If the array is large, III and IV are more efficient than I and II.
    d. If the array is large, II and IV are more efficient than I and III.
    e. All methods have the same efficiency. No method requires more work than any other.

13. Consider the following statements concerning operations with an `ArrayList`.

I. Inserting an element at position 0 of an `ArrayList`.
II. Inserting an element at the end of an `ArrayList`.
III. Removing an element from the beginning of an `ArrayList`.
IV. Removing an element from the end of an `ArrayList`.

Which of the following statements about the efficiency of these operations is true?

    a. If the `ArrayList` is large, I and II are more efficient than III and IV.
    b. If the `ArrayList` is large, I and III are more efficient than II and IV.
    c. If the `ArrayList` is large, III and IV are more efficient than I and II.
    d. If the `ArrayList` is large, II and IV are more efficient than I and III.
    e. All methods have the same efficiency. No method requires more work than any other.

14. An experiment consists of tossing ten 6-sided dice and counting the number of 1's that appear on one toss of ten dice. There are 11 possibilities (0–10).

This experiment is to be repeated 500 times. The results of the 500 experiments are to be printed in a frequency table for occurrences of 1's tossed. The table will show the number of the 500 experiments that resulted in 0 ones, the number that resulted in 1 one, the number that resulted in 2 ones, and so on.

Which of the following data structures is the best choice to hold the necessary information?

    a. An array of length 6.
    b. An array of length 11.
    c. An array of length 500.
    d. An `ArrayList` of size 100.
    e. An `ArrayList` of size 500.

(AB only) Questions 15 and 16 refer to the Person class below.

```
public class Person
{
    // Constructor
    public Person(String aName, int howOld)
    {
```

```
       name = aName;
       age = howOld;
    }
    // Returns name of person.
    public String getName() {...}

    // Returns age of person.
    public int getAge() {...}

    // Other methods here

    private int age;
    private String name;
}
```

The following statements are executed.

```
ArrayList people = new ArrayList();
people.add(new Person("Anna", 23));
people.add(new Person("Thomas", 17));
people.add(new Person("Lara", 19));
people.add(new Person("David", 34));
people.add(new Person("Karen", 22));
```

15. Which of the code segments below will correctly print the names of the `Person` objects in `people`?

I.
```
for (Iterator it = people.iterator(); it.hasNext();)
{
   Person temp = (Person)it.next();
   System.out.println(temp.getName());
}
```

II.
```
for (Iterator it = people.get(0); it.hasNext();)
{
   Person temp = (Person)it.next();
   System.out.println(temp.getName());
}
```

III.
```
Iterator it = people.iterator();
while (it.hasNext())
{
   Person temp = (Person)it.next();
   System.out.println(temp.getName());
}
```

    a.   I only
    b.   II only
    c.   III only
    d.   I and III only
    e.   I, II, and III

16. The following segment of code is executed.

```
Iterator it = people.iterator();
it.next();
it.next();
Person temp = (Person)it.next();
it.remove();
temp = (Person)it.next();
System.out.println(temp.getName());
```

What will be printed to the screen?

a. *Anna*
b. *Thomas*
c. *Lara*
d. *David*
e. *Karen*

17. **(AB only)** Consider the following code segment that is intended to fill and print a 2-dimensional array.

```
int x = 3; int y = 4; int z = 2;
int[][] tbl = new int[x][y];

for (int r = 0; r < x; r++)
{
   for (int c = 0; c < y; c++)
   {
      if (r != c)
         tbl[r][c] = y;
      else
         tbl[r][c] = z;
   }
}
for (int r = 0; r < x; r++)
{
   for (int c = 0; c < y; c++)
   {
      System.out.println(tbl[r][c]);
   }
   System.out.println();
}
```

Which of the following is the 2-dimensional array that is printed?

a. *422*
 242
 224

b. *2444*
    4244
    4424
    2222

c. *2444*
    4244
    4424

d. *4222*
    2422
    2242

e. *3222*
    2322
    2232

Free Response Questions

1. A `FooList` is a class that defines a list of strings and a string length. All strings in a `FooList` have the same length. There is no preset number of strings that a `FooList` can hold. For example,

The `FooList` list1 may contain the strings aa, bb, cc, and dd (all strings of length 2).

The `FooList` list2 may contain the strings cat, dog, pig, fox, bat, and eel (all strings of length 3).

An incomplete implementation of the `FooList` class appears below.

```
public class FooList
{
    // Constructor implementation initializes
    // fooLength (the length of the strings in FooList's list) and
    // availableFoos (FooList's list of strings).

    // Postcondition: Returns true if the string, key, is found in
    // the FooList's list of strings, false otherwise.
    public boolean found(String key)
    {
        // Code goes here
    }

    // Adds the string, entry, to FooList's list implementation if
    // it is the correct length and not already in the list. If the
    // string is already in the list or if the string is not the
    // correct length, it is not added.
    public void addFoo(String entry)
    {
```

```
        // Code goes here
    }

    // Removes and returns a random string entry from FooList's
    // list of strings.
    public String removeRandomFoo()
    {
        // Code goes here
    }

    // Returns the string in position i of FooList's list
    // implementation. The first string is in position 0.
    public String getFoo(int i) {...}

    // Returns length of a foo.
    public int getFooLength()

    // Fills FooList's list with strings input by the user.
    public void fillFooList() {...}

    // Private instance variables declared here
}
```

a.   You are to implement the `FooList` constructor. This constructor will have one parameter that will indicate the length of each string in `FooList`'s list. The constructor will initialize `fooLength` with this value and will initialize `FooList`'s list of strings, `availableFoos`, to have 0 entries.

b.   You are to implement the `FooList` method `found`. The method `found` returns `true` if its `String` parameter `key` is found in the list of strings, `false` otherwise. Use the header below when writing `found`.

```
    // Returns true if key is in FooList's list of strings, false
    // otherwise
    public boolean found(String key)
```

c.   You are to implement the method `addFoo` as specified in the method comment below. Use the following header in writing `addFoo`. You may call method `found` that is specified in part b of this problem. Assume that `found` works as intended regardless of what you wrote for part b.

```
    // Adds the string, entry, to FooList's list if it is the correct
    // length and not already in the list. If the string is already
    // in the list or if the string is not the correct length, it is
    // not added.
    public void addFoo(String entry)
```

d.   You are to implement the method `removeRandomFoo` that will remove a random string entry from `FooList`'s list of strings. Use the following header in writing `removeRandomFoo`.

```
// Removes and returns a random entry from FooList's list of
// strings.
public String removeRandomFoo()
```

2. Concentration is a game in which tiles are placed face-down in rows on a "concentration board". Each tile contains an image. For each tile, there is exactly one other tile with the same image. The player is to pick a tile, see which image it has, and try to find its match from the remaining face-down tiles. If the player fails to turn over its match, both tiles are turned face-down and the player attempts to pick a matching pair again. The game is over when all tiles on the board are turned face-up.

In this implementation of a simplified version of concentration,
*   Images will be strings chosen from a `FooList`. Assume that all `FooList` methods specified in Question 1 work as intended regardless of what you wrote.
*   The concentration board will contain an even number of `Tile`s.
*   The `Board` will be implemented as a one-dimensional array of `Tile`s.

For example, if the size of the concentration board is requested to be 4, the board will have 16 `Tile`s. The one-dimensional array, `gameboard`, can be viewed as a 4-by-4 concentration board as follows:

```
gameboard[0]      gameboard[1]      gameboard[2]      gameboard[3]
gameboard[4]      gameboard[5]      gameboard[6]      gameboard[7]
gameboard[8]      gameboard[9]      gameboard[10]     gameboard[11]
gameboard[12]     gameboard[13]     gameboard[14]     gameboard[15]
```

An incomplete implementation of the `Tile` class and an incomplete implementation of the `Board` class appear below.

```
public class Tile
{
    // Constructs a Tile whose faceUp shows word.
    public Tile(String word)
    {
        image = word;
        faceUp = false;
    }

    // Returns image on face of Tile.
    public String showFace() {...}

    // Returns true if Tile is face-up, false otherwise.
    public boolean isFaceUp() {...}

    // Returns true if the image on other is the same as this
    // image.
    public boolean equals(Object other) {...}

    // Postcondition: Tile is turned face-up.
    public void turnFaceUp() {...}
```

```
        // Postcondition: Tile is turned face-down.
        public void turnFaceDown() {...}

        private String image;
        private boolean faceUp;
    }
```

```
    public class Board
    {
        // Constructs n by n concentration board of Tiles whose values
        // are chosen from the already filled FooList list.
        // Precondition: n is the length of a side of the board,
        // n is an even positive integer
        // FooList contains at least n * n / 2 strings.
        public Board(int n, FooList list)
        {
            gameBoard = new Tile[n * n];   // concentration board
            size = gameBoard.length;   // board size
            numberOfTilesFaceUp = 0;   // number of Tiles face up
            rowLength = n;   // number of Tiles in a row
            possibleTileValues = list;   // possible tile images
            fillBoard();   // calls method to fill board with Tiles
        }

        // Randomly fills this concentration board with tiles. The
        // number of distinct tiles used on the board is size / 2.
        // Any one tile image appears exactly twice.
        // Precondition: number of positions on board is even,
        // possibleTileValues contains at least size / 2 elements
        private void fillBoard()
        {
            // Code goes here
        }

        // Precondition: Tile in position p is face-down.
        // Postcondition: Tile in position p is face-up.
        public void lookAtTile(int p)
        {
            // Code goes here
        }

        // Checks whether the Tiles in pos1 and pos2 have the same
        // image. If they do, the Tiles are turned face-up. If not, the
        // Tiles are turned face-down.
        // Precondition: gameBoard[pos1] is face-up,
        // gameBoard[pos2] is face-up.
        public void checkMatch(int pos1, int pos2)
        {
            // Code goes here
        }
```

```
// Board is printed for the player. If the Tile is turned face-
// up, the image is printed. If the Tile is turned face-down,
// the Tile position is printed.
public void printBoard()
{
    //  Code goes here
}

// Returns Tile in position pos.
public Tile pickTile(int pos) {...}

// Returns right-justified number with p places as a string.
public String format(int number, int p) {...}

// Returns right-justified word with p places.
public String format(String word, int p) {...}

// Returns true if all Tiles are turned face-up, false
// otherwise.
public boolean allTilesUp() {...}

private Tile[] gameBoard;   // concentration board of Tiles
private int size;   // number of Tiles on board
private int rowLength;   // number of Tiles printed in a row
int numberOfTilesFaceUp;   // number of Tiles face-up
private FooList possibleTileValues;   // possible Tile images
}
```

a.   Write the implementation for the `Board` method `fillBoard`. The method `fillBoard` will randomly fill the concentration `Board` with `Tiles` whose images are randomly chosen from strings contained in the `FooList` `possibleTileValues`. A tile image that appears on the board appears exactly twice on the board. Use the header below to write `fillBoard`.

```
// Randomly fills this concentration board with tiles. The
// number of distinct tiles used on the board is size / 2.
// Any one tile image appears exactly twice.
// Precondition: number of positions on board is even,
// possibleTileValues contains at least size / 2 elements.
private void fillBoard()
```

b.   Write the implementation for the `Board` method `lookAtTile`. This method will call the appropriate method of the `Tile` class to turn the `Tile` face-up. Assume that the method you wrote for part a and the other methods whose headers and comments are given in the problem specification work as intended. Use the header below to write `lookAtTile`.

```
// Precondition: Tile in position p is face-down.
// Postcondition: Tile in position p is face-up.
public void lookAtTile(int p)
```

c. Write the implementation for the `Board`'s method `checkMatch`. This method will check whether the tiles in its two integer parameter positions on `gameBoard` have the same image. If they do, the tiles will remain face-up. If they have different images, the tiless will be turned face-down. Assume that the methods you wrote for parts a and b and the other methods whose headers and comments were given in the problem specification work as intended. Use the header below to write `checkMatch`.

```
// Checks whether the Tiles in pos1 and pos2 have the same image.
// If they do, the Tiles remain face-up. If not, the Tiles are
// turned face-down.
// Precondition: gameBoard[pos1] is face-up,
// gameBoard[pos2] is face-up.
public void checkMatch(int pos1, int pos2)
```

d. Complete the implementation for `printBoard` so that the concentration board is printed as described in the comment and illustrated below. You should call the `Board` method `format` to right-justify the printing of the `Tile` image or the printing of the `Tile` position. For example, if `MAXPLACES = 5`,

```
System.out.print(format("go", MAXPLACES));
   // will print ["   go"]

i = 4;
System.out.print(format(i, MAXPLACES));
   // will print ["    4"]
```

Complete the implementation of `printBoard` that appears below.

```
// Board is printed for the player. If the tile is turned face-up,
// the image is printed. If the tile is turned face-down, the Tile
// position is printed.
public void printBoard()
{
    final int PADDING = 3;    // spacing of tiles
    int spacing = possibleTileValues.getFooLength() + PADDING;
    for (int i = 0; i < size; i++)
    {
        // Code goes here
    }
}
```

An example of `printBoard` for a 4 by 4 concentration board that is partially solved is shown below after 4 matches have been found. The `Foolist` passed as a parameter to the `Board` constructor contains strings of length 3.

fox	*fox*	*dog*	*dog*
cow	*5*	*6*	*7*
cow	*cat*	*10*	*11*
12	*13*	*14*	*cat*

3. **(AB only)** Suppose that the implementation of the concentration board constructed a two-dimensional array as an alternative to the one-dimensional array used in Question 2.

Board constructor

```
// Constructs n by n Concentration Board.
// n is an even positive integer
public Board(int n, FooList list)
{
   gameBoard = new Tile[n][n];   // Concentration board

   size = n * n;   // number of Tiles on Board
   numberOfTilesFaceUp = 0;   // number of Tiles face up
   rowLength = n;   // number of Tiles in a row
   possibleTileValues = list;   // possible Tile values
   fillBoard();   // calls method to fill board with Tiles
}
```

Private instance fields

```
private Tile[][] gameBoard;   // concentration board of Tiles
private int size;   // number of Tiles on board
private int rowLength;   // number of Tiles printed in a row
int numberOfTilesFaceUp;   // number of Tiles face-up
private FooList possibleTileValues;   // possible Tile values
```

a. Implement the `Board` method `fillBoard` using this two-dimensional array implementation. Use the header below to write `fillBoard`.

```
// Randomly fills this concentration board with tiles. The
// number of distinct tiles used on the board is size / 2.
// Any one tile image appears exactly twice.
// Precondition : number of positions on board is even,
// possibleTileValues contains at least size / 2 elements
private void fillBoard()
```

b. Implement the `Board` method `printBoard` using this two-dimensional array implementation. Use the header below to write `printBoard`.

```
// Board is printed for the player. If the Tile is turned face-up,
// the image is printed. If the Tile is turned face-down, the Tile
// position is printed.
public void printBoard()
```

CHAPTER **12**

Exception Handling

TOPIC OUTLINE

■ Topic Summary

12.1   Introduction to Exceptions

You plan a vacation to the Florida Keys to do some SCUBA diving. On the morning of your first day of diving, you arrive at the boat dock, prepared with all the appropriate equipment. Before launching the boat, the skipper listens to the weather report. The skipper finds out that the sea is far too rough, cancels the dive, and gives you a memo confirming cancellation. This is akin to *throwing an exception.* An exceptional situation causes abrupt termination of the normal processing (the SCUBA dive). Note that throwing an exception doesn't tell you how to *recover* from the exceptional situation. An example of recovery would be if the manager, upon seeing the cancellation memo, buys everyone breakfast, or refunds the dive trip costs. In Java, a *catch clause* is responsible for recovering from an exceptional condition.

Java provides an exception mechanism for handling *exceptional,* or abnormal, conditions in your programs. These problematic conditions prevent the continuation of the method execution. Exceptions in Java are represented by objects. These objects store information that includes the type of exception and where the exception was created. In the example, the cancellation memo confirmed this type of information about our SCUBA trip.

As we have seen in many of our programs, when we encounter run-time errors, a message on the screen describes the reason for that error. For example, the statements below are included in a program that compiles without error.

```
int[] numbers = new int[2];
numbers[0] = 54;
numbers[1] = 12;
numbers[2] = 14;
```

When the program is executed, the following message is printed.

Exception in thread "main" java.lang.ArrayIndexOutOfBoundsException
at ArrayTest.main(ArrayTest.java:12)

The segment of code *throws an exception* to indicate an error condition. The Java exception handling mechanism terminates the program with an error message. The information given includes the exception type (`ArrayIndexOutOfBoundsException`) and the location at which the exception was created (line 12 of the `main` method of the `ArrayTest` class in the file `ArrayTest.java`).

You can handle abnormal or problematic situations by including exception handling code in your program. For example, if a person tries to withdraw more money than their bank account has, you may wish to have the program terminated and indicate the reason rather than to alter the balance and cause unpredictable results later. The `throw` statement is used to invoke the exception handling mechanism. To throw an exception, you create an exception object with `new` and then throw it, using the `throw` keyword. The current flow of the method execution is terminated and the exception handler takes over.

There are two types of exceptions: checked exceptions and unchecked exceptions. Checked exceptions are compiler-enforced exceptions. This means that when you call a method that throws a *checked* exception, you *must* tell the compiler what you are going to do about the exception if it is thrown. Checked exceptions are due to external circumstances that the programmer cannot prevent. They are subclasses of the `Exception` class but are not subclasses of `RuntimeException`. Figure 2 in Section 14.2 of your text illustrates the inheritance hierarchy for exceptions. Checked exceptions are not part of the AP CS Java subset but they are discussed in Section 14.2 of your text.

Unchecked exceptions are run-time exceptions. In the programming of a method, a run-time exception is thrown to indicate an exceptional or problematic situation. We have already been exposed to several run-time exceptions. These include `NullPointerException`, `ClassCast-Exception`, `ArrayIndexOutOfBoundsException`, and `IllegalArgumentException`. These exceptions are subclasses of `java.lang.RuntimeException`.

12.2   Understanding Unchecked Exceptions

You are responsible for understanding the exceptions that are commonly generated in your Java programs. Table 12.1 lists some common exceptions and their meaning.

Table 12.1
Common Run-time (Unchecked) Exceptions

Exception	Exception Summary
ArithmeticException	Thrown when an illegal arithmetic operation has occurred. For example, an integer "divide by zero" throws an instance of this class.
ArrayIndexOutOfBoundsException	Thrown when there is an attempt to access an array index that is either negative or greater than or equal to the size of the array. This class is a subclass of the IndexOutOfBoundsException class.
ClassCastException	Thrown when there is an attempt to cast an object to a subclass of which it is not an instance.
IllegalArgumentException	Thrown when a method is passed an illegal or inappropriate argument.
IllegalStateException	Signals that a method has been invoked at an illegal or inappropriate time.
IndexOutOfBoundsException	Thrown when an index is out of range. ArrayIndexOutOfBoundsException and StringIndexOutOfBoundsException are subclasses of this class.
NoSuchElementException	Thrown when an attempt to access a nonexistent element is made.
NullPointerException	Thrown when there is an attempt to use null where an object is required.
NumberFormatException	Thrown when an attempt to convert a string to one of the numeric types is made when the string does not have the appropriate format. This class is a subclass of IllegalArgumentException.
StringIndexOutOfBoundsException	Thrown when an index is either negative or greater than the size of the string. This class is a subclass of the IndexOutOfBoundsException class.

Examples of various exceptions are given below.

ArithmeticException

If the following code were executed,

```
int num = some integer value;
int count = 0;
System.out.println(num / count);   // ArithmeticException
```

An ArithmeticException (division by 0) would occur in the System.out.println statement.

ClassCastException

The Manager is a subclass of the Employee class.

```
Employee worker1 = new Employee();
System.out.println((Manager)worker1);   // ClassCastException
```

`worker1` is an `Employee`, not a `Manager`.

IndexOutOfBoundsException
Consider the following code segment.

```
int[] anArray = new int[10];
anArray[11] = 0;   // ArrayIndexOutOfBoundsException

String s = "aString";
System.out.println(s.substring(0,8));
        // StringIndexOutOfBoundsException
```

The exceptions that are thrown are subclasses of the `IndexOutOfBoundsException` class.

NoSuchElementException
Consider the following code segment.

```
ArrayList friends = new ArrayList();

Iterator it2;
for (it2 = friends.iterator(); it2.hasNext();)
{
    String temp2 = (String)it2.next();
    System.out.println(temp2);
}
System.out.println(it2.next());   // NoSuchElementException
```

Assuming that the `Arraylist friends` is declared, the `for` loop has the iterator traverse the entire array. In the second `println` call, the iterator `it2` tries to access an element after the last one has been accessed. Iterators are part of the AP CS AB subset.

NullPointerException
```
Manager worker1 = null;
String temp = worker1.getName();   // NullPointerException
```

We cannot access an instance method of a null object.

NumberFormatException
```
int units = Integer.parseInt("1234a");
System.out.println(units + 1);
```

Although `parseInt` is not required in the AP CS subsets, it can be useful when getting input from the user. It can also lead to `NumberFormatExceptions`. In the above example, `"1234a"` is not a valid number so a `NumberFormatException` occurs. If `"1234a"` were replaced by `"12345"`, *12346* would be printed.

12.3   Throwing Exceptions (AB only)

Throwing exceptions allows you to insure certain conditions exist when your programs are executed. Although it is the responsibility of the calling procedure to meet the preconditions of a called method, it can be useful to check that the preconditions of your own methods are met. To do this, you can have your methods throw the appropriate exception if the precondition is not met. For example, the `Runner` class (Example 10.2 in this guide) has a method `race` that requires a `double` parameter. This parameter indicates the length of a race in miles. The length of a race should be a positive number. If the user passes a non-positive value to this method, you may choose to throw an exception.

IllegalArgumentException

```
public void race(double raceLength)
{
   if (raceLength <= 0)
   {
      throw new IllegalArgumentException("Race length must be
            greater than 0.");
   }
   System.out.println(getName() + " is racing in a " + raceLength
         + " mile race.");
   numberOfRaces++;
   milesRaced += raceLength;
}
```

When the exception is thrown, the method terminates immediately. Execution is transferred to the exception handler. You can pass whatever `String` makes sense for the error condition you are checking or you can call the default constructor by not passing any string parameter. Of course, it is more meaningful to pass a string parameter that adequately identifies the specific error.

IllegalStateException

An `IllegalStateException` might be thrown if a class invariant is violated. For example, a `BankAccount` is constructed with a non-negative balance. If an attempt is made to construct a `BankAccount` with a negative balance, an `IllegalStateException` could be thrown.

```
public BankAccount(double initialBalance)
{
   if (initialBalance < 0)
   {
      throw new IllegalStateException("Initial balance must be
            non-negative.");
   }
   balance = initialBalance;
}
```

AB students are expected to be able to throw the `IllegalStateException` and `NoSuchElementException` in their own methods.

■ Topics That Are Useful But Not Tested

- Checked exceptions are due to external circumstances that the programmer cannot prevent. The compiler checks that your program handles these exceptions. Checked exceptions are explained in Section 14.2 of your text.
- The `throws` specifier is used to indicate that a method may throw a checked exception. The `throws` specifier is discussed in Section 14.2 of your text.
- Designing your own exceptions can help to more accurately describe the exceptional situation. Designing your own exceptions is discussed in Section 14.3 of your text.
- Every exception should be handled somewhere in your program. The exceptions discussed in this chapter cause your program to terminate. The `try` block, `catch` clause, and `finally` clause describe a more professional way to handle exceptions. These topics are explained in Sections 14.4–14.6 of your text.

■ Things to Remember When Taking the AP Exam

- Know the conditions under which the common exceptions listed in this chapter are thrown.
- AB students should be able to throw the unchecked `IllegalStateException` and `NoSuchElementException` in their own methods.

■ Key Words

You should understand the terms below. The AP CS Exam questions may include references to these terms. The citations in parentheses next to each term identify the page numbers where it is defined and/or discussed in *Computing Concepts with Java Essentials*, 3rd ed., and *Big Java*.

checked exception (561)
exception handler (559)
`IllegalArgumentException` (559)

`RuntimeException` (561)
`throws` (561)
unchecked exception (561)

■ Connecting the Detailed Topic Outline to the Text

The citations in parentheses identify where information in the outline can be located in *Computing Concepts with Java Essentials*, 3rd ed., and *Big Java*.

- Introduction to Exceptions (557–561)
- Understanding Unchecked Exceptions (560–561)
- Throwing Exceptions **(AB only)** (558–561)

■ Practice Questions

Multiple Choice

1. Which of the following statements about checked and unchecked exceptions is true?

    a. Checked exceptions are run-time exceptions.
    b. Unchecked exceptions are run-time exceptions.
    c. Checked and unchecked exceptions generate compile-time errors.
    d. Unchecked exceptions are checked by the compiler and will not terminate your program.
    e. In order for an unchecked exception to be generated, you must include a `throws` clause in your method.

2. Which of the following exceptions will be generated when the code segment below is executed?

    ```
    int numerator = 10;
    int denominator = 0;
    int wholePart = numerator / denominator;
    ```

    a. `ArithmeticException`
    b. `IllegalArgumentException`
    c. `NumberFormatException`
    d. `IndexOutOfBoundsException`
    e. `IllegalStateException`

Questions 3 and 4 refer to the `Person` constructor below. The `Person` constructor has two `String` parameters, a first name and a last name. The constructor initializes the email address to the first letter of the first name followed by the first five letters of the last name followed by @ccj.com. If the last name has fewer than five letters, the email address will be the first letter of the first name followed by the entire last name followed by @ccj.com. Examples:

Name	email address
Jane Smith	JSmith@ccj.com
John Morris	JMorri@ccj.com
Mary Key	MKey@ccj.com

```
public Person(String fName, String lName)
{
    firstName = fName;
    lastName = lName;
    emailAddress = firstName.substring(0, 1)
        + lastName.substring(0, 5)
        + "@ccj.com";
}
```

3. Which of the following exceptions will be thrown in this constructor if it is called with the data given in the problem table?

   a. `ArithmeticException`
   b. `IllegalArgumentException`
   c. `NumberFormatException`
   d. `StringIndexOutOfBoundsException`
   e. `IllegalStateException`

4. Which of the following calls to the `Person` constructor will cause the exception in Question 3 to be thrown?

   a. `Person scm1 = new Person("Marian", "Jones");`
   b. `Person scm2 = new Person("Joe", "Thomas");`
   c. `Person scm3 = new Person("Harry", "Tote");`
   d. `Person scm4 = new Person("J", "Franks");`
   e. `Person scm5 = new Person("Ellen", "Johnson");`

Questions 5 and 6 refer to the `ArrayList friends` as declared below.

```
ArrayList friends = new ArrayList();
friends.add("Mary");
friends.add("James");
friends.add("Kevin");
friends.add(1, "Tanya");
```

5. Consider the method `search` defined below.

```
public static int search(String key, ArrayList a)
{
   int count = 0;
   String temp = (String)(a.get(count));
   while (count < a.size() && !temp.equals(key))
   {
      count++;
      temp = (String)(a.get(count));
   }
   if (count < a.size())
      return count;
   else
      return -1;
}
```

Suppose the following call to `search` was made.

```
int indexFound = search("John", friends);
```

Which of the following statements best describes the result of this call?

    a. −1 is returned.
    b. 0 is returned.
    c. 4 is returned.
    d. An `IndexOutOfBoundsException` is thrown.
    e. A compile-time error occurs.

6. What is the result of the call

```
String s = (String)friends.get(4);
```

    a. `s` is assigned the value `"Kevin"`
    b. A compile-time error occurs.
    c. A `ClassCastException` is thrown.
    d. An `IllegalArgumentException` is thrown.
    e. An `IndexOutOfBoundsException` is thrown.

Questions 7–9 refer to the `Employee` class and the `Manager` class incompletely defined below.

```java
public class Employee
{
   public void work()
   {
      System.out.println("Employee working.");
   }
}

public class Manager extends Employee
{
   public Manager()
   {
      firstName = null;
      lastName = null;
      salary = 0;
   }

   public Manager(String fName, String lName, double money)
   {
      firstName = fName;
      lastName = lName;
      salary = money;
   }

   public String getName()
   {
      return (firstName + " " + lastName);
   }

   public void work()
   {
```

```
        System.out.println("Manager working.");
    }
    private double salary;
    private String firstName;
    private String lastName;
}
```

The following code is executed.

```
ArrayList workers = new ArrayList();
workers.add(new Manager());
workers.add(new Employee());
workers.add(new Manager("John", "Doe", 20000));
```

7. Which of the following statements results in a `ClassCastException` being thrown?

I.   `Employee temp = (Manager)workers.get(0);`
II. `Employee temp = (Manager)workers.get(1);`
III. `Employee temp = (Manager)workers.get(2);`
IV. `Employee temp = (Manager)workers.get(3);`

   a. I only
   b. II only
   c. III only
   d. IV only
   e. None of the statements above cause a `ClassCastException` to be thrown.

8. Which of the statements below execute without run-time exceptions being thrown?

I.   `Employee temp = (Manager)workers.get(0);`
II. `Employee temp = (Manager)workers.get(1);`
III. `Employee temp = (Manager)workers.get(2);`
IV. `Employee temp = (Manager)workers.get(3);`

   a. I only
   b. I and II only
   c. I and III only
   d. I, II, III only
   e. I, II, III, and IV

9. The statement

```
String temp = ((Manager)(workers.get(2))).getName();
```

   a. Compiles and executes without error
   b. Reports a compile-time error: Incompatible types.
   c. Causes a `ClassCastException` to be thrown.
   d. Causes a `StringIndexOutOfBoundsException` to be thrown.
   e. Causes an `IllegalStateException` to be thrown.

10. Which of the following exceptions is **not** an unchecked exception?

    a. `IndexOutOfRangeException`
    b. `IOException`
    c. `IllegalArgumentException`
    d. `ArithmeticException`
    e. `NumberFormatException`

Free Response Questions

1. You are to design a `Teacher` class that is a subclass of the `Person` class whose incomplete definition is below.

```
public class Person
{
    public Person(String fName, String lName)
    {
        // Constructor code goes here.
        // Private instance variables are initialized.
    }

    public String getName()
    {
        return firstName + " " + lastName;
    }

    public String getEmail()
    {
        return emailAddress;
    }

    public String toString()
    {
        return ("name = " + getName()+ "\n" +
                "email address = " + getEmail());
    }

    private String firstName;
    private String lastName;
    private String emailAddress;
}
```

The `Teacher` inherits instance variables and methods from `Person`. In addition, a `Teacher` has a private instance field, `salary` (of type `double`) and a public instance method `getRaise`. The method `getRaise` has a `double` parameter and will increment the `Teacher`'s salary by the amount of its parameter. You are to implement the `Teacher` class according to the specifications given. The `Teacher` has one constructor that expects three parameters: a first name (`String`), a last name (`String`), and a salary (`double`). You should design your constructor to throw the appropriate exception if the salary passed is not a positive number. In writing `getRaise`, you should throw the appropriate exception if the parameter passed is not a positive number.

Note: AB students should include exceptions where indicated in the problem description. AP CS A students do **not** need to include the exception handling code.

2. For a study in probability, we want to simulate the tossing of coins. A `CoinTosser` object tosses a coin a random number of times and reports on its outcomes. It has the following public interface:

```
public class CoinTosser
{
   // Constructor
   public CoinTosser()
   {
      //  Code goes here
   }


   // Postcondition: returns true if the coin tosser has more
   // coin tosses to report.
   public boolean hasMoreTosses()
   {
      //  Code goes here
   }


   // Postcondition: returns "HEAD" or "TAIL"
   public String nextToss()
   {
      //  Code goes here
   }

   ...     //  Private implementation
}
```

a. You are to implement the `CoinTosser` constructor. In the constructor, construct a random number generator and generate a random integer between 0 and 20 (inclusive). That value determines how many tosses this particular coin tosser will carry out.

b. List the private instance fields.

c. Implement the `hasMoreTosses` method that returns `true` if there are tosses remaining, `false` otherwise.

d. The `nextToss` method generates a random integer between 0 and 1 (inclusive) and returns one of the two strings "HEADS" or "TAILS". You should **not** construct a new random number generator in this method.

(AB only) The `nextToss` method should throw a `NoSuchElementException` if it is called after the hasMoreTosses method has returned `false`.

CHAPTER **13**

System Design

■ Topic Summary

13.1 Designing Software Systems

The AP CS Topic Outline requires that all AP Computer Science students
- Understand encapsulation.
- Understand the *is-a* and *has-a* inheritance relationships
- Understand and be able to implement an inheritance class hierarchy according to given specifications.
- Design and implement a class according to given specifications.
- Understand when to use an interface and be able to design an interface.
- Extend a given class with inheritance.

In addition to the above, AP Computer Science AB students should be able to
- Discover and design classes.
- Determine relationships between classes
- Determine responsibilities of each class.
- Use object-oriented design to build a program from a set of interacting classes.

We have introduced many of these topics separately. This chapter will give you practice pulling the pieces together to design a program involving more than one class.

13.2 The Software Life Cycle

Process	Process Description
Analysis	The *analysis* phase is the time when you determine what your software system is intended to accomplish.
Design	The *design* phase is when you develop a plan to implement your system.
Implementation	The *implementation* phase is when you write the code according to the specifications made in the design phase.
Testing	During the *testing* phase you verify that the system works as intended.
Deployment	The *deployment* phase is when the intended user of the system installs and uses it.

Section 16.1 of your text explains this life cycle in detail.

13.3 Discovering Classes

In the design phase, you need to be able to describe a set of classes that can be used to implement the task(s) your software system is intended to accomplish. Look for *nouns*.

- Task: Print an invoice
  Candidate classes: `Invoice, Item, Customer`

- Task: Publish a book
  Candidate classes: `Book, Page, Binding`

- Task: Organize a 5-mile race
  Candidate classes: `Race, Runner, VolunteerWorker`

- Task: Play the lottery
  Candidate classes: `Ball, BallPicker, BallShaker`

- Task: Build a house
  Candidate classes: `Wall, Window, Roof`

Some of these classes may consist of objects defined by other classes. For example, a customer has a name (`String` object), a customer identification number (an `int`), an address (perhaps an object instantiating an `Address` class composed of a street address, a city, and a state).

13.4 Relationships between Classes

It is sometimes useful to classify relationships between classes. There are several different types of class relationships. The AP CS Topic Outline includes the following two relationships:
- inheritance (*is-a*) relationships
- association or composition (*has-a*) relationships

Using some of the examples already presented, we have:
- A `Bank` *has-a* `Customer`.
- A `Customer` *has-a* `BankAccount`.
- A `SavingsAccount` *is-a* `BankAccount`.

- A `Car` *is-a* `Vehicle`.
- A `Car` *has-a* `Tire`.

- A `Race` *has-a* `Runner`.
- A `Marathoner` *is-a* `Runner`.

- A `Purse` *has-a* `Coin`.

A class is *associated* with another class if the class has an instance field whose type is another class. Your textbook covers another relationship, the *uses-a* relationship or *dependency*. A class *depends* on another class if it *uses* an object of the other class. The original version of `Purse` *uses* a `Coin`. The `Purse` did not have a private instance field of type `Coin`, nor did it have an `ArrayList` that collected `Coin` objects. The distinction between *association* and *dependency* is not part of the AP CS subsets, but understanding this concept can help you in designing your software systems.

Remember, if many classes in a program depend on each other, there is high coupling. In designing system software, one should strive for low coupling and high cohesion.

13.5   Responsibilities of a Class

Once the set of classes has been identified, you need to define the responsibilities (behaviors) of each class. When you look for these behaviors, look for *verbs* in the task description. The verbs will define the candidate methods.
- Task: Print an invoice
  Candidate classes: `Invoice`, `Item`, `Customer`
  Example candidate methods:
  > Invoice has method `computeAmountDue`.
  > Item has method `getPrice`.
  > Customer has method `getName`.

- Task: Organize a 5-mile race
  Candidate classes: `Race`, `Runner`, `VolunteerWorker`
  Example candidate methods:
  > `Race` has methods `addRunner`, `getNumberOfRunners`.
  > `Runner` has methods `getRaceNumber`, `setFinishTime`.
  > `VolunteerWorker` has methods `getName`, `setJob`.

When designing a class, it is also useful to list the attributes (usually instance fields) that a class might have.
- A `Runner` has a `name`, a `raceNumber`, a `finishTime`.
- A `Race` has a *list* (probably an array list) of `Runner`s, a `raceDistance`, a *list* of `VolunteerWorker`s.

When trying to decide which class has what responsibilities, start by listing the tasks that your system needs to accomplish and assign each task to the class that is responsible for carrying out that task. If an action modifies the state (the private instance fields or attributes) of the object, it is the responsibility of the object itself. One way to ensure this is to keep the attributes of the object private.

One popular way to illustrate class relationships is with the use of CRC cards. CRC stands for "classes", "responsibilities", and "collaborators". CRC cards are discussed in Section 16.2 of your text. *HowTo 16.1* in your text lists the steps in the design process that will help you discover class interactions and responsibilities.

You may also need to provide a data representation for your software design. So far, we have studied arrays and array lists. You will need to choose a data representation consistent with the specifications given in the problem description.

Consider the New York (or any state) Lottery that we discussed in Chapter 7 of this guide. Each evening the lottery is televised and we observe the following. There is a container that holds the numbered balls and no two balls have the same number. There is a popper that "pops" a random ball. It is this popped ball's number that is one of the lottery number choices. The classes we might use are summarized below.

Classes:
- `Container` has a collection of `Ball`s. If asked for a ball, the `Container` will return the `Ball` that is requested.
- `Ball` has a number on it. It can return its number to whoever wants to know it.
- `Popper` will ask the `Container` how many `Ball`s it has and then will ask the `Random` class for a random number generator to generate a random number in the range of the numbers on the `Ball`s. The `Popper` will then ask the `Container` to remove a particular `Ball`.

The `Container` is a collection of `Ball` objects. A data representation that is consistent with the problem requirements needs to be chosen in order to implement the lottery game. Example 13.1 contains one such data representation in an incomplete implementation of the `Container` class.

Example 13.1

```
public class Container
{
    public Container(int numberOfBalls)
    {
        for (int i = 0; i < numberOfBalls; i++)
            lotteryBalls.add(new Ball(i));
    }

    // Other methods

    private ArrayList lotteryBalls = new ArrayList();
}
```

The data representation chosen in Example 13.1 is an array list. Array lists contain objects. In this problem, `Ball` objects need to be added to and removed from the `Container`. An array list is a reasonable choice for the following reasons:

- `add` and `remove` methods are defined for the `ArrayList`.
- The `Popper` will give the `Container` a random number. An array list gives immediate access ($O(1)$) to the `Ball` with that number.

■ Topics That Are Useful But Not Tested

- Using CRC (classes-responsibilities-collaborators) cards is an excellent way to discover class responsibilities and class collaborators. CRC cards are described in Section 16.2 of your text.
- UML diagrams can be used to illustrate class relationships. Section 16.3 discusses the UML diagrams used with inheritance, realization, class association, and class dependency.
- The association relationship is defined in great detail in *Advanced Topic 16.2* of your text. This relationship is presented using more detailed classifications.

■ Things to Remember When Taking the AP Exam

- Read the free-response questions very carefully. Hints to the answer may appear in the way the question is worded.
- Look for key words: "extends", "is a", "is a kind of". These phrases indicate an inheritance relationship.
- Look for key words: "has a", "has", "is made from", "uses". These phrases indicate a class association.
- Modifying the state of an object is the responsibility of the object itself.

Key Words

You should understand the terms below. The AP CS Exam questions may include references to these terms. The citation within parentheses next to each term identifies the page number where it is defined and/or discussed in *Computing Concepts with Java Essentials*, 3rd ed. and *Big Java*.

analysis (616)	deployment (616)	*is-a* relationship (624)
association (624)	design (616)	software life cycle (616)
collaborators (623)	*has-a* relationship (624)	testing (617)
dependency (625)	implementation (617)	uses (625)

■ Connecting the Detailed Topic Outline to the Text

The citations in parentheses identify where information in the outline can be located in *Computing Concepts with Java Essentials*, 3rd ed., and *Big Java*.

- Designing Software Systems (Appendix B of this guide, page *xxx*)
- The Software Life Cycle (616–621)
- Discovering Classes (621–623)
- Relationships between Classes (624–625)
- Responsibilities of a Class (622)

■ Practice Questions

Multiple Choice

1. Which of the following choices gives the correct order of the software development processes for a complex program?

   a. Analysis, Design, Implementation, Testing, Deployment
   b. Design, Analysis, Implementation, Testing, Deployment
   c. Design, Implementation, Testing, Analysis, Deployment
   d. Design, Implementation, Testing, Deployment, Analysis
   e. Analysis, Design, Implementation, Deployment, Testing

2. Which of the following pairs is not an inheritance (*is-a*) relationship?

   a. Violin, Instrument
   b. Car, Vehicle
   c. Tire, Car
   d. Student, Person
   e. Sedan, Car

3. Which of the following is an association (*has-a*) relationship?

   a. Student directory, Student
   b. Student, Person
   c. Truck, Vehicle
   d. Student, Freshman
   e. Fruit, Apple

4. You are to design a program that simulates a vending machine. Your design might include all of the following except

   a. `Product`
   b. `Coin`
   c. `VendingMachine`

    d. `Customer`

    e. `ChangeMachine`

5. In designing a software system, you should:

I. Look for nouns in the system description to identify candidate classes.
II. Look for verbs in the system description to identify class responsibilities.
III. Describe relationships among the candidate classes.

    a. I only
    b. II only
    c. III only
    d. I and II only
    e. I, II, and III

Questions 6 and 7 refer to the following design problem.

You are to create a software design that simulates a fast food restaurant. You will have food items (hamburgers, hot dogs, chicken sandwiches) and drink items (Coke, Sprite, root beer). The drinks come in various sizes given in ounces (for example: 12, 24, 48). Food items will be assigned a price when they are created. The price for drink items will be assigned according to the size of the drink.

6. Which of the following would be the best choice for the design of this system?

    a. The design should include the following classes: `Hamburger`, `HotDog`, `Chicken`, `Coke`, `Sprite`, and `RootBeer`.

    b. The design should include the following classes: `FoodItem` with `Hamburger`, `HotDog`, and `Chicken` extending `FoodItem` and `DrinkItem` with `Coke`, `Sprite`, and `RootBeer` extending `DrinkItem`.

    c. The design should include the following classes: `Item` with `FoodItem` and `DrinkItem` extending `Item`; `Hamburger`, `HotDog`, and `Chicken` extending `FoodItem`; and `DrinkItem` with `Coke`, `Sprite`, and `RootBeer` extending `DrinkItem`.

    d. The design should include the following classes: `FoodItem` and `DrinkItem`. The individual types of food and drink are only descriptions of the food or drink and should not be separate classes.

    e. The design should include the following classes: `Item` with `FoodItem` and `DrinkItem` extending `Item`. The individual types of food and drink are objects that are instances of these classes, not separate classes.

7. The fast food restaurant also offers value meals. A value meal is a drink and a food item purchased at the same time. A 10% discount off the full price of purchasing each separately is applied to the price of a value meal. A deluxe value meal costs $0.50 more than a value meal and includes apple pie for dessert. Which statement is true about this system design?

    a. `DeluxeValueMeal` should be a subclass of `ValueMeal`.
    b. `ValueMeal` should be a subclass of `DeluxeValueMeal`.

    c. Both `DeluxeValueMeal` and `ValueMeal` should be separate classes that have no inheritance relationship.

    d. `ValueMeal` has an association (*has-a*) relationship with `DeluxeValueMeal`.

    e. `ValueMeal` and `DeluxeValueMeal` both have an instance field of type `Meal` which is a superclass of both `ValueMeal` and `DeluxeValueMeal`.

Questions 8–10 refer to the problem stated below.

Your task is to automate the booking system of a travel agency. Some customers of the travel agency only purchase a single ticket, but others purchase whole trips consisting of multiple airline, boat, or train tickets, hotel stays, and car rentals.

8.   Consider these statements about a possible system design:

I.   A class `Ticket` has subclasses `AirlineTicket`, `BoatTicket`, `TrainTicket`.

II. A class `Trip` *has-a* collection of `Ticket` objects, describing all tickets needed for the trip.

III. To facilitate travelers who only buy a single ticket, we use inheritance so that a `Ticket` *is-a* `Trip`.

The following are true:

    a. I only

    b. II only

    c. III only

    d. I and II only

    e. I, II, and III

9.   A good travel agent is expected to check that a customer does not accidentally end up with mismatched reservations, such as a flight from New York to Rome and a hotel reservation in Karachi on the same night. Thus, there is a need to implement the responsibility "check trip" that flags itineraries with mismatched reservations. These flagged itineraries require special attention. Consider these statements about the assignment of this responsibility:

I.   The `Ticket` and `HotelReservation` class are jointly responsible for carrying out the "check trip" responsibility.

II. The "check trip" responsibility must lie with the `Trip` class.

III. It is useless to implement this responsibility because some customers might get a rental car and drive to an unknown destination.

The following are true:

    a. I only

    b. II only

    c. III only

    d. I and II only

    e. I, II, and III

10. Consider these statements about the implementation of the `Trip` class:

I.   The `Trip` class can use an `ArrayList` of `Ticket` objects to store a variable number of tickets.
II. The `Trip` class should have an instance field of type `CarRental`.
III. The `Trip` class must contain a field of type `String[]` to store hotel names.

The following are true:

   a.   I only
   b.   II only
   c.   III only
   d.   I and II only
   e.   I, II, and III

Free Response Questions

1.   A used car lot contains cars of various makes and models. The size of a car lot is fixed. The owner of the car lot wants to inventory the cars he has available. For the inventory, he needs the following information about each car:

Make (Toyota, Ford, etc.)
Year (1997, 2001, etc.)
Mileage (120734.6, 23555.2, etc.)
Cost (20000.00, 24500.00, etc.)

When a new car is created, the make, the car year, and the mileage are given. The cars are occasionally taken for test rides. A test ride alters the mileage of the car. The price of the car is set by the owner of the car lot. The car dealer will eventually need to print all of the information about each car in the lot.

a.   Implement the `Car` class. In implementing the class, you should:
   • Choose appropriate variable names, parameter names, and method names.
   • Properly identify access modifiers (private, public) of each method and instance field.
   • Include a method to print the information about a car.

Consider the `CarLot` class partially implemented below.

```
public class CarLot
{
    static final int MAX_CARS = 100;
    static int numberOfCars = 0;

    // Constructs an array of cars.
    public CarLot()
    {
        lot = new Car[MAX_CARS];
    }
```

```
    // Precondition: numberOfCars < MAX_CARS
    public void addCar(Car aNewCar)
    {
        // Code goes here
    }

    public void printCarsInLot()
    {
        // Code goes here
    }

    private Car[] lot;
}
```

b. Write the `CarLot` method, `addCar`, that will add a `Car` to the car lot in the next available place. (AB students: If there are no more spaces available, throw an appropriate exception.)

c. Write the `CarLot` method, `printCarsInLot`, that will print the year, make, and price of each car in the lot.

2. Consider the task of modeling record keeping for a real estate company. The company keeps records on each of its real estate agent employees. Each employee's record contains the following information:
    - The employee first name
    - The employee last name
    - The employee identification number (integer)
    - The total value of real estate property sold by the employee (decimal number)

When a new employee record is created, it is created with the employee's first name and last name. The next available employee identification number is assigned to the employee and the total real estate property sold is initialized to 0.

The company keeps a list of employees that is constantly updated so that newly hired employees are added to the list and employees that quit or are fired and removed from the list. A newly created real estate company has no employees.

Among the many tasks that need to be completed are:
    - Create a new employee record given the first and last name of the employee.
    - Add the value of real estate property sold to an employee record given the property value.
    - Gets commission earned to date for an employee. Commission earned is 6% of the total value of real estate property sold by the employee.
    - Create a new real estate company.
    - Add an employee to the company list of employees given the employee first and last name.
    - Remove an employee from the list of employees given the employee identification number.
    - Retrieve the employee who sold the highest value of real estate.

a.   **(AB only)** Design each class that is needed in the real estate system described above. The class design should include:
- Class name
- Constructor header for each constructor
- Method signatures (include parameters) and return type for each method
- Instance fields
- Static variables

In completing each class design, you should:
- Choose appropriate variable names, parameter names, and method names.
- Properly identify access modifiers (private, public) of each method, instance field, and static variable.

b.   Write the class header, declare and initialize any static and instance variables, and write the constructor(s) for the class that creates a new employee record. Follow the specifications given in the problem description.

c.   Write the class header, declare and initialize any static and instance variables, and write the constructor(s) for the class that creates a new real estate company. Follow the specifications given in the problem description.

3.   The game of Nim is a well-known game with a number of variants. We will consider the following variant, which has an interesting winning strategy. Two players alternately take marbles from a pile. In each move, a player chooses how many marbles to take. The player must take at least one but at most half of the marbles. Then the other player takes a turn. The player who takes the last marble loses.

You will design a program in which the computer plays against a human opponent. Nim specifications include:
- The initial size of the pile will be a random integer generated between two values passed to the constructor of `NimGame` by the calling method.
- A random integer between 0 and 1 inclusive will be generated to decide whether the computer or the human takes the first turn.
- A random integer between 0 and 1 inclusive will be generated to decide whether the computer plays smart or stupid. A computer knows if it is smart or stupid.
- A player that is not smart simply takes a random legal value (between 1 and $n/2$) from the pile whenever it has a turn.
- A smart player takes off enough marbles to make the size of the pile a power of two minus 1 that is, 3, 7, 15, 31, or 63. That is always a legal move, except if the size of the pile is currently one less than a power of two. In that case, the smart player makes a random legal move.
- A human player has a name that is given when asked. A human player is asked how many marbles s/he wishes to take.
- The computer's name is "ROBO COMPUTER".

You will note that a smart player cannot be beaten when it has the first move, unless the pile size happens to be 15, 31, or 63. Of course, a human player who has the first turn and knows the winning strategy can win against the computer.

In implementing this game, choose the following classes:

```
NimGame
NimPile
Player
HumanPlayer
SmartPlayer
```

The following methods are available to you in a Utilities class.

```
getRandomNumber
largestPowerOfTwoMinusOneBelow
readInt
readWord
```

The public interface for the Utilities class is below.

```java
public class Utilities
{
    /**
        Generates random integer in [low,high).
        Precondition: low is smallest integer generated, high - 1 is
        largest integer generated; low < high
        Postcondition: Returns a random integer in [low, high)
    */
    public static int getRandNumber(int low, int high) {...}

    /**
        Tests whether n has the form pow(2, k) - 1.
        Precondition: n > 0
        Postcondition: returns true if n is a power of two minus
        one, false otherwise.
    */
    boolean isPowerOfTwoMinusOne(int n) {...}

    /**
        Precondition: n > 0
        Postcondition: Returns the largest power of two minus one
        below a given number (the largest pow(2, k) - 1 < n).
    */
    int largestPowerOfTwoMinusOneBelow(int n) {...}

    /**
        Reads an integer from the keyboard.
        Returns integer entered by user
    */
    public static int readInt();

    /**
        Reads a String from the keyboard.
        Returns integer entered by user
```

```
    */
    public static String readWord();
}
```

The main method that invokes the game of Nim is:

```
public static void main(String[] args)
{
    NimGame nim = new NimGame(10, 100);
        // The pile will have a random number of marbles between
        // 10 inclusive and 100 exclusive.
    nim.playNim();
}
```

a. Find and list the *has-a* and *is-a* relationships between the following classes.
    - NimGame
    - NimPile
    - Player
    - HumanPlayer
    - SmartPlayer

b. Find the responsibilities of each of the classes in a, and provide the following for each class.
    - Class name
    - Constructor headers for each constructor
    - Method signatures (including parameters) and return type for each method
    - Instance fields

c. Implement the methods that you determined in the preceding step.

Note: It is highly improbably that the AP Exam will ask you to implement an entire program such as Nim. Consider part c a "just for fun" activity!

CHAPTER **14**

Recursion

TOPIC OUTLINE

■ Topic Summary

14.1   Thinking Recursively

In Chapter 5 we discussed iterative control structures (the `for` loop and the `while` loop). In this chapter we look at another method of repetition, recursion. A recursive computation solves a problem by calling itself to solve a smaller piece of the problem. There are three basic rules for developing recursive algorithms.

- Know how to take one step.
- Break each problem down into one step plus a smaller problem.
- Know how and when to stop.

Here is the method for converting and printing the decimal number 100 to a binary number (base 2) that was presented in Chapter 4

    100 / 2 = 50 remainder 0
    50 / 2 = 25 remainder 0
    25 / 2 = 12 remainder 1
    12 / 2 = 6 remainder 0
    6 / 2 = 3 remainder 0
    3 / 2 = 1 remainder 1
    1 / 2 = 0 remainder 1

Reading the remainders in reverse order, we have 1100100 which is the binary representation for the decimal number 100.

Now, let's look at this same problem recursively.
- First, know how to take one step: A step seems to be "Divide by 2; Note the quotient and the remainder."
- Second, break each problem down into one step plus a smaller problem:
  The quotient is smaller than the original number.
  The above process can be applied to the quotient.
  Therefore you have a smaller problem.
- Know how and when to stop: Stop when the quotient is 0. Actually, the recursion stops when the quotient <= 0. Print out the remainders when you reach a quotient of 0. Notice that in the original example from Chapter 4, the remainders were read "from bottom up". The last remainder must be printed first.

Now let's look at code.

Example 14.1

```
public static void convertToBin(int decimalNum)
{
    int quotient = decimalNum / 2;
    int remainder = decimalNum % 2;

    if (quotient > 0)
    {
        convertToBin(quotient);   // smaller problem
    }

    System.out.print(remainder);   // after all recursive calls
                                    // have been made, last
                                    // remainder printed first
}
```

Divide the decimal number by 2 and remember the remainder. Keep repeating this process with a smaller decimal number (quotient) until the quotient <= 0. Then, print out the remainder for each call. As long as the quotient is > 0, another recursive call is made (no printing occurs yet). When the quotient is <= 0, the `if` statement is not executed and the algorithm continues by executing the `System.out.print` statement. This statement is executed for each recursive call that was made beginning with the last. The "stack" of recursive calls is "unstacked." Thus, the remainders will be printed in the "correct" order. That is, the result on the screen will be the binary representation of the decimal number we started with.

Do you think this solution would work to convert decimal numbers to octal numbers? To hexadecimal numbers?

14.2   Permutations

Many gas pumps have displays that spin digits (either analog or digital) while the gas is being pumped into your car's gas tank. The display's digits change to indicate the amount of gas in the tank and the current price.

Figure 14.1

We'll look at one of these displays and recursively generate the spinning of the digits. Our GasPump class will allow us to create a "gas pump" display with a specified number of display places and will allow us to specify the highest digit in use. We will simplify a gas pump display by using a smaller display of only three digits where the digits are in the limited range of 0–4 inclusive.

Example 14.2

```java
public class GasPumpDisplay
{
   /**
      Constructor creates a display of digits.
      @param numberOfPositions is the number of positions diplayed
   */
   public GasPumpDisplay(int numberOfPositions)
   {
      digits = numberOfPositions;
      if (digits > 1)
         tail = new GasPumpDisplay(digits - 1);
      else
         tail = null;
      currentDigit = 0;
   }

   /**
      @return the next permutation display
   */
   public String nextElement()
   {
      String r = null;
      if (digits == 1)
```

```
        {
            r = currentDigit + "";
            currentDigit++;
            return r;
        }
        r = currentDigit + tail.nextElement();
        if (!tail.hasMoreElements())
        {
            currentDigit++;
            tail = new GasPumpDisplay(digits - 1);
        }
        return r;
    }

    /**
        @return true if there are more elements,
        false otherwise.
    */
    public boolean hasMoreElements()
    {
        return currentDigit <= MAX_DIGIT;
    }

    private int digits;
    private GasPumpDisplay tail;
    private int currentDigit;
    private static final MAX_DIGIT = 4;
}
```

```
    /**
        This program tests the permutation generator.
    */
    public class GasPumpTest
    {
        public static void main(String[] args)
        {
            GasPumpDisplay d = new GasPumpDisplay(3);   // 3 digits in
                                                        // display

            while (d.hasMoreElements())
                System.out.println(d.nextElement());
        }
    }
```

`GasPumpTest` prints the following permutations.

000 001 002 003 004 010 011 012 013 014 020 021 022 023 024 030 031 032 033 034
040 041 042 043 044 100 101 102 103 104 110 111 112 113 114 120 121 122 123 124
130 131 132 133 134 140 141 142 143 144 200 201 202 203 204 210 211 212 213 214
220 221 222 223 224 230 231 232 233 234 240 241 242 243 244 300 301 302 303 304
310 311 312 313 314 320 321 322 323 324 330 331 332 333 334 340 341 342 343 344

400 401 402 403 404 410 411 412 413 414 420 421 422 423 424 430 431 432 433 434 440 441 442 443 444

Section 17.2 of your text demonstrates a `PermutationGenerator` class that generates the permutations of a string using a similar approach.

14.3   Tracing Through Recursive Methods

The AP Exam may include multiple-choice questions that give a recursive algorithm and then ask questions about that algorithm. You need to be able to analyze the algorithm and hand-simulate (trace through) the algorithm. Consider the recursive method below.

Example 14.3

```
public class MysteryMaker
{
   /**
   Constructor
   */
   public MysteryMaker() {...}

   /**
   Precondition: x > 0, y > 0
   @return ?????
   */
   public int mystery(int x, int y)
   {
      if (y == 1)
         return x;
      else
         return x * mystery(x, y - 1);
   }
   ...
}
```

Suppose the statements

```
MysteryMaker magic = new MysteryMaker();
System.out.println(magic.mystery(2, 5));
```

were executed. Examining the method in Example 14.3, we see that our three rules of recursion are satisfied.

- Taking one step is defined in the general case (the `else` clause).
- `y` starts with a positive integer value and each recursive call is made with a smaller `y` (a smaller problem).
- The end condition (base case) occurs when `y = 1`.

Tracing through the program requires us to write down the work done for each recursive call. When the end condition is reached, work backwards, substituting values into the recursive calls.

Figure 14.2

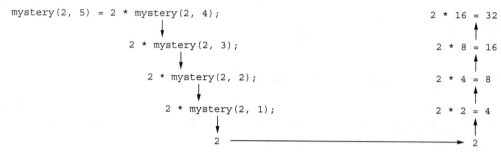

```
mystery(2, 5) = 2 * mystery(2, 4);                          2 * 16 = 32

              2 * mystery(2, 3);                            2 * 8 = 16

                  2 * mystery(2, 2);                        2 * 4 = 8

                      2 * mystery(2, 1);                    2 * 2 = 4

                              2                             2
```

From Figure 14.2, we can conclude the following:

- The statement System.out.println(mystery(2, 5)) would print *32*.
- The number of times the call to mystery was made, including the original call, is 5.
- mystery (x, y) returns x^y.

14.4   Recursive Helper Methods and Mutual Recursion

Section 17.3 of your text demonstrates the use of helper methods to simplify recursive solutions. Section 17.4 discusses mutual recursion. Neither of these topics is specifically listed in the AP CS Topic Outline but both are extensions of recursive solutions. You should read through the examples presented in your text.

14.5   A Word About Efficiency

Although recursion is always fun, it's not always the most efficient way to solve a problem. The example of finding the nth Fibonacci number, which is illustrated in Section 17.5 of your text, certainly demonstrates this!

One of the best known recursive functions, Ackerman's Function, is not very useful, but it is very interesting. For *lots* of practice with tracing a recursive function, try tracing this algorithm to evaluate acker(2, 3) (or any other call with small numbers). This function grows very fast! By tracing Ackerman's function, you can see that the same method call is executed multiple times.

$$
acker(x, y) = \begin{cases} y + 1 & \text{when } x = 0 \\ acker(x - 1, 1) & \text{when } x \,!= 0, \, y = 0 \\ acker(x - 1, acker(x, y - 1)) & \text{when } x \,!= 0, \, y \,!= 0 \end{cases}
$$

After you try this by hand, test it out by writing a recursive method to solve the problem. If you try to evaluate this function for large values your program will report a "stack fault". *Common Error 17.1* of your text discusses stack faults.

■ Things to Remember When Taking the AP Exam

- Recursion is a topic for both AP CS A and AP CS AB. The programming exercises given at the end of Chapter 17 in your text will provide great practice in writing recursive methods.
- It is a common error to use a `while` statement when an `if` statement should be used to check for the base case in a recursive function. Check your work!
- A recursive solution is not necessarily more efficient than an iterative solution to the same problem.
- Remember to include an end condition for recursive solutions. Infinite recursions are usually undesirable.
  - Write recursive solutions when the problem statement is defined recursively or when explicitly instructed to do so. Do not use recursion as a substitute for iteration.

■ Key Words

You should understand the terms below. The AP CS Exam questions may include references to these terms. The citations in parentheses next to each term identify the page numbers where it is defined and/or discussed in *Computing Concepts with Java Essentials*, 3rd ed., and *Big Java*.

infinite recursion (671)   permutation (672)   recursion (667)

■ Connecting the Detailed Topic Outline to the Text

The citations in parentheses identify where information in the outline can be located in *Computing Concepts with Java Essentials*, 3rd ed., and *Big Java*.

- Thinking Recursively (678–682)
- Permutations (672–676)
- Tracing through Recursive Methods (676)
- Recursive Helper Methods and Mutual Recursion (682–684)
- A Word about Efficiency (689–694)

■ Practice Questions

Multiple Choice

Questions 1 and 2 refer to the following three code segments.

```
I.    public static void mysteryPrint(int n)
      {
         if (n > 0)
         {
            mysteryPrint(n - 1);
```

```
        }
        System.out.println(n);
    }
```

II.   ```
        public static void mysteryPrint(int n)
        {
            if (n > 0)
            {
                mysteryPrint(n - 1);
                System.out.println(n);
            }
        }
        ```

III.    ```
        public static void mysteryPrint(int n)
        {
            if (n > 0)
            {
                mysteryPrint(n - 1);
            }
            else
            {
                System.out.println(n);
            }
        }
        ```

1. Assuming that the method `mysteryPrint` is called with a positive integer parameter, which statement about methods I, II, and III above is true?

    a. All three methods produce the same output.
    b. Methods I and II produce the same output that is different from the output produced by Method III.
    c. Methods I and III produce the same output that is different from the output produced by Method II.
    d. Methods II and III produce the same output that is different from the output produced by Method I.
    e. All three methods produce different outputs.

2. If the statement

```
        mysteryPrint(5);
```

were executed, what output would be produced by code segment II ?

a.	b.	c.	d.	e.
0	1	5	5	0
1	2	4	4	
2	3	3	3	
3	4	2	2	
4	5	1	1	
5		0		

3. Which of the following statements is true about recursive methods?

   a. Iterative methods are always easier to write than recursive methods.
   b. Recursive solutions to methods are always more efficient than iterative solutions.
   c. For recursion to terminate there must be a special case for simple inputs.
   d. If a problem is solved both iteratively and recursively, the solutions will always have the same efficiency.
   e. Recursion is the most elegant and appropriate way to solve all problems.

4. Consider the recursive method whose definition appears below.

```
public static String mysteryString(String s)
{
   if (s.length() == 1)
      return s;
   else
      return s.substring(s.length() - 1) +
            mysteryString(s.substring(0, s.length() - 1));
}
```

What is the result of the following call?

```
System.out.println(mysteryString("computer"));
```

   a. *computer* is printed to the screen.
   b. *retupmoc* is printed to the screen.
   c. *c* is printed to the screen.
   d. A stack fault occurs.
   e. A StringIndexOutOfBoundsException is thrown.

Questions 5 and 6 refer to the following recursive method definition.

```
public static int foo(int n)
{
   if (n < 10)
      return 1;
   else
      return 1 + foo(n / 10);
}
```

5. Which of the following statements best describes the value returned by method foo?

   a. foo returns the sum of the digits in its positive integer parameter.
   b. foo returns the sum of the digits in its integer parameter.
   c. foo returns the number of digits in its positive integer parameter.
   d. foo returns the number of digits in its integer parameter.
   e. foo returns the number of 1's in its integer parameter.

6. If the following statement is executed,

```
int n = foo(1234);
```

what is the total number of times the method `foo` is called (including the original call)?

a. 1
b. 2
c. 3
d. 4
e. 5

Questions 7–9 refer to the `ArraySearcher` class incompletely defined below.

```java
public class ArraySearcher
{
    public ArraySearcher(int[] anArray)
    {
        a = anArray;
    }

    public int searchFor(int n)
    {
        int low = 0;
        int high = a.length - 1;
        return search(low, high, n);
    }

    // Postcondition: Returns the index in the array a where key
    // occurs.
    // Returns -1 if key is not found in a.
    public int search(int low, int high, int key)
    {
        if (low > high)
            return -1;
        else
        {
            int mid = (low + high) / 2;
            if (key == a[mid])
                return mid;
            else if (key < a[mid])
                return search(low, mid - 1, key);
            else
                return search(mid + 1, high, key);
        }
    }
    private int[] a;
}
```

The recursive method `search` is intended to locate the value `key` in array `a`. The method is to return the index of the first location of `key` in `a` and return -1 if `key` is not found in `a`.

7. Under which conditions will this work as intended?

    a.   `search` will work as intended only if `key` is not found in `a`.
    b.   `search` will work as intended only if `key` is in position `0`.
    c.   `search` will work as intended only if array `a` is sorted in ascending order.
    d.   `search` will work as intended only if array `a` is sorted in descending order.
    e.   `search` will never work as intended.

8. Assume that a client program included the following declarations and method calls,

    ```
    int[] a = {1, 21, 32, 45, 58, 61, 72, 80, 99, 100, 101};
    ArraySearcher searcher = new ArraySearcher(a);
    int pos = searcher.searchFor(58);
    ```

    How many times is the method `search` called before a value is returned?

    a.   1
    b.   2
    c.   3
    d.   4
    e.   5

9. Assume that a client program included the following declarations and method calls,

    ```
    int[] a = {6, 5, 4, 3, 2, 1};
    ArraySearcher searcher = new ArraySearcher(a);
    int pos = searcher.searchFor(5);
    ```

    What value would be assigned to `pos`?

    a.   −1
    b.   0
    c.   1
    d.   No value would be assigned. There would be a compile-time error.
    e.   No value would be assigned. This would result in infinite recursion.

10. Consider the `Triangle` class defined below.

    ```
    public class Triangle
    {
        public Triangle(int aWidth)
        {
            width = aWidth;
        }

        public int getArea()
        {
            if (width <= 0) return 0;
            if (width == 1) return 1;
    ```

```
        Triangle smallerTriangle = new Triangle(width - 1);
        int smallerArea = smallerTriangle.getArea();
        return smallerArea + width;
    }

    private int width;
}
```

Suppose a client program included the following code segment.

```
Triangle t = new Triangle(4);
int area = t.getArea();
```

What value would be assigned to `area`?

   a. 1
   b. 4
   c. 5
   d. 10
   e. 15

Free Response Questions

1. Euclid's Algorithm can be used to find the greatest common divisor (gcd) of two integers. The algorithm works recursively as illustrated in the example below.

Method Call		Recursive Method Call
gcd(3388, 436)	3388 = 7 * 436 + 336	gcd(3388, 436) = gcd(436, 336)
gcd(3388, 336)	436 = 1 * 336 + 100	gcd(436, 336) = gcd(336, 100)
gcd(336, 100)	336 = 3 * 100 + 36	gcd(336, 100) = gcd(100, 36)
gcd(100, 36)	100 = 2 * 36 + 28	gcd(100, 36) = gcd(36, 28)
gcd(36, 28)	36 = 1 * 28 + 8	gcd(36, 28) = gcd(28, 8)
gcd(28, 8)	28 = 3 * 8 + 4	gcd(28, 8) = gcd(8, 4)
gcd(8, 4)	8 = 2 * 4 + 0	gcd(8, 4) = gcd(4, 0)
gcd(4, 0) = 4		

Therefore, `gcd(3388, 436) = 4`.

You are to implement the recursive method for Euclid's Algorithm. Write your method using the method header below.

```
// Precondition: num1 >= 0, num2 >= 0
// Returns the greatest common divisor of num1 and num2
public static int gcd(int num1, int num2)
```

2. It is well-known that the area of a triangle with corner points (x1, y1), (x2, y2), and (x3, y3) can be computed as:

$$A = \frac{|x1 * y2 + x2 * y3 + x3 * y1 - y2 * x1 - y3 * x2 - y1 * x3|}{2}$$

a. Write the method `triangleArea` that computes the area of its three `Point` parameters using the above formula. The incomplete `Point` class implementation appears below.

```
public class Point
{
    // Constructor
    Point(double x1, double y1)
    {
        x = x1;
        y = y1;
    }

    // Returns the x-coordinate of this point.
    public double getX() {...}

    // Returns the y-coordinate of this point.
    public double getY() {...}

    private double x;
    private double y;
}
```

Write your method `triangleArea` using the method header below.

```
public double triangleArea(Point p1, Point p2, Point p3)
```

b. To compute the area of a polygon with more than three corner points, you can chop off a triangle and recursively compute the area of the remaining polygon (which has one corner point less than the original).

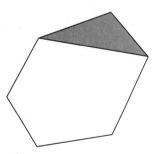

Refer to the incomplete `Polygon` class below.

```
import java.util.ArrayList;

// A polygon with a number of Point2D.Double corners.
public class Polygon
```

```
{
    // Constructs a Polygon object with no corners.
    public Polygon()
    {
        corners = new ArrayList();
    }

    // Adds a point p to the list.
    public void add(Point p)
    {
        corners.add(p);
    }

    // Returns the area of the triangle with the three vertices p1,
    // p2, and p3.
    public double triangleArea(Point p1, Point p2, Point p3) {...}

    // Recursively computes and returns the area of a polygon.
    // If this polygon has fewer than 3 vertices, return 0.
    // Otherwise, return the sum of the area of a triangle
    // and the area of a smaller polygon.
    public double getArea()
    {
        // Code goes here
    }

    private ArrayList corners;
}
```

In writing the method `getArea`, you may call the method `triangleArea`. Assume `triangleArea` works as specified regardless of what you wrote for part a. Write `getArea` using the method header below.

```
public double getArea()
```

CHAPTER 15

Sorting and Searching

■ Topic Summary

15.1 Selection Sort

The selection sort algorithm orders array elements by inspecting all elements in the array to find the smallest element. This element is exchanged with the first entry in the array. The smallest element is now first. The next step is to inspect the elements to find the second smallest element and exchange this element with the second entry in the array. The smallest two elements in the array are now in the first two positions of the array. This procedure continues until all elements in the array are in sorted order. The complete SelectionSorter class can be found in Section 18.1 of your text. Example 15.1 examines three key methods used in the selection sort.

Example 15.1   sort Method

```
public void sort()
   {
   // Loop invariant: Elements a[0]...a[i - 1] are in their final
   // positions.
   for (int i = 0; i < a.length - 1; i++)
      {
         int minPos = minimumPosition(i);
```

```
            swap(minPos, i);
        }
    }
```

The method `sort` calls the method `minimumPosition` to return the index of the smallest entry in the tail portion of the array beginning in position `i` and then calls the method `swap` to exchange the entries in these two positions of the array. This is the method that puts each element in its final position.

`minimumPosition` **Method**

```
private int minimumPosition(int from)
{
    int minPos = from;
    for (int i = from + 1; i < a.length; i++)
        if (a[i] < a[minPos]) minPos = i;
    return minPos;
}
```

The method `minimumPosition` searches the array for the smallest value beginning in position `from`. The index of the element with the smallest value in this portion of the array is returned.

`swap` **Method**

```
private void swap(int i, int j)
{
    int temp = a[i];
    a[i] = a[j];
    a[j] = temp;
}
```

The method `swap` has two parameters that represent indices of the array. `swap` exchanges the entries in these two positions in the array.

Your text uses the `ArrayUtil` class to fill the array with random values and to print the array values to the screen. The `ArrayUtil` class is a utility class (similar to the `Math` class). A utility class has no objects but it contains related static methods. These static methods are called by using the class name and passing the appropriate parameters. The statements

```
// Fills a 20 element array with integers in the range
// 0-99 inclusive.
int[a] = ArrayUtil.randomIntArray(20, 100);
```

and

```
// Prints the contents of the array.
ArrayUtil.print(a);
```

call static methods of the `ArrayUtil` utility class.

15.1.1 *Analyzing the Performance of the Selection Sort Algorithm*

We are sometimes asked to analyze the running time of an algorithm or to determine how many comparisons are made in a certain algorithm. Consider the following array:

Using the selection sort algorithm we have:

- Starting with position 0: 4 comparisons are made to determine that 1 is the smallest value in the array. 1 is swapped with 13.

| 1 | 34 | 13 | 50 | 21 |

1 is in its final position.

- Advancing to position 1: 3 comparisons are made to determine that 13 is the smallest value in the remaining part of the array. 13 is swapped with 34.

| 1 | 13 | 34 | 50 | 21 |

1 and **13** are in their final positions.

- Advancing to position 2: 2 comparisons are made to determine that 21 is the smallest value in the remaining part of the array. 34 is swapped with 21.

| 1 | 13 | 21 | 50 | 34 |

1, **13**, and **21** are in their final positions.

- Advancing to position 3: 1 comparison is made to determine that 34 is the smallest value in the remaining part of the array. 34 is swapped with 50.

| 1 | 13 | 21 | 34 | 50 |

All numbers are in their final positions.

The total number of comparisons made during this simulation of the selection sort is

$$4 + 3 + 2 + 1 = 10$$

For 5 elements, the number of comparisons made by the selection sort algorithm is the sum of the first 4 integers. For *n* elements, the number of comparisons would be the sum of the first *n*−1 integers:

$$(n-1) + (n-2) + (n-3) + \ldots + 3 + 2 + 1.$$

The formula for finding the sum of the first k integers is: $\sum_{i=1}^{k} i = \dfrac{(k)(k+1)}{2}$. In our example, the sum of the first 4 integers is $\dfrac{(4)(5)}{2}$.

The original order of the array elements has no effect on the number of comparisons made by the selection sort algorithm. The nested loop executes the same number of times regardless of the original ordering of the array elements.

For the AP CS A Exam, you should be able to count comparisons (or statement executions) for a given algorithm. For the AB Exam, you need to be able to classify algorithms based on their performance efficiency.

(AB only) As explained above, the number of comparisons made to sort an array with n elements is the sum of the first $n-1$ integers. In general, for an n-element array, this computation evaluates to

$$\frac{n(n-1)}{2} = \frac{n^2}{2} - \frac{n}{2}$$

We classify the selection sort as a *quadratic* sort because it has complexity of the form $y = an^2$, where n is the number of elements being sorted and y is the run-time complexity (in our case, the number of comparisons), and a is some constant. We use the expression $O(n^2)$ (read as "big-Oh of n squared") to represent the complexity of this algorithm. We are generally concerned with what happens to a sorting algorithm's behavior and efficiency as the number of elements, n, gets very large. The curves $y = n^2$, $y = \frac{n^2}{2}$, and $y = \frac{n^2}{2} - \frac{n}{2}$ have the same basic shape and are all classified as $O(n^2)$.

15.2 Insertion Sort

The insertion sort algorithm takes each element of the array and inserts it into an already sorted portion of the array. Although insertion sort is not found in your text, it is outlined below and covered in Chapter 20A in Appendix A of this guide.

To sort our original array using insertion sort:

| 13 | 34 | 1 | 50 | 21 |

- Starting with position 1:   Ready to insert 34.

| 34 | | | | |

| 13 | | 1 | 50 | 21 |

> 34 is compared to 13. Since 13 is not greater than 34, it is not shifted.
> 34 is inserted into position 1.

| 13 | 34 | 1 | 50 | 21 |

- Advancing to position 2: Ready to insert 1.

```
        1
┌──┬──┬──┬──┬──┐
│13│34│  │50│21│
└──┴──┴──┴──┴──┘
```

1 is compared to 34. Since 34 is greater than 1, 34 is shifted.

```
      1
┌──┬──┬──┬──┬──┐
│13│  │34│50│21│
└──┴──┴──┴──┴──┘
```

1 is compared to 13. Since 13 is greater than 1, 13 is shifted.

```
 1
┌──┬──┬──┬──┬──┐
│  │13│34│50│21│
└──┴──┴──┴──┴──┘
```

1 is inserted into position 0.

```
┌──┬──┬──┬──┬──┐
│ 1│13│34│50│21│
└──┴──┴──┴──┴──┘
```

- Advancing to position 3: Ready to insert 50.

```
         50
┌──┬──┬──┬──┬──┐
│ 1│13│34│  │21│
└──┴──┴──┴──┴──┘
```

50 is compared to 34. Since 34 is not greater than 50, no entry is shifted.
50 is inserted into position 3.

```
┌──┬──┬──┬──┬──┐
│ 1│13│34│50│21│
└──┴──┴──┴──┴──┘
```

- Advancing to position 4: Ready to insert 21.

```
            21
┌──┬──┬──┬──┬──┐
│ 1│13│34│50│  │
└──┴──┴──┴──┴──┘
```

21 is compared to 50. Since 50 is greater than 21, 50 is shifted.

```
         21
┌──┬──┬──┬──┬──┐
│ 1│13│34│  │50│
└──┴──┴──┴──┴──┘
```

21 is compared to 34. Since 34 is greater than 21, 34 is shifted.

```
      21
┌──┬──┬──┬──┬──┐
│ 1│13│  │34│50│
└──┴──┴──┴──┴──┘
```

21 is compared to 13. Since 13 is not greater than 21, no other entries are shifted. 21 is inserted into position 2.

1	13	21	34	50

The array is now sorted. Example 15.2 shows the `sort` method of the `InsertionSorter` class.

Example 15.2

```java
public void sort()
{
    for (int i = 1; i < a.length; i++)
    {
        int temp = a[i];
        int pos = i;
        while (0 < pos && temp < a[pos - 1])
        {
            a[pos] = a[pos - 1];
            pos--;
        }
    }
    a[pos] = temp
}
```

15.2.1 Analyzing the Performance of the Insertion Sort Algorithm

When insertion sort is used to sort the array

13	34	1	50	21

we see that the number of comparisons and the number of shifts made was dependent on the original order of the array. The insertion sort algorithm only compares terms until the correct position of the element to insert is determined. If the original array were in increasing order, there would be only one comparison (and no shifts) for each element we insert. Many more comparisons and shifts are needed if the original array is in decreasing order.

(AB only) For the insertion sort algorithm, the number of comparisons made to sort an array with n elements in the worst case (when the array is in reverse order) will take $(n - 1) + (n - 2) + \ldots + 2 + 1$ comparisons (and shifts). This is

$$\frac{n(n - 1)}{2} = \frac{n^2}{2} - \frac{n}{2}$$

We see that the insertion sort is also an $O(n^2)$ sorting algorithm. Of course if we start with a sorted array, the complexity is $O(n)$ because only one comparison is made for each of the $n-1$ elements visited. Wouldn't it be nice if all of the arrays we had to sort were already sorted!

15.3 Merge Sort

The merge sort algorithm sorts an array by cutting the array in half, recursively sorting each half, and then merging the sorted halves. Section 18.4 of your text shows the `MergeSorter` class. Let's look at the basic parts of the merge sort algorithm.

Example 15.3   `sort` Method

```java
public void sort()
{
   if (a.length <= 1) return;
   int[] first = new int[a.length / 2];
   int[] second = new int[a.length - first.length];
   // System.arraycopy(a, 0, first, 0, first.length);
   int j = 0;
   for (int i = 0; i < first.length; i++)
   {
      first[j] = a[i];
      j++;
   }
   // System.arraycopy(a, first.length, second, 0, second.length);
   j = 0;
   for (int i = first.length; i < second.length + first.length;
        i++)
   {
      second[j] = a[i];
      j++;
   }
   MergeSorter firstSorter = new MergeSorter(first);
   MergeSorter secondSorter = new MergeSorter(second);
   firstSorter.sort();    // recursive call on first half
   secondSorter.sort();   // recursive call on second half
   merge(first, second);  // merge two sorted halves
}
```

This `sort` method contains 2 recursive calls, each calling itself with a smaller array. This process continues with each of the smaller arrays until the array has 1 or fewer elements. Since `System.arraycopy` is not part of the AP subset, the call to `System.arraycopy` has been commented out and replaced by a `for` loop that performs the same task.

Let's look at the merge sort algorithm with a sample array containing 8 elements. One call to `sort` is made to sort 8 elements

| 12 | 34 | 7 | 2 | 63 | 45 | 17 | 20 |

`sort` now makes 2 recursive calls to sort 2 smaller arrays, each with 8/2 or 4 elements.

| 12 | 34 | 7 | 2 | | 63 | 45 | 17 | 20 |

And now, 4 recursive calls to sort 4 smaller arrays, each with 8/4 or 2 elements.

| 12 | 34 | | 7 | 2 | | 63 | 45 | | 17 | 20 |

Finally, 8 recursive calls are made to sort 8 arrays, each of size 1.

| 12 | | 34 | | 7 | | 2 | | 63 | | 45 | | 17 | | 20 |

Then the method `merge` is called to merge two adjacent sorted arrays.

Example 15.4 `merge` **Method**

```java
private void merge(int[] first, int[] second)
{
   // Merge both halves into the temporary array
   int iFirst = 0;    // Next element in first half to look at
   int iSecond = 0;   // Next element in second half to look at
   int j = 0;         // Next open position in a

   // Merging the 2 arrays
   while (iFirst < first.length && iSecond < second.length)
   {
      if (first[iFirst] < second[iSecond])
      {
         a[j] = first[iFirst];
         iFirst++;
      }
      else
      {
         a[j] = second[iSecond];
         iSecond++;
      }
      j++;
   }

   // Exactly one of the two following loops will be executed.

   // Copy any remaining entries of the first half
   for (int i = iFirst; i < first.length; i++)
   {
      a[j] = first[i];
      j++;
   }

   // Copy any remaining entries of the second half
   for (int i = iSecond; i < second.length; i++)
   {
      a[j] = second[i];
      j++;
   }
}
```

The `System.arraycopy` statements have again been replaced by equivalent `for` loops.

After recursive calls to `sort` we have

```
12   34   7   2   63   45   17   20
```

Now, the `merge` method is called to merge two adjacent sorted arrays.

```
12 34   2 7   45 63   17 20
```

We merge two adjacent sorted arrays again,

```
2 7 12 34   17 20 45 63
```

And again.

```
2 7 12 17 20 34 45 63
```

15.3.1 *Analyzing the Performance of the Merge Sort Algorithm*

In almost all cases, merge sort is more efficient than insertion sort and in all cases merge sort is more efficient than selection sort.

(AB only) Suppose that the original size of our array is n where $n = 2^m$. The recursive calls to `sort` create m levels that we must merge.

Each level merges n elements so the complexity of the merge sort algorithm can be informally classified as $O(nm)$. If we apply our rules for logarithms, since $n = 2^m$ we have $m = \log_2(n)$. The shape of logarithm curves is the same regardless of the base. Substituting $\log_2(n)$ for m, we have $O(n \log_2(n))$ and we classify merge sort as an $O(n \log(n))$ algorithm. A more formal analysis of merge sort is in Section 18.5 of your text.

15.4 Quicksort (AB only)

Another $O(n \log(n))$ sort is quicksort. Unlike merge sort, quicksort does not need a temporary array. The algorithm chooses an element from the array (pivot) and then partitions the array into two smaller arrays so that those elements to the left of the partition are less than or equal to `pivot` and those elements to the right of the partition are greater than or equal to `pivot`. Example 15.5 shows the recursive quicksort `sort` method and the `partition` method.

Example 15.5 `sort` Method

```
public void sort(int from, int to)
{
    if (from >= to) return;   // There are elements to sort.

    int p = partition(from, to);   // Array partitioned.
    // So that the elements a[from]...a[p] (left partition) are
```

```
                    // less than the elements a[p+1]...a[to]  (right partition)

                    sort(from, p);    // Sort left partition
                    sort(p + 1, to);    // Sort right partition
                }
```

`sort` calls `partition` to divide the array into two partitions such that all elements in the left partition are less than or equal to `pivot` and those elements in the right partition are greater than or equal to `pivot`. `sort` then recursively calls itself to do the same on the left partition and the right partition.

`partition` **Method**

```
        private int partition(int from, int to)
        {
            int pivot = a[from];
            int i = from - 1;
            int j = to + 1;
            while (i < j)
            {
                i++;
                while (a[i] < pivot)
                    i++;
                j--;
                while (a[j] > pivot)
                    j--;
                if (i < j) swap(i, j);
            }
            return j;
        }
```

`partition` returns an index, `j`, in the array such that the elements `a[from]...a[j]` are less than the elements `a[j + 1]...a[to]`.

Consider the array: `a = {7   9   1   6   4   8   2   5}`

The `partition` method chooses the first element in the array (7) as `pivot`.

After the call to `partition`, the array is partitioned into two smaller arrays.

```
    {5   2   1   6   4}    {8   9   7}
```

The elements in the left partition are all less than or equal to 7 and the elements in the right partition are all greater than or equal to 7. Then `sort` is called with each smaller array and each smaller array is partitioned. You are encouraged to trace through this code for the example presented so that you can understand how the `partition` method and the quicksort algorithm work.

15.4.1 *Analyzing the Performance of the Quicksort Algorithm (AB only)*

The most efficient behavior of quicksort occurs when the partition is always found to be in the center of the array (approximately the same number of elements to the left of the partition as there are to the right of the partition). Assume that the number of elements, n, is a power of 2. Then $n = 2^m$. Assume also that the position of the partition is in the exact middle of the subarray.

Table 15.1   Quicksort Comparisons

Number of subarrays	Number of elements in each subarray	Number of comparisonss in each subarray	Total number of comparisons
1	n	$n - 1 \approx n$	$1(n)$
2	$\dfrac{n}{2}$	$\dfrac{n}{2} - 1 \approx \dfrac{n}{2}$	$2\left(\dfrac{n}{2}\right)$
4	$\dfrac{n}{4}$	$\dfrac{n}{4} - 1 \approx \dfrac{n}{4}$	$4\left(\dfrac{n}{4}\right)$
8	$\dfrac{n}{8}$	$\dfrac{n}{8} - 1 \approx \dfrac{n}{8}$	$8\left(\dfrac{n}{8}\right)$
...	...	...	...
...	...	...	$n + 2\left(\dfrac{n}{2}\right) + 4\left(\dfrac{n}{4}\right) + ... + n\left(\dfrac{n}{n}\right)$

After dividing m times, there are n partitions of size 1.

$$\begin{aligned}
\text{Total comparisons} &= n + 2\left(\frac{n}{2}\right) + 4\left(\frac{n}{4}\right) + 8\left(\frac{n}{8}\right) + ... + n\left(\frac{n}{n}\right) \\
&= n + n + n + ... + n \; \{m \text{ times}\} \\
&= nm
\end{aligned}$$

But, if $n = 2^m$, then $m = \log_2(n)$, so substituting, we have

$$\text{Total comparisons} = n \log_2(n)$$

which classifies the quicksort algorithm as $O(n \log(n))$.

15.5 Comparing $O(n^2)$ with $O(n \log(n))$ (AB only)

We are generally concerned with what happens to a sorting algorithm's behavior and efficiency as the number of elements, n, gets very large. The curves $y = n^2$, $y = n \log(n)$, and $y = n$ are graphed in Figure 15.1 for values of n ranging from 1 to 20. This graph shows that $y = n^2$ increases in value much faster than $y = n \log(n)$.

Figure 15.1   Comparing $y = n^2$, $y = n \log(n)$, and $y = n$

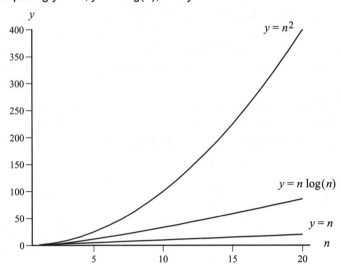

If you look at Table 15.2, you can see that the difference in running times is more pronounced when the number of elements is very large.

Table 15.2   Comparing $O(n^2)$ with $O(n \log(n))$

n	n^2	$n \log(n)$
100	10,000	664
300	90,000	2,468
500	250,000	4,482
800	640,000	7,715
1,000	1,000,000	9,965
10,000	100,000,000	132,877
100,000	10,000,000,000	1,660,964

Table 15.2 uses $\log_2$. Remember that $\log_2(x) = \log(x) / \log(2)$. You can calculate the values in Table 15.2 using your calculator and this $\log_2$ relationship.

15.6   Sequential Search

A sequential (or linear) search examines each element in the array until the required match is found or the end of the array is reached. In the best case, the element is found in the first position of the array. In the worst case, the element is not found in the array, so all of the elements in the array are visited. The sequential search does not depend on any particular ordering of the array elements.

15.6.1   Analyzing the Performance of the Sequential Search Algorithm (AB only)

In the worst case, the sequential search is $O(n)$. If you are lucky enough to find the element in position 0 of the array, then the search is $O(1)$. The average number of elements examined with the sequential search is $n/2$ and therefore, the sequential search is classified as an $O(n)$ algorithm.

15.7   Binary Search

The binary search algorithm is used to search a sorted array. Binary search locates a value in a sorted array by determining whether the value occurs in the first half or the second half of the array. This process is repeated in the half where it is likely to be found.

The game of *High-Low* is a game where one person thinks of a number between 1 and 100. The other person is to guess that number. The first person responds "Correct!", "Too high!", or "Too low!" for each guess. What would be your first guess? If you are familiar with the binary search, you can guess the number with no more than 7 tries! A person who attempts to play this game using a sequential search may take 100 guesses before being successful.

15.7.1   Analyzing the Performance of the Binary Search Algorithm

The formal analysis of the binary search is explained in Section 18.7 of your text. Informally, let's assume an array has 8 elements whose values are 11–18. Suppose you are searching for the value 13.

```
a = {11   12   13   14   15   16   17   18}
```

You know how to play this game. You guess 14. The answer is "Too high." You guess 12. The answer is "Too low." You guess 13. If there is no case of "cheating," you will guess the correct value in at most 3 guesses. Notice that $2^3 = 8$.

The maximum number of guesses for *High–Low* is the smallest power of 2 that results in a value greater than or equal to the number of numbers from which we are guessing. For our 1–100 *High–Low* game, the maximum number of guesses is 7 (if you know how to play the game efficiently) because $2^7 > 100$. 7 is the smallest power of 2 that results in a value greater than or equal to 100.

The `BinarySearcher` class is shown in Section 18.7 of your text. Example 15.6 shows the search method from `BinarySearcher`. The search method returns the index of the value v in the array. If v is not found in the array, -1 is returned.

Example 15.6

```java
public int search(int v)
{
   int low = 0;
   int high = a.length - 1;
   while (low <= high)
   {
      int mid = (low + high) / 2;
      int diff = a[mid] - v;

      if (diff == 0)   // a[mid] == v
         return mid;
      else if (diff < 0)   // a[mid] < v
         low = mid + 1;
      else
         high = mid - 1;
   }
```

```
        return -1;
    }
```

(AB only) If there are *n* elements in a sorted array, and $n = 2^m$, then $m = log_2(n)$. The maximum number of visits in the array is log(*n*). The binary search is a $O(log(n))$ algorithm.

15.8   Comparing *O(n)* and *O(log(n))* (AB only)

We are again primarily concerned with what happens to an algorithm's behavior and efficiency as the number of elements, *n*, gets very large. The curve $y = n$ and $y = log(n)$ are graphed below for values ranging from 1 to 20. You can see in Figure 15.2 that $y = n$ increases in value much faster than $y = log(n)$.

Figure 15.2   Comparing *O(n)* and *O(log(n))*

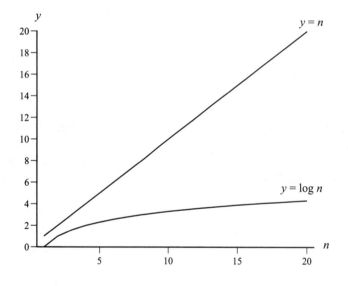

In Table 15.3, you can see that the difference between *n* and log(*n*) is again more pronounced when the number of elements, *n*, is very large.

Table 15.3

n	log(*n*)
100	6.64
300	8.22
500	8.97
800	9.64
1000	9.97
10,000	13.28
100,000	16.61

Using a binary search with 100,000 elements will require no more than 17 visits but a sequential search may require 100,000! However, the binary search requires that the array is sorted.

An interesting relationship to remember is that $\log_{10}(n)$ is the number of decimal digits of n, $\log_2(n)$ is the number of binary digits of n. The $\log_2(n)$ is approximately $(10/3) * \log_{10}(n)$.

■ Expanded Coverage of Material That is Not Found in the Text

- The insertion sort algorithm is not covered in your text but is explained in Chapter 20A in Appendix A of this guide and reviewed in Section 15.2 of this chapter.

■ Topics That Are Useful But Not Tested

- The Java `Arrays` class contains methods for searching and sorting collections of objects. These methods are discussed in Section 18.8 of your text.
- Defining a class that realizes the *strategy interface* `Comparator` is one way to sort objects of a class that we do not own and that does not implement the `Comparable` interface. The `Comparator` interface can also be used to sort objects in a way other than that which is defined in the class. This is explained in Section 18.8 of your text.
- The `Collections` class contains sort methods that can sort array lists.

■ Things to Remember When Taking the AP Exam

- When given a particular algorithm, you should be able to count the number of times a specific statement is executed.
- The merge sort is more efficient than the insertion sort and selection sort algorithms but requires a temporary array.
- When writing a sorting algorithm, there are many places where off-by-1 errors can occur. Be careful when choosing between 0 and 1, < and <=, and `a.length` and `a.length − 1` for loop initializations. Walk through your code carefully.
- When given an algorithm similar to the binary search algorithm and an algorithm similar to the sequential search algorithm, you should be able to choose the algorithm that is more efficient for a specific set of data.
- Remember that an array has to be sorted in order to use binary search.
- Binary search generally is more efficient than sequential search if the array is sorted.
- (**AB only**) Merge sort and quicksort are $O(n \log(n))$ algorithms. Insertion and selection sorts are $O(n^2)$.
- (**AB only**) The worst case for the quicksort algorithm is when the array is originally in order or in reverse order. This makes the quicksort running time $O(n^2)$.
- (**AB only**) Algorithms that are $O(n \log(n))$ are more efficient than algorithms that are $O(n^2)$.
- (**AB only**) When given an algorithm, you should be able to classify it as $O(1)$, $O(n)$, $O(\log(n))$, $O(n^2)$, or $O(n \log(n))$.

- **(AB only)** Do not classify an algorithm as $O(2n)$, $O(3)$, or $O(n^2 + 2n + 1)$. These are $O(n)$, $O(1)$, and $O(n^2)$ respectively.
- **(AB only)** Do not count loops when determining the big-Oh running time. Consecutive loop algorithms are most often $O(n)$. Nested loop algorithms tend to be $O(n^2)$.

■ Key Words

You should understand the terms below. The AP CS Exam questions may include references to these terms. The citations in parentheses next to each term identify the page numbers where it is defined and/or discussed in *Computing Concepts with Java Essentials*, 3rd ed., and *Big Java*.

big-Oh notation (711)   merge sort (713)   sequential search (722)
binary search (724)   quicksort (720)   worst-case run-time
linear search (722)   selection sort (704)   behavior (721)

■ Connecting the Detailed Topic Outline to the Text

The citations in parentheses identify where information in the outline can be located in *Computing Concepts with Java Essentials*, 3rd ed., and *Big Java*.

- Selection Sort (704–710)
    - Analyzing the Performance of the Selection Sort Algorithm (710–712)
- Insertion Sort (A–20A:412–414)
    - Analyzing the Performance of the Insertion Sort Algorithm (A–20A:412–414)
- Merge Sort (712–715)
    - Analyzing the Performance of the Merge Sort Algorithm (715–718)
- Quicksort (720–721)
    - Analyzing the Performance of the Quicksort Algorithm (721)
- Comparing $O(n^2)$ and $O(n \log(n))$ **(AB only)** (715-716)
- Sequential Search (722–723)
    - Analyzing the Performance of the Sequential Search Algorithm (722)
- Binary Search (724–725)
    - Analyzing the Performance of the Binary Search Algorithm (725–726)
- Comparing $O(n)$ and $O(\log(n))$ **(AB only)** (A–20A:413

■ Practice Questions

Multiple Choice

Questions 1 and 2 refer to the incomplete definition of the `SelectionSorter` class below.

```
public class SelectionSorter
{
   public SelectionSorter(int[] anArray)
   {
      a = anArray;
   }

   public void sort()
   {
      for (int i = 0; i < a.length - 1; i++)
      {
         int minPos = minimumPosition(i);
         swap(minPos, i);
      }
   }

   // Returns the position of the smallest element
   // in a[from]...a[a.length - 1]
   private int minimumPosition(int from) {...}

   // Exchanges a[i] with a[j]
   swap(int i, int j) {...}

   private int[] a;
}
```

The following segment of code is executed.

```
SelectionSorter sorter = new SelectionSorter(a);
sorter.sort();
```

Consider arrays initialized with the values below.

I.   {2, 3, 4, 5, 6}
II. {6, 5, 4, 3, 2}
III. {2, 6, 1, 5, 4}

1. Which of the following statements regarding the number of comparisons made to sort the array is true?

   a. I takes fewer comparisons than both II and III.
   b. II takes fewer comparisons than both I and III.
   c. III takes fewer comparisons than both I and II.

    d. I and II require the same number of comparisons, which is different from the number of comparisons required to sort III.

    e. I, II, and III require the same number of comparisons.

2. Consider the `SelectionSorter` method `sort`.

```
public void sort()
{
    for (int i = 0; i < a.length - 1; i++)
    {
        int minPos = minimumPosition(i);
        swap(minPos, i);
    }
}
```

Which of the following statements is true at the beginning of each iteration of the loop?

I   For all `j`, such that `0 <= j < i`, `0 <= a[j] <= a[i]`.
II. For all `j`, such that `0 <= j < i`, `a[j]` is in its final position in the sorted array.
III. For all `j`, such that `0 <= j < i`, `a[0]...a[j]` is sorted.

    a. I only
    b. II only
    c. III only
    d. II and III only
    e. I, II, and III

3. **(AB only)** Consider the following algorithms to accomplish the task of removing duplicates from an array list `list`.

I. For each element in `list` (x_i), look at x_i. Now look at each element in `list` and count how many times x_i occurs in `list`. If the count is larger than 1, remove x_i.

II. Sort the array list with an efficient sort algorithm. For each x_i in `list`, look at its next neighbor to decide whether it is present more than once. If it is, remove x_i.

III. Sort the array list, `list`, with an efficient algorithm. Traverse the array list looking at each x_i in `list`. Whenever the element after x_i is strictly larger than x_i, append x_i to a second (initially empty) array list, `list2`. Find the difference, `diff`, in the sizes of `list` and `list2`. Beginning with the last element of `list`, delete `diff` elements from `list`. Then, copy the elements of `list2` back into `list`.

Of the following, which best describes the running time of these algorithms?

    a. I, II, and III are all $O(n^2)$.
    b. I and II are $O(n^2)$, III is $O(n \log(n))$.
    c. I is $O(n^2)$, II and III are $O(n \log(n))$.
    d. I and III are $O(n^2)$, II is $O(n \log(n))$.
    e. I, II, and III are $O(n \log(n))$.

4. The method `removeDupes` is intended to remove duplicates from array a, returning n, the number of elements in a after duplicates have been removed. For example, if array a has the values

```
{4, 7, 11, 4, 9, 5, 11, 7, 3, 5}
```

before `removeDupes` is called, then after duplicates are removed, a will be {4, 7, 11, 5, 9, 3} and 6 will be returned.

```java
public static int removeDupes(int[] a)
{
    int n = a.length;
    for (int i = 0; i < n; i++)
    {
        int current = a[i];
        int j = i + 1;
        while (j < n)
        {
            if (current == a[j])
            {
                a[j] = a[n - 1];
                n--;
            }
            else
                j++;
        }
    }
    return n;
}
```

How many times is the comparison

```
(current == a[j])
```

executed in `removeDupes`?

    a. 45
    b. 42
    c. 36
    d. 25
    e. 21

5. The method `removeDupes` is intended to remove duplicates from array a, returning n, the number of elements in a after duplicates have been removed. For example, if array a has the values

```
{4, 7, 11, 4, 9, 5, 11, 7, 3, 5}
```

before `removeDupes` is called, then after duplicates are removed, a will be {4, 7, 11, 5, 9, 3} and 6 will be returned.

Consider the following three implementations of removeDupes.

I.
```java
public static int removeDupes(int[] a)
{
    int n = a.length;
    for (int i = 0; i < n; i++)
    {
        int current = a[i];
        int j = i + 1;
        while (j < n)
        {
            if (current == a[j])
            {
                a[j] = a[n - 1];
                n--;
            }
            else
                j++;
        }
    }
    return n;
}
```

II.
```java
public static int removeDupes(int[] a)
{
    int n = a.length;
    for (int i = 0; i < n; i++)
    {
        int current = a[i];
        for (int j = 0; j < n; j++)
        {
            if (i != j && current == a[j])
            {
                a[j] = a[n - 1];
                n--;
            }
        }
    }
    return n;
}
```

III.
```java
public static int removeDupes(int[] a)
{
    int n = a.length;
    int count = 0;
    int i = o;
    while (i < n)
    {
        int j = i + 1;
        boolean found = false;
        while (!found && j < n)
        {
```

```
            if (a[i] == a[j])
            {
                a[j] = a[n - 1];
                n--;
                found = true;
            }
            j++;
        }
        if (!found)
            i++;
    }
    return n;
}
```

Which of the code segments above requires the fewest number of operations?

    a. I
    b. II
    c. III
    d. All choices require the same number of operations.
    e. It is impossible to determine which segment requires the fewest operations.

6.   Which of the following statements about searching is **not** true?

    a. The linear search examines all values in an array until it finds a match or until it reaches the end.
    b. A binary search is generally more efficient than a linear search.
    c. A binary search can only be used to search for an item in a sorted array.
    d. A sequential search generally takes more comparisons than a binary search.
    e. A binary search is always faster than a sequential search.

7. **(AB only)** The quicksort algorithm is to be used to sort an array of integers in decreasing order. Which of the cases below describes the worst case for the quicksort algorithm?

    I.   The original array is in increasing order.
    II. The original array is in decreasing order.
    III. The original array is in random order.

    a. I only
    b. II only
    c. III only
    d. I and II only
    e. I, II, and III all take the same number of comparisons.

8. Consider the `search` method (of some class) below which is intended to return the index of the position in array `a` where `key` is found. If `key` is not in the array `a`, `-1` is returned.

```
public int search(int key)
{
    int low = 0;
```

```
    int high = a.length - 1;
    while (low <= high)
    {
        int mid = (low + high) / 2;
        int diff = a[mid] - key;

        if (diff == 0)    // a[mid] == key
            return mid;
        else if (diff < 0)    // a[mid] < key
            low = mid + 1;
        else
            high = mid - 1;
    }
    return -1;
}
private int[] a;
```

Suppose:

```
a = {8, 10, 1, 5, 7, 9, 6, 2}
```

What value will search(2) return?

   a. 8
   b. 4
   c. 3
   d. −1
   e. No value will be returned. An `ArrayIndexOutOfBoundsException` is thrown.

9. What is the maximum number of elements that will be visited by the binary search algorithm when searching a sorted 45-element array?

   a. 1
   b. 6
   c. 7
   d. 22
   e. 45

10. An array, a, is initialized to contain the following values.

```
a = {1, 23, 44, 56, 77, 81, 88, 90, 99}
```

The following search algorithm is provided.

```
public int search(int v, int high)
{
    int low = 0;
    while (low <= high)
    {
        int mid = (low + high) / 2;
```

```
        int diff = a[mid] - v;

        if (diff == 0)
            return mid;
        else if (diff < 0)
            low = mid + 1;
        else
            high = mid - 1;
    }
    return -low - 1;
}
```

When the call `search(60, 9)` is invoked, what is returned by this method call?

    a. −1
    b. −4
    c. −5
    d. 3
    e. 7

Free Response Questions

1. Two words are anagrams if one of the words is made by transposing the letters of the other word. For example, "stop" and "tops" are anagrams. This problem involves reading a dictionary of words, storing the words in a list, and then generating and printing all words in the dictionary that are anagrams of a given word. The problem uses the `Word` and `AnagramList` classes whose incomplete implementations are below.

Word class

```
// Holds words in two forms: the original word and the word with
// its letters in sorted order.
public class Word
{
    // Constructs a word.
    public Word(String theWord)
    {
        originalWord = theWord;
        sortedWord = sortWord();
    }

    // Sorts the letters of the word.
    // Returns the sorted word.
    // Example: if originalWord = "apple",
    // "aelpp" is returned.
    private String sortWord()
    {
        // Code goes here
    }

    // Returns the original word.
    public String getWord() {...}
```

```
        // Returns the sorted word.
        public String getSortedWord() {...}

        private String originalWord;
        private String sortedWord;
    }
```

AnagramList **class**

```
        // Holds a list of Words.
        public class AnagramList
        {
            // Constructs an empty list.
            public AnagramList()
            {
                wordList = new ArrayList();
            }

            // Adds a Word, whose original order is
            // newString, to wordList.
            public void addWord(String newString) {...}

            // Returns true if aWord and anotherWord have original
            // strings that are anagrams (words composed of the same
            // letters), otherwise returns false.
            public boolean checkAnagram(Word aWord, Word anotherWord)
            {
                // Code goes here
            }

            // Prints original words of all Words in wordList that
            // are anagrams of key.
            public void printAnagrams(String key)
            {
                // Code goes here
            }

            private ArrayList wordList;
        }
```

a. One way to check whether two words are anagrams is to sort the letters of each word and compare the sorted words. If the sorted words contain the same sequence of letters and are the same length, the original words are anagrams.

You are to write the sortWord method of the Word class. sortWord will return a string that contains the letters of originalWord in sorted order. For example,

originalWord	sortWord *returns*
cat	act
apple	aelpp
table	abelt

Use the method header below to write `sortWord`.

```
// Sorts the letters of the originalWord.
// Returns the sorted word.
// Example: if originalWord = "apple",
// "aelpp" is returned.
private String sortWord()
```

b. Write the `AnagramList` method `checkAnagram`. `checkAnagram` returns `true` if its two `Word` parameters have original words that are anagrams. If not, `checkAnagram` returns `false`. Use the method header below to write `checkAnagram`. Assume that all `Word` methods work as intended regardless of what you wrote for part a.

```
// Returns true if aWord and anotherWord have original
// words that are anagrams (words composed of the same
// letters), otherwise returns false.
public boolean checkAnagram(Word aWord, Word anotherWord)
```

c. Write the `AnagramList` method `printAnagrams`. `printAnagrams` prints the original words of all `Words` in `wordList` that are anagrams of `key`. Use the method header below to write `printAnagrams`. Assume that all `Word` methods work as intended regardless of what you wrote for part a. You may call `checkAnagram` in writing `printAnagrams`. Assume that `checkAnagram` works as intended regardless of what you wrote in part b. Use the method header below to write `printAnagrams`.

```
// Prints original words of all Words in wordList that
// are anagrams of key.
public void printAnagrams(String key)
```

2. An `AddressBook` contains an unknown number of entries. Each entry contains a person's first and last names and an email address. The `Person` class, whose incomplete definition is below, is used to represent an entry.

```java
public class Person implements Comparable
{
    // Constructs a person with first name (fName), and last
    // name (lName). The email address of the person is set.
    public Person(String fName, String lName)
    {
        firstName = fName;
        lastName = lName;
        emailAddress = makeEmailAddress();
    }

    // Returns an email address based on a person's name
    private String makeEmailAddress() {...}

    // Returns name of person in the form 'last, first'.
    public String getName() {...}

    // Returns email address of person.
```

```
        public String getEmailAddress() {...}

        // Compares two persons by the alphabetical ordering of
        // name (lastName, firstName).
        public int compareTo(Object o)
        {
            // Code goes here
        }
        private String firstName;
        private String lastName;
        private String emailAddress;
    }
```

Some useful public methods in the `AddressBook` class include:

```
    addEntry    // adds entry of type Person to address book.
    printEntries    // Prints information in address book.
    sortByLastName    // Sorts the information by last name.
    sortByEmailAddress    // Sorts the information by email address.
    search    // Returns the email address given the person's name.
```

The incomplete `AddressBook` class appears below.

```
    public class AddressBook
    {
        // Creates an empty address book of Persons.
        public AddressBook()
        {
            list = new ArrayList();
        }

        // Adds an entry to the address book.
        public void addEntry(Person p) {...}

        // Prints the entries in the address book.
        public void printEntries() {...}

        // Uses selection sort algorithm to sort the
        // address book entries by last name.
        public void sortByLastName()
        {
            for (int i = 0; i < list.size() - 1; i++)
            {
                int minPos = minimumPosition(i);
                swap(minPos, i);
            }
        }

        // Returns the index of smallest element
        // in a tail range of the ArrayList.
        private int minimumPosition(int from)
        {
```

```
        // Code goes here
    }

    // Sorts the address book entries by email address.
    public void sortByEmailAddress()
    {
        for (int i = 0; i < list.size() - 1; i++)
        {
            int minPos = minimumEmailPosition(i);
            swap(minPos, i);
        }
    }

    // Returns the index of smallest element in a tail
    // range of the array.
    private int minimumEmailPosition(int from)
    {
        // Code goes here
    }

    // Swaps the entry in the ith position of the address
    // book with the entry in the jth position of the
    // address book.
    private void swap(int i, int j) {...}

    private ArrayList list;
}
```

a. `Person` implements `Comparable`. You are to write the method `compareTo` for the `Person` class. `compareTo` for the `Person` class compares two `Person` objects by the alphabetical ordering of their names (last, first). You may call `Person`'s method `getName` in writing `compareTo`. Assume `getName` works as intended.

compareTo Summary	
`int compareTo(Object other)`	Returns a value < 0 if this Person is less than other.
	Returns 0 if this Person is equal to other.
	Returns a value > 0 if this person is greater than other.

Use the method header below to write `compareTo`.

```
    // Compares two persons by the alphabetical ordering of
    // name (lastName, firstName).
    public int compareTo(Object obj)
```

b. The `AddressBook` class has a method `sortByLastName` that uses the selection sort algorithm to sort the address book entries by last name. `sortByLastName` calls the method `minimumPosition` that returns the index of the `AddressBook` entry that has the minimum value (the entry whose name (last, first) comes alphabetically before other names in a portion of the `AddressBook`). You are to write the method `minimumPosition`. You may (and should) use the `Person` method `compareTo` when writing your solution. Assume `compareTo` works as specified regardless of what you wrote in part a.

```
// Returns the index of smallest element
// in a tail range of the ArrayList.
private int minimumPosition(int from)
```

c. In order to be able to sort by email address as well as by last name, a `Comparator` is used. The `PersonComparator` class is defined below. **(Note: The Comparator interface is not part of the AP subset.)**

```
public class PersonComparator implements Comparator
{
   public int compare(Object first, Object second)
   {
      Person firstPerson = (Person) first;
      Person secondPerson = (Person) second;
      String firstEmail = firstPerson.getEmailAddress();
      String secondEmail = secondPerson.getEmailAddress();
      if (firstEmail.compareTo(secondEmail) < 0) return -1;
      if (firstEmail.compareTo(secondEmail) == 0) return 0;
      return 1;
   }
}
```

The `AddressBook` class uses this `PersonComparator` class to sort entries alphabetically by email address. The `AddressBook` class has a method `sortByEmailAddress` that uses the selection sort algorithm to sort the address book entries alphabetically by email addresses. `sortByEmailAddress` calls the method `minimumEmailPosition` that returns the index of the `AddressBook` entry that has the minimum email value (the entry whose email comes alphabetically before other entries in a portion of the `AddressBook`). You are to complete the method `minimumEmailPosition`. You may (and should) use the `PersonComparator` method `compare` (defined above) when writing your solution.

```
// Returns the index of element with an email address
// that is alphabetically less than other email
// addresses in a tail range of the ArrayList.
private int minimumEmailPosition(int from)
{
   int minPos = from;
   Comparator comp = new PersonComparator();

   // Code goes here

   return minPos;
}
```

CHAPTER 16

An Introduction to Data Structures
(AB only)

■ Topic Summary

16.1 Using Linked Lists

A linked list is a sequence of elements. Each element stores an object and a reference to the next element.

Figure 16.1

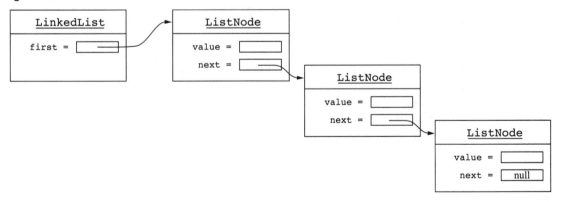

The figures in Section 19.1 of your text illustrate this concept in detail. The Java library provides a LinkedList class in the java.util package. LinkedList implements java.util.List. Table 16.1 lists the List methods that are included in the AP subset.

Table 16.1
`java.util.List`

Method	Method Summary
`void add(Object obj)`	Appends the object `obj` to the end of this list.
`Object get(int index)`	Returns the element at position `index` in this list.
`Iterator iterator()`	Returns an iterator for the elements in this list.
`ListIterator listIterator()`	Returns a list iterator for the elements in this list.
`Object set(int index, Object obj)`	Replaces the element at position index in this list with the specified element.
`int size()`	Returns the number of elements in the list.

Both the `ArrayList` and the `LinkedList` implement the `List` interface. Example 16.1 illustrates this.

Example 16.1

```
1       import java.util.List;
2       import java.util.ArrayList;
3       // import java.util.LinkedList;
4       import java.util.Iterator;

5       public class ArrayListTest
6       {
7          public static void main(String[] args)
8          {
9             ArrayList staff = new ArrayList();
10               // Construct an empty ArrayList
11            // LinkedList staff = new LinkedList();
12               // Construct an empty LinkedList
13            staff.add("Dick");    // Objects added to end of list
14            staff.add("Harry");
15            staff.add("Romeo");
16            staff.add("Tom");
17            printList(staff);    // Dick Harry Romeo Tom
18            System.out.println(staff.get(2));    // Romeo
19            staff.set(2, "Karen");    // Dick Harry Karen Tom
20            printList(staff);    // Dick Harry Karen Tom
21         }

22         public static void printList(List staff)
23         {
24            System.out.println();
25            Iterator iter = staff.iterator();
26            while (iter.hasNext())
27               System.out.println(iter.next());
28         }
29      }
```

Since `ArrayList` and `LinkedList` both implement `List`, the implementation used in Example 16.1 can be changed from an `ArrayList` implementation to a `LinkedList` implementation with two modifications:

- The import statement (Replace line 2 with line 3).
- The declaration (Replace line 9 with line 11).

The `printList` method (line 22) takes a `List` as a parameter and so no changes are necessary here.

As we will discuss in more detail later, some of these `List` methods are extremely inefficient when used with a `LinkedList` implementation.

In addition to the `List` methods, the `LinkedList` also implements methods from the `java.util.LinkedList` class. The `LinkedList` methods that are included in the AP subset are listed in Table 16.2.

Table 16.2
class java.util.LinkedList implements java.util.List

Method	Method Summary
void addFirst(Object obj)	Inserts the object `obj` at the beginning of this list.
void addLast(Object obj)	Appends the object `obj` to the end of this list.
Object getFirst()	Returns the first element in the list.
Object getLast()	Returns the last element in the list.
Object removeFirst()	Removes and returns the first element from this list.
Object removeLast()	Removes and returns the last element from this list.

To access elements in a `LinkedList`, you can use a list iterator. Table 16.3 contains the iterator methods and Table 16.4 contains the additional list iterator methods that are included in the AP subset. The list iterator works in the same way as the `ArrayList` iterator introduced in Chapter 11 of this study guide.

Table 16.3
java.util.Iterator

bMethod	Method Summary
boolean hasNext()	Returns `true` if this list iterator has more elements when traversing the list in the forward direction.
Object next()	Moves the iterator past the next element and returns the traversed element.
void remove()	Removes from the list the last element that was returned by `next`.

In addition to the operations `hasNext`, `next`, and `remove` that the `Iterator` interface provides, the `List` interface provides a special iterator, called a `ListIterator` (extending `Iterator`), that allows for element insertion and replacement. The `LinkedList` class provides a method to obtain a list iterator. The statement

```
ListIterator iter = staff.listIterator();
```

calls this method for the `LinkedList` staff.

Table 16.4

`interface java.util.ListIterator extends java.util.Iterator`

Method	Method Summary
`void add(Object obj)`	Inserts the specified element into the list before the current iterator position and moves the iterator past the inserted element.
`set(Object obj)`	Replaces the last element returned by `next` with `obj`.

Example 16.2 demonstrates the `LinkedList` and `ListIterator` methods included in the AP testable subset. Remember that the iterator position is *between* two list elements.

Example 16.2

```java
import java.util.LinkedList;
import java.util.ListIterator;
/**
    A program that demonstrates the LinkedList methods and
    ListIterator methods in AP subset.
*/
public class LinkedListTest
{
    public static void main(String[] args)
    {
        // Demonstrating LinkedList methods
        LinkedList staff = new LinkedList();    // Construct empty
                                                // list.

        staff.addFirst("Dave");    // Add to front of list, D
        staff.addFirst("Harry");    // H D
        staff.addFirst("Romeo");    // R H D
        staff.addFirst("Tom");    // T R H D
        staff.addLast("Mary");    // Add to end of list, T R H D M
        staff.addLast("Sue");    // T R H D M S

        System.out.println(staff.getFirst());    // Tom
        System.out.println(staff.getLast());    // Sue

        staff.removeFirst();    // R H D M S
        staff.removeLast();    // R H D M

        staff.add("George");    // R H D M G

        System.out.println(staff.size());    // 5
        System.out.println(staff.get(2));    // Dave
        staff.set(2, "Kevin");    // R H K M G

        // Demonstrating additional ListIterator methods
```

```
// | indicates iterator position

ListIterator iter = staff.listIterator(); // | R H K M G

iter.next();    // R | H K M G
iter.next();    // R H | K M G
iter.remove();   // R | K M G
iter.next();    // R K | M G
iter = staff.listIterator();    // | R K M G
iter.next();    //R | K M G

iter.set("Cathy");    // C | K M G

iter = staff.listIterator();
iter.next();    // C | K M G
iter.remove();   // | K M G
iter.add("Nina");    // N | K M G

iter = staff.listIterator();
while(iter.hasNext())
{
   System.out.print (iter.next()+ " ");
        // Nina Kevin Mary George
}
   }
}
```

The `ListIterator` method `remove` removes the last element returned by the iterator. This method can be called only once after a call to `next`.

Example 16.2 includes calls to the methods `get` and `set` because `java.util.LinkedList` implements `java.util.List` and the `List` class includes these methods. However, the `List` methods `get` and `set` are primarily used with the `ArrayList` implementation and *not* with a `LinkedList` implementation. Because array lists allow for random access, the call

```
System.out.println(arrayListName.get(x));
```

gives immediate access to the object whose index is x. This operation is $O(1)$. With a linked list, the list must be traversed to arrive at the element in position x. This operation is $O(n)$. That is, in Example 16.2, Romeo and Harry were visited before Dave with execution of the statement

```
System.out.println(staff.get(2));    // Dave
```

Think about the consequences of the `printList` method when a linked list is passed as the parameter!

```
public static void printList(List staff)
{
   for (int i = 0; i < staff.size(); i++)
```

```
        System.out.println((String)staff.get(i));
    }
```

Each call to `get` traverses the list. We can see why iterating over the elements in a linked list with an iterator is typically preferable to accessing the elements by indexing through the list!

The same is true for the `List` method `set`. The statement

```
    staff.set(2, "Kevin");
```

must traverse the list to arrive at position 2 in order to set the object to "Kevin" (a $O(n)$ operation). In an `ArrayList`, the statement

```
    arrayListName.set(2, "Kevin");
```

provides immediate access to the element in position 2 (a $O(1)$ operation).

An iterator should be used to access the elements of a `LinkedList`. Do not use `get` and `set` with linked lists.

16.2   Implementing Linked Lists

Since the implementation of a linked list is a part of the AB course, we will look at pieces of this implementation and discuss how the elements of a linked list are manipulated.

Elements in a linked list are called *nodes*. Nodes are visited in sequential order. Unlike an array, there is no random access in a linked list. Your text uses the `Link` class to define a node. To facilitate a consistency in the exam questions, the AP Exam uses the `ListNode`[1] class shown in Example 16.3 to define a node and its methods.

Example 16.3

```
public class ListNode
{
    public ListNode(Object initValue, ListNode initNext)
    {
        value = initValue;
        next = initNext;
    }

    /**
        Returns the value of a List node.
        @return value of list node
    */
    public Object getValue()
    {
        return value;
    }
```

---

[1] College Board's AP Computer Science AB: Implementation Classes and Interfaces

```
/**
    Returns the next field of a List node.
    @return next field of list node
*/
public ListNode getNext()
{
    return next;
}

/**
    Sets the value of the list node to theNewValue.
    @param theNewValue is the new value of the list node
*/
public void setValue(Object theNewValue)
{
    value = theNewValue;
}

/**
    Sets the list node's next field to a new reference.
    @param theNewNext is the new reference for the next
    field of the list node
*/
public void setNext(ListNode theNewNext)
{
    next = theNewNext;
}

private Object value;
private ListNode next;
}
```

A description of the ListNode class will appear at the beginning of the exam booklet. (The comments may not be included!)

Since the ListNode class does not implement equals, if two ListNodes are compared using equals, references are being compared (using the inherited Object equals method). For example, if node1 and node2 are references to ListNodes, the expression

```
node1.equals(node2)
```

evaluates to true only if node1 and node2 reference the same ListNode.

The implementation of a linked list involves the ListNode and the LinkedList classes. Example 16.4 contains the methods that directly involve manipulating the first element in a linked list. These methods are getFirst, addFirst, and removeFirst. The ListNode class is used in this implementation. Your text uses the private inner class Link that implements these same methods. Inner classes are not included in the AP subset.

Example 16.4

```
public class LinkedList
{
   /**
      Constructs an empty list.
   */
   public LinkedList()
   {
      first = null;
   }

   /**
      Returns the first object in the list if there is one.
      @return first object in the list if there is one
   */
   public Object getFirst()
   {
      if (first == null)
         throw new NoSuchElementException();
      return first.getValue();
   }

   /**
      Adds an object to the front of the list.
      @param the object to be added to the list
   */
   public void addFirst(Object obj)
   {
      ListNode newNode = new ListNode(obj, first);
      first = newNode;
   }

   /**
      Removes and returns the first object in the list if there
      is one.
      @return first object in the list if there is one
   */
   public Object removeFirst()
   {
      if (first == null)
         throw new NoSuchElementException();
      Object obj = first.getValue();
      first = first.getNext();
      return obj;
   }

   private ListNode first;
}
```

Figures 4 and 5 in Section 19.2 of your text provide illustrations of adding to and removing from the front of the linked list.

It is also useful to be able to add and remove from the end of a linked list. The Java class library implementation of a linked list provides immediate access to the beginning and the end of the list as illustrated in Figure 16.2.

Figure 16.2

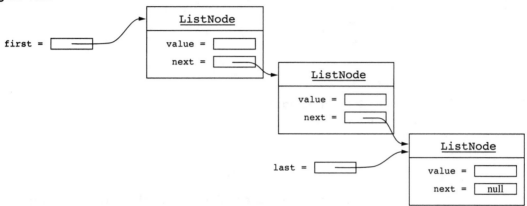

We can write our own linked list implementation with end-of-list access by adding a private instance field that keeps track of the last `ListNode` in the linked list. Example 16.5 includes the methods that directly manipulate the last element in a linked list. In Section 19.2 of your text, the `LinkedList` class defines a private inner class `LinkedListIterator` and its implementation. The iterator is used to traverse the linked list. Example 16.5 traverses the list without the use of an iterator.

Example 16.5

```
public class LinkedList
{
   /**
       Constructs an empty list.
   */
   public LinkedList()
   {
      first = null;
      last = null;
   }

   /**
       Returns the last object in the list if there is one.
       @return last object in the list if there is one
   */
   public Object getLast()
   {
      if (first == null)    // The list is empty.
         throw new NoSuchElementException();
      return last.getValue();
   }

   /**
       Adds an object to the end of the list.
       @param the object to be added to the list
```

```
   */
   public void addLast(Object obj)
   {
      ListNode newNode = new ListNode(obj, null);
      if (first == null)   // The list is empty.
      {
         first = newNode;
         last = newNode;
      }
      else
      {
         last.setNext(newNode);
         last = newNode;
      }
   }

   /**
      Removes and returns the last object in the list if there
      is one.
      @return last object in the list if there is one
   */
   public Object removeLast()
   {
      if (first == null)   // The list is empty.
         throw new NoSuchElementException();
      ListNode temp = first;
      if (first.getNext() == null)   // Only 1 node in list.
      {
         Object obj = first.getValue();   // first = last
         first = null;
         last = null;
         return obj;
      }
      while (temp.getNext() != last)   // More than 1 node in list
      {
         temp = temp.getNext();   // Looking for the node
      }                           // before the last node.

      Object obj = last.getValue();
      temp.setNext(null);
      last = temp;
      return obj;
   }
}
```

Now, what happens if you don't have that private instance field, last? In order to implement any of the methods above, the list must be traversed. Example 16.6 demonstrates traversing the list to do the same tasks as in Example 16.5.

Example 16.6

```java
    public Object getLast()
    {
        if (first == null)   // The list is empty.
            throw new NoSuchElementException();
        ListNode temp = first;   // Must traverse to find the end.
        while (temp.getNext() != null)
            temp = temp.getNext();
        return temp.getValue();
    }

    public void addLast(Object obj)
    {
        ListNode newNode = new ListNode(obj, null);
        ListNode temp = first;   // Must traverse to find the end.
        while (temp.getNext() != null)
            temp = temp.getNext();
        temp.setNext(newNode);
    }

        public Object removeLast()
        {
        if (first == null)   // The list is empty.
            throw new NoSuchElementException();

        if (first.getNext() == null)   // Only 1 node in list.
        {
            Object obj = first.getValue();
            first = null;
            return obj;
        }
        ListNode temp = first;      // Must traverse to find the end
        ListNode follower = temp;   // and the node before the last.
        while (temp.getNext() != null)
        {
            follower = temp;
            temp = temp.getNext();
        }
        follower.setNext(null);
        return temp.getValue();
        }
    }
```

It's a good exercise to trace the implementation above and draw pictures similar to Figure 5 in Section 19.2 of your text as you walk through the code. Try walking through the test program in Example 16.7. Go through each method implementation and sketch your ListNode additions and deletions.

Example 16.7

```java
    public static void main(String[] args)
    {
```

```
        LinkedList staff = new LinkedList();    // Construct empty
                                                // list.
        staff.addLast("Dick");    // D
        staff.addFirst("Harry");    // H D
        staff.addLast("Romeo");    // H D R
        staff.addFirst("Tom");     //T H D R
        staff.removeLast();    // T H D
        staff.printList();
        staff.removeFirst();    // H D
        System.out.println(staff.getFirst());    // Harry
        System.out.println(staff.getLast());    // Dick
    }
```

Finally, what happens if we want to add to the middle of a linked list? Suppose you have a linked list that maintains its elements in order. How do you insert or delete an element from this list? Let's look at inserting a `ListNode` whose value is a string. We wish to insert the node so that the strings are in alphabetical order. We will use our linked list implementation without the `last` instance field.

Our list is initialized to be empty.

```
        ListNode first = null;
```

Our new `ListNode` is created to hold the new string value (`name`).

```
        ListNode newNode = new ListNode(name, null);
```

Now, let's insert. First check to see if we are inserting into an empty list.

```
        if (first == null)
        {
            first = newNode;
        }
```

If the list is not empty, check to see if the new node should be inserted in the front of the list.

```
        String firstValue = (String)first.getValue();
        String newValue = (String)newNode.getValue();
        if (firstValue.compareTo(newValue) >= 0)    // New node goes first
        {
            newNode.setNext(first);
            first = newNode;
        }
```

If the new node isn't inserted in the front of the list, see if it belongs in the middle or at the end of the list.

```
        String newValue = (String)newNode.getValue();
        ListNode temp = first;
        ListNode follower = temp;
```

```
// Checking for end and for order
while (temp.getNext() != null &&
       newValue.compareTo((String)temp.getValue()) > 0)
{
   follower = temp;
   temp = temp.getNext();
}

// Stopped because end of list OR correct position found in middle
// Does it belong in the middle?
if (newValue.compareTo((String)temp.getValue()) < 0)
{
   follower.setNext(newNode);
   newNode.setNext(temp);
}
// Or does it belong at the end?
else
{
   temp.setNext(newNode);
}
```

Deleting a node from our linked list of `ListNodes` follows a similar coding pattern. You should first make sure that you are not trying to delete a node from an empty list. Then check to see if you are deleting the first node. If so, `first` will have to be adjusted. And finally, consider deleting from the middle or end of the list, setting the `next` fields where required.

When using the Java Library's `LinkedList` class, inserting nodes in order follows a similar pattern.

First, start with an empty list.

```
LinkedList list = new LinkedList();
```

Now, are you adding to an empty list?

```
if (list.size() == 0)
{
   list.addFirst(name);
}
```

If the list is not empty, does the new node belong in the front of the list?

```
String firstValue = (String)list.getFirst();
if (name.compareTo(firstValue) <= 0)
{
   list.addFirst(name);
}
```

If the node doesn't belong in the front of the list, then check to see if it belongs in the middle or at the end of the list.

```
ListIterator iter = list.listIterator();
boolean foundLarger = false;
while (!foundLarger && iter.hasNext())
{
    // Does object belong in the middle?
    if (name.compareTo((String)iter.next()) < 0)
    {
        foundLarger = true;
        iter.previous();   // previous is not tested on the AP Exam
        iter.add(name);
    }
}

// Or does it belong at the end?
if (!iter.hasNext())
    list.addLast(name);
```

The `ListIterator` has a `previous` method that allows us to traverse in reverse. `previous` is very useful when inserting or deleting from the middle or from the end of a `LinkedList`. The use of `previous` will not be tested on the AP Exam.

The preceding code inserts `String` objects into a linked list in alphabetical order. Suppose you wish to keep an ordered linked list of `Integers`, or `Coins`, or `Students`. How could we modify our code so that it can be used by any of these classes? To "order" objects of a class, what must be true of the class (what interface should the class implement)?

16.2.1 Doubly Linked Lists

In addition to linked lists that have a `next` field referencing the next node in the list, we can have a doubly linked list. In a doubly linked list, the node contains a value, a reference to the next node in the list, and a reference to the previous node in the list.

Figure 16.3

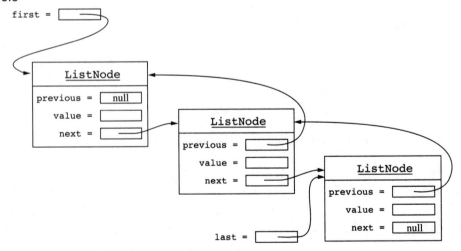

Suppose our `ListNode` class were modified to be a `DLListNode` class. Example 16.8 modifies the `ListNode` constructor for the `DLListNode` class. A doubly linked list *is a* linked list with another instance field.

Example 16.8

```
public DLListNode(DLListNode initPrevious,
    Object initValue, DLListNode initNext)
{
   previous = initPrevious;
   value = initValue;
   next = initNext;
}
```

When adding a node to this doubly linked list, you must make a few more node adjustments! Before writing any code, draw pictures of the intended adjustments. Figure 16.4 and Example 16.9 show adjustments necessary to add a DLListNode to the middle of a doubly linked list.

Figure 16.4

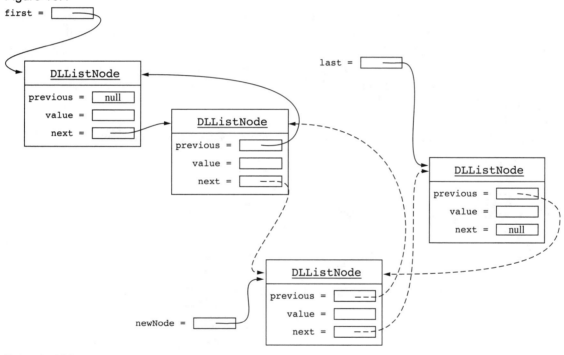

Example 16.9

```
// Adding a node to middle or end of an ordered doubly linked
// list.
Comparable newValue = (Comparable)newNode.getValue();
DLListNode temp = first;
while (temp.getNext() != null &&
    newValue.compareTo((Comparable)temp.getValue()) > 0)
{
   temp = temp.getNext();
}

if (newValue.compareTo((Comparable)temp.getValue()) <= 0)
{
   // Adding to middle.
```

```
    // Four references must be set.
    DLListNode hold = temp.getPrevious();
    hold.setNext(newNode);
    newNode.setNext(temp);
    newNode.setPrevious(temp.getPrevious());
    temp.setPrevious(newNode);
}
else
{
    // Adding to end.
    // Two references must be set.
    temp.setNext(newNode);
    newNode.setPrevious(temp);
}
```

To delete a node from a doubly linked list (and a singly linked list), you need to consider the same cases as you do when you insert into a linked list. Is the list empty? Is the node that is to be deleted the first node of the list? Is it in the middle? Is it the last node? Is the node to be deleted even in the list? If the node is not in the list, what should happen? If there is more than one node with the same value as the node to be deleted, should only the first occurrence be deleted or all nodes with that value?

To delete from the middle of a doubly linked list, you must adjust two references.

Figure 16.5

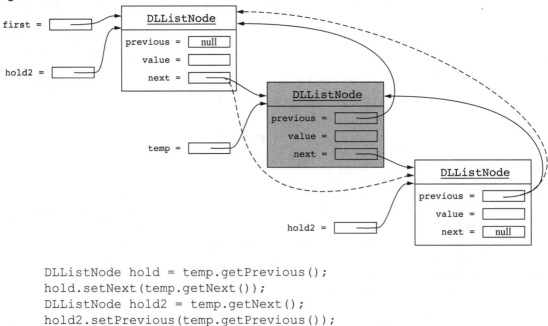

```
DLListNode hold = temp.getPrevious();
hold.setNext(temp.getNext());
DLListNode hold2 = temp.getNext();
hold2.setPrevious(temp.getPrevious());
```

It is a good exercise to draw the nodes of a doubly linked list and write the code necessary to delete the first and last nodes of the list.

The `Link` class described in Section 19.1 of your text is actually a node in a doubly linked list. It stores two links: one to the next element and one to the previous one.

The Java `LinkedList` class is implemented using a doubly linked list with references to the first node and to the last node. Operations that index into the list (accessing the ith node) will traverse the list from the beginning or the end, whichever is closer to the specified index (i).

16.2.2   Circularly Linked Lists

A circularly linked list is a list whose last node references the first node. The implementation works much like the singly linked list implementation except that, when traversing the list with the `temp`, the last node of the list is found when

```
temp.getNext() == first
```

evaluates to `true`. Figure 16.6 illustrates a circularly linked list.

Figure 16.6

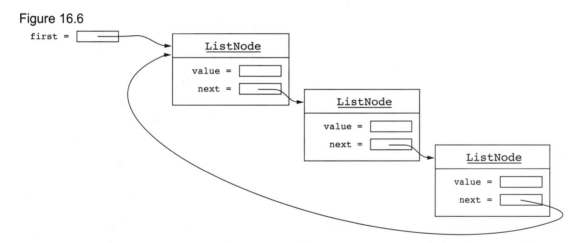

And, if you want to be challenged even more, you can implement a doubly-circularly linked list!

16.2.3   Header and Trailer Nodes

When implementing a linked list or a doubly linked list, you considered several cases: adding to the empty list, adding or removing the first node, adding or removing the last node, adding or removing a middle node. A *header* node is a node that comes before all other nodes in the list. A *trailer* node is a node that comes after all of the nodes in the list. If a list has a header node and a trailer node, most of these cases are eliminated. We are left only with adding and deleting from the middle of the list. The header and trailer nodes are not included when printing the list contents or searching the list. They can be considered "dummy" nodes.

The constructor of a linked list implementation that has a header and trailer node would create a list similar to the one illustrated in Figure 16.7.

Figure 16.7

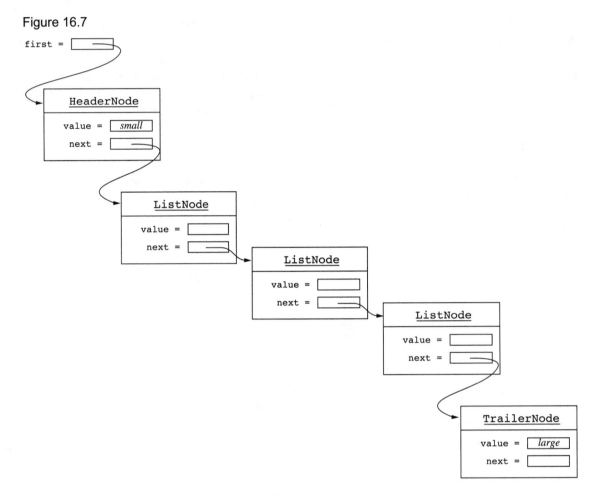

You may see these terms used on the AP Exam but when implementing linked lists on the free-response questions on the AP Exam, do not use header and trailer nodes unless explicitly told to do so.

16.3   Abstract and Concrete Data Types

An abstract data type defines the fundamental operations on the data but does not specify the implementation. When we refer to a list, we think of an ordered sequence of elements in which an element can be inserted or removed. The concrete representation of a list may be a `LinkedList` or an `ArrayList`. Although the operations performed on both implementations appear to have the same outcome, the performance efficiency of these operations can be quite different. As we discussed in Example 16.1, the implementation of the `List` methods is quite different for the `LinkedList` and the `ArrayList`. The `ArrayList` has random access. The `LinkedList` is accessed sequentially. Figures 8 and 10 in Section 19.3 of your text illustrate the differences. Table 16.5 summarizes the efficiency of some of the more common operations on lists of elements that maintain their order.

Table 16.5

Operation	ArrayList	LinkedList (Java library class)
Insert at front	$O(n)$	$O(1)$
Insert at end	$O(1)$	$O(1)$
Remove from front	$O(n)$	$O(1)$
Remove from end	$O(1)$	$O(1)$
Linear Traversal	$O(n)$	$O(n)$
Random Access	$O(1)$	$O(n)$

As you can see, if random access to list elements is important and done frequently, an ArrayList may be a better choice than a linked list.

16.4 Stacks

A stack is an abstract data type to which elements can be added and removed at one end only. Think about a stack of dinner plates in your kitchen cabinet. Each plate you add to the stack is placed on the top of the stack. When you remove a plate, you remove the topmost plate first. A stack is a collection of items with "last in first out" (LIFO) retrieval. The stack's insert method is push. The remove method is pop. The stack can also "look at" the top element without removing it with the peekTop method. To facilitate a consistency in the exam questions, the AP Exam uses the Stack interface[2] shown in Example 16.10.

Example 16.10

```
public interface Stack
{
   /**
      Postcondition: Returns true if stack is empty, false
      otherwise.
   */
   boolean isEmpty();

   /**
      Precondition: stack is [e1, e2, ..., en] with n >= 0
      Postcondition: stack is [e1, e2, ..., en, x]
   */
   void push(Object x);

   /**
      Precondition: stack is [e1, e2, ..., en] with n >= 1
      Postcondition: stack is [e1, e2, ..., e(n-1)];
      Returns en
      Throws an unchecked exception if the stack is empty.
   */
   Object pop();

   /**
```

---

[2] College Board's AP Computer Science AB: Implementation Classes and Interfaces

```
        Precondition: stack is [e1, e2, ..., en] with n >= 1
        Postcondition: Returns en
        Throws an unchecked exception if the stack is empty.
    */
    Object peekTop();
}
```

A description of this `Stack` interface will appear in the exam booklet.

Now, let's look at the concrete data implementation. Stacks can be implemented using an array, an `ArrayList`, or a linked list. Of course, if the stack were implemented using an array (fixed size), an `isFull` method would be useful. Think about implementing the stack using the Java `LinkedList` class. Implementing the methods in the `Stack` interface defined in Example 16.10 is not complicated at all. Consider the `peekTop` method. Suppose that the stack implementation adds to and removes from the front of the stack. `peekTop` returns the element on the top of the stack without modifying the stack contents.

Example 16.11

```
// Stack implementation using LinkedList
public Object peekTop()
{
    if (s.isEmpty())
        throw new NoSuchElementException();
    return(s.getFirst());
}
```

Are there any advantages to using the front of the list? `push` and `pop` are $O(1)$. Would this change if we were to implement `push` and `pop` using the back of the list as the top of the stack (`addLast` and `removeLast`)? Does this depend on the linked list implementation used?

You can also use an `ArrayList` implementation for a stack[3]. One such implementation is listed in the *AP Computer Science AB: Implementation Classes and Interfaces* that is available on the College Board Web site. Example 16.12 contains this implementation.

For the `ArrayList` implementation, the top of the stack is the element with the highest index. With this implementation `push` and `pop` are $O(1)$.

Example 16.12

```
public class ArrayStack implements Stack
{
    public ArrayStack()
    {
        array = new ArrayList();
    }

    public void push(Object x)
    {
```

```
            array.add(x);
        }

        public Object pop()
        {
            return array.remove(array.size() - 1);
        }

        public Object peekTop()
        {
            return array.get(array.size() - 1);
        }

        public boolean isEmpty()
        {
            return array.size() == 0;
        }

        private ArrayList array;
    }
```

Some applications where stacks might be useful include:
- Evaluation of postfix expressions.
- Testing the balancing of nested parentheses (symbols) in an algebraic expressions.
  $\{a + (b - [c + d]) / e + (f - g - h)\}$
- Keeping track of variable declarations inside nested { } inside a compiler.

Example 16.13 shows a test program for our LinkedList implementation of a stack. If you are providing an array implementation, ArrayStack, for stack, you would only replace the constructor call in Example 16.13.

Example 16.13

```
    public class StackTest
    {
        public static void main(String[] args)
        {
            Stack s = new ListStack();    // Constructor call
            s.push("Dick");
            s.push("Harry");
            s.push("Romeo");
            s.push("Tom");

            while (!(s.isEmpty()))
            {
                System.out.println(s.pop());
            }
        }
    }
```

The resulting output is:

Tom
Romeo
Harry
Dick

16.5 Queues

A queue is an abstract data type to which you add elements at one end and remove elements from the other end. Think about a queue being a water fountain line or a cafeteria line. The first person in the line is the first person out of the line. When one is added to the line, he is added to the rear of the line. A queue is a collection of items with "first in first out" (FIFO) retrieval. The insert method that we will use for a queue is enqueue. To remove an element from a queue, we will use the dequeue method. We can "look at" the front element in a queue without removing it with the method peekFront. To facilitate a consistency in the exam questions, the AP Exam uses the Queue interface[4] shown in Example 16.14.

Example 16.14

```
public interface Queue
{
   /**
      Postcondition: Returns true if queue is empty, false
      otherwise.
   */
   boolean isEmpty();

   /**
      Precondition:  queue is [e1, e2, ..., en] with n >= 0
      Postcondition: queue is [e1, e2, ..., en, x]
   */
   void enqueue(Object x);

   /**
      Precondition: queue is [e1, e2, ..., en] with n >= 1
      Postcondition: queue is [e2, ..., en];
      Returns e1
      Throws an unchecked exception if the queue is empty.
   */
   Object dequeue();

   /**
      Precondition:  queue is [e1, e2, ..., en] with n >= 1
      Returns e1
      Throws an unchecked exception if the queue is empty.
   */
```

[4] College Board's AP Computer Science AB: Implementation Classes and Interfaces

```
        Object peekFront();
}
```

A description of the Queue interface will appear in the exam booklet.

One possible implementation of a queue might be a linked list implementation as shown in Example 16.15.

Example 16.15

```
public class ListQueue implements Queue
{
    /**
        Constructs an empty queue.
    */
    public ListQueue()
    {
        que = new LinkedList();
    }

    /**
        Adds obj to queue.
        @param obj is added to queue.
    */
    public void enqueue(Object obj)
    {
        que.addLast(obj);
    }

    /**
        The first object is removed from the queue.
    */
    public Object dequeue()
    {
        if (que.isEmpty())
            throw new NoSuchElementException();
        return que.removeFirst();
    }

    /**
        The first object in the queue is returned but not removed.
        @return the first object in queue
    */
    public Object peekFront()
    {
        return que.getFirst();
    }

    /**
        @return true if the queue has no elements, false otherwise.
    */
    public boolean isEmpty()
```

```
        {
            return que.size() == 0;
        }

        private LinkedList que;
    }
```

Example 16.16 shows a test program for our `LinkedList` implementation of a queue.

Example 16.16

```
        public class QueueTest
        {
            public static void main(String[] args)
            {
                Queue que = new ListQueue();

                que.enqueue("Harry");
                que.enqueue("Romeo");
                que.enqueue("Tom");

                while (!(que.isEmpty()))
                {
                    System.out.println(que.dequeue());
                }
            }
        }
```

The resulting output is:

> *Harry*
> *Romeo*
> *Tom*

Some applications where queues might be useful include:
- Airport simulation of planes on a runway.
- A printer queue (where your print requests are held while the printer is busy).
- A queue of user interface events (button clicks, keystrokes) that need to be processed.
- Other simulations, e.g., customers waiting in a line at a bank.
- Other requests, e.g., service requests for a web-based application.

■ Expanded Coverage of Material That is Not Found in the Text

- Circularly linked lists are not covered in your text but are explained in Section 16.3.2 of this guide.
- Header and trailer nodes are not covered in your text but are explained in Section 16.3.3 of this guide.

■ Topics That Are Useful But Not Tested

- The `ListIterator` includes the methods `hasPrevious` and `previous`. These methods are used to determine if there is a previous node and to move the iterator position backwards.
- Your text implements a linked list using inner classes for `Link` (a `ListNode` class) and `LinkedListIterator` (the list iterator). Inner classes are very useful here and allow for simpler implementation of the linked list methods. This is demonstrated in Section 19.2 of your text.

■ Things to Remember When Taking the AP Exam

- Inserting and deleting from a `LinkedList` is efficient because these operations do not require shifting the other elements in the list.
- Stacks are LIFO (last-in, first-out). Queues are FIFO (first-in, first-out).
- If an application requires many look-ups (searches), use an implementation that provides $O(1)$ access whenever possible. Specifically, use an array when you need random access to individual elements (e.g., sorting algorithms) and use a linked list when you frequently need to insert or remove in the middle of the list (e.g., simulation of cars on a freeway with entrance/exit ramps).
- Be sure to check whether the list data structure is empty before you try to remove an item from it.
- Become familiar with the `ListNode` class, the `Stack` interface, and the `Queue` interface. The AB Quick Reference Guide that you will be given during the AP Exam contains examples similar to Examples 16.3, 16.10, and 16.14 of this guide (minus the comments).
- Be careful when implementing code that adds or removes nodes from a linked list. Ask yourself the following questions:
  - Does this code handle the empty list case?
  - Does this code handle the front of the list case?
  - Does this code handle the end of the list case?
  - Does this code handle the middle of the list case?
  - Does this code handle the list with only one node?
- Use a list iterator to access elements of a `LinkedList`. DO NOT use `get/set/insert`.
- Check for `null` pointers! Whenever calling `p.next`, `p.data`, etc., ask yourself "Can `p` be empty? If so, am I checking for it? If not, why not?"

■ Key Words

You should understand the terms below. The AP CS Exam questions may include references to these terms. The citations in parentheses next to each term identify the page numbers where it is defined and/or discussed in *Computing Concepts with Java Essentials*, 3rd ed., and *Big Java*.

abstract data type (754)	LIFO (758)	push (758)
concrete implementation (754)	linked list (738)	queue (758)
	links (738)	stack (757)
doubly linked list (740)	list iterator (740)	stack top (757)
FIFO (758)	pop (758)	

■ Connecting the Detailed Topic Outline to the Text

The citations in parentheses identify where information in the outline can be located in *Computing Concepts with Java Essentials*, 3rd ed., and *Big Java*.

- Using Linked Lists (738–742)
- Implementing Linked Lists (742–753)
  - Doubly Linked Lists (740)
  - Circularly Linked Lists
  - Header and Trailer Nodes
- Abstract and Concrete Data Types (754)
- Stacks (757–758)
- Queues (758–760)

■ Practice Questions

Multiple Choice

1. What is printed to the screen when the following code segment is executed?

```
LinkedList staff = new LinkedList();
staff.addFirst("Mary");
staff.addFirst("Joe");
staff.addLast("Fran");
System.out.print(staff.removeLast() + " ");
System.out.print(staff.removeFirst()+ " ");
System.out.println(staff.removeFirst());
```

   a. *Joe Mary Fran*
   b. *Fran Joe Mary*
   c. *Mary Joe Fran*
   d. *Fran Mary Joe*
   e. *Joe Fran Mary*

2. An application is being written to simulate planes waiting to take off on an airport runway. Which of the following data structures is the best choice for this application?

    a.   A fixed-length array
    b.   An `ArrayList`
    c.   A singly-linked list
    d.   A queue
    e.   A stack

3. Suppose the following code segment is executed.

    ```
    LinkedList list = new LinkedList();
    ListIterator iter = list.listIterator();
    iter.add("David");
    iter.add("Juliet");
    iter.add("Gail");
    iter.add("Chris");
    iter = list.listIterator();
    iter.next();
    iter.remove();
    iter.add("Mom");
    ```

    What does the linked list, `list`, contain after this code segment is executed?

    a.   David Mom Gail Chris
    b.   Mom Gail Juliet David
    c.   Chris Mom Juliet David
    d.   Mom Juliet Gail Chris
    e.   Mom David Gail Chris

4. For the Java library `LinkedList` class, which operations are constant time ($O(1)$) in the worst case?

I.   `addFirst`
II. `addLast`
III. `getLast`

    a.   I only
    b.   II only
    c.   III only
    d.   II and II only
    e.   I, II, and III

5. A client program wishes to test to see if two `ListNodes`, `node1` and `node2`, have the same `String` values in their value fields. Which of the following conditions properly checks this?

    a.   `node1 == node2`
    b.   `node1.equals(node2)`
    c.   `node1.value == node2.value`

    d.   `(node1.value).equals(node2.value)`
    e.   `(node1.getValue()).equals(node2.getValue())`

6. Which of the following conditions tests whether two `ListNodes`, `node1` and `node2`, reference the same node?

I.   `node1 == node2`
II. `node1.equals(node2)`
III. `node2.equals(node1)`

    a. I only
    b. II only
    c. III only
    d. II and III only
    e. I, II, and III

7. Consider a partially-filled array implementation of a stack, `stck`. Suppose the implementation uses `stck[0]` as the top of the stack and the last filled position of the array as the bottom of the stack. Which of the following statements about this implementation is true?

    a. `push`, `pop`, and `peekTop` are $O(n)$.
    b. `push`, `pop`, and `peekTop` are $O(1)$.
    c. `push` and `pop` are $O(1)$; `peekTop` is $O(n)$.
    d. `push` and `pop` are $O(n)$; `peekTop` is $O(1)$.
    e. `pop` and `peekTop` are $O(n)$; `push` is $O(1)$.

8. Consider a partially-filled array implementation of a stack, `stck`. Suppose the implementation uses `stck[0]` as the bottom of the stack and the last filled position of the array as the top of the stack. Which of the following statements about this implementation is true?

    a. `push`, `pop`, and `peekTop` are $O(n)$.
    b. `push`, `pop`, and `peekTop` are $O(1)$.
    c. `push` and `pop` are $O(1)$; `peekTop` is $O(n)$.
    d. `push` and `pop` are $O(n)$; `peekTop` is $O(1)$.
    e. `pop` and `peekTop` are $O(n)$; `push` is $O(1)$.

9. The `Integers` 1, 2, 3, 4, and 5 are enqueued in a queue (in that order), then dequeued one at a time and pushed on a stack. The stack is popped three times. What element is now on the top of the stack?

    a. 1
    b. 2
    c. 3
    d. 4
    e. 5

10. Which statement is true about an abstract data type?

    a. An abstract data type defines the fundamental operations on the data but does not specify an implementation.

    b. An abstract data type is an abstract class. It cannot be instantiated.

    c. An abstract data type defines the implementation choices made.

    d. An abstract data type is more efficient than a concrete data type.

    e. An abstract data type is another name for an interface.

11. Suppose you need to organize a collection of phone numbers for a company. There are currently over 6,000 employees. You know the phone switch can handle at most 10,000 phone numbers. You expect several hundred lookups against the collection every day. What would be the best choice for a data structure in implementing this simulation?

    a. array

    b. linked list

    c. doubly linked list

    d. stack

    e. queue

12. Consider the following algorithm.

    • The `Integers` from 1 to 5 inclusive are enqueued into an initially empty queue, `q`, in that order.

    • The `Integers` from 1 to 5 inclusive are pushed onto an initially empty stack, `s`, in that order.

The following code is executed.

```
for (int x = 1; x <= 5; x++)
{
   Integer y, z;
   y = (Integer)q.dequeue();
   if (y.intValue() % 2 == 0)
      s.push(y);
   else
      q.enqueue(y);

   z = (Integer)s.pop();
   if (z.intValue() % 2 == 0)
      s.push(z);
   else
      q.enqueue(z);
}

while (!s.isEmpty())
{
   System.out.print(s.pop() + " ");
}
while (!q.isEmpty())
```

```
    {
        System.out.print(q.dequeue() + " ");
    }
```

What will be printed?

    a. *4 4 3 2 1 5 1 5 3 5*
    b. *1 2 3 4 2 4 1 5 3 5*
    c. *1 2 3 4 2 4 1 5 3 5*
    d. *4 2 4 3 2 1 1 5 3 5*
    e. *4 4 3 2 1 1 5 3 5 5*

13. The following implementations of the method `reverse` are intended to reverse the order of the elements in a `LinkedList`. The `IntStack` class implements the `Stack` interface and the `IntQueue` class implements the `Queue` interface found in Examples 16.10 and 16.14 (or in the AB Quick Reference Guide).

I.
```
    public static void reverse(LinkedList aList)
    {
        LinkedList temp = new LinkedList();
        while (aList.size() > 0)
            temp.addLast(aList.removeFirst());
        while (temp.size() > 0)
            aList.addFirst(temp.removeFirst());
    }
```

II.
```
    public static void reverse(LinkedList aList)
    {
        IntQueue temp = new IntQueue();
        while (aList.size() > 0)
            temp.enqueue(aList.removeFirst());
        while (!temp.isEmpty() )
            aList.addFirst(temp.dequeue());
    }
```

III.
```
    public static void reverse(LinkedList aList)
    {
        IntStack temp = new IntStack();
        while (aList.size() > 0)
            temp.push(aList.removeLast());
        while (!temp.isEmpty() )
            aList.addFirst(temp.pop());
    }
```

Which of the choices above perform the intended task successfully?

    a. I only
    b. II only
    c. III only

    d. II and III only

    e. I, II, and III

Questions 14 and 15 refer to the following problem statement.

Consider the algorithm for determining whether a sequence of parentheses is balanced (has correct nesting). The pseudocode for this algorithm appears below.

> *Initialize a boolean variable* `validExpression` *to true.*
> *while (there are more symbols in the expression)*
> *{*
>   *look at the next* `symbol`
>   *if* `symbol` *is a {, [, or (*
>   *push it on the stack*
>   *if it is a },], or)*
>   *{*
>   *if the stack is empty then return false*
>   *else pop the stack*
>   *}*
>   *if the element popped is not the match for* `symbol` *then return false*
> *}*
> *if the stack is not empty then return false else return true.*

14. What is the maximum number of symbols that will appear on the stack at any one time for the sequence { [( )] [( )] [( )] }?

    a. 1

    b. 2

    c. 3

    d. 4

    e. 5

15. What sequence of elements is on the stack after processing the input { [( )] [(( ))] { [(? (The top of the stack is to the right.)

    a. { [( )] [(( ))] { [(

    b. { [([(({ [(

    c.)]))]

    d. { { [(

    e. ([{ {

Questions 16 and 17 refer to the postfix problem statement below.

We normally write algebraic expressions with an arithmetic operator between two operands (numbers). A postfix expression is an expression in which the operator is written after the operands. For example, the postfix notation for the expression 2 + 3 is 2 3 +.

The following algorithm describes the evaluation of a postfix expression using a stack. The postfix expression is evaluated from left to right. If a number is read, it is pushed on the stack. If an operator is read, two numbers are popped off the stack, the operator is applied to the two popped values and the answer is pushed on the stack. When all has been read from the expression, what's left on the stack is the answer.

16. Using the above algorithm, the postfix expression:

3 4 + 5 * 3 4 * 6 / 8 * +

evaluates to:

   a. 0
   b. 4
   c. 19
   d. 51
   e. 192

17. What is the maximum number of numbers on the stack at any one time?

   a. 2
   b. 3
   c. 4
   d. 5
   e. 6

18. You are implementing a program for tracking appointments. You have a class `Person` and a class `Appointment`. A person can have multiple appointments. Each appointment has a start time, an end time, and a description. You keep the appointments in order sorted by start time. Which of the following statements are correct?

I. If appointments are frequently deleted and inserted, then a linked list of appointments is more efficient than an array.
II. Using a linked list of appointments makes it efficient to use the binary search algorithm for finding an appointment that falls on a given time.
III. Appointments should be kept on a stack so that the most important appointment is always on the top of the stack.

   a. I only
   b. II only
   c. III only
   d. I and II only
   e. I and III only

19. You are implementing a word processor. You need to find an appropriate data structure to store a sequence of characters. Users will frequently insert and remove characters from the middle of a document. Which of the following statements are true?

I.   Storing all characters in a single array is inefficient, particularly for long documents.

II. The characters should be stored in a stack so that the most recently inserted character can be immediately deleted when the user hits the "Backspace" key.

III. A singly linked list of characters is not an appropriate data structure for the document because each node would need to store one character and one link, which uses a lot of storage.

    a.   I only

    b.   II only

    c.   II and III only

    d.   I and III only

    e.   I, II, and III

20. Suppose we have a stack, `aStack`, implemented using an array of size of 10. The methods `push` and `pop` are implemented without shifting elements in the array. Also suppose that the stack has 5 items stored in it. A new item is to be pushed onto the stack and 2 items are popped off the stack. In what position of the array will the next item pushed be placed?

    a.   `aStack [0]`

    b.   `aStack [1]`

    c.   `aStack [4]`

    d.   `aStack [5]`

    e.   `aStack [6]`

Free Response Questions

1.   `DLListNode` *is a* `ListNode` with an additional instance field that references the previous node in a doubly linked list. Refer to the `ListNode` implementation in Example 16.3 or the `ListNode` class in the AB Quick Reference Guide to answer this question.

a.   Which methods (if any) of the `ListNode` class need to be modified?

b.   What additional methods should be added?

c.   Given the class header for `DLListNode` below,

```
public class DLListNode extends ListNode
```

implement the DLListNode constructor.

d.   Indicate the efficiency of each operation listed in the table below for the doubly linked list of `DLListNode`s illustrated.

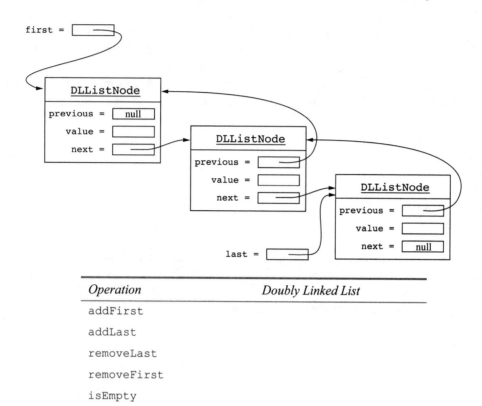

Operation	Doubly Linked List
addFirst	
addLast	
removeLast	
removeFirst	
isEmpty	
Linear Traversal	
Random Access	

Consider the doubly linked list class whose incomplete implementation appears below. This list has two private instance variables, `first`, that accesses the first node of the list, and `last`, that accesses the last node of the list. The list does not contain header or trailer nodes.

```java
// Invariant: All nodes in the DLList are DLListNodes.
public class DLList
{
    public DLList()    // Constructs an empty list.
    {
        first = null;
        last = null;
    }

    // Inserts a new node containing key in the list.
    public void insert(Object key) {...}

    // Prints the contents of the nodes in the list.
    public void printList() {...}

    // Postcondition: Returns a reference to the first node
    // containing key. If key is not found in the list, null is
    // returned.
    public DLListNode search(Object key)
    {
```

```
        //  Code goes here
    }

    // Removes the first node that contains key if that node
    // exists.
    public void removeOne(Object key)
    {
        //  Code goes here
    }

    // Removes all nodes in the list that contain key.
    public void removeAll(Object key)
    {
        //  Code goes here
    }
    private DLListNode first;
    private DLListNode last;
}
```

e. Implement the method `search` that takes one parameter, `key`, and searches the doubly linked list for the first occurrence of `key` in the list and returns a reference to this node. If `key` is not in the list, `search` returns `null`. Assume that all `DLListNode` methods and constructors work as intended. In writing `search`, use the method header below.

```
        public DLListNode search(Object key)
```

f. Implement the method `removeOne`. `removeOne` removes the first node in the list whose value is the same as its one parameter, `key`. You may call `search` in writing `removeOne`. Assume that `search` works as intended regardless of what you wrote in part e. Also assume that all `DLListNode` methods and constructors work as intended. In writing `removeOne`, use the method header below.

```
        public void removeOne(Object key)
```

g. Implement the method `removeAll`. `removeAll` removes all nodes in the list whose value is the same as its parameter `key`. You may call `search` and/or `removeOne` in writing `removeAll`. Assume that all methods and constructors written in parts a–f of this problem work as intended regardless of what you wrote. In writing `removeAll`, use the header below.

```
        public void removeAll(Object key)
```

2. A stack can be used to convert decimal numbers to binary numbers.

a. You are to write the method `displayBinary` that will convert a decimal number into a binary number using a stack. Assume that `intStack` is a class that correctly implements the `Stack` interface found in Example 16.10 and in the AB Quick Reference Guide. The pseudocode for an algorithm that converts a decimal number to a binary number is given below.

```
        public static void displayBinary(int decimalNum)
        {
```

```
intStack stck = new intStack();
while decimalNum not equal to 0
{
    find remainder when decimalNum is divided by 2
    push remainder on the stack
    divide the decimalNum by 2
}
while stack isn't empty
    pop num off the stack and display
```

Use the following header in writing your method `displayBinary`.

```
// Precondition: decimalNum > 0
// Displays the binary representation of decimalNum.
public static void displayBinary(int decimalNum)
```

b. Implement a method `displayOtherBase` that will convert a decimal number to a number in any base less than or equal to 16 (hexadecimal numbers). Examples of conversions are given in the table below. Assume that `intStack` is a class that correctly implements the `Stack` interface found in Example 16.10 and in the AB Quick Reference Guide.

Decimal number	Converted to this base	Results in
21	2	10101
100	2	1100100
64	8	100
73	8	111
74	16	4A
447	16	1BF

In writing `displayOtherBase`, use the header given below.

```
// Precondition: num > 0, 0 < base, and base <= 16
// Displays the decimal number converted to base, base.
public static void displayOtherBase(int num, int base)
```

3. A graphical user interface (GUI) system (such as *Microsoft Windows* or an *X Windows* window manager in *Linux*) keeps track of all of the windows on the user's screen. One of the windows is the *top* window. It has a specially marked title bar and is displayed on top of the other windows. The GUI has an operation to *cycle* through the windows, typically with a keystroke such as ALT + TAB. That operation moves the current top window to the bottom and the other windows up by one position. It also has operations to open a new window, which now becomes the top window, and to close the top window, so that the next window under it becomes the top window.

Your task is to implement a class `WindowManager` that manages a collection of objects of type `Window`. Each `Window` has a `Rectangle` indicating its size, and a `String` indicating the message on the title bar. (Real windows would know how to draw their contents, but we will ignore that aspect in this problem.)

The Rectangle constructor takes four parameters: *x*- and *y*-coordinates of its top left point, its width, and its height. The Rectangle toString method returns the String representing the Rectangle object's coordinate and size values.

Operations of the WindowManager are:
- add: Adds a new Window as the top window.
- remove: Removes the top window.
- cycle: Moves the current top window to the bottom and the other windows up by one position.
- print: Prints the windows from top to bottom. The toString method of Window returns a "printable" Window.

The implementation of Window and an incomplete implementation of WindowManager are below.

```java
public class Window
{
    // Constructs a rectangular Window with title, winTitle.
    public Window(String winTitle, Rectangle winBounds)
    {
        title = winTitle;
        bounds = winBounds;
    }

    // Returns the string representation of the Rectangular window
    // that includes the window title and dimensions.
    public String toString()
    {
        return "Window[title=" + title + ", bounds=" + bounds + "]";
    }

    private String title;
    private Rectangle bounds;
}

public class WindowManager
{
    // Adds window w. w now becomes the top window.
    public void add(Window w)
    {
        // Code goes here
    }

    // Removes the top window.
    public void remove()
    {
        // Code goes here
```

```
        }

        // Moves the current top window to the bottom and the other
        // windows are moved up by one position.
        public void cycle()
        {
            // Code goes here
        }

        // Prints the windows from top to bottom.
        public void print()
        {
            // Code goes here
        }

        // Private stuff here
    }
```

A Sample Client Program

```
    import java.awt.Rectangle;

    public class WindowManagerTest
    {
        public static void main(String[] args)
        {
            WindowManager manager = new WindowManager();
            manager.add(new Window("A", new Rectangle(5, 10, 15, 20)));
            manager.add(new Window("B", new Rectangle(15, 20, 15, 20)));
            manager.add(new Window("C", new Rectangle(25, 30, 15, 20)));
            manager.print();
            manager.cycle();
            manager.print();
            manager.remove();
            manager.print();
        }
    }
```

The program run is:

```
Window[title=C, bounds=java.awt.Rectangle[x=25,y=30,width=15,height=20]]
Window[title=B, bounds=java.awt.Rectangle[x=15,y=20,width=15,height=20]]
Window[title=A, bounds=java.awt.Rectangle[x=5,y=10,width=15,height=20]]

Window[title=B, bounds=java.awt.Rectangle[x=15,y=20,width=15,height=20]]
Window[title=A, bounds=java.awt.Rectangle[x=5,y=10,width=15,height=20]]
Window[title=C, bounds=java.awt.Rectangle[x=25,y=30,width=15,height=20]]

Window[title=A, bounds=java.awt.Rectangle[x=5,y=10,width=15,height=20]]
Window[title=C, bounds=java.awt.Rectangle[x=25,y=30,width=15,height=20]]
```

a.   What data structure is most appropriate for storing the collection of `Window` objects? Choose from an array, a linked list, a stack, and a queue. Justify your choice.

b.   Use your chosen data structure to implement the method `add`. Use the method header below when writing `add`.

```
public void add(Window w)
```

c.   Use your chosen data structure to implement the method `remove`. Use the method header below when writing `remove`.

```
public void remove()
```

d.   Given the incomplete implementation of the `WindowManager` class above, use your chosen data structure to implement the method `cycle`. Use the method header below when writing `cycle`.

```
public void cycle()
```

e.   Given the incomplete implementation of the `WindowManager` class above, use your chosen data structure to implement the method `print`. Use the method header below when writing `print`. `print` should print the windows from top to bottom. The `toString` method of `Window` returns a "printable" `Window`. If `w` is a `Window`,

```
System.out.println(w);
```

will print the correct `Window` information in the format displayed in the execution shown above.

CHAPTER **17**

Advanced Data Structures
(AB only)

■ Topic Summary

17.1 Sets

A *set* is an unordered collection of distinct elements. Unlike linked lists, stacks, and queues, sets contain no duplicate items. Elements can be added to, located in, and removed from a set. The AP subset contains the set methods listed in Table 17.1

Table 17.1
interface java.util.Set

Method	Method Summary
boolean add(Object obj)	Adds the parameter obj as an element to this set if it is not already in the set and returns true. If the element is already in the set, returns false.
boolean contains(Object obj)	Returns true if this set contains the element obj, otherwise returns false.
boolean remove(Object obj)	Removes the element obj from this set and returns true if the obj is in this set; if the element is not present, returns false.
int size()	Returns the number of elements in this set.
Iterator iterator()	Returns an Iterator that provides access to the elements of this set.

The elements of a set are accessed using a set iterator. Since sets are unordered, the iterator may visit the set elements in a different order from the order in which the elements were added to the set. The set iterator includes the methods listed in Table 17.2.

Table 17.2
`interface java.util.Iterator`

Method	Method Summary
`boolean hasNext()`	Returns `true` if the iteration has more elements.
`Object next()`	Returns the next element in the iteration.
`void remove()`	Removes the last element returned by next.

We do not use the `ListIterator` methods `add`, `set`, and `previous` with sets. The list iterator methods `previous` and `add` are dependent on iterating the elements in some order and adding an element to a specific place. This makes no sense with sets since sets are not ordered. The list iterator method `set` allows replacement of an element. Because there are no duplicates in a set, calling a method to replace an element in a set could be dangerous because the replacement may already exist in the set.

Since `Set` is an interface, we cannot instantiate a `Set`. In other words, we can't create an object of type `Set`. Section 20.1 in Appendix A of this guide instantiates a `HashSet` object that implements the `Set` interface. Section 20.6 in Appendix A of this guide instantiates a `TreeSet` object that implements the `Set` interface. Both `HashSet` and `TreeSet` are data structures that enable quick retrievals (searches). To search for a particular element in a linked list, we must search the list sequentially ($O(n)$). To search an ordered array or an ordered `ArrayList` we can use the binary search which improves the retrieval time ($O(\log(n))$). A `HashSet` can be implemented using a hash table which can search in $O(1)$ time and a `TreeSet` can be implemented for searching in $O(\log(n))$ time. `HashSet` and `TreeSet` will be tested on the AP Exam.

```
class java.util.HashSet implements java.util.Set
class java.util.TreeSet implements java.util.Set
```

We will look at these data structures in more detail later in this Chapter.

17.2   Maps

A *map* is a data type that keeps associations between *keys* and *values*. Each *key* in a map has a unique *value*. But a value may be associated with more than one *key*. Some examples:
- A mapping of names to phone numbers ("Gail Thomas" maps to "212-555-1234").
- A mapping of your college friends to the university that they attend. ("Cay Horstmann" maps to "San Jose State University", "Fran Trees" maps to "Drew University").
- A mapping of animals to animal sounds ("cat" maps to "meow").
- A mapping of a coin name to its value ("Quarter" maps to 0.25).
- A mapping of a car model to its make ("4-Runner" maps to "Toyota").

- A mapping of case numbers of medical patients to the medical technician handling the case.
- A mapping of login IDs to passwords.

Each association has a *key* mapped to a *value*. Figure 3 in Section 20.2 of Appendix A in this guide illustrates this mapping relationship. Associations can be put in, changed, and located in a map. The Map interface methods that will be tested on the AP CS Exam are listed in Table 17.3.

Table 17.3
interface java.util.Map

Method	Method Summary
Object put(Object key, Object value)	Associates value with key in this map so that get(key) returns value. If the map previously contained a mapping for this key, the old value is replaced by the specified value.
Object get(Object key)	Returns the value associated with key in this map, or null if there is no value associated with key.
Object remove(Object key)	Removes the mapping for key from this map if it is present.
boolean containsKey(Object key)	Returns true if there is a value associated with key in this map, otherwise returns false.
int size()	Returns the number of keys in this map.
Set keySet()	Returns a Set of the keys in the map.

Since a Map is an interface, we cannot create an object of type Map. The AP CS subset includes the HashMap and TreeMap classes that implement Map.

```
class java.util.HashMap implements java.util.Map
class java.util.TreeMap implements java.util.Map
```

The Map interface requires that the keySet method be implemented. The keySet method produces a Set of keys. We can visit all of the elements of a HashMap or TreeMap by iterating through the keys in the set that the keySet method produces. The Map method get will return the value associated with a map key. HashMap and TreeMap differ in implementation. A HashMap does not keep the elements ordered. In fact, the order may not even remain the same throughout the implementation. A TreeMap keeps the elements in an order (according to the key) from smallest to largest. The choice as to which implementation to use for a given application depends largely on the requirements of that particular application. We will discuss this more as we look at each of the different data structures. Before we talk about a HashSet or a HashMap, we need to understand what *hashing* is and why it is used. Before we talk about a TreeSet and a TreeMap, we need to understand binary search trees and their implementation.

17.3 Hash Tables

Hashing is an efficient way to store data for quick insertion and retrieval. Hashing involves the use of a hash function that computes and returns an integer value. This value can be used to determine the place in the hash table in which the object will be inserted or can be found. A well constructed hash table allows for quick insertion and quick look-up. Figure 6 in Chapter 20 in Appendix A of this guide illustrates a simple example of a hash table that stores names. The hash table illustrated in this example is an array of *buckets* that hold names (`String` objects). Each bucket holds all the names that produce the hash code that corresponds to the index of the bucket. Figure 17.1 illustrates a small portion of this hash table.

Figure 17.1

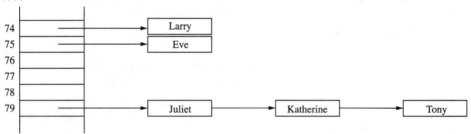

The hash code returned for the name Larry is 74. The names Juliet, Katherine, and Tony return the same hash code, 79. When two objects have the same hash code, a *collision* occurs. The goal of a good hash function is to minimize the number of collisions. If the hash function distributes the elements so that there is one element per bucket (which would be the ideal goal) then searching for a particular name is $O(1)$.

Suppose that a search for the name "Eve" is to be done. First, the hash code for "Eve" is calculated by calling the `hashCode` method of the `String` class (because the object is a `String`). This hash code determines the array index (bucket) in which "Eve" should be found. Searching a hash table is $O(1)$ if the `hashCode` method uniformly distributes the elements in the hash table. A very bad hash function would put all names in the same bucket. Retrieving an element in this worst case would then be $O(n)$. All objects in that bucket would have to be traversed.

17.3.1 Using HashSet

A hash table can be implemented using a `HashSet`. A hash set stores an unordered collection of objects. First, we will look at a test program that uses the Java library class `HashSet`. We will add the names that appear in Figure 17.1 to our hash set.

Example 17.1

```
import java.util.Iterator;
import java.util.Set;
import java.util.HashSet;

/**
    This program tests the hash set class.
*/
public class SetTest
{
    public static void main(String[] args)
```

```
    {
        Set names = new HashSet(101);    // 101 (the size of our hash
                                         // table) is a prime
        names.add("Larry");
        names.add("Tony");
        names.add("Katherine");
        names.add("Eve");
        names.add("Juliet");
        System.out.println(names.size());
        Iterator iter = names.iterator();
        while (iter.hasNext())
            System.out.println(iter.next());
    }
}
```

The output of the above test program is:

5
Larry
Eve
Juliet
Katherine
Tony

You can see that the iterator returns the elements in the hash table by visiting each bucket and sequentially traversing the elements in the bucket. Example 17.1 uses a table size of 101. Research shows that the best size for a hash table is a prime number larger than the number of elements your table is expected to hold. An excess of approximately 30% is typical. This means that, if *s* is the number of slots in the table and *e* is the number of elements, then $s = a\ prime\ number \geq \frac{4}{3} * e$. Table 17.4 lists the HashSet methods in the AP subset as well as two constructors that can be used to instantiate a HashSet.

Table 17.4
class java.util.HashSet

Method	Method Summary
HashSet()	Constructs a new, empty hash table with default initial capacity.
HashSet(int initialSize)	Constructs a new, empty hash table with an initial capacity of initialSize.
boolean add(Object obj)	Adds the parameter obj as an element to this set if it is not already stored in this set and returns true. If the element is already in the set, returns false.
boolean contains(Object obj)	Returns true if this set contains the element obj, otherwise returns false.
boolean remove(Object obj)	Removes the argument obj from this set and returns true if the argument is in this set; if it is not present, returns false.
int size()	Returns the number of elements in this set.
Iterator iterator()	Returns an Iterator that provides access to the elements of this set.

The HashSet class has a default constructor. This constructor will create an initial hash table with a default size. If the table gets too full, a new table twice the size is created and all the elements are inserted into the new table. The statement

```
HashSet names = new HashSet();
```

constructs a hash set by calling the HashSet default constructor. Example 17.2 extends Example 17.1 to show calls to the other HashSet methods in Table 17.4.

Example 17.2

```
names.add("Tony");
names.remove("Eve");
System.out.println(names.size());
iter = names.iterator();
while (iter.hasNext())
    System.out.println(iter.next());
if (names.contains("Fran"))
    System.out.println("Fran found.");
else
    System.out.println("Fran NOT found.");
```

The additional code in Example 17.2 extends Example 17.1 so the resulting output is:

4
Katherine
Juliet
Tony
Larry
Fran NOT found.

The objects added to and removed from the `HashSet` names in Examples 17.1 and 17.2 were done so using the `HashSet` methods `add` and `remove`. How did the method `add` know in which bucket to insert a given name? How did the method `remove` find the appropriate name to remove? `HashSet` `add` calls the `hashCode` method of its `Object` parameter. The objects in our example are `String` objects. The `HashSet` `add` method uses the `String` `hashCode` method and the table size to determine where to place (or where to look for) the object. Although the `String` `hashCode` method will not be tested on the AP Exam, it's important to understand how hashing works. It's not magic!

When you are using the `HashSet` class to store objects instantiated by your own classes, you need to be careful. You must define an `equals` method and a `hashCode` method for your class. For example, do you wish to store `Student` objects in a hash table according to the student's name, the ID number, the GPA, or a combination of these instance field values? Forgetting to define `hashCode` is an error that is discussed in *Common Error 20.1* in Appendix A of this guide. Although implementing the `equals` method and the `hashCode` method will not be tested on the AP Exam, hashing concepts will be tested.

17.3.2 Implementing `HashSet`

Section 20.3 in Appendix A of this guide implements the `HashSet` as an array of `Link`s using the inner classes `Link` and `HashSetIterator`. Our AP implementation would implement a hash table as an array of `ListNode`s. This method of hashing is often referred to as *chaining* because a bucket contains a *chain* of `ListNode`s with the same hash value. Example 17.3 demonstrates this implementation.

Example 17.3

```
/**
    A hash set stores an unordered collection of objects, using
    a hash table.
*/
public class HashSet
{
   /**
      Constructs a hash table.
      @param bucketsLength the length of the buckets array
   */
   public HashSet(int bucketsLength)
   {
      buckets = new ListNode[bucketsLength];
      size = 0;
   }

   /**
      Tests for set membership.
      @param x an object to search for
      @return true if x is an element of this set
   */
   public boolean contains(Object x)
   {
      int h = getBucketIndex(x);
```

```java
      ListNode current = buckets[h];
      while (current != null)
      {
         if ((current.getValue()).equals(x))
               return true;    // x is already in bucket
         current = current.getNext();
      }
      return false;    // x not found in this bucket
   }

   /**
      Adds an element to this set.
      @param x an object
      @return true if x is a new object, false if x was already in
      the set
   */
   public boolean add(Object x)
   {
      int h = getBucketIndex(x);
      ListNode current = buckets[h];    // Go to bucket
      while (current != null)
      {
         if ((current.getValue()).equals(x))
            return false;    // x is already in the set
         current = current.getNext();
      }
      ListNode newListNode = new ListNode(x, buckets[h]);

      buckets[h] = newListNode;    // Add x to bucket
      size++;
      return true;
   }

   /**
      Removes an object from this set.
      @param x an object
      @return true if x was removed from this set, false if x was
      not an element of this set
   */
   public boolean remove(Object x)
   {
      int h = getBucketIndex(x);
      ListNode current = buckets[h];
      ListNode previous = null;
      while (current != null)
      {
         if ((current.getValue()).equals(x))    // Is x in bucket?
         {
            if (previous == null) buckets[h] = current.getNext();
            else previous.setNext(current.getNext());
            size--;
            return true;  // If found, x is removed.
```

```
        }
        previous = current;
        current = current.getNext();
    }
    return false;
}


/**
    Gets the number of elements in this set.
    @return the number of elements
*/
public int size()
{
    return size;
}


 public void printHashSet()
{
    for (int i = 0; i < buckets.length; i++)
    {
        ListNode temp = buckets[i];
        while(temp != null)
        {
            System.out.println(temp.getValue());
            temp = temp.getNext();
        }
    }
}


/**
    Determines bucket in which x belongs.
    @param x an object to find bucket for
    @return index (bucket) in which x belongs
*/
private int getBucketIndex(Object x)
{
    int h = x.hashCode();    // Calls String hashCode method
    if (h < 0) h = -h;
    h = h % buckets.length;    // Finding bucket index
    return h;
}

private ListNode[] buckets;    // Array of ListNodes
private int size;
}
```

17.3.3 Using *HashMap*

The HashMap class implements the Map interface and uses hashing as the technique to store entries. Each entry of a hash map consists of a *key* and a *value*. A HashMap stores pairs (key, value) according to the hash code determined by the key. Assuming that the hashCode method defined for the key object distributes the entries uniformly in the hash table, searching, insertion, and removal of an entry in the hash map is constant time ($O(1)$). The HashMap methods included in the AP subset are listed in Table 17.5.

Table 17.5
interface java.util.HashMap

Method	Method Summary
HashMap()	Constructs an empty HashMap with default size.
Object put(Object key, Object value)	Associates value with key in this map so that get(key) returns value. If the map previously contained a mapping for this key, the old value is replaced by the specified value.
Object get(Object key)	Return the value associated with key in this map, or null if there is no value associated with key.
Object remove(Object key)	Removes the mapping for key from this map if it is present.
boolean containsKey(Object key)	Returns true if there is a value associated with key in this map, otherwise returns false.
int size()	Returns the number of keys in this map.
Set keySet()	Returns a Set of the keys in the map.

Example 17.4 demonstrates the HashMap methods with the case number for a medical patient mapped to the name of the medical technician handling the case.

Example 17.4

```java
import java.util.Iterator;
import java.util.Map;
import java.util.HashMap;
import java.util.Set;

/**
    This program tests the hash map class.
*/
public class HashMapTest
{
    public static void main(String[] args)
    {
        Map names = new HashMap( );   // Constructs an empty HashMap
        names.put(new Integer(1435), "Smith");
        names.put(new Integer(1110), "Thomas");
        names.put(new Integer(1425), "Jones");
        names.put(new Integer(987), "Evans");
        names.put(new Integer(1323), "Murray");

        System.out.println("Number of cases: " + names.size()); // 5

        Integer lookfor = new Integer(1435);
        if (names.containsKey(lookfor))
           System.out.println("Key found.");
        else
```

```
            System.out.println("Key NOT found.");

        Set namesSet = names.keySet();
        Iterator iter = namesSet.iterator();
        while (iter.hasNext())
        {
            Integer caseNumber = (Integer)iter.next();
            System.out.println(caseNumber + " handled by " +
                    names.get(caseNumber));
        }
    }
}
```

The resulting output is:

Number of cases: 5
Key found.
1323 handled by Murray
987 handled by Evans
1435 handled by Smith
1110 handled by Thomas
1425 handled by Jones

If the statements that insert keys and values into the HashMap were changed to:

```
names.put(new Integer(1435), "Smith");
names.put(new Integer(1110), "Thomas");
names.put(new Integer(1425), "Jones");
names.put(new Integer(987), "Evans");
names.put(new Integer(1323), "Murray");
names.put(new Integer(1323), "Duplicate");
```

The resulting output would be:

Number of cases: 5
Key found.
1323 handled by Duplicate
987 handled by Evans
1435 handled by Smith
1110 handled by Thomas
1425 handled by Jones

Notice that case #1323 is handled by Duplicate, not by Murray. If a duplicate key entry is attempted, the original one is replaced.

Section 20.2 in Appendix A of this guide includes another example of instantiating a HashMap object that implements the Map interface.

17.3.4 Implementing `HashMap`

Our implementation of `HashMap` would be similar to the implementation for `HashSet` in Example 17.3. The differences are

- A class `MapEntry` is defined. `MapEntry` has a `key` field, a `value` field, and the appropriate constructors and accessor methods.
- The `ListNode` will contain an object, `MapEntry`.
- When the `hashCode` method is called on a table entry, it is called on the `key` field of a `MapEntry` object.

17.4 Computing Hash Codes

A hash function should be easy and fast to compute and should scatter the data evenly throughout the hash table. Choose a table size that has more space than is actually needed and develop a function to compute the hash address. Remember that a good table size is a prime number greater than or equal to 4/3 times the expected number of elements. You can define `hashCode` methods for your own classes by combining the hash codes for the individual instance variables. Section 20.4 in Appendix A of this guide describes how to do this is detail. The implementation of `hashCode` methods is not part of the AP subset but hashing concepts will be tested. You should understand the goal of a good hash function.

17.5 Binary Search Trees

A binary tree consists of nodes, each of which has two child nodes (which may be `null` references). A *leaf* of a binary tree is a node that has two `null` children. A *complete* binary tree is binary tree where each leaf is at the same level and each non-leaf has exactly two non-`null` children. A complete binary tree is illustrated in Figure 17.2.

Figure 17.2

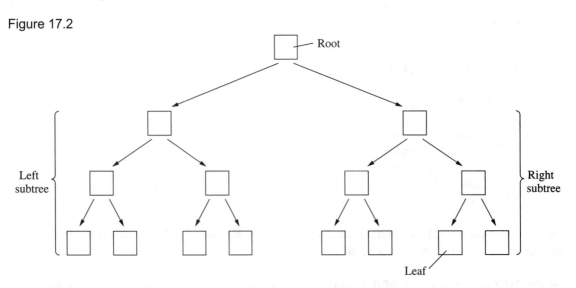

A *binary search tree* (*BST*) is a binary tree in which the descendents to the left of a node have smaller values than the node value field and the descendents to the right have values that are greater than or equal to the node value field. Figure 17.2 illustrates a binary search tree of `Integer`s.

Figure 17.3

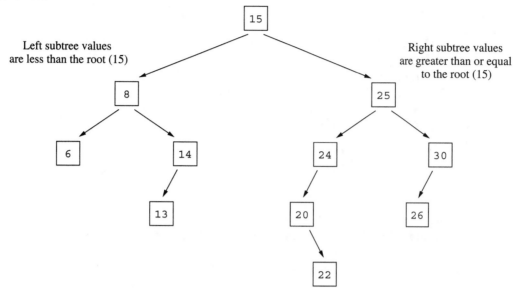

A binary tree is made up of nodes that have an info field and two reference fields. In Figure 17.3, a node is illustrated as a square containing a number (info field) and left and right arrows (reference fields). To facilitate a consistency in the exam questions, the AB exam uses the TreeNode[1] class shown in Example 17.5 to define a node and its methods.

Example 17.5

```
public class TreeNode
{
   public TreeNode(Object initValue,
        TreeNode initLeft, TreeNode initRight)
   {
      value = initValue;
      left = initLeft;
      right = initRight;
   }

   /**
      Returns the value of tree node.
      @return value of tree node.
   */
   public Object getValue()
   {
      return value;
   }

   /**
      Returns the left field of tree node.
      @return left field of tree node.
   */
   public TreeNode getLeft()
```

[1] College Board's AP Computer Science AB: Implementation Classes and Interfaces

```
    {
        return left;
    }

    /**
        Returns the right field of tree node.
        @return right field of tree node.
    */
    public TreeNode getRight()
    {
        return right;
    }

    /**
        Sets the value of the tree node to theNewValue.
        @param theNewValue is the new value of the tree node.
    */
    public void setValue(Object theNewValue)
    {
        value = theNewValue;
    }

    /**
        Sets the tree node's left field to a new reference.
        @param theNewLeft is the new reference for the left
        field of the tree node
    */

    public void setLeft(TreeNode theNewLeft)
    {
        left = theNewLeft;
    }

    /**
        Sets the tree node's right field to a new reference.
        @param theNewRight is the new reference for the right
        field of the tree node
    */
    public void setRight(TreeNode theNewRight)
    {
        right = theNewRight;
    }

    private Object value;
    private TreeNode left;
    private TreeNode right;
}
```

A description of the `TreeNode` class will appear at the beginning of the exam booklet.

Figure 7 in Chapter 20 of Appendix A in this guide illustrates a binary search tree. Figure 8 illustrates a binary tree that is not a binary search tree. In order to build a binary search tree, we must be able to compare the objects in the value field of the `TreeNode`. This means that the objects that we are inserting into the binary search tree must implement `Comparable` and define `compareTo`. To insert a node into a binary search tree we check first to see if the tree is empty. If it is, then the root of the tree references the new node.

```
public void insert(Comparable obj)
{
   Node newNode = new TreeNode(null, obj, null);
   if (root == null) root = newNode;
   else root.insertNode(newNode);
}
```

If the tree is not empty, the new node must be inserted to the left if the new value is smaller than the present node's value, and to the right if the new node's value is greater than or equal to the value of the current node. An implementation of the binary search tree using the `TreeNode` class appears in Example 17.6.

Example 17.6

```
/**
    This class implements a binary search tree whose
    nodes hold objects that implement the Comparable
    interface.
*/
public class Tree
{
   /**
      Constructs an empty tree.
   */
   public Tree()
   {
      root = null;
   }

   /**
      Inserts a new node into the tree.
      @param obj the object to insert
   */
   public void insert(Comparable obj)
   {
      TreeNode newNode = new TreeNode(obj, null, null);
      if (root == null)
         root = newNode;
      else
         insertNode(root, newNode);
   }

   /**
      Prints the contents of the tree in sorted order.
   */
```

```java
      public void print()
      {
         if (root != null)
            printNodes(root);
      }

      /**
         A TreeNode of a tree stores a data item and references
         to the child TreeNodes to the left and to the right.
      */
      public void insertNode(TreeNode current, TreeNode newNode)
      {
         Comparable newValue = (Comparable)newNode.getValue();
         Comparable currValue = (Comparable)current.getValue();
         if (newValue.compareTo(currValue) < 0)
         {
            if (current.getLeft() == null)
               current.setLeft(newNode);
            else
               insertNode(current.getLeft(), newNode);
         }
         else
         {
            if (current.getRight() == null)
               current.setRight(newNode);
            else
               insertNode(current.getRight(), newNode);
         }
      }

      /**
         Prints this TreeNode and all of its descendants
         in sorted order.
      */
      public void printNodes(TreeNode current)
      {
         if (current != null)
         {
            printNodes(current.getLeft());
            System.out.println(current.getValue());
            printNodes(current.getRight());
         }
      }
      private TreeNode root;
   }
```

Example 17.7 tests this binary search tree implementation for `String` objects and for `Integer` objects.

Example 17.7

```
/**
    This program tests the binary search tree class.
*/
public class TreeTest
{
    public static void main(String[] args)
    {
        Tree names = new Tree();
        names.insert("Romeo");
        names.insert("Juliet");
        names.insert("Tom");
        names.insert("Dick");
        names.insert("Harry");
        names.print();    // Dick Harry Juliet Romeo Tom

        // Inserting 15 8 25 6 14 24 20 22 30 13 26
        Tree numbers = new Tree();
        numbers.insert(new Integer(15));
        numbers.insert(new Integer(8));
        numbers.insert(new Integer(25));
        numbers.insert(new Integer(6));
        numbers.insert(new Integer(14));
        numbers.insert(new Integer(24));
        numbers.insert(new Integer(20));
        numbers.insert(new Integer(22));
        numbers.insert(new Integer(30));
        numbers.insert(new Integer(13));
        numbers.insert(new Integer(26));
        numbers.print();    // 6 8 13 14 15 20 22 24 25 26 30
    }
}
```

17.5.1 Binary Tree Traversals

Notice that the tree node values are printed in order. The print method does an *inorder* traversal of the `TreeNodes`. This means the left subtree is printed, the root value is printed, and then the right subtree is printed. Because the `insert` algorithm inserts nodes with values less than the current node value in the left subtree and nodes with values greater than or equal to the current node value in the right subtree, the inorder traversal results in an ordered printing of the node values. *Preorder* and *postorder* traversals are explained in Section 20A.3 in Appendix A of this guide. The inorder traversal visits nodes in the order: left, root, right. Preorder traversal visits root, left, right. Postorder traversal visits left, right, root. Consider the binary search tree in Figure 17.3.

- Inorder traversal yields: 6 8 13 14 15 20 22 24 25 26 30
- Preorder traversal yields: 15 8 6 14 13 25 24 20 22 30 26
- Postorder traversal yields: 6 13 14 8 22 20 24 26 30 25 15

The postorder traversal of an expression tree (Figure 3 in Chapter 20A in Appendix A of this guide) gives a postfix expression which can be evaluated using a stack. The stack is illustrated in Figure 4 of Section 20A.3 in Appendix A of this guide. Preorder traversal of an arithmetic expression will result in Lukasiewicz notation (prefix notation). Prefix notation is discussed in *Random Fact 20A.1* in Appendix A of this guide. The operators precede the operands. Prefix and postfix expressions do not need parentheses. Although prefix and postfix are not topics explicitly listed in the AP CS Topic Outline, they are applications involving binary trees and stacks and questions related to these traversals and applications may appear on the AP Exam.

17.5.2 Searching a Binary Search Tree

Searching a binary search tree follows the same basic algorithm as a binary search of an array. If the key is less than the current value, go left, otherwise go right.

Example 17.8

```
/**
    Searches for key in the tree.
    @param key is value to search for in tree.
    @return true if key found in tree, false otherwise.
*/
public boolean find(Comparable key)
{
    if (root == null)
        return false;
    else
        return findNode(root, key);
}


/**
    A TreeNode of a tree stores a data item and references
    to the child TreeNodes to the left and to the right.
*/
public boolean findNode(TreeNode current, Comparable key)
{
    if (current == null)
        return false;
    else
    {
        Comparable currValue = (Comparable)current.getValue();
        if (key.compareTo(currValue) == 0)
            return true;
        else if (key.compareTo(currValue) < 0)
            return findNode(current.getLeft(), key);
        else
            return findNode(current.getRight(),key);
    }
}
```

As with a binary search on an array, searching for a value in a binary search tree (BST) is $O(\log(n))$. Since inserting an element into a BST follows the same algorithm, and since a BST is a sorted collection of elements, when traversed with an inorder traversal, the binary search tree (when reasonably balanced) is a $O(n \log(n))$ sort. A *balanced* tree contains approximately as many children in the left subtree as in the right subtree. However, if the `Integers 1-10` were inserted into a binary search tree (in that order), a very unbalanced tree would result. The tree, in fact, would be linked as a linked list. The efficiency of searching this tree is $O(n)$. Trace through the insertion algorithm for the numbers 1–10 and sketch your resulting tree.

17.5.3   Removing a Node from a Binary Search Tree

Removing a node from a binary search tree is not as intuitive. There are three basic situations: removing a node with no children, removing a node with one child, and removing a node with two children.

To remove a node with no children: set the appropriate field of the parent to `null`. Delete 22.

Figure 17.4

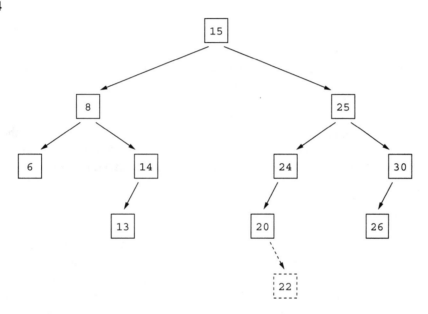

To remove a node with one child, replace the node with its child. Delete 30.

Figure 17.5

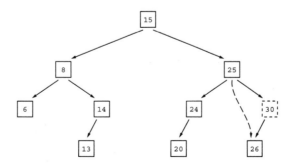

The node containing 30 is replaced with the node containing 26.

To remove a node with two children, go right once then all the way left. The smallest value in the right subtree of the node we are deleting will replace the deleted node. Delete 15.

Figure 17.6

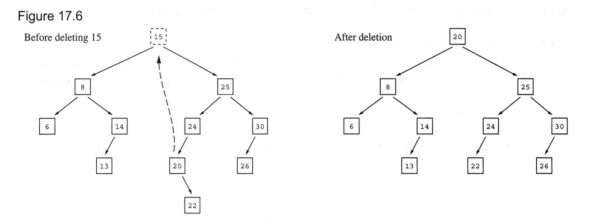

The node containing 15 is replaced by the node containing 20.

Section 20A.2 in Appendix A of this guide includes the enhanced `Tree` class implementation. This implementation contains the `remove` method and a non-recursive `find` method using an inner `Node` class. Chapters 20 and 20A in Appendix A of this guide implement some of the BST methods using inner classes. Inner classes will not be tested on the AP Exam.

17.6   Using Tree Sets and Tree Maps

The `TreeSet` class uses a form of balanced binary trees that guarantees that adding and removing an element takes $O(\log(n))$ time. We know that a good hashing function can give us a retrieval with efficiency $O(1)$ but if we also wanted to be able to list our data in order, a hash table would not be the appropriate choice. Binary search trees, when traversed with an inorder traversal, allow for an efficient search ($O(\log(n))$) and can also be traversed so that elements can be printed in order. The `TreeSet` class implements the `Set` interface. Table 17.6 lists the methods of `TreeSet` that may be tested on the AP Exam.

Table 17.6

class java.util.TreeSet

Method	*Method Summary*
TreeSet()	Constructs a new, empty tree set.
boolean add(Object obj)	Adds the parameter obj as an element if it is not already stored in this set and returns true. If the element is already in the set, returns false.
boolean contains(Object obj)	Returns true if this set contains the element obj, otherwise returns false.
boolean remove(Object obj)	Removes the argument obj from this set and returns true if the argument is in this set; if it is not present, returns false.
int size()	Returns the number of elements in this set.
Iterator iterator()	Returns an Iterator that provides access to the elements of this set.

A TreeSet requires that its elements be comparable. That means that compareTo is defined for the objects placed in the TreeSet. This is important because the elements in a tree are ordered (unlike a HashSet). For your own classes, you must realize the Comparable interface and define compareTo or provide a Comparator (explained in Section 20.6 in Appendix A; Comparator is not tested on the AP Exam) in order to use the TreeSet. Since a TreeSet implements Set, a TreeSet contains no duplicates. Example 17.9 demonstrates a test program for TreeSet.

Example 17.9

```
import java.util.Iterator;
import java.util.Set;
import java.util.TreeSet;

/**
   This program tests the tree set class.
*/
public class TreeSetTest
{
   public static void main(String[] args)
   {
      Set names = new TreeSet();
      names.add("Larry");
      names.add("Tony");
      names.add("Katherine");
      names.add("Eve");
      names.add("Juliet");

      System.out.println(names.size());
      Iterator iter = names.iterator();
      while (iter.hasNext())
         System.out.println(iter.next());
      System.out.println();

      names.add("Tony");   // Attempting to add duplicate.
```

```
                    // Duplicate is not added. (Sets do not contain duplicates.)
                    names.remove("Eve");    // Removing name.
                    iter = names.iterator();
                    while (iter.hasNext())
                        System.out.println(iter.next());
                    System.out.println();
                }
            }
```

The resulting output is:

```
5
Eve
Juliet
Katherine
Larry
Tony

Juliet
Katherine
Larry
Tony
```

A `TreeSet` guarantees reasonable search performance ($O(\log(n))$) and allows for visiting the elements in the tree set in order. Because traversing a `TreeSet` with an iterator visits the tree set in order, the first call to the iterator's `next` method takes $O(\log(n))$ time.

A `TreeMap` also requires that the objects belong to a class that realizes the `Comparable` interface and defines `compareTo` for the keys. There is no requirement for the values. The `TreeMap` methods included in the AP subset are listed in Table 17.7 and demonstrated in Example 17.10.

Table 17.7

interface java.util.TreeMap

Method	Method Summary
TreeMap()	Constructs a new, empty map, sorted according to the keys' natural order.
Object put(Object key, Object value)	Associates value with key in this map so that get(key) returns value. If the map previously contained a mapping for this key, the old value is replaced by the specified value.
Object get(Object key)	Returns the value associated with key in this map, or null if there is no value associated with key.
Object remove(Object key)	Removes the mapping for key from this map if it is present.
boolean containsKey(Object key)	Returns true if there is a value associated with key in this map, otherwise returns false.
int size()	Returns the number of keys in this map.
Set keySet()	Returns a Set of the keys in the map.

Example 17.10

```java
import java.util.Iterator;
import java.util.Map;
import java.util.TreeMap;
import java.util.Set;
/**
    This program tests the TreeMap class.
*/
public class TreeMapTest
{
    public static void main(String[] args)
    {
        Map names = new TreeMap( );
        names.put(new Integer(1435), "Smith");
        names.put(new Integer(1110), "Thomas");
        names.put(new Integer(1425), "Jones");
        names.put(new Integer(987), "Evans");
        names.put(new Integer(1323), "Murray");

        System.out.println("Number of cases: " + names.size());

        Integer lookfor = new Integer(1435);
        if (names.containsKey(lookfor))
            System.out.println("Key found");
        else
            System.out.println("Key NOT found");

        Set namesSet = names.keySet();
        Iterator iter = namesSet.iterator();
        while (iter.hasNext())
```

```
        {
            Integer caseNumber = (Integer)iter.next();
            System.out.println(caseNumber + " handled by " +
            names.get(caseNumber));
        }
    }
}
```

The resulting output is:

Number of cases: 5
Key found
987 handled by Evans
1110 handled by Thomas
1323 handled by Murray
1425 handled by Jones
1435 handled by Smith

Note that the iterator loop casts `caseNumber` to `Integer`. There is no *need* to cast here if you just want to print the value. But if the code is later changed to do anything else with this value, you would then have to go back and change the variable type.

If the same test program were executed replacing

```
names.put(new Integer(1435), "Smith");
names.put(new Integer(1110), "Thomas");
names.put(new Integer(1425), "Jones");
names.put(new Integer(987), "Evans");
names.put(new Integer(1323), "Murray");
```

with

```
names.put("Smith", new Integer(1435));
names.put("Thomas", new Integer(1110));
names.put("Jones", new Integer(1425));
names.put("Evans", new Integer(987));
names.put("Murray", new Integer(1323));
```

and the iterator code was replaced by

```
while(iter.hasNext())
{
    String who = (String)iter.next();
    System.out.println(who + " handled " + names.get(who));
}
```

the resulting output would be:

Number of cases: 5
Evans handled 987

Jones handled 1425
Murray handled 1323
Smith handled 1435
Thomas handled 1110

In both executions, the nodes are visited in order according to the key field's natural ordering.

The examples of binary search trees that have been discussed so far contain integer and string values. Recall that a `TreeNode` stores any comparable object. Suppose `Student` objects were to be stored in a binary search tree. The `Student` class must implement the `Comparable` interface. This means `compareTo` must be defined in the `Student` class. The decision is made to compare students by the alphabetical ordering of last name, first name, and then ID. Example 17.11 demonstrates this.

Example 17.11

```
/**
    A student with an ID.
*/
public class Student implements Comparable
{
    /**
        Constructs a Student object.
        @param aFirstName the first name
        @param aLastName the last name
        @param anId the ID
    */
    public Student(String aFirstName, String aLastName, int anId)
    {
        firstName = aFirstName;
        lastName = aLastName;
        id = anId;
    }

    /**
        Gets the student's first name
        @return firstName the first name
    */
    public String getFirstName() {...}

    /**
        Gets the student's last name
        @return lastName the last name
    */
    public String getLastName() {...}

    /**
        Gets the student's ID
        @return id the ID
    */
    public int getId() {...}
```

```
public int compareTo(Object obj)
{
    if (obj == null)
        return -1;
    String thisName = lastName + " " + firstName + " " + id;
    String objName = ((Student)obj).lastName + " " +
            ((Student)obj).firstName + " " + ((Student)obj).id;
    return thisName.compareTo(objName);
}

/**
    Determines if the students are equal.
    @param otherObject the other student
    @return true if the students are equal, false otherwise
*/
public boolean equals(Object otherObject)
{
    return compareTo(otherObject) == 0;
}

/**
    Displays a string representation of the student object.
    @return a string describing the student object.
*/
public String toString() {...}

private String firstName;
private String lastName;
private int id;
}
```

The program segment below adds students to a binary search tree and prints the students using an inorder traversal.

```
Tree drewCsiClass = new Tree();
drewCsiClass.insert(new Student("Ann", "Brown", 111));
drewCsiClass.insert(new Student("Alan", "Frazee", 122));
drewCsiClass.insert(new Student("Bob", "Brown", 132));
drewCsiClass.insert(new Student("Ann", "Bergin", 451));
drewCsiClass.insert(new Student("Tim", "Brown", 112));
drewCsiClass.insert(new Student("Tom", "Casper", 171));
drewCsiClass.inOrderPrint();
```

The result is:

Student[First name=Ann,Last name=Bergin,ID=451]
Student[First name=Ann,Last name=Brown,ID=111]
Student[First name=Bob,Last name=Brown,ID=132]
Student[First name=Tim,Last name=Brown,ID=112]

Student[First name=Tom,Last name=Casper,ID=171]
Student[First name=Alan,Last name=Frazee,ID=122]

Because it may also be important to list students by ID number, a `Comparator` is implemented for `Student`. Example 17.12 shows this `StudentComparator` implementation and a test program that stores `Student` objects in a `TreeSet` ordered by ID numbers.

Example 17.12

```
import java.util.Comparator;
public class StudentComparator implements Comparator
{
   public int compare(Object firstObject, Object secondObject)
   {
      Student first = (Student)firstObject;
      Student second = (Student)secondObject;
      if (first.getId() < second.getId())
         return -1;
      else if (first.getId() == second.getId())
         return 0;
      else
         return 1;
   }
}
```

The program segment below adds students to a `TreeSet` using the `StudentComparator` that compares student ID numbers.

```
Comparator comp = new StudentComparator();
Set studentsByID = new TreeSet(comp);

studentsByID.add(new Student("Ann", "Brown", 111));
studentsByID.add(new Student("Alan", "Frazee", 122));
studentsByID.add(new Student("Bob", "Brown", 132));
studentsByID.add(new Student("Ann", "Bergin", 451));
studentsByID.add(new Student("Tim", "Brown", 112));
studentsByID.add(new Student("Tom", "Casper", 171));

System.out.println();
Iterator iter = studentsByID.iterator();
while (iter.hasNext())
   System.out.println(iter.next());
```

The result is:

Student[First name=Ann,Last name=Brown,ID=111]
Student[First name=Tim,Last name=Brown,ID=112]
Student[First name=Alan,Last name=Frazee,ID=122]
Student[First name=Bob,Last name=Brown,ID=132]

Student[First name=Tom,Last name=Casper,ID=171]
Student[First name=Ann,Last name=Bergin,ID=451]

17.7   Priority Queues

A priority queue is an abstract data type that has two operations: add an element and delete the element with the highest priority. Unfortunately, the Java class library does not provide a class for a priority queue.

When you send your job to a printer, it is placed on a queue. In some systems, some printing jobs may have a higher priority than other jobs because of their importance. If we assign each of these printing jobs a number to indicate its priority in the queue, then the smaller number is assigned to the most important job indicating that it should be handled first. The AP `PriorityQueue` interface defines a priority queue in which the item with the smallest value is the one with the highest priority and is deleted from the priority queue first (similar to the printer queue example).

To facilitate a consistency in the exam questions, the AB exam uses the `PriorityQueue` interface[2] shown in Example 17.13.

Example 17.13

```
/**
    The "highest priority" is defined as the smallest item in this
    priority queue.
*/
public interface PriorityQueue
{
  /**
     Postcondition: returns true if the number of elements in
     the priority queue is 0; otherwise, returns false
  */
  boolean isEmpty();

  /**
     Postcondition: x has been added to the priority queue; the
     number of elements in the priority queue is increased by 1.
  */
  void add(Object x);

  /**
     Postcondition: The smallest item in the priority queue is
     removed and returned; the number of elements in the priority
     queue is decreased by 1. Throws unchecked exception if
     priority queue is empty.
  */
  Object removeMin();

  /**
     Postcondition: The smallest item in the priority queue is
```

---

[2] College Board's AP Computer Science AB: Implementation Classes and Interfaces

```
        returned; the priority queue is unchanged. Throws unchecked
        exception if priority queue is empty.
    */
    Object peekMin();
}
```

The AP `PriorityQueue` interface defines the "highest priority" as the smallest item in the priority queue. When the method `removeMin()` is implemented, the item with the smallest value should be returned. Let's consider some options for implementing a priority queue and discuss their limitations.

An unsorted array (or `ArrayList`)
- Adding an element is $O(1)$.
  Elements will be added to the end of the array.
- `removeMin` is $O(n)$.
  In order to delete this element from the array, the smallest value must be found ($O(n)$) and deleted.

A sorted array (or `ArrayList`)
- Adding an element is $O(n)$.
  The array must searched for the correct place and then elements must be shifted to accommodate the insertion. We should keep the list sorted so that the element with the smallest value is last.
- `removeMin` is $O(1)$ if this element is stored in last position.

An unsorted linked list
- Adding an element is $O(1)$.
  Elements will be added to the front of the list.
- `removeMin` is $O(n)$.
  We must search the linked list to find the element ($O(n)$) and then delete the element.

A sorted linked list
- Adding an element is $O(n)$.
  Must search for the correct place and then insert it. The list will be sorted in ascending order so that the element with the smallest value is first.
- `removeMin` is $O(1)$ because we are removing the first element of the linked list.

A tree set
- Adding an element is $O(\log(n))$.
- `removeMin` is $O(\log(n))$.

Example 17.14 is an example of the `TreeSet` implementation of `PriorityQueue`.

Example 17.14

```java
import java.util.TreeSet;
import java.util.Iterator;

public class TreePriorityQueue implements PriorityQueue
{
    public TreePriorityQueue()
    {
        tree = new TreeSet();
    }
```

```java
/**
    Postcondition: returns true if the number of elements
    in the priority queue is 0; otherwise, returns false
*/
public boolean isEmpty()
{
    return tree.size() == 0;
}

/**
    Postcondition: x has been added to the priority queue; the
    number of elements in the priority queue is increased by 1.
*/
public void add(Object x)
{
    tree.add(x);
}

/**
    Postcondition: The smallest item in the priority queue is
    removed and returned; the number of elements in the priority
    queue is decreased by 1. Throws unchecked exception if
    priority queue is empty.
*/
public Object removeMin()
{
    Iterator iter = tree.iterator();
    Object r = iter.next();
    iter.remove();
    return r;
}

/**
    Postcondition: The smallest item in the priority queue is
    returned; the priority queue is unchanged. Throws unchecked
    exception if priority queue is empty.
*/
public Object peekMin()
{
    Iterator iter = tree.iterator();
    Object r = iter.next();
    return r;
}

private TreeSet tree;
}
```

Now, let's look at another data implementation called a *heap*.

17.8   Heaps

A *max-heap* is a binary tree with the following properties:
1. It is complete or almost complete, which means that every level of the tree is completely filled, except maybe the bottom level. If the bottom level is not filled, the nodes are in the leftmost positions (See Figure 5 in Section 20A.5 of Appendix A of this guide).
2. The object stored at each node is at least as large as the values stored in its children.

These properties are maintained with each addition to the heap. Figure 17.7 illustrates a max-heap.

Figure 17.7

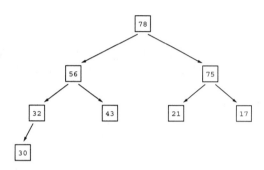

Figure 7 in Section 20A.5 in Appendix A of this guide illustrates creating a max-heap and adding elements to the heap. It is easy to see that the element with the largest value is the root of the binary tree. To remove this element, replace the root with the "last" element in the heap and readjust the heap elements so that the max-heap properties are maintained (See Figure 8 in Section 20A.5 of Appendix A in this guide).

Figure 17.8

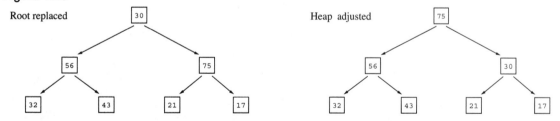

With the conclusion of each operation, the properties of a max-heap are satisfied. The algorithms used for insertions to and deletions from a heap are based on a binary tree-making each of the operations $O(\log(n))$.

Now, consider the min-heap defined as a binary tree with the following properties:
*   It is complete or almost complete, which means that every level of the tree is completely filled, except maybe the bottom level. If the bottom level is not filled, the nodes are in the leftmost positions. (This is true for all heaps.)
*   The object stored at each node is at least as large as the value stored in its *parent* node. (In the max-heap, the word *parent* was *child*.)

In this case, the root would contain the smallest value, rather than the largest value. If we implement the `PriorityQueue` interface with this heap implementation, we have:

- Adding an element is $O(\log(n))$. (This is the same as for our max-heap insertion.)
- Deleting with `removeMin` is $O(\log(n))$. The smallest value is deleted (not the largest). (This is the same as our max-heap deletion.)

17.8.1   Implementing a Heap

Section 20A.5 in Appendix A of this guide implements a heap using an `ArrayList`. The elements from the tree are mapped to indices in an array list. The root of the heap is placed in index `1`. The left child of the node in position `x` is placed in index `2x` and the right child is place in index `2x + 1`. Figure 9 in Section 20A.5 of Appendix A in this guide illustraces this and the `ArrayList` implementation of the heap is given following the illustration.

17.8.2   The Heapsort Algorithm

Heaps are also used to implement an efficient sorting algorithm, heapsort. This sorting algorithm is $O(n \log(n))$. There are n items in the heap. Each insertion and removal is $O(\log(n))$. Let's look at a very simplified description of the heapsort algorithm. Figure 17.9 illustrates this pseudocode.

Start with a max-heap (an array) of size n.

```
for (int n = heapName.size() - 1; n >= 0; n--)
{
    swap h[n-1] with root (h[0])
    readjust heap from 1 ... n - 2
}
```

While readjusting to maintain max-heap properties, if we need to demote a node, we swap it with its oldest child.

Figure 17.9

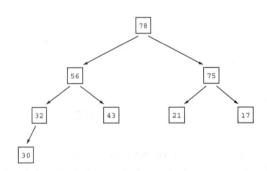

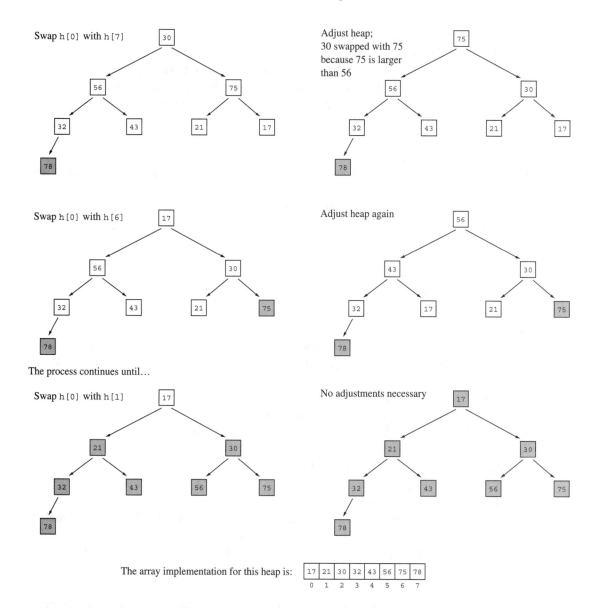

The array implementation for this heap is:

17	21	30	32	43	56	75	78
0	1	2	3	4	5	6	7

When we traverse the array beginning with the first array element, the elements visited are in increasing order.

17.9   Choosing a Container

HowTo 20.1 in Appendix A of this guide reviews how to pick the appropriate container (implementation) for your application. The questions you should ask yourself and the possible answers to each question are summarized below. As you read the questions and choose an answer, think about the container that you would use. The Comments below the questions discuss possible choices.

Your container choices: arrays, array lists, linked lists, sets, and maps.

1. How will elements be accessed?
   a. The method of accessing doesn't matter in this application.
   b. Accessing elements needs to be by index for immediate retrieval.
   c. The accessing will be done by key (like an ID number or a bank account number).
   d. Accessing is done by an index pair such as a row and column.

2. Does order matter?
   a. Order doesn't matter.
   b. The order of the entries needs to be kept in the order in which the entries were entered.
   c. The entries need to be kept in sorted order.

3. Which operations need to be fast?
   a. It doesn't matter.
   b. Adding and/or removing elements needs to be fast.
   c. Finding an element needs to be fast.

Comments:
- If the answers to all of the questions is doesn't matter, then use an array list. It's an easy and straightforward implementation.
- If the answer to 1 is b, use an array or array list.
- If the answer to 1 is c, use a map.
- If the answer to 1 is d, use a two-dimensional array.
- If the answer to 2 is b, use an array, an array list, or a linked list.
- If the answer to 2 is c, use a tree set.
- If the answer to 3 is b, use linked lists.
- If the answer to 3 is c, use a set.
- If you need a set or a map, remember
    - A `HashSet` and a `HashMap` need a `hashCode` method. Check to see that the class of your object implements this method.
    - Trees need to implement `Comparable` or define a `Comparator`. Check to see that the class of your object has `compareTo` defined. `Comparator` is not included in the AP subset.
- Sets do not contain duplicates. If your application is meant to include duplicates, a set is not your choice.

■ Expanded Coverage of Material That is Not Found in the Text

- Appendix A contains *Big Java* Chapter 20 (referenced as A–20). Material that is not covered in *Computing Concepts with Java Essentials*, 3rd ed., or *Big Java* is found in Appendix A, Chapter 20A (referenced as A–20A).
- A *min-heap* is a binary tree with the following properties:
    - It is complete or almost complete, which means that every level of the tree is completely filled, except maybe the bottom level. If the bottom level is not filled, the nodes are in the leftmost positions (similar to a heap).
    - The object stored at each node is at least as large as the value stored in its *parent* node.

- The min-heap is another representation of *heap*. The min-heap implementation has the root contain the smallest value, rather than the largest value (as in the max-heap presented in this guide and in your text).
- The method we used to implement our hash table involved *chaining*. Another method of storing elements in a hash table is called *linear probing*. With linear probing, each bucket contains at most one element. If an attempt is made to add an element to a bucket that already has an element in it, the new element would be added to the next available (empty) bucket.

■ Topics That Are Useful But Not Tested

- The `String` class, `Double` class and `Integer` class provide a `hashCode` method that returns an integer hash code. When writing your own hash function, you may wish to call these methods. The `Coin` example in Section 20.4 in Appendix A of this guide calls the `Double hashCode` method.
- Computing hash codes is covered in Section 20.4 of Appendix A of this guide. Implementing `hashCode` will not be tested.

■ Things to Remember When Taking the AP Exam

- Do not change the objects in a set. Sets do not contain duplicates. If you change an item in a set it may become the same as another item in the set. Moreover, this WILL upset the set data structure since it may change the hash code or the sort order!
- Sets are not ordered.
- Use an iterator to list all elements in a set.
- An iterator for a `HashSet` does not return the elements in any specific order.
- For a `HashSet`, an iterator can iterate through all elements in $O(n)$ time where n is the sum of the `HashSet` instance's size (the number of elements) and the number of buckets.
- You cannot add an element to a set at an iterator position.
- A hash function computes an integer value from an object.
- A good hash function will distribute entries uniformly in a hash table.
- A map associates keys with values.
- In a hash map, only the keys are hashed. In a tree map, only the keys are sorted.
- For `HashSet` and `HashMap`, the operations `add`, `remove`, and `contains` have an expected time of $O(1)$ and are $O(n)$ in the worst case.
- When a class redefines `equals`, it should redefine `hashCode` to be compatible. Implementing these functions is not tested on the AP Exam.
- If a binary search tree is balanced, locating, adding, and removing an element is $O(\log(n))$.
- To use a tree set or a tree map, the elements must be comparable.
- `TreeSets` and `TreeMaps` are implemented as balanced binary trees so the operations `add`, `remove`, and `contains` are $O(\log(n))$.
- For a `TreeSet` iterator, the first call to `next()` takes $O(\log(n))$ time.

- Know the difference between preorder, postorder, and inorder traversals of a binary tree.
- Removing an element from a priority queue will remove the element with the highest priority.
- The heap sort algorithm is $O(n \log(n))$.

■ Key Words

You should understand the terms below. The AP CS Exam questions may include references to these terms. The citations in parentheses next to each term identify the page numbers where it is defined and/or discussed in Appendix A of this guide.

balanced binary search tree (A-20:398)
binary tree (A-20:392)
binary search tree (A-20:391)
buckets (A-20:382)
children (A-20:392)
collision (A-20:380)
descendant (A-20:392)
hash code (A-20:380)
hash function (A-20:380)

hash map (A-20:378)
hash set (A-20:374)
hash table (A-20:375)
heap (A-20A:422)
heapsort (A-20A:433)
inorder (A-20A:419)
key set (A-20:401)
map (A-20:378)
postorder (A-20A:419)

preorder (A-20A:419)
priority queue (A-20:402, A-20A:422)
root (A-20:392)
set (A-20:374)
table size (A-20:382)
tree map (A-20:378)
tree set (A-20:375)
value set (A-20:378)

■ Connecting the Detailed Topic Outline to the Text

The citations in parentheses identify where information in the outline can be located in Appendix A of this guide.

- Sets (A-20:374–378)
- Maps (A-20:378–380)
- Hash Tables (A-20:380–387)
  - Using `HashSet` (A-20:376–377)
  - Implementing `HashSet` (A-20:383–386)
  - Using `HashMap` (A-20:378–380)
  - Implementing `HashMap` (*Guide Chapter 17*, pages 308-309)
- Computing Hash Codes (A-20:387–391)
- Binary Search Trees (A-20:391–401)
  - Binary Tree Traversals (A-20A:419)
  - Searching a Binary Search Tree (A-20A:416)
  - Removing a Node from a Binary Search Tree (A-20A:414–419)
- Using Tree Sets and Tree Maps (A-20:401–402)
- Priority Queues (A-20:402–403, A-20A:422)

■ Practice Questions

Multiple Choice

1. A hash function computes an integer value from an object. The goal of a good hash function is to:

   a. determine the size of the hash table.
   b. provide space for the object that is to be inserted.
   c. provide a method of dealing with collisions.
   d. provide a key for efficiently sorting the objects in the hash table.
   e. provide an integer value for the object so that the objects are uniformly distributed in the hash table.

Questions 2, 3, and 4 refer to the incomplete binary search tree implementation given below. The class `Tree` is a binary search tree of `TreeNodes`. Refer to the *AB Quick Reference Guide* or Example 17.5 for the `TreeNode` implementation. The Tree method `printXxx` calls `xxxPrint` to print the values in the nodes of the binary search tree.

```
/*
    This class implements a binary search tree whose
    nodes are TreeNodes that hold objects that
    implement the Comparable interface.
*/
public class Tree
{
    // Constructs an empty tree.
    public Tree()
    {
        root = null;
    }

    // Other Binary Search Tree methods here

    public void printXxx()
    {
        if (root != null)
            xxxPrint(root);
    }

    public void xxxPrint(TreeNode current)
    {
        ListQueue q = new ListQueue();
        q.enqueue(current);
```

```
        while (!q.isEmpty())
        {
           Object temp = q.dequeue();
           current = (TreeNode)temp;
           System.out.print(current.getValue() + " ");
           if (current.getLeft() != null)
              q.enqueue(current.getLeft());
           if (current.getRight() != null)
              q.enqueue(current.getRight());
        }
    }

    private TreeNode root;
}
```

The following declaration is made.

```
Tree numbers = new Tree();
```

The following `Integer` values are inserted, in the order below, into an initially empty binary search tree, `numbers`.

```
15 8 25 6 14 24 20 22 30 13 26
```

2. What is printed when the statement

```
numbers.printXxx();
```

is executed in a client program of the `Tree` class?

a. *6 8 13 14 15 20 22 24 25 26 30*
b. *6 13 14 8 22 20 24 26 30 25 15*
c. *15 8 6 14 13 25 24 29 22 30 26*
d. *15 8 25 6 14 24 30 13 20 26 22*
e. *15 25 8 30 24 14 6 26 20 13 22*

3. Suppose the statements

```
if (current.getLeft() != null)
   q.enqueue(current.getLeft());
```

and

```
if (current.getRight() != null)
   q.enqueue(current.getRight());
```

were exchanged. What would be printed when the statement

```
numbers.printXxx();
```

is executed in a client program of the `Tree` class?

   a. *6 8 13 14 15 20 22 24 25 26 30*
   b. *6 13 14 8 22 20 24 26 30 25 15*
   c. *15 8 6 14 13 25 24 29 22 30 26*
   d. *15 8 25 6 14 24 30 13 20 26 22*
   e. *15 25 8 30 24 14 6 26 20 13 22*

4. Suppose the following methods were added to the `Tree` class above.

```
public int mysterySum(TreeNode current)
{
   if (current == null)
      return 0;
   else
      return (1 + mysterySum(current.getLeft()) +
            mysterySum(current.getRight()));
}

public int mystery()
{
   return mysterySum(root);
}
```

The following `Integer` values are inserted, in the order below, into the binary search tree, `numbers`.

```
8 3 10 2 5
```

What would be printed when the statement

```
System.out.println(numbers.mystery());
```

is executed in a client program of the `Tree` class?

   a. *0*
   b. *1*
   c. *5*
   d. *28*
   e. Nothing is printed, a run-time error occurs.

5. Which of the following statements about maps and sets is true?

   a. A `HashMap` can have two keys with the same value but two values will not have the same key.
   b. A `HashMap` can have two values with the same key but two keys will not have the same value.
   c. Each key in a `HashMap` must have a unique value and each value in a `HashMap` has a unique key.

d. A `HashMap` can have two values with the same key and two keys with the same value.

e. A `HashMap` can have values that do not belong to any key.

Questions 6 and 7 refer to the problem statement below.

The following `Integer` values are pushed onto a stack, s, that implements the `Stack` interface that is defined in Example 16.10 and in the *AB Quick Reference Guide*. The values are pushed onto s in the order that they appear below (left to right).

```
1 7 4 6 10 9
```

6. Consider a priority queue, `priQueue` that is instantiated from a class `priorityQueueList` implementing the `PriorityQueue` interface defined in Example 17.13 and in the *AB Quick Reference Guide*. The following declarations are made.

```
PriorityQueue priQue = new PriorityQueueList();
// PriorityQueueList implements PriorityQueue
```

Values are popped off the stack, s, and as each value is popped off the stack, it is inserted into the priority queue, `priQue`. The following code is then executed.

```
while (!priQue.isEmpty())
{
    System.out.println(priQue.removeMin())
}
```

The numbers printed to the screen would be:

a. *1 7 4 6 10 9*
b. *9 10 6 4 7 1*
c. *1 4 6 7 9 10*
d. *10 9 7 6 4 1*
e. *9 6 4 1 7 10*

7. The values are pushed onto stack s in the order that they appear below (left to right).

```
1 7 4 6 10 9
```

The values are then popped off the stack. As each value is popped off the stack, it is inserted into a binary search tree. The values in the tree are printed by visiting the nodes in the tree with a preorder traversal. The numbers printed to the screen would be:

a. *1 7 4 6 10 9*
b. *6 4 9 10 7 1*
c. *1 4 6 7 9 10*
d. *10 9 7 6 4 1*
e. *9 6 4 1 7 10*

8. Which of the following is **not** a fundamental operation for a Set?

    a. Adding elements to the set.
    b. Removing elements from the set.
    c. Listing elements in the set.
    d. Testing the set to see if an element is contained in the set.
    e. Returning the number of times a given element appears in the set.

9. Which of the following statements is true?

    a. A set iterator visits the elements in the order in which you inserted them.
    b. When adding elements to a set, you should use the `add` method of the set iterator.
    c. Elements can be removed from a set using the iterator method `remove` or the `Set` method `remove` that is defined by the class that implements `Set`.
    d. You should not attempt to add duplicates to a set because a run-time error will occur.
    e. To insert an element in a particular place in the set, use the set iterator to find the set position.

10. Which of the following lines of code will add an association of a person and a university in the `Map friends`?

    a. `friends.add("Mary");`
    b. `friends.add("Mary", "University of Delaware");`
    c. `friends.put("Mary", "University of Delaware");`
    d. `friends.addValue("Mary", "University of Delaware");`
    e. `friends.putValue("Mary", "University of Delaware");`

11. Which of the following describes how to print all of the keys, with their associated values, of a class that implements `Map`?

    a. Store all values and keys in a `TreeNode` and insert the `TreeNode` in a binary search tree. Then, traverse the tree using an inorder traversal.
    b. Store all values and keys in a `TreeNode` and insert the `TreeNode` in a binary search tree. Then, use a tree iterator to retrieve the values.
    c. Iterate through the set returned by the class's `keySet` method to retrieve the key and use the class's `get` method to retrieve the value associated with the key.
    d. Iterate through the set returned by the class's `keySet` method to retrieve the value and use the class's `get` method to retrieve the key associated with the value.
    e. Store the elements in an array list and the corresponding values in a set. Iterate through the array list and the set simultaneously to retrieve and print the keys and values.

12. If there are no collisions in the hash table, then locating a hash table element takes

    a. $O(1)$
    b. $O(\log(n))$
    c. $O(n)$
    d. $O(n \log(n))$
    e. $O(n^2)$

13. Consider the following sorting algorithms.

I.   Merge sort
II. Quicksort
III. Heapsort

In the worst case, which of the algorithms is $O(n \log(n))$?

    a. I only
    b. II only
    c. III only
    d. I and III only
    e. I, II, and III

14. Consider the following definition of a heap.

A *heap* is a binary tree with the following properties:
- It is complete or almost complete, which means that every level of the tree is completely filled, except maybe the bottom level. If the bottom level is not filled, the nodes are in the leftmost positions.
- The object stored at each node is at least as large as the values stored in its children.
- Adding an element to the heap maintains the heap properties.

The following Integers are added to an initially empty heap in the order they are listed. The heap properties are maintained with each insertion.

    9 25 32 90 15 4 23

If the heap is represented by a binary tree and an inorder traversal is done on this binary tree, the resulting order of the visited Integers is:

    a. 9 32 15 90 4 25 23
    b. 4 9 15 23 25 32 90
    c. 90 32 25 23 15 9 4
    d. 90 32 25 9 15 4 23
    e. 9 15 32 4 23 25 90

15. Consider the following two methods for sorting a set of strings in descending order.

Method 1
- Construct an empty binary search tree.
- Insert all strings into the binary search tree.
- Repeatedly get the maximum element (by following the rightmost path) and remove it.

Method 2
- Construct an empty heap.
- Insert all strings into the heap.
- Repeatedly get the maximum element (stored in the root) and remove it.

Which of the following statements is true?

   a. Method 2 is more efficient than Method 1 if the resulting trees are both balanced after inserting all elements.

   b. Method 1 is more efficient than Method 2 if the input set is already sorted.

   c. Method 1 has $O(n \log(n))$ efficiency in the best case.

   d. Method 2 has $O(n^2)$ efficiency in the worst case.

   e. Method 1 and Method 2 are both less efficient than selection sort.

16. Your job is to choose a data structure to implement polynomials whose coefficients are positive integers, such as $17x^4 + 4x^3 + 0x^2 + 6x^1 + 12x^0$.

Here are three possible implementations.

I. As a two-dimensional array of boolean values: coeff[c][i] is true if and only if $c * x^i$ is a term of the polynomial.

II. As a tree map with `Integer` keys and values. If $c * x^i$ is a term of the polynomial, then we add the following correspondence to the map:

```
coeff.put(new Integer(i), new Integer(c))
```

III. As a hash set of objects of type

```
class Term
{
    ...
    private int coefficient;
    private int power;
}
```

Which of the following statements is *false*?

   a. Implementation I requires more space than implementations II and III.

   b. Implementation II makes it easy to print the polynomial in its natural order (by decreasing powers).

   c. Implementation II requires $O(n)$ time to find the coefficient of a term with a given power, where n is the number of terms in the polynomial.

   d. Implementation III is impossible to carry out because one cannot define a hash code for terms.

   e. If the hash code is assumed to run in constant time, implementation III requires $O(1)$ time to find the coefficient of a term with a given power.

17. The principal advantage that heapsort has over the merge sort algorithm is

   a. Heapsort is related to priority queues.

   b. Heapsort doesn't require a second array for intermediate storage.

   c. Heapsort is a $O(n \log(n))$ algorithm.

    d.   Heapsort uses binary search trees.

    e.   Heapsort does not require recursion.

18. Consider the following max-heap:

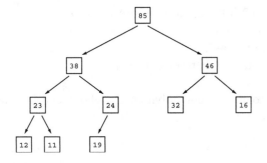

The array representation of this heap is

    a.   11 12 16 19 23 24 38 46 85

    b.   85 38 46 23 24 32 16 12 11 19

    c.   12 11 19 24 24 32 16 38 46 85

    d.   85 38 23 12 11 24 19 46 32 16

    e.   None of the above—the tree doesn't fulfill the max-heap conditions.

19.   Consider the following binary trees:

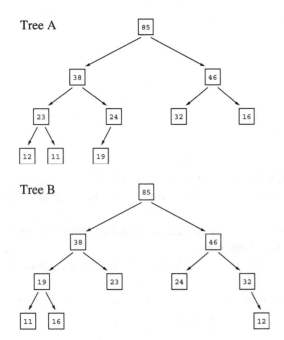

Tree C

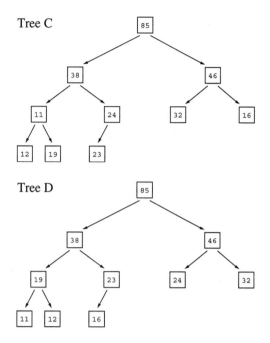

Tree D

Which of the binary trees above are heaps?

a.   All of the trees above are heaps.
b.   A and B only
c.   C and D only
d.   B and D only
e.   A and D only

20. Consider the following mystery function on a binary tree (not necessarily a binary search tree).

```
public int mystery(TreeNode cur)
{
    if (cur == null)
        return 0;
    else
    {
        int r = mystery(cur.getLeft()) + mystery(cur.getRight());
        if (cur.getLeft() != null && ((Integer)cur.getLeft()
                .getValue()).compareTo(cur.getValue()) > 0) ||
                (cur.getRight() != null && ((Integer)cur.getRight()
                .getValue()).compareTo(cur.getValue()) < 0))
        r++;
        return r;
    }

    public int mystery()
    {
        return mystery(root);
    }
}
```

What is the result when applying the function to the following tree?

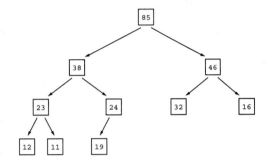

a. 5
b. 4
c. 6
d. 10
e. 306

Free Response Questions

1. The class `TreeSetWithOps` is a subclass of `TreeSet`. `TreeSetWithOps` has functionality that includes the methods `setIntersection`, `setUnion`, `setDifference`, `isSubset`, and `isProperSubset`. The incomplete definition of `TreeSetWithOps` appears below.

```
import java.util.Set;
import java.util.TreeSet;
import java.util.Iterator;

public class TreeSetWithOps extends TreeSet
{

    /*
        set2 is the set with whom the intersection is determined.
        Returns the intersection of this TreeSet with set2
    */
    public Set setIntersection(Set set2)
    {
        // Code goes here
    }

    /*
        set2 is a set with whom the set union is determined.
        Returns the union of this TreeSet with set2
    */
    public Set setUnion(Set set2)
    {
        // Code goes here
    }

    /*
```

```
            set2 is a set with whom the set difference is determined.
            Returns the difference of this TreeSet with set2
        */
        public Set setDifference(Set set2)
        {
            // Code goes here
        }


        /*
            set2 is a set to be evaluated as a subset.
            Returns true if set2 is a subset of this set,
            false otherwise
        */
        public boolean isSubset(Set set2)
        {
            // Code goes here
        }


        /*
            set2 is a set to be evaluated as a proper subset.
            Returns true if set2 is a proper subset of this set,
            false otherwise
        */
        public boolean isProperSubset(Set set2)
        {
            // Code goes here
        }
    }
```

a.   You are to implement the `TreeSetWithOps` method `setIntersection`. The intersection of two sets is a set whose members are common to both sets. The method `setIntersection` will return the intersection of `this` set with its `Set` parameter. For example, if

set1 is the set `{"Ginger", "Harry", "Mary", "Thomas"}`

and

set2 is the set `{"Frank", "Harry", "Kevin", "Mary", "Nancy"}`

and the statement

```
        Set set3 = set1.setIntersection(set2);
```

were executed, set3 would contain `{"Harry", "Mary"}`.

If the two sets have no elements in common, `null` is returned. Use the method header below to write the method `setIntersection`.

```
        public Set setIntersection(Set set2)
```

b.   You are to implement the `TreeSetWithOps` method `setUnion`. The union of two sets is a set whose members are in at least one of the sets. The method `setUnion` will return the union of `this` set with its `Set` parameter. For example, if

`set1` is the set `{"Ginger", "Harry", "Mary", "Thomas"}`

and

`set2` is the set `{"Frank", "Harry", "Kevin", "Mary", "Nancy"}`

and the statement

```
Set set3 = set1.setUnion(set2);
```

were executed, `set3` would contain `{"Frank", "Ginger", "Harry", "Kevin", "Mary", "Nancy", "Thomas"}`.

Use the method header below to write the method `setUnion`.

```
public Set setUnion(Set set2)
```

c.   You are to implement the `TreeSetWithOps` method `setDifference`. The difference of `set1` minus `set2` is the set whose members are in `set1` but are not in `set2`. The method `setDifference` will return the difference of `this` set with its `Set` parameter. For example, if

`set1` is the set `{"Ginger", "Harry", "Mary", "Thomas"}`

and

`set2` is the set `{"Frank", "Harry", "Kevin", "Mary", "Nancy"}`

and the statement

```
Set set3 = set1.setDifference(set2);
```

were executed, `set3` would contain `{"Ginger", "Thomas"}`.

Use the method header below to write the method `setDifference`.

```
public Set setDifference(Set set2)
```

d.   You are to implement the `TreeSetWithOps` method `isSubset`. The method `isSubset` will return `true` if every element of `set2` is also an element of `set1`. The set `set1` may have exactly the same elements as `set2`. For example, if

set1	set2	set1.*isSubset(set2)*
{1,2,3,4,5}	{1,2,3}	true
{1,2,3,4}	{1,2,3,4}	true
{1,2,3,4,5}	{1,2,3,6}	false

Use the method header below to write the method isSubset.

```
public boolean isSubset(Set set2)
```

e. You are to implement the `TreeSetWithOps` method isProperSubset. The method isProperSubset will return true if every element of set2 is also an element of set1 and set1 has some elements that are not in set2. For example, if

set1	set2	set1.*isProperSubset(set2)*
{1,2,3,4,5}	{1,2,3}	true
{1,2,3,4}	{1,2,3,4}	false
{1,2,3,4,5}	{1,2,3,6}	false

In writing isProperSubset, you may call the method isSubset described in part d of this problem. Assume isSubset works as intended regardless of what you wrote for part d. Use the method header below to write the method isProperSubset.

```
public boolean isProperSubset(Set set2)
```

2. A concordance is an alphabetical wordlist for a passage of text. Each word in the concordance is mapped to an `Integer` indicating the frequency of the word's occurrence. The constructor of `Concordance` has one `String` parameter that identifies the text file to be read. An incomplete `Concordance` class is below.

```
public class Concordance
{
   // Constructor
   public Concordance(String nameOfFile)
   {
      concord = new TreeMap();
      createConcordance(nameOfFile);
   }

   // Create and return a TreeMap of words mapped to their
   // Integer frequencies.
   public void createConcordance(String fileName)
   {
      // Code goes here
   }

   // Prints the alphabetized list of words paired with their
      frequencies.
   public void printConcordance()
```

```
    {
        // Code goes here
    }

    private Map concord;
}
```

a. The method `createConcordance` will fill `concord`, a `TreeMap` of words mapped to their `Integer` frequencies. Complete the method `createConcordance` below. You may assume that all words in the passage are made up of lowercase letters.

```
public static TreeMap createConcordance(String fileName)
{
    // infile(fileName) is open for reading.
    while (!(infile.eof()))
    {
        String word = inFile.readWord();   // reads word from infile
        // More code goes here
    }
}
```

b. Write the method `printConcordance` that will print the alphabetized list of words paired with their frequencies. If the text file contains the following text:

> *hickory dickory dock*
> *the mouse ran up the clock*
> *the clock struck one*
> *the mouse ran down*
> *hickory dickory dock*

`printConcordance` will print:

> *clock occurs 2 time(s).*
> *dickory occurs 2 time(s).*
> *dock occurs 2 time(s).*
> *down occurs 1 time(s).*
> *hickory occurs 2 time(s).*
> *mouse occurs 2 time(s).*
> *one occurs 1 time(s).*
> *ran occurs 2 time(s).*
> *struck occurs 1 time(s).*
> *the occurs 4 time(s).*
> *up occurs 1 time(s).*

Use the method header below in writing `printConcordance`.

```
public void printConcordance()
```

c.   Suppose, in addition to the method `printConcordance`, you wish to include a method `printByFrequency` that would print the words ordered by frequency. The method `printByFrequency` will print:

> *down occurs 1 time(s).*
> *one occurs 1 time(s).*
> *struck occurs 1 time(s).*
> *up occurs 1 time(s).*
> *clock occurs 2 time(s).*
> *dickory occurs 2 time(s).*
> *dock occurs 2 time(s).*
> *hickory occurs 2 time(s).*
> *mouse occurs 2 time(s).*
> *ran occurs 2 time(s).*
> *the occurs 4 time(s).*

Words with the same frequency can be printed in any order. Describe the data structure(s) and algorithms that you would use to write `printByFrequency`. Comment on the time complexity of your algorithm.

CHAPTER **18**

The AP Exam Case Study

■ Topic Summary

18.1   What Is a Case Study?

A case study is a document that includes a problem statement, a program that solves the problem, and a narrative discussing the steps taken and the decisions made in developing the problem solution. Case studies have been used for years to teach law, medicine, business, and science. Case studies were added to the AP Computer Science curriculum in 1994. The AP CS Case Study contains a large program, written by experts, that is meant to serve as a good programming example. The narrative discusses the development of this program. Within the narrative there are exercises and analysis questions. Through these questions and the questions posed within the narrative, development options are explored as they would be before development decisions are made. This enables you, the student, to act as an apprentice in the programming situation. You will be learning from the experts as you work through the program. The case study narrative makes it clear that having a program that just "works" should never be the focus of a software system — the process of arriving at a solution is just as important as the final product itself. In Chapter 13 we discussed the software life cycle. This cycle consists of five distinct processes.

- Analysis
- Design
- Implementation
- Testing
- Deployment

The focus of the case study is to become familiar with each of these five processes as they relate to the particular case study problem. You will be able to study the different alternatives to a problem solution and you will understand why certain choices were made in each step of the software life cycle.

The exercises and analysis questions guide you through the software life cycle for the case study problem. Do not skip these questions and do not "leave them for later." Completing the questions as you go through the case study document allows for an understanding of the complete development process.

18.2   Why Are Case Studies Included in AP CS?

The AP CS Exam consists of 40 multiple-choice questions and 4 free-response questions. Answering these types of questions would not necessarily indicate that you have ever worked with a program of any size. Since AP Computer Science parallels the first semester or two of university-level computer science courses, and since universities generally require the development and completion of larger programs, the case study offers a method for ensuring that AP CS students have some experience with a large program. This case study program requires you to read a very large program written by someone else. By working with the case study, you will again experience modifying and extending a large program, and you will be exposed to a good programming example written by experts. The exercises throughout the case study deal with all stages of development and encourage you think through design and implementation tradeoffs.

18.3   How Do I Use the Case Study During the School Year?

The case study will help develop critical thinking skills. You should begin reading the case study very early in the year. It is important that you become familiar with the current case study documents. If possible, you should visit the case study several times throughout the AP CS course. Do not wait until two weeks before the exam to look at the document for the first time. The case study will help you learn computer science concepts. Studying the case study will improve your performance throughout the course, not just on the case study exam questions. Complete all of the exercises and analysis questions as you go through the case study. These questions will help you understand the design decisions and programming alternatives. Research has indicated that the more time spent on the case study, the better the mastery of all AP CS material.

18.4   How Do I Prepare for the Case Study Questions on the AP Exam?

Familiarize yourself with the goal of the case study. Review the exercises and analysis questions before the exam. There may be different requirements for the A and AB Exams. Be aware of the material that is covered on the AP Exam that you will be taking. You can find this information on the College Board Web site listed at the end of this chapter.

You will be given certain documents during the AP CS Exam. You may use these documents throughout the multiple-choice and free-response parts of the exam. These documents include the AP CS A or AB Quick Reference Guide and portions of the case study document. The case study materials will include the source code for the visible classes, a summary of class documentation for the black box classes (the classes whose code you are not responsible for knowing), and an index for the source code. All of these documents are available to you during the school year and are found in the case study narrative document. Become familiar with these resources.

Be familiar with the classes that are included in the case study. Understand the constructors, accessor methods, and modifier methods for each class. Know the class dependencies and inheritance hierarchies. Be able to modify and extend the existing classes. You should have quite a bit of experience with this already if you have been faithfully completing the questions and exercises and implementing these changes in the case study.

Remember that there will be 5–10 multiple-choice questions and one free-response question directly related to the case study. These questions may include tasks such as:
- Extend the case study code by writing a new method, class, or subclass.
- Give a different design for a class.
- Design an entirely new class.
- Design a set of interacting classes. **(AB only)**
- Give an alternative choice of data structure.
- Implement a given method using an alternative data structure or approach.
- Develop test data for a particular implementation.
- Explain the interaction and dependencies among classes.
- Analyze given code, explaining how it might be made more efficient.
- Give the big-Oh analysis for a particular algorithm. **(AB only)**
- Modify classes based on an alternative problem description.

Do not wait until the exam to look at the case study resources! Time is very valuable during the exam period. Read the exam questions carefully. They may be simple modifications of problems that you have already done.

18.5   Where Do I Get the Case Study?

The case study consists of several parts. The required material is available for you to download from the College Board Web site. Important College Board links are listed below.

Information on the current case study:
http://www.collegeboard.com/ap/students/compsci/download.html

You can access general information about the Advanced Placement Program at:
http://www.collegeboard.com/ap/students/index.html

Current information about AP Computer Science:
http://www.collegeboard.com/ap/students/compsci/index.html

CHAPTER **19**

Help with Common Compilers

■ Topic Summary

19.1 Java™ 2 Platform

Java is a language developed by Sun Microsystems. You can download the Java Software Development Kit (SDK) at no charge from the Sun site at http://java.sun.com/j2se/ (for Windows and Linux; see below for the Macintosh version).

To get started with the SDK, download the most recent edition of Java™ 2 Platform, Standard Edition (J2SE™). At the time this book was printed, the most recent edition (not beta version) was J2SE 1.4.1.

- Follow the Download link from the Java 2 Platform, Standard Edition page.
- Choose to download the SDK (Standard Development Kit) for your operating system. This will be an .exe file for Windows.
- To install, double click on the .exe file. Follow the setup instructions. Use the default directories for easy installation.
- Before you leave the site, also download the SDK documentation. From the download page (where you chose your platform), go to the bottom of the page and look for "J2SE v 1.4.1 Documentation." Download this documentation so you have a local copy to which you can easily and quickly refer.

After installing the SDK, you should add the location of the SDK program files to the PATH environment variable. This is necessary so that the commands can be executed when you type them into a command shell, or when they are issued by a text editor with Java support. Directions for setting the path can be found at http://horstmann.com/bigj/help/sdk/index.html.

For Mac OS X, you need to download the developer tools from Apple (http://developer.apple.com/tools). The developer tools include the Java SDK.

Before you continue, test your installation. Steps for checking installations for Windows, Linux, and Mac OS X are given at http://horstmann.com/bigj/help/sdk/index.html.

You can now run Java as a command line application or you can download an Integrated Development Environment (IDE) that will work with the Java SDK.

19.2   Command Line Programming

You do not *need* an IDE to write, compile, and execute a Java program. Many professional programmers prefer to use the Java SDK and a text editor.

After downloading the Java 2 SDK, open your favorite text editor. If you don't have one, you can download one such as TextPad (http://www.textpad.com) or JEdit (http://jedit.org). To make it easier to use, you may wish to customize the text editor's settings to set tabs for indenting your code, determine the display of line numbers, and set font colors. Customizing your editor is usually done by choosing from a Configure menu.

It is always a good practice to keep all classes for one program in a separate folder. As you write each class, save the class with a `.java` extension in the proper folder. To compile and run the program, open a command prompt window or DOS window. Keep both your text editor and your command shell window open at all times.

Overview of Writing, Compiling, and Running a Java program
Navigate to change your current directory to the directory where your program (`.java` file) is located. To compile the code, execute the `javac` command in the command shell window.

```
javac MyProg.java
```

If the compilation is successful, then the file `MyProg.class` is created (possibly with other `.class` files).

You must compile all `.java` files that are included in your program. You can do this by using the wild card symbol when compiling:

```
javac *.java
```

To execute the program, issue the command

```
java ClassName
```

from the command shell window. You should execute the file containing the `main` method.

Comments

- Knowing the SDK tool set is essential for understanding what an IDE does "under the hood."
- More detailed directions for downloading and using the SDK and a text editor are found at: http://horstmann.com/bigj/help/sdk/index.html.
- To extract `javadoc` comments from your source code, from the command shell window change to the directory that contains the program code. Then issue the command

```
javadoc *.java
```

The `javadoc` program generates the HTML documentation files for all classes in the current directory.

19.3   Common Integrated Development Environments

A common question among Java students and teachers is, "What IDE is best?" There is not one correct answer to that question. The IDE you choose should be easy, fast, and it should run on the computer(s) that you will be using. This chapter introduces a few of the more popular IDEs used in high schools and by first-year computer science college students. It will be in your best interest to use the same environment on your home computer as you are using in school (if possible). This way, you do not need to learn more than one environment. Your Java programs, however, will run without modification using different IDEs. More complete instructions for many of these IDEs can be found at http://horstmann.com/bigj/help/.

19.3.1   BlueJ

BlueJ provides a free environment for the Java language that emphasizes visualization and object-oriented programming. It is an interactive environment that is easy to use and facilitates the understanding of basic object-oriented principles. You can use BlueJ to run any Java programs, but to make the best use of the environment, it is better if you reorganize your programs so that you create objects through the environment instead of including a `main` method.

BlueJ Requirements

BlueJ can be installed on any machine that has the Java 2 SDK version 1.3 or higher. You should have the SDK installed before installing BlueJ. On MacOS X, the SDK is installed by default and you do not need to install it. BlueJ is written in Java and runs on any platform with a Java 2 runtime, such as Linux, Solaris, Windows, or Mac OS X.

BlueJ Installation Instructions

The BlueJ download is free and available at http://www.bluej.org/.
- Choose the Download option.
- Choose the file to download according to the system you will be using.

After downloading the appropriate file to your computer, double click the file name and follow the setup directions. Make sure you answer the questions about the location of J2SE 1.4.1 correctly.

Overview of Writing, Compiling, and Running a Java Program in BlueJ

BlueJ programs do not have (or need) a `public static void main`. You first create a new project. To do this, use the **Project → New Project** menu command. After you have answered the questions about your project location, you can create a new class by clicking on the **New Class** button. Again, you will be asked for the name of your class. After answering the questions, your class is visually displayed. Double click on the class picture to enter code. You can compile the program in edit mode or in visual mode by choosing **Compile**. If your class has diagonal lines through it, it needs to be compiled. To instantiate an object belonging to this class, right click the mouse and choose a constructor. The object (a red representation of the object) appears. Right-click the object to see the available methods for the object. BlueJ allows for easy incremental testing of your classes.

Comments

- Detailed instructions for running BlueJ can be found at http://horstmann.com/bigj/help/bluej/index.html.
- A tutorial for BlueJ is available at http://www.bluej.org/doc/documentation.html.
- In BlueJ, you should have a subdirectory for each program. Simply make a new subdirectory every time you write or test a new program, and copy the source files (all of the `.java` files) that you want into that directory.
- Hints for setting up the Java Marine Biology Simulation Case Study with BlueJ can be found at http://www.bluej.org/help/ap.html.
- If your Java file code includes `javadoc` comments, when the code window is open, choose **interface** (in the **implementation/interface** pull down menu at the top of the screen) to view the `javadoc` pages.

19.3.2 Eclipse

Eclipse is a free open-source Java environment available from http://eclipse.org. Eclipse is a Java program, but it uses a custom user interface toolkit that does not run on all platforms that support Java 2. Eclipse supports tools to manipulate HTML, Java, C, JSP, EJB, XML, and GIF.

Eclipse Requirements

Eclipse requires a Java 2 runtime, so you need to install the Java 2 SDK first before installing Eclipse. Eclipse supports a number of platforms including Windows, Linux, and Mac OSX (requires OSX 10.2 Jaguar). Check http://eclipse.org for currently supported platforms.

Eclipse Installation Instructions

You can download Eclipse at http://www.eclipse.org/downloads/index.php.

Once downloaded, it is a good idea to set preferences for your editor. These can be found in the **Window → Preferences** menu. Select **Java → Appearance → Code Formatter** from the tree in the left panel. Click on the **Style** tab to change your tab setting to 3.

Overview of Writing, Compiling, and Running a Java Program in Eclipse

If you already have your program in a Java file (or a directory containing multiple Java files), then you need to make a project that contains the file. **Select File → New → Project** from the menu. Select the **Java** option and click on the **Next** button. Give the name and full path directory information. Click **Finish**. Select **File → Save**. To compile a program in Eclipse, select the project in the pane on the left-hand side. Then select **Project** → **Rebuild Project** from the menu. To run a program, select the **Run** → **Run as ...** → **Java Application** menu option.

If you write a program from scratch, then you can start your work in Eclipse. It is always best to place each of your programs into a separate directory. Eclipse will create the directory for you. Select **File** → **New** → **Project** from the menu. You will get the **New Project** dialog. Select the **Java** option and click on the **Next** button. In the following dialog, give a name to the project. A good choice for the name is the directory that contains the files. Then uncheck the **Use** default box, and provide the full path of the directory that contains the files. Click on the **Finish** button. Now locate the name of your new project in the left hand panel. Right-click on it. Select **New** → **Class** from the menu. Supply the name of the class. If you want a `main` method for this class, check the box `public static void main(String[] args)`. Enter and save your file(s).

To compile your program, select **Project** → **Rebuild Project** from the menu. If there are no errors, select the **Run** → **Run as ...** → **Java Application** menu option. The program runs.

Comments

- You may enjoy the "method completion" feature of Eclipse. If you type the name of an object and then wait for a short time, a dialog shows all possible methods, together with their comments. Just pick the one you want from the list.
- To generate `javadoc` comments, select **Project** → **Generate Javadoc** from the menu. You will get a dialog. Make sure that the destination directory is correct. Click on **Finish**.
- More detailed instructions on downloading and using Eclipse are found at: http://horstmann.com/bigj/help/eclipse/index.html.

19.3.3   JCreator

JCreator™ is a trademark of Xinox Software. JCreator is an IDE that provides a project management system, project templates, a debugger interface, an editor with syntax highlighting, and many other options. Since it is written in C++, the compiler is fast. The IDE is easy to use. There are two versions of JCreator. JCreator Learning Edition (LE) is freeware. JCreator Pro has a few additional features and is not free. Information on the differences between the two versions and downloading JCreator can be found at http://www.jcreator.com/.

JCreator Requirements

The current minimum system requirement for JCreator is Microsoft Windows 95, 98, ME, XP, NT4 or 2000.

JCreator Installation Instructions

Download JCreatorLE v2.50 from http://www.jcreator.com.
- Choose to download JCreatorv2.5 (freeware).
- Accept all default options during download.
- During SETUP, JCreator should find the correct home directory for the Java 2 SDK. It should be c:\j2sdk1.4.1_xx.
- You must browse to give it the documentation home directory: It should be: c:\j2sdk1.4.1_xx\docs

- JCreator should open automatically.
- To configure JCreator: choose **Configure → Options**. Expand the **Editor** options on the left and choose **Java** and the following settings: Insert spaces (choose 3), AutoIndent brackets ANSI style, Auto end of line, Compatibility (check all). Choose **Directories** (on left) and for the Default Project Directory, browse to choose the directory in which you want to save your JCreator work.

Overview of Writing, Compiling, and Running a Java Program in JCreator

JCreator has a workspace organization. It is a good practice to create a new workspace for each chapter in your text and then create a new project for each problem. That way, you will be able to find your programs quickly.

Choose **File → New → Workspace → Empty Workspace**. Give your workspace a name (`Chapter1WS`). Choose **File → New → Project → Empty Project**. Give your project a name (`HelloProject`). Choose **File → New → File → Java File.** Give your file a name (It must be the same name as the class name). Write your Java file code. **File → Save All** often!

To compile, choose **Build → Compile Project.** To run your compiled program, choose **Build → Execute project.**

Comments

- To generate `javadoc` comments, choose **Configure → Options**. Choose **Tools**. Click on the **New** button. Choose **Program**. Browse to C:\j2sdk1.4.1\bin directory (or wherever the bin directory for java resides). Choose `javadoc.exe`. From the list on the left, click on `javdoc` under **Tools**.
  - For Arguments, choose **Java Project Files**.
  - For initial directory, choose **project directory**.
  - Under Tool Options, check **Close Console on exit**.
  To run your newly created `javadoc` tool, on the **Tools** menu, choose `javadoc`, click on the first wrench picture, or type Ctrl-1.
- More detailed information on installing and using JCreator can be found at: http://horstmann.com/bigj/help/jcreator/index.html.

19.3.4 JJ

JJ is a Java educational system that runs online. With either a personal JJ account or a student JJ account setup by the teacher, anyone can learn Java from any browser. Lessons, presentations, labs, references, and much more are immediately accessible to you.

JJ Installation Instructions

There is no installation with JJ. Your school can register to use JJ at http://www.psvm.org or www.LearnJavaNow.com. For the complete JJ package, there is a cost. The cost varies for school accounts based on the number of student accounts created for the school. JJ is also available for an individual subscription industry user.

JJ Requirements

You need a browser to use JJ! The JJ system itself runs online.

Overview of Writing, Compiling, and Running a Java Program in JJ

You can try JJ without having a JJ account by starting at JJ's partner's page: http://www.psvm.com/partners.html. If you have a JJ account, you login and JJ will maintain a folder with all your Java programs. You can logoff and log back in from any computer (from anywhere) and you have immediate access to all of your homework, assignments, programs, submitted solutions, and teacher's comments. Once in JJ from either a partner's visit or your own JJ account, there are three buttons to press:

1. **CheckIt** (compile)
2. **RunIt** (execute)
3. **Start**

If your program uses input/output, press the **Start** button again to run a different set of tests so that your teacher can see the input and output for your chosen test data as well as your Java program code.

Comments

- JJ is a Java educational system that runs online. No downloading is necessary. Beginners avoid start-up frustrations because there is no need to install software. You run your program online.
- You submit your work (with test cases) to be graded online.

19.3.5   MetroWerks CodeWarrior

CodeWarrior is a multi-language, multi-platform IDE. The CodeWarrior Learning Edition supports C, C++, and Java on Windows and Mac OS X. CodeWarrior includes a *project manager* to manage your files and multiple projects, an e*ditor* to write and edit your code, a *compiler and linker* to turn your newly written code into an application, and a *debugger* to test your program and locate errors. The Development Tools for Mac OS and Windows, Learning Edition have been specifically developed to be used by AP Computer Science teachers and students. The Learning Edition is significantly less expensive than the professional edition.

CodeWarrior Requirements

For Windows: Microsoft Windows 98/ME/2000/XP, or Windows NT 4.0 with Service Pack 6a or later, 66 MHz Pentium II class or higher or AMD-K6™ processor or higher, 128 MB of RAM, 850 MB for full installation, CD-ROM drive for installation.

For Mac OS X: Mac OS X v.10.1.3 or greater, G3 processor or higher (G4 recommended), 128 MB of RAM, 900 MB for full installation, CD-ROM drive for installation.

CodeWarrior Installation Instructions

Install CodeWarrior software from the CodeWarrior Learning Edition CD. Follow the on-screen instructions.

Overview of Writing, Compiling, and Running a Java Program in CodeWarrior

Choose **File → New → Java J2SE Stationery**. Enter the name of your project and set the location (navigate to the directory where you want the project to reside). Metrowerks will create a separate folder for the new project. Click **OK** once you've set the location.

A **Project Stationery** menu is now presented. Expand the group by clicking the + sign. Select **Java Application** and click **OK**.

In the project window is a folder called **Sources**. Click the + sign to see what source files are present. There should be only one: `TrivialApplication.java` (the default source file for any new project). **Edit → Remove** and add your own Java source files to the project.

To compile and run a program, make sure the **MyApplication.mcp** window is active and select **Run** from the **Project** menu.

If the program compiles correctly, it will be automatically run. If there are syntax errors in any files in the program, they will be noted.

To create and edit a new Java file, choose **File → New → File → Text File**. Name the file (it should have the same name as the class name and end in `.java`). Write your code in the resulting window and **Save**. Once saved, add the file to your project by choosing **Project → Add FileName.java**.

Specify the `main` class name by choosing **Edit → JavaApplication Release Settings**. Click **Java Target**. Enter the correct name of the class containing `main`. Click **Apply**.

Comments

- You do not need to download Java SDK from the Sun Web site. Metrowerks CodeWarrior provides everything that you need.
- Metrowerks has developed their own AP Resource Center, a web-delivered collection of materials that can be used in conjunction with your textbook and this guide.
- The latest version of CodeWarrior Learning Edition includes the final AP CS libraries and Java Marine Biology Simulation Case Study.
- The latest version also includes a voice-over multimedia tutorial that walks the user through the CodeWarrior IDE.
- More detailed instructions on downloading and using Metrowerks CodeWarrior are found at: http://horstmann.com/bigj/help/metrowerks/index.html.

19.3.6 NetBeans

NetBeans is a free open-source Java environment available from http://netbeans.org with no restrictions on how it can be used. The NetBeans IDE is a development environment that allows you to write, compile, debug, and deploy your programs. NetBeans is written in Java but supports other languages and technologies including C++, XML, HTML, Java Server Pages, and more. NetBeans is a complex program with many options for professional programmers. You can safely ignore most of the options if you use NetBeans only to compile and run simple Java programs.

NetBeans Requirements

NetBeans is a pure Java program that runs on all platforms that support Java 2 such as Linux, Solaris, Windows, or Mac OS X. NetBeans requires a Java 2 runtime, so you need to install the Java 2 SDK before installing NetBeans.

NetBeans Installation Instructions

The NetBeans download is free and available at http://netbeans.org.
- Choose the Download option.
- Choose the file to download according to the system you will be using.
- After downloading the appropriate file to your computer, double click the file name and follow the setup directions. Using the default directories is usually the easiest.

Overview of Writing, Compiling, and Running a Java Program in NetBeans

When you start NetBeans, a startup screen appears, and the program spends some time loading various modules. To load an already existing program, use the **File → Open File** menu command.

If you write a program from scratch, it is always best to place each of your programs into a separate directory. Select the **File → New menu** command. Now select **Empty** and click on **Next**. Name the class and select the appropriate directory in the "Filesystems" tree. Click **Finish**. Finally, you get an editor window into which you can type your program.

To compile a program in NetBeans, select **Build → Compile** from the menu. After your program compiles successfully, select the **Build → Execute** menu option.

Comments
- It is always best to place each of your programs into a separate directory.
- In NetBeans, it is very easy to load programs that you created in some other way, without having to fuss with projects.
- More detailed instructions on downloading and using NetBeans can be found at http://horstmann.com/bigj/help/netbeans/index.html.

APPENDIX A

Advanced Data Structures and Algorithms

Chapter 20

Advanced Data Structures

CHAPTER GOALS

- ▶ To learn about the set and map data types
- ▶ To understand the implementation of hash tables
- ▶ To be able to program hash functions
- ▶ To learn about binary trees
- ▶ To be able to use tree sets and tree maps

In this chapter we study data structures that are more complex than arrays or lists. These data structures take control of organizing their elements, rather than keeping them in a fixed position. In return, they can offer better performance for adding, removing, and finding elements.

You will learn about the abstract set and map data types and the implementations that the standard library offers for these abstract types. You will see how two completely different implementations—hash tables and trees—can be used to implement these abstract types efficiently.

20.1 Sets

In the preceding chapter you encountered two important data structures: arrays and lists. Both have one characteristic in common: These data structures keep the elements in the same order in which you inserted them. However, in many applications, you don't really care about the order of the elements in a collection. For example, a server may keep a collection of objects representing available printers (see Figure 1). The order of the objects doesn't really matter.

> A set is an unordered collection of distinct elements. Elements can be added, located, and removed.

In mathematics, such an unordered collection is called a *set*. You have probably learned some set theory in a course in mathematics, and you may know that sets are a fundamental mathematical notion.

But what does that mean for data structures? If the data structure is no longer responsible for remembering the order of element insertion, can it give us better performance for some of its operations? It turns out that it can indeed, as you will see later in this chapter.

Let's list the fundamental operations on a set:

- Adding an element
- Removing an element
- Containment testing (does the set contain a given object?)
- Listing all elements (in arbitrary order)

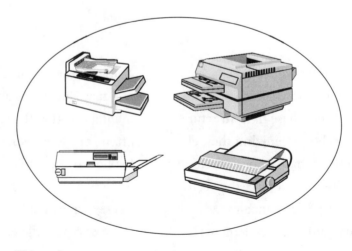

Figure 1

A Set of Printers

> Sets don't have duplicates. Adding a duplicate of an element that is already present is silently ignored.

In mathematics, a set rejects duplicates. If an object is already in the set, an attempt to add it again is ignored. That's useful in many programming situations as well. For example, if we keep a set of available printers, each printer should occur at most once in the set. Thus, we will interpret the **add** and **remove** operations of sets just as we do in mathematics: Adding an element has no effect if the element is already in the set, and attempting to remove an element that isn't in the set is silently ignored.

Of course, we could use a linked list to implement a set. But adding, removing, and containment testing would be relatively slow, because they all have to do a linear search through the list. (Adding requires a search through the list to make sure that we don't add a duplicate.) As you will see later in this chapter, there are data structures that can handle these operations much more quickly.

> Both the HashSet and TreeSet classes realize the Set interface.

In fact, there are two different data structures for that purpose, called *hash tables* and *trees*. The standard Java library provides set implementations based on both data structures, called **HashSet** and **TreeSet**. Both of these data structures realize the **Set** interface (see Figure 2).

You will see later in this chapter when it is better to choose a hash set or a tree set. For now, let's look at an example where we choose a hash set. To keep the example simple, we'll just store strings, not **Printer** objects.

```
Set names = new HashSet();
```

Note that we store the reference to the **HashSet** object in a **Set** variable. After you construct the collection object, it no longer matters what kind of set implementation it is; only the interface is important.

Adding and removing set elements is straightforward:

```
names.add("Romeo");
names.remove("Juliet");
```

The **contains** method tests whether an element is contained in the set:

```
if (names.contains("Juliet")) ...
```

> Use an iterator to list all elements in a set.

Finally, to list all elements in the set, you get an iterator. As with list iterators, you use the **next** and **hasNext** methods to step through the set.

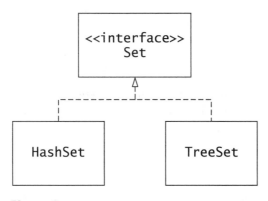

Figure 2

Set Classes and Interfaces in the Standard Library

```
Iterator iter = names.iterator();
    while (iter.hasNext())
    {
        String name = (String)iter.next();
        do something with name
    }
```

> A set iterator does not visit the elements in the order in which you inserted them. The set implementation rearranges the elements so that it can locate them quickly.

Note that the elements are *not* visited in the order in which you inserted them. Instead, they are visited in the order in which the HashSet keeps them for rapid execution of its methods.

There is an important difference between the `Iterator` that you obtain from a set and the `ListIterator` that a list yields. The `ListIterator` has an `add` method to add an element at the list iterator position. The `Iterator` interface has no such method. It makes no sense to add an element at a particular position in a set, because the set can order the elements any way it likes. Thus, you always add elements directly to a set, never to an iterator of the set.

> You cannot add an element to a set at an iterator position.

However, you can remove a set element at an iterator position, just as you do with list iterators.

Also, the `Iterator` interface has no `previous` method to go backwards through the elements. Since the elements are not ordered, it is not meaningful to distinguish between "going forward" and "going backward".

The following test program lets you add and remove elements from a set. After each command, it prints out the current contents of the set. When you run this program, try adding strings that are already contained in the set and removing strings that aren't present in the set.

File SetTest.java

```
1  import java.util.HashSet;
2  import java.util.Iterator;
3  import java.util.Set;
4  import javax.swing.JOptionPane;
5
6  /**
7      This program demonstrates a set of strings. The user
8      can add and remove strings.
9  */
10 public class SetTest
11 {
12     public static void main(String[] args)
13     {
14         Set names = new HashSet();
15
16         boolean done = false;
17         while (!done)
18         {
19             String input = JOptionPane.showInputDialog(
20                 "Add name, Cancel when done");
21             if (input == null)
22                 done = true;
23             else
24             {
25                 names.add(input);
26                 print(names);
27             }
28         }
```

```
29
30          done = false;
31          while (!done)
32          {
33             String input = JOptionPane.showInputDialog(
34                "Remove name, Cancel when done");
35             if (input == null)
36                done = true;
37             else
38             {
39                names.remove(input);
40                print(names);
41             }
42          }
43          System.exit(0);
44       }
45
46       /**
47          Prints the contents of a set.
48          @param s a set
49       */
50       private static void print(Set s)
51       {
52          Iterator iter = s.iterator();
53          System.out.print("{ ");
54          while (iter.hasNext())
55          {
56             System.out.print(iter.next());
57             System.out.print(" ");
58          }
59          System.out.println("}");
60       }
61    }
```

Quality Tip 20.1

Use Interface References to Manipulate Data Structures

It is considered good style to store a reference to a HashSet or TreeSet in a variable of type Set.

```
Set names = new HashSet();
```

That way, you have to change only one line if you decide to use a TreeSet instead.

Also, methods that operate on sets should specify parameters of type Set:

```
public static void print(Set s)
```

Then the method can be used for all set implementations.

In theory, we should make the same recommendation for linked lists, namely to save LinkedList references in variables of type List. However, in the Java library, the List interface is common to both the ArrayList and the LinkedList class. In particular, it has get and set methods for random access, even though these methods are very inefficient for linked lists. You can't write efficient code if you don't know whether random access is efficient or not. This is plainly a serious design error in the standard library, and I

▼ cannot recommend using the List interface for that reason. (To see just how embarrassing that error is, have a look at the source code for the binarySearch method of the

▼ Collections class. That method takes a List parameter, but binary search makes no sense for a linked list. The code then clumsily tries to discover whether the list is a linked list, and then switches to a linear search!)

▼ The Set interface and the Map interface, which you will see in the next section, are well-designed, and you should use them.

20.2 Maps

> A map keeps associations between key and value objects.

A map is a data type that keeps associations between *keys and values*. Figure 3 gives a typical example: a map that associates names with colors. This map might describe the favorite colors of various people.

Mathematically speaking, a map is a function from one set, the *key set*, to another set, the *value set*. Every key in the map has a unique value, but a value may be associated with several keys.

> Both the HashMap and TreeMap classes realize the Map interface.

Just as there are two kinds of set implementations, the Java library has two implementations for maps: HashMap and TreeMap. Both of them realize the Map interface (see Figure 4).

After constructing a HashMap or TreeMap, you should store the reference to the map object in a Map reference:

```
Map favoriteColors = new HashMap();
```

Use the put method to add an association:

```
favoriteColors.put("Juliet", Color.pink);
```

You can change the value of an existing association, simply by calling put again:

```
favoriteColors.put("Juliet", Color.red);
```

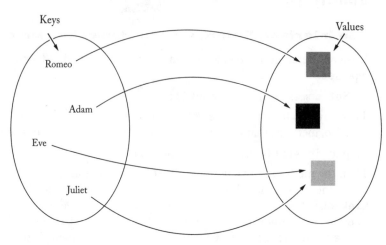

Figure 3

A Map

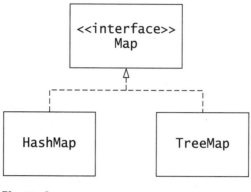

Figure 4

Map Classes and Interfaces in the Standard Library

The `get` method returns the value associated with a key.

```
Color julietsFavoriteColor =
   favoriteColors.get("Juliet");
```

If you ask for a key that isn't associated with any values, then the `get` method returns `null`.

To remove a key and its associated value, use the `remove` method:

```
favoriteColors.remove("Juliet");
```

> To find all keys and values in a map, iterate through the key set and find the values that correspond to the keys.

Sometimes you want to enumerate all keys in a map. The `keySet` method yields the set of keys. You can then ask the key set for an iterator and get all keys. From each key, you can find the associated value with the `get` method. Thus, the following instructions print all key/value pairs in a map m:

```
Set keySet = m.keySet();
Iterator iter = keySet.iterator();
while (iter.hasNext())
{
   Object key = iter.next();
   Object value = m.get(key);
   System.out.println(key + "->" + value);
}
```

The sample program at the end of this section shows a map in action.

File MapTest.java

```
1  import java.awt.Color;
2  import java.util.HashMap;
3  import java.util.Iterator;
4  import java.util.Map;
5  import java.util.Set;
6
7  /**
8     This program tests a map that maps names to colors.
9  */
10 public class MapTest
```

```
11  {
12      public static void main(String[] args)
13      {
14
15          Map favoriteColors = new HashMap();
16          favoriteColors.put("Juliet", Color.pink);
17          favoriteColors.put("Romeo", Color.green);
18          favoriteColors.put("Adam", Color.blue);
19          favoriteColors.put("Eve", Color.pink);
20          print(favoriteColors);
21      }
22
23      /**
24          Prints the contents of a map.
25          @param m a map
26      */
27      private static void print(Map m)
28      {
29          Set keySet = m.keySet();
30          Iterator iter = keySet.iterator();
31          while (iter.hasNext())
32          {
33              Object key = iter.next();
34              Object value = m.get(key);
35              System.out.println(key + "->" + value);
36          }
37      }
38  }
```

20.3   Hash Tables

In this section, you will see how the technique of *hashing* can be used to find elements in a data structure quickly, without making a linear search through all elements. Hashing gives rise to the *hash table*, which can be used to implement sets and maps.

> A hash function computes an integer value from an object.

A *hash function* is a function that computes an integer value, the *hash code*, from an object, in such a way that different objects are likely to yield different hash codes. The Object class has a hashCode method that other classes need to redefine. The call

```
int h = x.hashCode();
```

computes the hash code of the object x.

> A good hash function minimizes *collisions*, identical hash codes for different objects.

It is possible that two or more distinct objects have the same hash code. That is called a *collision*. A good hash function minimizes collisions. For example, the String class defines a hash function for strings that does a good job of producing different integer values for different strings. Table 1 shows some examples of strings and their hash codes.

You will see in Section 20.4 how these values are obtained.

Section 20.4 explains how you should redefine the hashCode method for other classes.

A hash code is used as an array index into a hash table. In the simplest implementation of a hash table, you could make an array and insert each object at the location of its hash code (see Figure 5).

String	Hash Code
"Adam"	2035631
"Eve"	70069
"Harry"	69496448
"Jim"	74478
"Joe"	74656
"Juliet"	−2065036585
"Katherine"	2079199209
"Sue"	83491

Table 1

Sample Strings and Their Hash Codes

Then it is a very simple matter to find out whether an object is already present in the set or not. Compute its hash code and check whether the array position with that hash code is already occupied. This doesn't require a search through the entire array!

However, there are two problems with this simplistic approach. First, it is not possible to allocate an array that is large enough to hold all possible integer index positions. Therefore, we must pick an array of some reasonable size and then reduce the hash code to fall inside the array:

```
int h = x.hashCode();
if (h < 0) h = -h;
h = h % size;
```

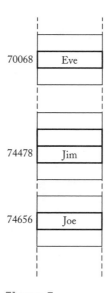

Figure 5

A Simplistic Implementation of a Hash Table

> A hash table can be implemented as an array of *buckets,* sequences of links that hold elements with the same hash code.

Furthermore, it is possible that two different objects have the same hash code. After reducing the hash code modulo a smaller array size, it becomes even more likely that several objects collide and need to share a position in the array.

To store multiple objects in the same array position, we use (short, we hope) link sequences for the elements with the same hash code (see Figure 6). These link sequences are called *buckets.*

Now the algorithm for finding an object x in a hash table is quite simple.

1. Compute the hash code and reduce it modulo the table size. This gives an index h into the hash table.

2. Iterate through the elements of the bucket at position h. For each element of the bucket, check whether it is equal to x.

3. If a match is found among the elements of that bucket, then x is in the set. Otherwise, it is not.

> If there are no or only a few collisions, then adding, locating, and removing hash table elements takes constant or $O(1)$ time.

In the best case, in which there are no collisions, all buckets either are empty or have a single element. Then checking for containment takes constant or $O(1)$ time.

More generally, for this algorithm to be effective, the bucket sizes must be small. If the table only has a few entries, then collisions are unavoidable, and each bucket will get quite full. Then the linear search through a bucket is time-consuming. In the worst case, where all elements end up in the same bucket, a hash table degenerates into a linked list!

> The table size should be a prime number, larger than the expected number of elements.

Therefore, it is recommended to make the table somewhat larger than the number of elements that you expect to insert. Then there is a good chance for avoiding collisions altogether. An excess capacity of about 30 percent is typical. According to some researchers, the hash table size should be chosen to be a prime number to minimize the number of collisions.

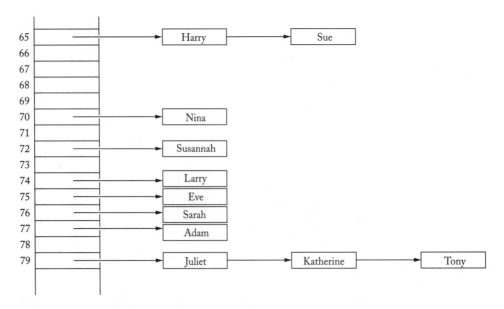

Figure 6

A Hash Table with Linked Lists to Store Elements with the Same Hash Code

Adding an element is a simple extension of the algorithm for finding an object. First compute the hash code to locate the bucket in which the element should be inserted. Try finding the object in that bucket. If it is already present, do nothing. Otherwise, insert it.

Removing an element is equally simple. First compute the hash code to locate the bucket in which the element should be inserted. Try finding the object in that bucket. If it is present, remove it. Otherwise, do nothing.

As long as there are few collisions, an element can also be added or removed in constant or $O(1)$ time.

At the end of this section you will find the code for a simple implementation of a hash set. That implementation takes advantage of the AbstractSet class, which already implements most of the methods of the Set interface.

In this implementation you must specify the size of the hash table. In the standard library, you don't need to supply a table size. If the hash table gets too full, a new table of twice the size is created, and all elements are inserted into the new table.

File HashSet.java

```
1  import java.util.Iterator;
2  import java.util.AbstractSet;
3
4  /**
5      A hash set stores an unordered collection of objects, using
6      a hash table.
7  */
8  public class HashSet extends AbstractSet
9  {
10     /**
11        Constructs a hash table.
12        @param bucketsLength the length of the buckets array
13     */
14     public HashSet(int bucketsLength)
15     {
16        buckets = new Link[bucketsLength];
17        size = 0;
18     }
19
20     /**
21        Tests for set membership.
22        @param x an object
23        @return true if x is an element of this set
24     */
25     public boolean contains(Object x)
26     {
27        int h = x.hashCode();
28        if (h < 0) h = -h;
29        h = h % buckets.length;
30
31        Link current = buckets[h];
32        while (current != null)
33        {
34           if (current.data.equals(x)) return true;
35           current = current.next;
36        }
37        return false;
38     }
39
```

```
40    /**
41        Adds an element to this set.
42        @param x  an object
43        @return true if x is a new object, false if x was
44           already in the set
45    */
46    public boolean add(Object x)
47    {
48       int h = x.hashCode();
49       if (h < 0) h = -h;
50       h = h % buckets.length;
51
52       Link current = buckets[h];
53       while (current != null)
54       {
55          if (current.data.equals(x))
56             return false; // already in the set
57          current = current.next;
58       }
59       Link newLink = new Link();
60       newLink.data = x;
61       newLink.next = buckets[h];
62       buckets[h] = newLink;
63       size++;
64       return true;
65    }
66
67    /**
68        Removes an object from this set.
69        @param x  an object
70        @return true if x was removed from this set, false
71           if x was not an element of this set
72    */
73    public boolean remove(Object x)
74    {
75       int h = x.hashCode();
76       if (h < 0) h = -h;
77       h = h % buckets.length;
78
79       Link current = buckets[h];
80       Link previous = null;
81       while (current != null)
82       {
83          if (current.data.equals(x))
84          {
85             if (previous == null)
86                buckets[h] = current.next;
87             else previous.next = current.next;
88             size--;
89             return true;
90          }
91          previous = current;
92          current = current.next;
93       }
94       return false;
95    }
96
97    /**
```

```
98          Returns an iterator that traverses the elements of this set.
99          @param a  hash set iterator
100      */
101      public Iterator iterator()
102      {
103          return new HashSetIterator();
104      }
105
106      /**
107          Gets the number of elements in this set.
108          @return  the number of elements
109      */
110      public int size()
111      {
112          return size;
113      }
114
115      private Link[] buckets;
116      private int size;
117
118      private class Link
119      {
120          public Object data;
121          public Link next;
122      }
123
124      private class HashSetIterator implements Iterator
125      {
126
127          /**
128              Constructs a hash set iterator that points to the
129              first element of the hash set.
130          */
131          public HashSetIterator()
132          {
133              bucket = 0;
134              previous = null;
135              previousBucket = buckets.length;
136
137              // set bucket to the index of the first nonempty bucket
138              while (bucket < buckets.length
139                      && buckets[bucket] == null)
140                  bucket++;
141              if (bucket < buckets.length)
142                  current = buckets[bucket];
143              else current = null;
144          }
145
146          public boolean hasNext()
147          {
148              return current != null;
149          }
150
151          public Object next()
152          {
153              Object r = current.data;
154
155              if (current.next == null) // move to next bucket
```

```
156                 {
157                     previousBucket = bucket;
158                     bucket++;
159
160                     while (bucket < buckets.length
161                             && buckets[bucket] == null)
162                         bucket++;
163                     if (bucket < buckets.length)
164                         current = buckets[bucket];
165                     else
166                         current = null;
167                 }
168                 else // move to next element in bucket
169                 {
170                     previous = current;
171                     current = current.next;
172                 }
173
174                 return r;
175             }
176
177             public void remove()
178             {
179                 if (previous != null)
180                     previous.next = previous.next.next;
181                 else if (previousBucket < buckets.length)
182                     buckets[previousBucket] = null;
183                 else
184                     throw new IllegalStateException();
185                 previous = null;
186                 previousBucket = buckets.length;
187             }
188
189             private int bucket;
190             private Link current;
191             private int previousBucket;
192             private Link previous;
193         }
194 }
```

File SetTest.java

```
1  import java.util.Iterator;
2  import java.util.Set;
3
4  /**
5      This program tests the hash set class.
6  */
7  public class SetTest
8  {
9      public static void main(String[] args)
10     {
11         Set names = new HashSet(101); // 101 is a prime
12
13         names.add("Sue");
14         names.add("Harry");
15         names.add("Nina");
```

```
16        names.add("Susannah");
17        names.add("Larry");
18        names.add("Eve");
19        names.add("Sarah");
20        names.add("Adam");
21        names.add("Tony");
22        names.add("Katherine");
23        names.add("Juliet");
24        names.add("Romeo");
25        names.remove("Romeo");
26        names.remove("George");
27
28        Iterator iter = names.iterator();
29        while (iter.hasNext())
30            System.out.println(iter.next());
31    }
32 }
```

20.4 Computing Hash Codes

A hash function computes an integer hash code from an object, so that different objects are likely to have different hash codes. Let us first look at how you can compute a hash code from a string. Clearly, you need to combine the character values of the string to yield some integer. You could, for example, add up the character values:

```
int h = 0;
for (int i = 0; i < s.length(); i++)
   h = h + s.charAt(i);
```

However, that would not be a good idea. It doesn't scramble the character values enough. Strings that are permutations of another (such as "eat" and "tea") all have the same hash code.

Here is the method that the standard library uses to compute the hash code for a string.

```
final int HASH_MULTIPLIER = 31;
int h = 0;
for (int i = 0; i < s.length(); i++)
   h = HASH_MULTIPLIER * h + s.charAt(i);
```

For example, the hash code of "eat" is

$$31 * (31 * 'e' + 'a') + 't' = 100184$$

The hash code of "tea" is quite different, namely

$$31 * (31 * 't' + 'e') + 'a' = 114704$$

> Define hashCode methods for your own classes by combining the hash codes for the instance variables.

(Use a Unicode table to look up the character values: 'a' is 97, 'e' is 101, and 't' is 116.)

For your own classes, you should make up a hash code that combines the hash codes of the instance fields in a similar way. For example, let us define a hashCode method for the Coin class. There are two instance fields: the coin name and the coin value. First, compute their hash code. You know how to compute the hash code of a string. To compute the hash code of a floating-point number, first wrap the floating-point number into a Double object, and then compute its hash code.

```
class Coin
{
   public int hashCode()
   {
      int h1 = name.hashCode();
      int h2 = new Double(value).hashCode();
      ...
   }
}
```

Then combine the two hash codes.

```
final int HASH_MULTIPLIER = 29;
int h = HASH_MULTIPLIER * h1 + h2;
return h;
```

Use a prime number as the hash multiplier—it scrambles the values better.

If you have more than two instance fields, then combine their hash codes as follows:

```
int h = HASH_MULTIPLIER * h1 + h2;
h = HASH_MULTIPLIER * h + h3;
h = HASH_MULTIPLIER * h + h4;

...

return h;
```

> Your hashCode method must be compatible with the equals method.

If one of the instance fields is an integer, just use the field value as its hash code.

When you add objects of your class into a hash table, you need to double-check that it is *compatible* with the equals method of your class. Two objects that are equal must yield the same hash code:

```
If x.equals(y), then x.hashCode() == y.hashCode()
```

After all, if x and y are equal to another, then you don't want to insert both of them into a set—sets don't store duplicates. But if their hash codes are different, x and y may end up in different buckets, and the add method would never notice that they are actually duplicates.

Of course, the converse of the compatibility condition is generally not true. It is possible for two objects to have the same hash code without being equal.

For the Coin class, the compatibility condition holds. We define two coins to be equal to another if their names and values are equal. In that case, their hash codes will also be equal, because the hash code is computed from the hash codes of the name and value fields.

You get into trouble if your class defines an equals method but not a hashCode method. Suppose we forget to define a hashCode method for the Coin class. Then it inherits the hash code method from the Object superclass. That method computes a hash code from the *memory location* of the object. The effect is that any two objects are very likely to have a different hash code.

```
Coin coin1 = new Coin(0.25, "quarter");
Coin coin2 = new Coin(0.25, "quarter");
```

Now coin1.hashCode() is derived from the memory location of coin1, and coin2.hashCode() is derived from the memory location of coin2. Even though coin1.equals(coin2) is true, their hash codes differ.

However, if you define *neither* equals or hashCode, then there is no problem. The equals method of the Object class considers two objects equal only if their memory location is the same. That is, the Object class has compatible equals and hashCode methods. Of course, then the notion of equality is very restricted: Only identical objects are considered equal. That is not necessarily a bad notion of equality: If you want to collect a set of coins in a purse, you may not want to lump coins of equal value together.

Whenever you use a hash set, you need to make sure that an appropriate hash function exists for the type of the objects that you add to the set. Check the `equals` method of your class. It tells you when two objects are considered equal. There are two possibilities. Either `equals` hasn't been defined or it has been. If `equals` has not been defined, only identical objects are considered equal. In that case, don't define `hashCode` either. However, if the `equals` method has been defined, look at its implementation. Typically, two objects are considered equal if some or all of the instance fields are equal. Sometimes, not all instance fields are used in the comparison. Two `Student` objects may be considered equal if their `studentID` fields are equal. Define the `hashCode` method to combine the hash codes of the fields that are compared in the `equals` method.

> In a hash map, only the keys are hashed.

When you use a `HashMap`, only the keys are hashed. They need compatible `hashCode` and `equals` methods. The values are never hashed or compared. The reason is simple—the map only needs to find, add, and remove keys quickly.

What can you do if the objects of your class have `equals` and `hashCode` methods defined that don't work for your situation, or if you don't want to bother defining an appropriate `hashCode` method? Maybe you can use a `TreeSet` or `TreeMap` instead. Trees are the subject of the next section.

File Coin.java

```java
1  /**
2      A coin with a monetary value.
3  */
4  public class Coin
5  {
6      /**
7          Constructs a coin.
8          @param aValue  the monetary value of the coin
9          @param aName  the name of the coin
10     */
11     public Coin(double aValue, String aName)
12     {
13         value = aValue;
14         name = aName;
15     }
16
17     /**
18         Gets the coin value.
19         @return  the value
20     */
21     public double getValue()
22     {
23         return value;
24     }
25
26     /**
27         Gets the coin name.
28         @return  the name
29     */
30     public String getName()
31     {
32         return name;
```

```
33      }
34
35      public boolean equals(Object otherObject)
36      {
37         if (otherObject == null) return false;
38         if (getClass() != otherObject.getClass())
39            return false;
40         Coin other = (Coin)otherObject;
41         return (
42            value == other.value
43            && name.equals(other.name));
44      }
45
46      public int hashCode()
47      {
48         int h1 = name.hashCode();
49         int h2 = new Double(value).hashCode();
50         final int HASH_MULTIPLIER = 29;
51         int h = HASH_MULTIPLIER * h1 + h2;
52         return h;
53      }
54
55      public String toString()
56      {
57         return
58            "Coin[value=" + value + ",name=" + name + "]";
59      }
60
61      private double value;
62      private String name;
63   }
```

File HashCodeTest.java

```
1  import java.util.HashSet;
2  import java.util.Iterator;
3  import java.util.Set;
4
5  /**
6     A program to test hash codes of coins.
7  */
8  public class HashCodeTest
9  {
10     public static void main(String[] args)
11     {
12        Coin coin1 = new Coin(0.25, "quarter");
13        Coin coin2 = new Coin(0.25, "quarter");
14        Coin coin3 = new Coin(0.05, "nickel");
15
16        System.out.println("hash code of coin1="
17           + coin1.hashCode());
18        System.out.println("hash code of coin2="
19           + coin2.hashCode());
20        System.out.println("hash code of coin3="
21           + coin3.hashCode());
22
23        Set coins = new HashSet();
```

```
24          coins.add(coin1);
25          coins.add(coin2);
26          coins.add(coin3);
27
28          Iterator iter = coins.iterator();
29          while (iter.hasNext())
30              System.out.println(iter.next());
31      }
32  }
```

▼ ⊗ **Common Error** **20.1**

Forgetting to Define hashCode

When putting elements into a hash table, make sure that the hashCode method is defined. (The only exception is that you don't need to define hashCode if equals isn't defined either, and you consider any two objects of your class different, even if they have matching contents.)

If you forget to implement the hashCode method, then you inherit the hashCode method of the Object class. That method computes a hash code of the memory location of the object. For example, suppose that you do *not* define the hashCode method of the Coin class. Then the following code is likely to fail:

```
Coin coin1 = new Coin(0.25, "quarter");
Set coins = new HashSet();
coins.add(new Coin(0.25, "quarter"));
// the following comparison will probably fail if hashCode not defined
if (coins.contains(new Coin(0.25, "quarter"))
    System.out.println("The set contains a quarter.");
```

The two Coin objects are constructed at different memory locations, so the hashCode method of the Object class will probably compute different hash codes for them. (As always with hash codes, there is a small chance that the hash codes happen to collide.) Then the contains method will inspect the wrong bucket and never find the matching coin.

The remedy is to define a hashCode method in the Coin class.

20.5 Binary Search Trees

A set implementation is allowed to rearrange its elements in any way it chooses so that it can find elements quickly. Suppose a set implementation *sorts* its entries. Then it can use *binary search* to locate elements quickly. Binary search takes $O(\log(n))$ steps, where n is the size of the set. For example, binary search in an array of 1000 elements is able to locate an element in about 10 steps by cutting the size of the search interval in half in each step.

There is just one wrinkle with this idea. We can't use an array to store the elements of a set, because insertion and removal in an array is slow; an $O(n)$ operation.

> A binary tree consists of nodes, each of which has two child nodes.

In this section we will introduce the simplest of many *treelike* data structures that computer scientists have invented to overcome that problem. Binary search trees allow fast insertion and removal of elements, *and* they are specially designed for fast searching.

> All nodes in a binary search tree fulfill the property that the descendants to the left have smaller data values than the node data value, and the descendants to the right have larger data values.

A linked list is a one-dimensional data structure. Every link has a reference to the next link. You can imagine that all links are arranged in line. In contrast, a *binary tree* is made of nodes with *two* references, called the *left* and *right children*. You should visualize it as a tree, except that it is traditional to draw the tree upside down, like a family tree or hierarchy chart (see Figure 7). In a binary tree, every node has at most two children; hence the name *binary*.

Finally, a *binary search tree* is carefully constructed to have the following important property:

- The data values of *all* descendants to the left of *any* node are less than the data value stored in that node, and *all* descendants to the right have greater data values.

The tree in Figure 7 has this property. To verify the binary search property, you must check each node. Consider the node "Juliet". All descendants to the left have data before "Juliet". All descendants on the right have data after "Juliet". Move on to "Eve". There is a single descendant to the left, with data "Adam" before "Eve", and a single descendant to the right, with data "Harry" after "Eve". Check the remaining nodes in the same way.

Figure 8 shows a binary tree that is not a binary search tree. Look carefully—the *root node* passes the test, but its two children do not.

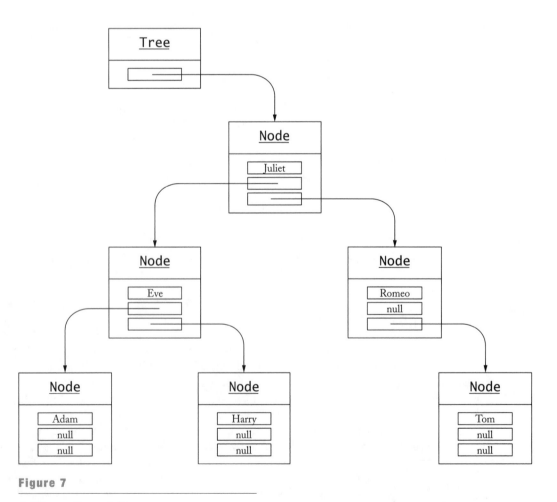

Figure 7

A Binary Search Tree

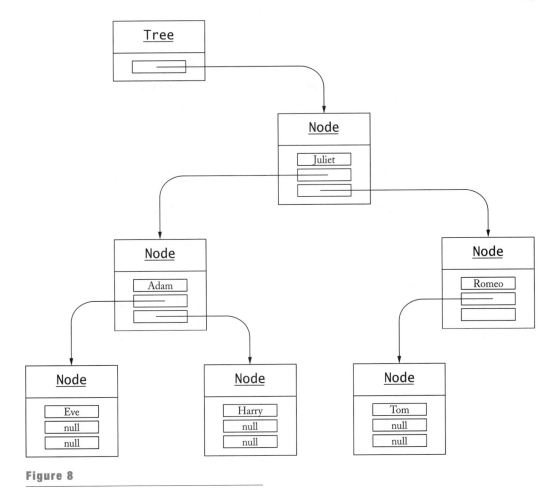

Figure 8

A Binary Tree That Is Not a Binary Search Tree

Let us implement these tree classes. Just as you needed classes for lists and their links, you need one class for the tree, containing a reference to the root node, and a separate class for the nodes. Each node contains two references (to the left and right child nodes) and a data field. At the fringes of the tree, one or two of the child references are `null`. The `data` field has type `Comparable`, not `Object`, because you must be able to compare the values in a binary search tree in order to place them into the correct position.

```
class Tree
{
   public Tree() { ... }
   public void insert(Comparable obj) { ... }
   public void print() { ... }

   private Node root;

   private class Node
   {
      public void insertNode(Node newNode) { ... }
      public void printNodes() { ... }
      public Comparable data;
      public Node left;
      public Node right;
```

```
    }
}
```

To insert data into the tree, use the following algorithm:

- If you encounter a non-null node pointer, look at its data value. If the data value of that node is larger than the one you want to insert, continue the process with the left subtree. If the existing data value is smaller, continue the process with the right subtree.

- If you encounter a null node pointer, replace it with the new node.

For example, consider the tree in Figure 9. We want to insert a new element Romeo into it.

Start with the root, Juliet. Romeo comes after Juliet, so you move to the right subtree. You encounter the node Tom. Romeo comes before Tom, so you move to the left subtree. But there is no left subtree. Hence, you insert a new Romeo node as the left child of Tom (see Figure 10).

You should convince yourself that the resulting tree is still a binary search tree. When Romeo is inserted, it must end up as a right descendant of Juliet–that is what the binary search tree condition means for the root node Juliet. The root node doesn't care where in the right subtree the new node ends up. Moving along to Tom, the right child of Juliet, all it cares about is that the new node Romeo ends up somewhere on its left.

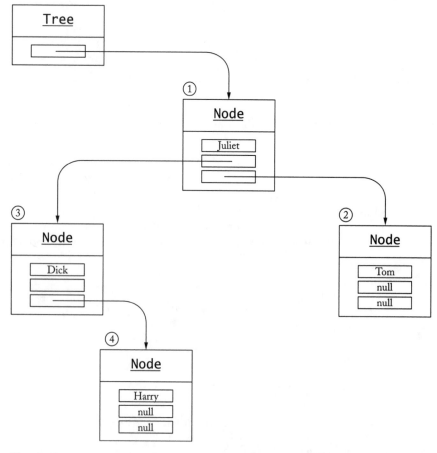

Figure 9

Binary Search Tree after Four Insertions

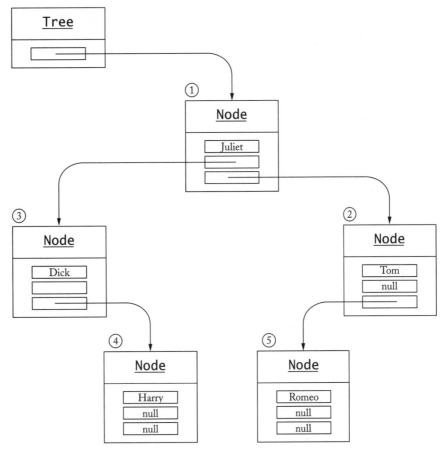

Figure 10

Binary Search Tree after Five Insertions

There is nothing to its left, so `Romeo` becomes the new left child, and the resulting tree is again a binary search tree.

Here is the code for the `insert` method of the `Tree` class:

```
class Tree
{
   ...
   public void insert(Comparable obj)
   {
      Node newNode = new Node();
      newNode.data = obj;
      newNode.left = null;
      newNode.right = null;
      if (root == null) root = newNode;
      else root.insertNode(newNode);
   }
   ...
}
```

If the tree is empty, simply set its root to the new node. Otherwise, you know that the new node must be inserted somewhere within the nodes, and you can ask the root node to perform the insertion. That node object calls the `insertNode` method of the `Node` class, which checks whether the new object is less than the object stored in the node. If so, the element is inserted in the left subtree; if not, it is inserted in the right subtree:

```
private class Node
{
    ...
    public void insertNode(Node newNode)
    {
        if (newNode.data.compareTo(data) < 0)
        {
            if (left == null) left = newNode;
            else left.insertNode(newNode);
        }
        else
        {
            if (right == null) right = newNode;
            else right.insertNode(newNode);
        }
    }
    ...
}
```

Let us trace the calls to `insertNode` when inserting `Romeo` into the tree in Figure 9. The first call to `insertNode` is

```
root.insertNode(newNode)
```

Because `root` points to `Juliet`, compare `Juliet` with `Romeo` and find that you must call

```
root.right.insertNode(newNode)
```

The node `root.right` is Tom. Compare the data values again (`Tom` vs. `Romeo`) and find that you must now move to the left. Since `root.right.left` is `null`, set `root.right.left` to `newNode`, and the insertion is complete (see Figure 10).

Now that the data are inserted in the tree, what can you do with them? It turns out to be surprisingly simple to print all elements in sorted order. You *know* that all data in the left subtree of any node must come before the node and before all data in the right subtree. That is, the following algorithm will print the elements in sorted order:

1. Print the left subtree.
2. Print the data.
3. Print the right subtree.

Let's try this out with the tree in Figure 10. The algorithm tells us to

1. Print the left subtree of `Juliet`; that is, `Dick` and children.
2. Print `Juliet`.
3. Print the right subtree of `Juliet`; that is, `Tom` and children.

How do you print the subtree starting at `Dick`?

1. Print the left subtree of `Dick`. There is nothing to print.
2. Print `Dick`.
3. Print the right subtree of `Dick`, that is, `Harry`.

That is, the left subtree of `Juliet` is printed as

```
Dick
Harry
```

The right subtree of Juliet is the subtree starting at Tom. How is it printed? Again, using the same algorithm:

1. Print the left subtree of Tom, that is, Romeo.
2. Print Tom.
3. Print the right subtree of Tom. There is nothing to print.

Thus, the right subtree of Juliet is printed as

```
Romeo
Tom
```

Now put it all together: the left subtree, Juliet, and the right subtree:

```
Dick
Harry
Juliet
Romeo
Tom
```

The tree is printed in sorted order.

Let us implement the print method. You need a worker method printNodes of the Node class:

```java
private class Node
{
   ...
   public void printNodes()
   {
      if (left != null)
         left.printNodes();
      System.out.println(data);

      if (right != null)
         right.printNodes();
   }
   ...
}
```

To print the entire tree, start this recursive printing process at the root, with the following method of the Tree class.

```java
class Tree
{
   ...
   public void print()
   {
      if (root != null)
         root.printNodes();
   }
   ...
}
```

At the end of this section you will find a complete program to insert data into a tree and to print them out in sorted order.

Unlike a linked list or an array, and like a hash table, a binary tree has no *insert positions*. You cannot select the position where you would like to insert an element into a binary search tree. The data structure is *self-organizing*; that is, each element finds its own place.

Deleting an element from a binary search tree is a little more complicated, because the children of the deleted node must be rearranged. We will leave that topic to a course on data structures. You can find the details in reference [1].

> If a binary search tree is approximately balanced, then adding an element takes $O(\log(n))$ time.

Now that you have implemented this complex data structure, you may well wonder whether it is any good. Like links in a list, nodes are allocated one at a time. No existing elements need to be moved when a new element is inserted in the tree; that is an advantage. How fast insertion is, however, depends on the shape of the tree. If the tree is *balanced*—that is, if each node has approximately as many children on the left as on the right—then insertion is very fast, because about half of the nodes are eliminated in each step. On the other hand, if the tree happens to be *unbalanced*, then insertion can be slow—perhaps as slow as insertion into a linked list. (See Figure 11.)

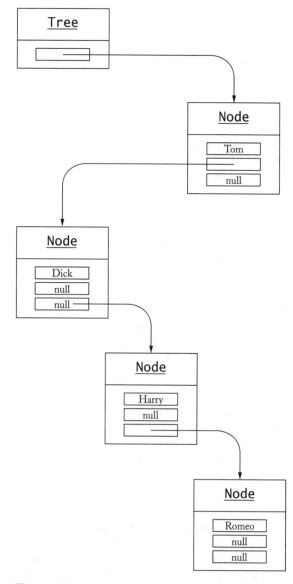

Figure 11

An Unbalanced Binary Search Tree

If new elements are fairly random, the resulting tree is likely to be well balanced. However, if the incoming elements happen to be already in sorted order, then the resulting tree is completely unbalanced. Each new element is inserted at the end, and the entire tree must be traversed every time to find that end!

Binary search trees work well for random data, but if you suspect that the data in your application might be sorted or have long runs of sorted data, you should not use a binary search tree. There are more sophisticated tree structures whose methods keep trees balanced at all times. In these tree structures, one can guarantee that finding, adding, and removing elements takes $O(\log(n))$ time. To learn more about those advanced data structures, you may want to enroll in a course about data structures.

The standard Java library uses *red-black trees*, a special form of balanced binary trees, to implement sets and maps. You will see in the next section what you need to do to use the TreeSet and TreeMap classes. For information on how to implement a red-black tree yourself, see reference [1].

File TreeTest.java

```
1  /**
2       This program tests the binary search tree class.
3  */
4  public class TreeTest
5  {
6     public static void main(String[] args)
7     {
8        Tree names = new Tree();
9        names.insert("Romeo");
10       names.insert("Juliet");
11       names.insert("Tom");
12       names.insert("Dick");
13       names.insert("Harry");
14
15       names.print();
16    }
17 }
```

File Tree.java

```
1  /**
2       This class implements a binary search tree whose
3       nodes hold objects that implement the Comparable
4       interface.
5  */
6  public class Tree
7  {
8     /**
9          Constructs an empty tree.
10    */
11    public Tree()
12    {
13       root = null;
14    }
15
16    /**
17         Inserts a new node into the tree.
18         @param obj  the object to insert
19    */
20    public void insert(Comparable obj)
```

```
21      {
22         Node newNode = new Node();
23         newNode.data = obj;
24         newNode.left = null;
25         newNode.right = null;
26         if (root == null) root = newNode;
27         else root.insertNode(newNode);
28      }
29
30      /**
31         Prints the contents of the tree in sorted order.
32      */
33      public void print()
34      {
35         if (root != null)
36            root.printNodes();
37      }
38
39      private Node root;
40
41      /**
42         A node of a tree stores a data item and references
43         to the child nodes on the left and on the right.
44      */
45      private class Node
46      {
47         /**
48            Inserts a new node as a descendant of this node.
49            @param newNode the node to insert
50         */
51         public void insertNode(Node newNode)
52         {
53            if (newNode.data.compareTo(data) < 0)
54            {
55               if (left == null) left = newNode;
56               else left.insertNode(newNode);
57            }
58            else
59            {
60               if (right == null) right = newNode;
61               else right.insertNode(newNode);
62            }
63         }
64
65         /**
66            Prints this node and all of its descendants
67            in sorted order.
68         */
69         public void printNodes()
70         {
71            if (left != null)
72               left.printNodes();
73            System.out.println(data);
74            if (right != null)
75               right.printNodes();
76         }
77
78         public Comparable data;
```

```
79          public Node left;
80          public Node right;
81    }
82 }
```

20.6   Using Tree Sets and Tree Maps

> The TreeSet class uses a form of balanced binary trees that guarantees that adding and removing an element takes $O(\log(n))$ time.

Both the HashSet and the TreeSet classes implement the Set interface. Thus, if you need a set of objects, you have a choice which one to use.

If you have a good hash function for your objects, then hashing is usually faster than tree-based algorithms. But the balanced trees used in the TreeSet class can *guarantee* reasonable performance, whereas the HashSet is entirely at the mercy of the hash function.

If you don't want to define a hash function, then a tree set is an attractive option. Tree sets have another advantage: The iterators visit elements in *sorted order* rather than the completely random order given by the hash codes.

> To use a tree set, the elements must be comparable.

To use a TreeSet, either your objects must belong to a class that realizes the Comparable interface, or you must supply a Comparator object. That is exactly the same requirement that you saw in Section 18.8 for using the sort and binarySearch methods in the standard library.

To use a TreeMap, the same requirement holds for the *keys*. There is no requirement for the values.

For example, the String class realizes the Comparable interface. The compareTo method compares strings in dictionary order. Thus, you can form tree sets of strings, and use strings as keys for tree maps.

> If the class of the tree set elements doesn't implement the Comparable interface, you must supply a comparator.

If your class doesn't realize the Comparable interface, or the sort order of the compareTo method isn't the one you want, then you can define your own comparison by supplying a Comparator object to the TreeSet or TreeMap constructor. For example,

```
Comparator comp = new CoinComparator();
Set s = new TreeSet(comp);
```

Recall from Section 18.8 that a Comparator object compares two elements and returns a negative integer if the first is less than the second, zero if they are identical, and a positive value otherwise. The example program at the end of this section constructs a TreeSet of Coin objects, using the coin comparator of Section 18.8.

File TreeSetTest.java

```
1 import java.util.Comparator;
2 import java.util.Iterator;
3 import java.util.Set;
4 import java.util.TreeSet;
5
6 /**
7     A program to test hash codes of coins.
8 */
9 public class TreeSetTest
10 {
11    public static void main(String[] args)
12    {
13       Coin coin1 = new Coin(0.25, "quarter");
```

```
14        Coin coin2 = new Coin(0.25, "quarter");
15        Coin coin3 = new Coin(0.01, "penny");
16        Coin coin4 = new Coin(0.05, "nickel");
17
18        class CoinComparator implements Comparator
19        {
20           public int compare(
21              Object firstObject, Object secondObject)
22           {
23              Coin first = (Coin)firstObject;
24              Coin second = (Coin)secondObject;
25              if (first.getValue() < second.getValue())
26                 return -1;
27              if (first.getValue() == second.getValue())
28                 return 0;
29              return 1;
30           }
31        }
32
33        Comparator comp = new CoinComparator();
34        Set coins = new TreeSet(comp);
35        coins.add(coin1);
36        coins.add(coin2);
37        coins.add(coin3);
38        coins.add(coin4);
39
40        Iterator iter = coins.iterator();
41        while (iter.hasNext())
42           System.out.println(iter.next());
43     }
44 }
```

▼ AT **Advanced Topic**   **20.1**

Priority Queues

▼

A priority queue is an abstract data type that has many practical applications. It has two fundamental operations:

▼

- Add an element.

- Remove the element with the highest priority.

▼

One example of a priority queue is an event queue. User interface events are inserted in random order. Whenever there is time to process an event, the one with the smallest time stamp is removed. Generally, the "highest" priority is often the one with the minimum value. We will follow that convention in this section.

▼

To implement a priority queue, it is not necessary to sort the entire set of elements. In fact, the fastest implementations of priority queues do not keep the elements sorted but instead use a tree structure that is optimized for quickly finding the minimum and for efficiently reorganizing the elements when the minimum is removed. We refer you to reference [1] for more information on the implementation of priority queues.

▼

The standard Java library does not supply any priority queue interfaces or implementations. But you can easily turn a TreeSet into a priority queue as follows:

```
public class TreePriorityQueue
{
   public TreePriorityQueue(Comparator comp)
   {
      tree = new TreeSet(comp);
   }

   public void add(Object x)
   {
      tree.add(x);
   }

   public int size()
   {
      return tree.size();
   }

   public Object removeFirst()
   {
      Iterator iter = tree.iterator();
      Object r = iter.next();
      iter.remove();
      return r;
   }

   private TreeSet tree;
}
```

 Random Fact   20.1

Software Piracy

As you read this, you have written a few computer programs, and you have experienced firsthand how much effort it takes to write even the humblest of programs. Writing a real software product, such as a financial application or a computer game, takes a lot of time and money. Few people, and fewer companies, are going to spend that kind of time and money if they don't have a reasonable chance to make more money from their effort. (Actually, some companies give away their software in the hope that users will upgrade to more elaborate paid versions. Other companies give away the software that enables users to read and use files but sell the software needed to create those files. Finally, there are individuals who donate their time, out of enthusiasm, and produce programs that you can copy freely.)

When selling software, a company must rely on the honesty of its customers. It is an easy matter for an unscrupulous person to make copies of computer programs without paying for them. In most countries that is illegal. Most governments provide legal protection, such as copyright laws and patents, to encourage the development of new products. Countries that tolerate widespread piracy have found that they have an ample cheap supply of foreign software, but that no local manufacturer is stupid enough to design good software for their own citizens, such as word processors in the local script or financial programs adapted to the local tax laws.

When a mass market for software first appeared, vendors were enraged by the money they lost through piracy. They tried to fight back by various schemes to ensure that only the legitimate owner could use the software. Some manufacturers used *key disks:* floppy disks with a special pattern of holes burned in by a laser, which couldn't be copied. Others used *dongles:* devices that are attached between the computer and a printer port. Legitimate users hated these measures. They paid for the software, but they had to suffer through the inconvenience of inserting a key disk every time they started the software or having multiple dongles stick out from the back of their computer. In the United States, market pressures forced most vendors to give up on these copy protection schemes, but they are still commonplace in other parts of the world.

Because it is so easy and inexpensive to pirate software, and the chance of being found out is minimal, you have to make a moral choice for yourself. If a package that you would really like to have is too expensive for your budget, do you steal it, or do you stay honest and get by with a more affordable product?

Of course, piracy is not limited to software. The same issues arise for other digital products as well. You may have had the opportunity to obtain copies of songs or movies without payment. Or you may have been frustrated by a copy protection device on your music player that made it difficult for you to listen to songs that you paid for. Admittedly, it can be difficult to have a lot of sympathy for a musical ensemble whose publisher charges a lot of money for what seems to have been very little effort on their part, at least when compared to the effort that goes into designing and implementing a software package. Nevertheless, it seems only fair that artists and authors receive some compensation for their effort. How to pay artists, authors, and programmers fairly, without burdening honest customers, is an unsolved problem at the time of this writing, and many computer scientists are engaged in research in this area.

HOWTO 20.1

Choosing a Container

Suppose you need to store objects in a container. You have now seen a number of different data structures. This HOWTO reviews how to pick an appropriate container for your application.

Step 1 Determine how you access the elements

You store elements in a container so that you can later retrieve them. How do you want to access individual elements? You have several choices.

- It doesn't matter. Elements are always accessed "in bulk", by visiting all elements and doing something with them.
- Access by key. Elements are accessed by a special key. Example: Retrieve a bank account by the account number.
- Access by integer index. Elements have a position that is naturally an integer or a pair of integers. Example: A piece on a chess board is accessed by a row and column index.

If you need keyed access, use a map. If you need access by integer index, use an array list or array. For an index pair, use a two-dimensional array.

Step 2 Determine whether element order matters

When you retrieve elements from a container, do you care about the order in which they are retrieved? You have several choices.

- It doesn't matter. As long as you get to visit all elements, you don't care in which order.
- Elements must be sorted.
- Elements must be in the same order in which they were inserted.

To keep elements sorted, use a `TreeSet`.

To keep elements in the order in which you inserted them, use a `LinkedList`, `Array-List`, or array.

Step 3 Determine which operations need to be fast

You have several choices.

- It doesn't matter. You collect so few elements that you aren't concerned about speed.
- Adding and removing elements must be fast.
- Finding elements must be fast.

Linked lists let you add and remove elements efficiently, provided you are already near the location of the change. Changing either end of the linked list is always fast.

If you need to find an element quickly, use a set.

At this point, you should have narrowed down your selection to a particular container. If you answered "It doesn't matter" for each of the choices, then just use an `ArrayList`. It's a simple container that you already know well.

Step 4 For sets and maps, choose between hash tables and trees

If you decided that you need a set or map, you need to pick a particular implementation, either a hash table or a tree.

If your elements (or keys, in case of a map) are strings, use a hash table. It's more efficient.

If your elements or keys belong to a type that someone else defined, check whether the class implements its own `hashCode` and `equals` methods. The inherited `hashCode` method of the `Object` class takes only the object's memory address into account, not its contents. If there is no satisfactory `hashCode` method, then you must use a tree.

If your elements or keys belong to your own class, you usually want to use hashing. Define a `hashCode` and compatible `equals` method.

Step 5 If you use a tree, decide whether to supply a comparator

Look at the class of the elements or keys that the tree manages. Does that class implement the `Comparable` interface? If so, is the sort order given by the `compareTo` method the one you want. Then you don't need to do anything further.

Otherwise, you need to define a class that implements the `Comparator` interface and define the `compare` method. Supply an object of the comparator class to the `TreeSet` or `TreeMap` constructor.

CHAPTER SUMMARY

1. A set is an unordered collection of distinct elements. Elements can be added, located, and removed.

2. Sets don't have duplicates. Adding a duplicate of an element that is already present is silently ignored.

3. Both the HashSet and TreeSet classes realize the Set interface.

4. Use an iterator to list all elements in a set.

5. A set iterator does not visit the elements in the order in which you inserted them. The set implementation rearranges the elements so that it can locate them quickly.

6. You cannot add an element to a set at an iterator position.

7. A map keeps associations between key and value objects.

8. Both the HashMap and TreeMap classes realize the Map interface.

9. To find all keys and values in a map, iterate through the key set and find the values that correspond to the keys.

10. A hash function computes an integer value from an object.

11. A good hash function minimizes *collisions*, identical hash codes for different objects.

12. A hash table can be implemented as an array of *buckets*, sequences of links that hold elements with the same hash code.

13. If there are no or only a few collisions, then adding, locating, and removing hash table elements takes constant or $O(1)$ time.

14. The table size should be a prime number, larger than the expected number of elements.

15. Define hashCode methods for your own classes by combining the hash codes for the instance variables.

16. Your hashCode method must be compatible with the equals method.

17. In a hash map, only the keys are hashed.

18. A binary tree consists of nodes, each of which has two child nodes.

19. All nodes in a binary search tree fulfill the property that the descendants to the left have smaller data values than the node data value, and the descendants to the right have larger data values.

20. If a binary search tree is approximately balanced, then adding an element takes $O(\log(n))$ time.

21. The TreeSet class uses a form of balanced binary trees that guarantees that adding and removing an element takes $O(\log(n))$ time.

22. To use a tree set, the elements must be comparable.

23. If the class of the tree set elements doesn't implement the Comparable interface, you must supply a comparator.

CLASSES, OBJECTS, AND METHODS INTRODUCED IN THIS CHAPTER

```
java.util.HashMap
java.util.HashSet
java.util.Iterator
    hasNext
    next
    remove
java.util.Map
    get
    put
    keySet
    remove
java.util.Set
    add
    contains
    iterator
    remove
    size
java.util.TreeMap
java.util.TreeSet
```

Further Reading

[1] Thomas H. Cormen, Charles E. Leiserson, Ronald L. Rivest, *Introduction to Algorithms*, MIT Press, 1990.

REVIEW EXERCISES

Exercise R20.1. What is the difference between a set and a map?

Exercise R20.2. What implementations does the Java library provide for the abstract set type?

Exercise R20.3. What are the fundamental operations on the abstract set type? What additional methods does the Set interface provide? (Look up the interface in the API documentation.)

Exercise R20.4. The union of two sets *A* and *B* is the set of all elements that are contained in *A*, *B*, or both. The intersection is the set of all elements that are contained in *A* and *B*. How can you compute the union and intersection of two sets, using the fundamental set operations?

Exercise R20.5. How can you compute the union and intersection of two sets, using some of the methods that the Set interface provides? (Look up the interface in the API documentation.)

Exercise R20.6. Can a map have two keys with the same value? Two values with the same key?

Exercise R20.7. A map can be implemented as a set of (*key, value*) pairs. Explain.

Exercise R20.8. When implementing a hash map as a set of (*key, value*) pairs, what hash function should be used?

Exercise R20.9. Verify the hash codes of the strings `"Jim"` and `"Joe"` in Table 1.

Exercise R20.10. From the hash codes in Table 1, show that Figure 6 accurately shows the locations of the strings if the hash table size is 101.

Exercise R20.11. What is the difference between a binary tree and a binary search tree? Give examples of each.

Exercise R20.12. What is the difference between a balanced tree and an unbalanced tree? Give examples of each.

Exercise R20.13. The following elements are inserted into a binary search tree. Make a drawing that shows the resulting tree after each insertion.

```
Adam
Eve
Romeo
Juliet
Tom
Dick
Harry
```

Exercise R20.14. Insert the elements of the preceding exercise in opposite order. Then determine how the `Tree.print` method prints out both the tree from the preceding exercise and this tree. Explain how the printouts are related.

Exercise R20.15. Consider the following tree. In which order are the nodes printed by the `Tree.print` method?

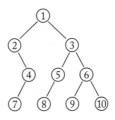

PROGRAMMING EXERCISES

Exercise P20.1. Write a program that reads text from `System.in` and breaks it up into individual words, just like the `Split` program in Chapter 6. Insert the words into a tree set. At the end of the input file, print all words, followed by the size of the resulting set. This program determines how many unique words a text file has.

Exercise P20.2. Insert the 13 standard colors that the `Color` class predefines (that is, `Color.pink`, `Color.green`, and so on) into a set. Prompt the user to enter a color by specifying red, green, and blue values between 0 and 1. Then tell the user whether the resulting color is in the set.

Exercise P20.3. Add a `debug` method to the `HashSet` implementation in Section 20.3 that prints the nonempty buckets of the hash table. Run the test program at the end of Section 20.3. Call the `debug` method after all additions and removals and verify that Figure 6 accurately represents the state of the hash table.

Exercise P20.4. Write a program that keeps a map in which both keys and values are strings—the names of students and their course grades. Prompt the user of the program to add or remove students, to modify grades, or to print all grades. The printout should be sorted by name and formatted like this:

```
Carl: B+
Joe: C
Sarah: A
```

Exercise P20.5. Reimplement the preceding exercise so that the keys of the map are objects of class `Student`. A student should have a first name, a last name, and an integer ID. The printout should be sorted by last name. If two students have the same last name, then use the first name as tie breaker. If the first names are also identical, then use the integer ID.

Exercise P20.6. Supply compatible `hashCode` and `equals` methods to the `Student` class described in the preceding exercise. Test the hash code by adding `Student` objects to a hash set.

Exercise P20.7. Supply compatible `hashCode` and `equals` methods to the `BankAccount` class. Test the `hashCode` method by printing out hash codes and by adding `BankAccount` objects to a hash set.

Exercise P20.8. Design a data structure `IntSet` that can hold a set of integers. Hide the private implementation: a tree set of `Integer` objects. Provide the following methods:

- A constructor to make an empty set
- `add(int x)` to add x if it is not present
- `remove(int x)` to remove x if it is present
- `print()` to print all elements currently in the set

Exercise P20.9. Enhance the set class from the previous example by supplying an iterator object that supports only the `hasNext`/`next` methods.

```
IntSetIterator iterator = mySet.iterator();
while (iterator.hasNext())
   System.out.println(iterator.next());
```

Note that the `next` method returns an `int`, not an object. For that reason, you cannot simply return the iterator of the tree set.

Exercise P20.10. Enhance the set class from the previous examples by supplying methods

```
IntSet union(IntSet other)
IntSet intersection(IntSet other)
```

that compute the union and intersection of two sets.

Exercise P20.11. Implement the *sieve of Eratosthenes*: a method for computing prime numbers, known to the ancient Greeks. Choose an *n*. This method will compute all prime numbers up to *n*. First insert all numbers from 2 to *n* into a set. Then erase all multiples of 2 (except 2); that is, 4, 6, 8, 10, 12, ... Erase all multiples of 3; that is, 6, 9, 12, 15, ... Go up to $\sqrt{n}$. The remaining numbers are all primes. Of course, you should use only the public interface of the `IntSet` data structure.

Exercise P20.12. Design an `IntTree` class that stores just integers, not objects. Support the same methods as the `Tree` class in the book.

Exercise P20.13. Write a method of the `Tree` class

    Comparable smallest()

that returns the smallest element of a tree. You will also need to add a method to the `Node` class.

Exercise P20.14. Change the `print` method to print the tree as a tree shape. You can print the tree sideways. Extra credit if you instead display the tree graphically, with the root node centered on the top.

Exercise P20.15. The `print` method of the tree class prints a tree according to the following algorithm:

1. Print the left subtree.
2. Print the current node.
3. Print the right subtree.

This is called *inorder traversal*. There are two other traversal schemes, namely *preorder traversal*,

1. Print the current node.
2. Print the left subtree.
3. Print the right subtree.

and *postorder traversal*,

1. Print the left subtree.
2. Print the right subtree.
3. Print the current node.

Write a program that builds a tree of strings from user input and then prints the user's choice of preorder, inorder, or postorder traversal.

Additional Algorithms and Data Structures

CHAPTER GOALS

▶ To learn about additional algorithms and data structures that are required for the AP CS Examination

▶ To understand the insertion sort algorithm

▶ To learn more about binary search trees

▶ To understand tree traversal

▶ To become familiar with the heap data structure

▶ To learn how to implement the priority queue data type

▶ To understand how to use heaps for sorting

This chapter contains supplemental material that may be covered on the AP CS Examination. You will learn about another simple sorting algorithm, insertion sort, that is comparable to selection sort. This chapter also continues the discussion of tree structures. In particular, you will learn how to use a special tree structure, called a heap, to implement priority queues and an efficient sorting algorithm.

20A.1 Insertion Sort

In Section 18.1, you learned about the selection sort algorithm. The selection sort algorithm is simple to understand, but it is not particularly efficient.

> The insertion sort algorithm sorts an array by repeatedly inserting elements into a sequence that is kept sorted.

The insertion sort algorithm is another simple sorting algorithm. In this algorithm, we assume that the initial sequence

    a[0] a[1] ... a[k]

of an array is already sorted. (When the algorithm starts, we set k to 0.) We enlarge that initial sequence by inserting the next array element, a[k+1], at the proper location. When we reach the end of the array, the sorting process is complete.

For example, suppose we start with the array

| 11 | 9 | 16 | 5 | 7 |

Of course, the initial sequence of length 1 is already sorted. We now add a[1], which has the value 9. The element needs to be inserted before the element 11. The result is

| 9 | 11 | 16 | 5 | 7 |

Next, we add a[2], which has the value 16. As it happens, the element does not have to be moved.

| 9 | 11 | 16 | 5 | 7 |

We repeat the process, inserting a[3] or 5 at the very beginning of the initial sequence.

| 5 | 9 | 11 | 16 | 7 |

Finally, a[4] or 7 is inserted in its correct position, and the sorting is completed.

The program at the end of this section contains the code for the algorithm.

How efficient is this algorithm? Let n denote the size of the array. We carry out $n-1$ iterations. In the kth iteration, we have a sequence of k elements that is already sorted, and we need to insert a new element into the sequence. For each insertion, we need to visit the elements of the initial sequence until we have found the location in which the new element can be inserted. Then we need to move up the remaining elements of the sequence. Thus, $k + 1$ array elements are visited. Therefore, the total number of visits is

$$2+3+\ldots+n = n \cdot (n+1)/2 - 1$$

> Insertion sort is an $O(n^2)$ algorithm.

We conclude that insertion sort is an $O(n^2)$ algorithm, on the same order of efficiency as selection sort and less efficient than the mergesort algorithm.

Obviously, this algorithm is inefficient in part because array elements need to be shifted whenever an element is inserted. You may wonder if one can avoid this inefficiency if one stores the data in a linked list rather than an array.

Indeed, the insertion sort algorithm can be adapted to a linked list (see Exercise P20A.1). The algorithm is then somewhat faster. In the kth iteration, it takes an average of $(k+1)/2$ visits to find the insertion location, and constant time to remove the element from the old location and add it to the new location. If we count the latter as two visits, then the total number of visits can be estimated as

$$2/2 + 2 + 3/2 + 2 + \ldots + n/2 + 2 = n \cdot (n-1)/4 - 1/2 + 2 \cdot (n-1)$$

That is a lower number of visits, but it is still $O(n^2)$. Thus, even for linked lists, insertion sort is not a particularly efficient sorting algorithm.

File InsertionSorter.java

```
 1 /**
 2     This class sorts an array, using the insertion sort
 3     algorithm.
 4 */
 5 public class InsertionSorter
 6 {
 7     /**
 8         Constructs an insertion sorter.
 9         @param anArray the array to sort
10     */
11     public InsertionSorter(int[] anArray)
12     {
13         a = anArray;
14     }
15
16     /**
17         Sorts the array managed by this insertion sorter.
18     */
19     public void sort()
20     {
21         for (int i = 1; i < a.length; i++)
22         {
23             int next = a[i];
24             // find the insertion location
25             // move all larger elements up
26             int j = i;
27             while (j > 0 && a[j - 1] > next)
28             {
29                 a[j] = a[j - 1];
30                 j--;
31             }
32             // insert the element
33             a[j] = next;
34         }
35     }
36
37     private int[] a;
38 }
```

20A.2   Removing Elements from a Binary Search Tree

In Chapter 20, you saw how to insert elements into a binary search tree. In that chapter, we did not discuss how to remove a value from a binary search tree because that algorithm is quite a bit more complex than the insertion algorithm.

We will now discuss the removal algorithm. Our task is to remove a node from the tree. Of course, we must first *find* the node to be removed. That is a simple matter, due to the characteristic property of a binary search tree. Compare the data value to be removed with the data value that is stored in the root node. If it is smaller, keep looking in the left subtree. Otherwise, keep looking in the right subtree.

Let us now assume that we have located the node that needs to be removed. First, let us consider an easy case, when that node has only one child (see Figure 1).

> When removing a node with only one child from a binary search tree, the child replaces the node to be removed.

To remove the node, simply modify the parent link that points to the node so that it points to the child instead.

If the node to be removed has no children at all, then the parent link is simply set to `null`.

> When removing a node with two children from a binary search tree, replace it with the smallest node of the right subtree.

The case in which the node to be removed has two children is more challenging. Rather than removing the node, it is easier to replace its data value with the next larger value in the tree. That replacement preserves the binary search tree property. (Alternatively, you could use the largest element of the left subtree—see Exercise P20A.2).

To locate the next larger value, go to the right subtree and find its smallest data value. Keep following the left child links. Once you reach a node that has no left child, you have found the node containing the smallest data value of the subtree. Now remove that node—it is easily removed because it has at most one child to the right. Then store its data value in the original node that was slated for removal. Figure 2 shows the details. You will find the complete code at the end of this section.

There is a remaining complexity. As you have seen, removal of a node may force a change in one of the parent links. If the removed node is the root, then the link to the root needs to be updated. The tedium of tracking the parents can be avoided with a simple trick. Just as the `insert` method of the `Tree` class calls a recursive `insertNode` method

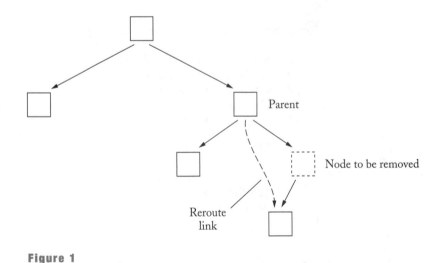

Figure 1

Removing a Node with One Child

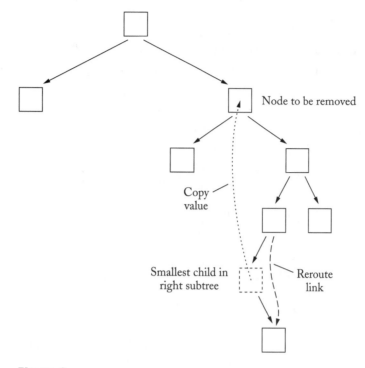

Node to be removed

Copy
value

Smallest child in
right subtree

Reroute
link

Figure 2

Removing a Node with Two Children

of the `Node` class, the `remove` method of the `Tree` class calls a recursive `removeNode` method of the `Node` class. However, the `removeNode` method returns a reference to the root of a subtree, after removing the requested value. That may be a reference to a child node, if the current node is removed, or a reference to the same node if the removal happens farther down in the tree.

Then the `remove` method of the `Tree` class attaches the return value of the `removeNode` method to the `root` field:

```
if (root != null)
    root = root.removeNode(obj);
```

Similarly, the `removeNode` method of the `Node` class updates the `left` and `right` links in its recursive calls:

```
public Node removeNode(Comparable obj)
{
    int d = data.compareTo(obj);
    if (d > 0)
    {
        if (left != null)
            left = left.removeNode(obj);
    }
    if (d < 0)
    {
        if (right != null)
            right = right.removeNode(obj);
    }
    ...
}
```

In most cases, the removeNode method returns this, a reference to the current node. However, when removeNode is called on a node that contains the data value to be removed, and when the node has at most one child, then removeNode returns the child.

```
public Node removeNode(Comparable obj)
{
    ...
    if (d != 0) return this;

    // this node contains obj

    // if one of the subtrees is empty, return the other

    if (left == null) return right;
    if (right == null) return left;

    // if neither subtree is empty
    // replace data with smallest value from right subtree

    ...
    return this;
}
```

Here is the source code for the enhanced Tree class. It contains the remove method that was just described, as well as a find method that tests whether a value is present in a binary search tree.

File Tree.java

```
1  /**
2     This class implements a binary search tree whose
3     nodes hold objects that implement the Comparable
4     interface.
5  */
6  public class Tree
7  {
8     /**
9        Constructs an empty tree.
10    */
11    public Tree()
12    {
13       root = null;
14    }
15
16    /**
17       Inserts a new node into the tree.
18       @param obj the object to insert
19    */
20    public void insert(Comparable obj)
21    {
22       Node newNode = new Node();
23       newNode.data = obj;
24       newNode.left = null;
25       newNode.right = null;
26       if (root == null) root = newNode;
27       else root.insertNode(newNode);
28    }
29
```

```
30    /**
31        Tries to find an object in the tree.
32        @param obj  the object to find
33        @return true  if the object is contained in the tree
34    */
35    public boolean find(Comparable obj)
36    {
37        Node current = root;
38        while (current != null)
39        {
40            int d = current.data.compareTo(obj);
41            if (d == 0) return true;
42            else if (d > 0) current = current.left;
43            else current = current.right;
44        }
45        return false;
46    }
47
48    /**
49        Tries to remove an object from the tree. Does nothing
50        if the object is not contained in the tree.
51        @param obj  the object to remove
52    */
53    public void remove(Comparable obj)
54    {
55        if (root != null)
56            root = root.removeNode(obj);
57    }
58
59    /**
60        Prints the contents of the tree in sorted order.
61    */
62    public void print()
63    {
64        if (root != null)
65            root.printNodes();
66    }
67
68    private Node root;
69
70    /**
71        A node of a tree stores a data item and references
72        to the child nodes to the left and to the right.
73    */
74    private class Node
75    {
76        /**
77            Inserts a new node as a descendant of this node.
78            @param newNode  the node to insert
79        */
80        public void insertNode(Node newNode)
81        {
82            if (newNode.data.compareTo(data) < 0)
83            {
84                if (left == null) left = newNode;
85                else left.insertNode(newNode);
86            }
87            else
```

```
88          {
89              if (right == null) right = newNode;
90              else right.insertNode(newNode);
91          }
92      }
93
94      /**
95          Tries to remove an object from this node or its descendants.
96          @param obj the object to remove
97          @return the root of the subtree that results from the removal
98      */
99      public Node removeNode(Comparable obj)
100     {
101         int d = data.compareTo(obj);
102         if (d > 0)
103         {
104             if (left != null)
105                 left = left.removeNode(obj);
106         }
107         if (d < 0)
108         {
109             if (right != null)
110                 right = right.removeNode(obj);
111         }
112
113         if (d != 0) return this;
114
115         // this node contains obj
116
117         // if one of the subtrees is empty, return the other
118
119         if (left == null) return right;
120         if (right == null) return left;
121
122         // neither subtree is empty
123
124         // find smallest element of the right subtree
125
126         Node parent = null;
127         Node child = right;
128         while (child.left != null)
129         {
130             parent = child;
131             child = child.left;
132         }
133
134         // move contents, unlink child
135
136         data = child.data;
137         if (parent == null) right = right.right;
138         else parent.left = child.right;
139
140         return this;
141     }
142
```

```
143        /**
144             Prints this node and all of its descendants
145             in sorted order.
146        */
147        public void printNodes()
148        {
149            if (left != null)
150                left.printNodes();
151            System.out.println(data);
152            if (right != null)
153                right.printNodes();
154        }
155
156        public Comparable data;
157        public Node left;
158        public Node right;
159    }
160 }
```

20A.3   Tree Traversal

When printing a binary search tree, we use the following recursive algorithm:

- Print the left subtree
- Print the root value
- Print the right subtree

Because the values of all nodes of the tree lie between the values of their left and right subtrees, this arrangement prints the node values in sorted order.

> Tree traversal schemes include preorder traversal, inorder traversal, and postorder traversal.

This visitation scheme is called *inorder traversal*. There are two other traversal schemes, called *preorder traversal* and *postorder traversal*.

In preorder traversal,

- Visit the root
- Visit the left subtree
- Visit the right subtree

In postorder traversal,

- Visit the left subtree
- Visit the right subtree
- Visit the root

These two visitation schemes will not print the tree in sorted order. However, they are important in other applications of binary trees. Here is an example.

In Chapter 19, we presented an algorithm for parsing arithmetic expressions such as

```
(3 + 4) * 5
3 + 4 * 5
```

It is customary to draw these expressions in tree form—see Figure 3. If all operators have two arguments, then the resulting tree is a binary tree. Its leaves store numbers, and its interior nodes store operators.

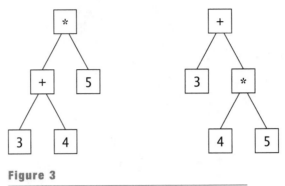

Figure 3

Expression Trees

Note that the expression trees describe the order in which the operators are applied. This order becomes visible when applying the postorder traversal of the expression tree. The first tree yields

3 4 + 5 *

whereas the second tree yields

3 4 5 * +

> Postorder traversal of an expression tree yields the instructions for evaluating the expression on a stack-based calculator.

You can interpret these sequences as instructions for a stack-based calculator. A number means:

- Push the number on the stack.

An operator means:

- Pop the top two numbers off the stack.
- Apply the operator to these two numbers.
- Push the result back on the stack.

Figure 4 shows the computation sequences for the two expressions.

This observation yields an algorithm for evaluating arithmetic expressions. First, turn the expression into a tree. Then carry out a postorder traversal of the expression tree and apply the operations in the given order. The result is the value of the expression.

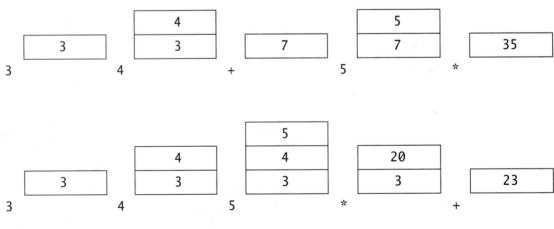

Figure 4

A Stack-Based Calculator

▼ **Random Fact** 20A.1

Reverse Polish Notation

In the 1920s, the Polish mathematician Jan Lukasiewicz realized that it is possible to dispense with parentheses in arithmetic expressions, provided that you write the operators *before* their arguments. For example,

Standard Notation	Lukasiewicz Notation
3 + 4	+ 3 4
3 + 4 * 5	+ 3 * 4 5
3 * (4 + 5)	* 3 + 4 5
(3 + 4) * 5	* + 3 4 5
3 + 4 + 5	+ + 3 4 5

The Lukasiewicz notation might look strange to you, but that is just an accident of history. Had earlier mathematicians realized its advantages, schoolchildren would not now learn an inferior notation with arbitrary precedence rules and parentheses.

Of course, an entrenched notation is not easily displaced, even when it has distinct disadvantages, and Lukasiewicz's discovery did not cause much of a stir for about 50 years.

However, in 1972, Hewlett-Packard introduced the HP 35 calculator that used *reverse Polish notation* or RPN. RPN is simply Lukasiewicz's notation in reverse, with the operators after their arguments. For example, to compute 3 + 4 * 5, you enter 3 4 5 * +. RPN calculators have no keys labeled with parentheses or an equals symbol. There is just a key labeled ENTER to push a number onto a stack. For that reason, Hewlett-Packard's marketing department used to refer to their product as "the calculators that have no equal". Indeed, the Hewlett-Packard calculators were a great advance over competing models that were unable to handle algebraic notation and left users with no other choice but to write intermediate results on paper.

Over time, developers of high quality calculators have adapted to the standard algebraic notation rather than forcing its users to learn a new notation. However, those users who have made the effort of learning RPN tend to be fanatic proponents, and to this day, some Hewlett-Packard calculator models still support it.

Photo courtesy Nigel Tout

20A.4 Priority Queues

In Section 19.4, you encountered two common abstract data types: stacks and queues. In this section, we will discuss another important abstract data type. A *priority* queue collects elements, each of which has a *priority*. A typical example of a priority queue is a collection of work requests, some of which may be more urgent than others.

> When removing an element from a priority queue, the element with the highest priority is retrieved.

Unlike a regular queue, the priority queue does not maintain a first-in, first-out discipline. Instead, elements are retrieved according to their priority. In other words, new items can be inserted in any order. But whenever an item is removed, that item has maximum priority.

For example, consider this sample code:

```
PriorityQueue q = ...;
q.add(new WorkOrder(5, "Replace light bulb"));
q.add(new WorkOrder(10, "Fix overflowing sink"));
q.add(new WorkOrder(2, "Clean coffee maker"));
```

When calling `q.remove()` for the first time, the work order with priority 10 is removed. The next call to `q.remove()` removes the work order whose priority is highest among those remaining in the queue—in our example, the work order with priority 5.

Actually, there is no `PriorityQueue` class in the standard Java library. However, you will learn in this chapter how to supply your own implementation.

Keep in mind that the priority queue is an *abstract* data type. You do not know how a priority queue organizes its elements. There are several concrete data structures that can be used to implement priority queues.

Of course, one implementation comes to mind immediately. Just store the elements in a linked list, adding new elements to the head of the list. The `remove` method then traverses the linked list and removes the element with the highest priority. In this implementation, adding elements is quick, but removing them is slow.

Another implementation strategy is to keep the elements in sorted order, for example in a binary search tree. Then it is an easy matter to locate and remove the largest element. However, as you will learn in the next section, another data structure, called a *heap*, is even more suitable for implementing priority queues.

20A.5 Heaps

> A heap is an almost complete tree in which the values of all nodes are at least as large as those of their children.

A heap is a binary tree with two special properties.

1. A heap is *almost complete*: all nodes are filled in, except the last level may have some nodes missing toward the right (see Figure 5).
2. The tree fulfills the *heap property*: all nodes store values that are at least as large as the values stored in their children (see Figure 6).

It is easy to see that the heap property ensures that the largest element is stored in the root.

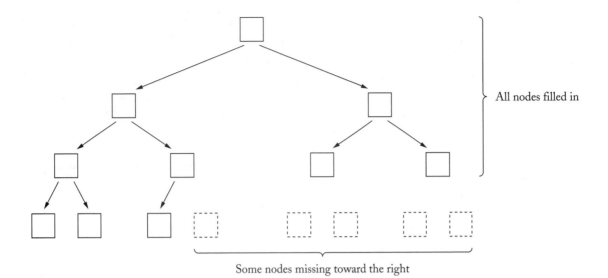

Figure 5

An Almost Complete Tree

A heap is superficially similar to a binary search tree, but there are two important differences.

1. The shape of a heap is very regular. Binary search trees can have arbitrary shapes.
2. In a heap, both the left and right subtrees store elements that are smaller than the root element. In contrast, in a binary search tree, smaller elements are stored in the left subtree and larger elements are stored in the right subtree.

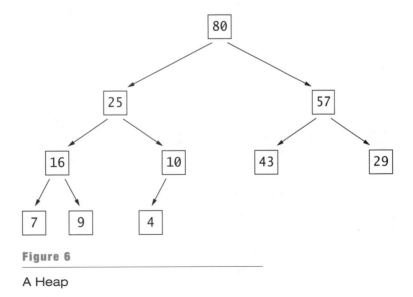

Figure 6

A Heap

Suppose we have a heap and want to insert a new element. Afterwards, the heap property should again be fulfilled. The following algorithm carries out the insertion (see Figure 7).

1. First, add a vacant slot to the end of the tree.

2. Next, *demote* the parent of the empty slot if it is smaller than the element to be inserted. That is, move the parent value into the vacant slot, and move the vacant slot up. Repeat this demotion as long as the parent of the vacant slot is smaller than the element to be inserted.

3. At this point, either the vacant slot is at the root, or the parent of the vacant slot is larger than the element to be inserted. Insert the element into the vacant slot.

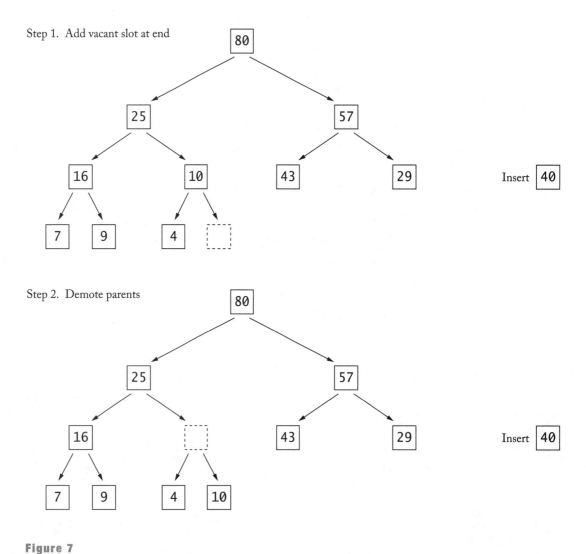

Figure 7

Inserting an Element into a Heap

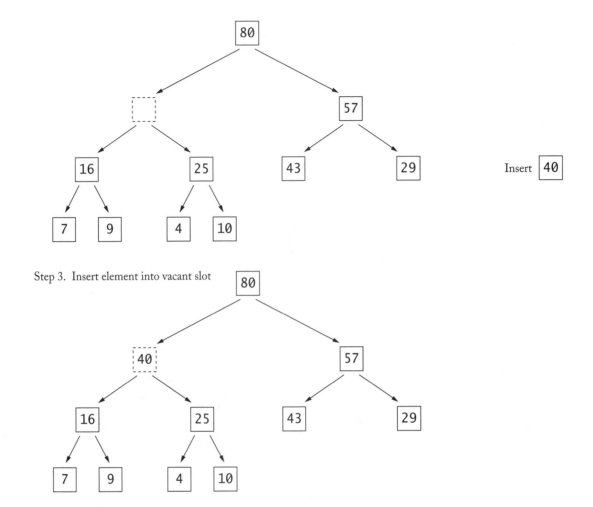

Step 3. Insert element into vacant slot

Figure 7 (continued)

Inserting an Element into a Heap

We will not consider an algorithm for removing an arbitrary node from a heap. The only node that we will remove is the root node which contains the maximum of all of the values in the heap. Figure 8 shows the algorithm in action.

1. Extract the root node value.
2. Move the value of the last node of the heap into the root node, and remove the last node. Now the heap property may be violated for the root node, since one or both of its children may be larger.
3. Promote the larger child of the root node if it is larger than the root node. Now the root node again fulfills the heap property. Repeat this process with the demoted child. That is, promote the larger of its children. Continue until the demoted child has no larger children. The heap property is now fulfilled again. This process is called "fixing the heap".

Step 1. Remove the maximum element from the root

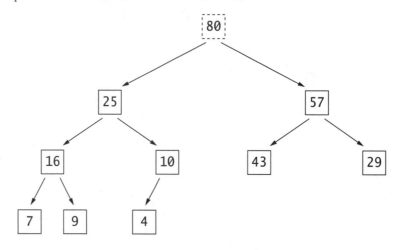

Step 2. Move the last element into the root

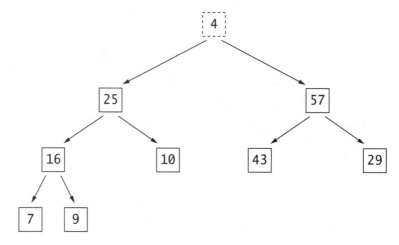

Step 3. Fix the heap

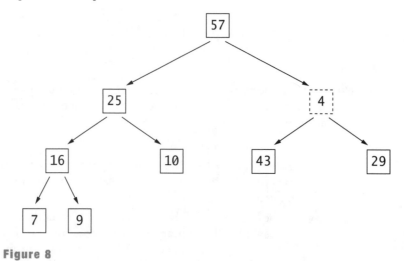

Figure 8

Removing the Maximum Value from a Heap

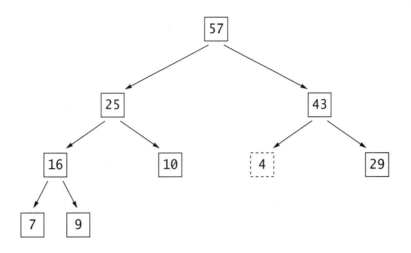

Figure 8 (continued)

Removing the Maximum Value from a Heap

Inserting and removing heap elements is very efficient. The reason lies in the balanced shape of a heap. The insertion and removal operations visit at most h nodes, where h is the height of the tree. A heap of height h contains at least 2^{h-1} elements but less than 2^h elements. In other words, if n is the number of elements, then

$$2^{h-1} \le n < 2^h$$

or

$$h - 1 \le \log_2 n < h$$

This argument shows that the insertion and removal operations in a heap with n elements take $O(\log(n))$ steps.

> Inserting or removing a heap element is an $O(\log(n))$ operation.

Contrast this finding with the situation of binary search trees. When a binary search tree is unbalanced, then it can degenerate into a linked list, so that in the worst case insertion and removal are $O(n)$ operations.

> The regular layout of a heap makes it possible to store heap nodes efficiently in an array.

Heaps have another major advantage. Because of the regular layout of the heap nodes, it is easy to store the node values in an array. First store the first layer, then the second, and so on (see Figure 9). For convenience, we leave the 0 element of the array empty. Then the child nodes of the node with index i have index $2 \cdot i$ and $2 \cdot i + 1$, and the parent node of the node with index i has index $i/2$. For example, as you can see in Figure 9, the children of node 4 are nodes 8 and 9, and the parent is node 2.

Storing the heap values in an array may not be intuitive, but it is very efficient. There is no need to allocate individual nodes or to store the links to the child nodes. Instead, child and parent positions can be determined by very simple computations.

The program at the end of this section contains an implementation of a heap. For greater clarity, the computation of the parent and child index positions is carried out in methods `getParentIndex`, `getLeftChildIndex`, and `getRightChildIndex`. For

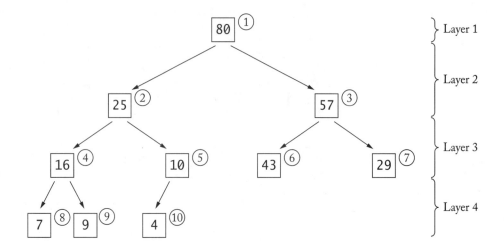

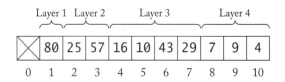

Figure 9

Storing a Heap in an Array

greater efficiency, the method calls could be avoided by using expressions `index/2`, `2 * index`, and `2 * index + 1` directly.

In this section, we have organized our heaps such that the largest element is stored in the root. It is also possible to store the smallest element in the root, simply by reversing all comparisons in the heap building algorithm. If there is a possibility of misunderstandings, it is best to refer to the data structures as max-heap or min-heap.

The test program demonstrates how to use a max-heap as a priority queue.

File MaxHeap.java

```
 1  import java.util.*;
 2
 3  /**
 4      This class implements a heap.
 5  */
 6  public class MaxHeap
 7  {
 8     /**
 9         Constructs an empty heap.
10     */
11     public MaxHeap()
12     {
13        elements = new ArrayList();
14        elements.add(null);
15     }
16
17     /**
18         Adds a new element to this heap.
19         @param newElement the element to add
```

```
20     */
21     public void add(Comparable newElement)
22     {
23        // add a new leaf
24        elements.add(null);
25        int index = elements.size() - 1;
26
27        // demote parents that are smaller than the new element
28        while (index > 1
29           && getParent(index).compareTo(newElement) < 0)
30        {
31           elements.set(index, getParent(index));
32           index = getParentIndex(index);
33        }
34
35        // store the new element into the vacant slot
36        elements.set(index, newElement);
37     }
38
39     /**
40        Gets the maximum element stored in this heap.
41        @return the maximum element
42     */
43     public Comparable getMaximum()
44     {
45        return (Comparable)elements.get(1);
46     }
47
48     /**
49        Removes the maximum element from this heap.
50        @return the maximum element
51     */
52     public Comparable removeMaximum()
53     {
54        Comparable maximum = (Comparable)elements.get(1);
55
56        // remove last element
57        int lastIndex = elements.size() - 1;
58        Comparable last = (Comparable)elements.remove(lastIndex);
59
60        if (lastIndex > 1)
61        {
62           elements.set(1, last);
63           fixHeap();
64        }
65
66        return maximum;
67     }
68
69     /**
70        Turns the tree back into a heap, provided only the root
71        node violates the heap condition.
72     */
73     private void fixHeap()
74     {
75        Comparable root = (Comparable)elements.get(1);
76
77        int lastIndex = elements.size() - 1;
```

```
78          //  promote children of removed root while they are larger than last
79
80          int index = 1;
81          boolean more = true;
82          while (more)
83          {
84             int childIndex = getLeftChildIndex(index);
85             if (childIndex <= lastIndex)
86             {
87                // get larger child
88
89                // get left child first
90                Comparable child = getLeftChild(index);
91
92                // use right child instead if it is larger
93                if (getRightChildIndex(index) <= lastIndex
94                   && getRightChild(index).compareTo(child) > 0)
95                {
96                   childIndex = getRightChildIndex(index);
97                   child = getRightChild(index);
98                }
99
100               // check if larger child is larger than root
101               if (child.compareTo(root) > 0)
102               {
103                  // promote child
104                  elements.set(index, child);
105                  index = childIndex;
106               }
107               else
108               {
109                  // root is larger than both children
110                  more = false;
111               }
112            }
113            else
114            {
115               // no children
116               more = false;
117            }
118         }
119
120         // store root element in vacant slot
121         elements.set(index, root);
122      }
123
124      /**
125         Returns the number of elements in this heap.
126      */
127      public int size()
128      {
129         return elements.size() - 1;
130      }
131
132      /**
133         Returns the index of the left child.
134         @param index the index of a node in this heap
135         @return the index of the left child of the given node
```

```
136        */
137        private static int getLeftChildIndex(int index)
138        {
139            return 2 * index;
140        }
141
142        /**
143            Returns the index of the right child.
144            @param index  the index of a node in this heap
145            @return  the index of the right child of the given node
146        */
147        private static int getRightChildIndex(int index)
148        {
149            return 2 * index + 1;
150        }
151
152        /**
153            Returns the index of the parent.
154            @param index  the index of a node in this heap
155            @return  the index of the parent of the given node
156        */
157        private static int getParentIndex(int index)
158        {
159            return index / 2;
160        }
161
162        /**
163            Returns the value of the left child.
164            @param index  the index of a node in this heap
165            @return  the value of the left child of the given node
166        */
167        private Comparable getLeftChild(int index)
168        {
169            return (Comparable)elements.get(2 * index);
170        }
171
172        /**
173            Returns the value of the right child.
174            @param index  the index of a node in this heap
175            @return  the value of the right child of the given node
176        */
177        private Comparable getRightChild(int index)
178        {
179            return (Comparable)elements.get(2 * index + 1);
180        }
181
182        /**
183            Returns the value of the parent.
184            @param index  the index of a node in this heap
185            @return  the value of the parent of the given node
186        */
187        private Comparable getParent(int index)
188        {
189            return (Comparable)elements.get(index / 2);
190        }
191
192        private ArrayList elements;
193    }
```

File HeapTest.java

```java
1  /**
2      This program demonstrates the use of a heap as a priority queue.
3  */
4  public class HeapTest
5  {
6     public static void main(String[] args)
7     {
8        MaxHeap h = new MaxHeap();
9        h.add(new WorkOrder(4, "Empty trash"));
10       h.add(new WorkOrder(3, "Water plants"));
11       h.add(new WorkOrder(1, "Remove pencil sharpener shavings"));
12       h.add(new WorkOrder(5, "Replace light bulb"));
13       h.add(new WorkOrder(10, "Fix broken sink"));
14       h.add(new WorkOrder(2, "Clean coffee maker"));
15       h.add(new WorkOrder(8, "Order cleaning supplies"));
16       h.add(new WorkOrder(7, "Shampoo carpets"));
17
18       while (h.size() > 0)
19          System.out.println(h.removeMaximum());
20    }
21 }
```

File WorkOrder.java

```java
1  /**
2      This class encapsulates a work order with a priority.
3  */
4  public class WorkOrder implements Comparable
5  {
6     /**
7         Constructs a work order with a given priority and description.
8         @param aPriority the priority of this work order
9         @param aDescription the description of this work order
10    */
11    public WorkOrder(int aPriority, String aDescription)
12    {
13       priority = aPriority;
14       description = aDescription;
15    }
16
17    public String toString()
18    {
19       return "priority=" + priority + ", description=" +
20             description;
21    }
22
23    public int compareTo(Object otherObject)
24    {
25       WorkOrder other = (WorkOrder)otherObject;
26       if (priority < other.priority) return -1;
27       if (priority > other.priority) return 1;
28       return 0;
29    }
30
31    private int priority;
32    private String description;
33 }
```

The Heapsort Algorithm

> The heapsort algorithm is based on inserting elements into a heap and removing them in sorted order.

Heaps are not only useful for implementing priority queues, they also give rise to an efficient sorting algorithm. In its simplest form, the algorithm works as follows. First insert all elements to be sorted into the heap, then keep extracting the maximum. The elements are retrieved in descending order. In order to obtain the elements in ascending order, we will fill them into an array in reverse order, starting at the end.

> Heapsort is an $O(n \log(n))$ algorithm.

This simple algorithm is an $O(n \log(n))$ algorithm: each insertion and removal is $O(\log(n))$, and these steps are repeated n times, once for each element in the sequence that is to be sorted. However, it is customary to speed up the algorithm further by simplifying the repeated insertion of elements.

Rather than inserting the elements one at a time, we will start with a sequence of values in an array. Of course, that array does not represent a heap. We will use the procedure of "fixing the heap" that you encountered in the preceding section as part of the element removal algorithm. "Fixing the heap" operates on a binary tree whose children are heaps but whose root value may not be larger than the child values. The procedure turns the tree into a heap, by repeatedly promoting the largest child value, moving the root value to its proper location.

Of course, we cannot simply apply this procedure to the initial sequence of unsorted values—the children of the root are not likely to be heaps. But we can first fix small subtrees into heaps, then fix larger trees. Since trees of size 1 are automatically heaps, we can begin the fixing procedure with the subtrees whose roots are located in the next-to-lowest level of the tree.

The sorting algorithm uses a generalized `fixHeap` method that fixes a subtree with a given root index:

```
void fixHeap(int rootIndex, int lastIndex)
```

Here, `lastIndex` is the index of the last node in the full tree. That method needs to be invoked on all subtrees whose roots are in the next-to-last level. Then the subtrees whose roots are in the next level above are fixed, and so on. Finally, the fixup is applied to the root node, and the tree is turned into a heap (see Figure 10).

Step 1.

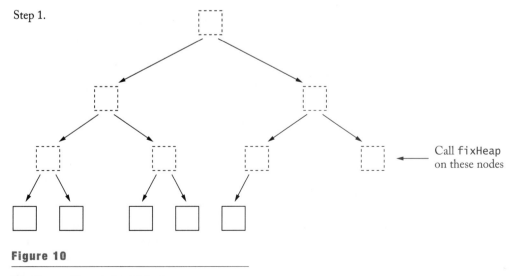

Call `fixHeap` on these nodes

Figure 10

Turning a Tree into a Heap

Step 2.

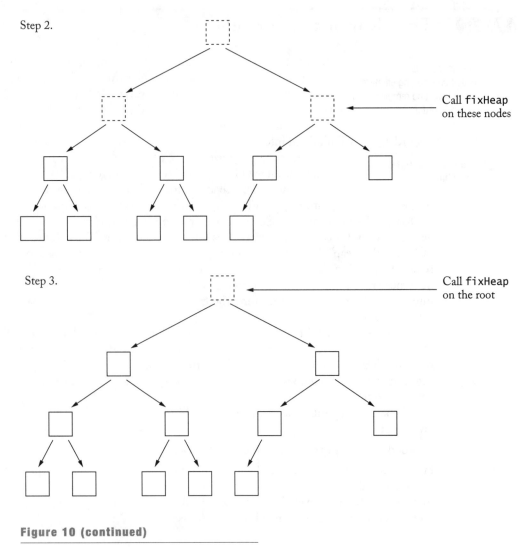

Call `fixHeap` on these nodes

Step 3.

Call `fixHeap` on the root

Figure 10 (continued)

Turning a Tree into a Heap

That repetition can be programmed easily. Start with the *last* node on the next-to-lowest level and work toward the left. Then go to the next higher level. The node index values then simply run backwards from the index of the last node to the index of the root.

```
int n = a.length - 1;
for (int i = (n - 1) / 2; i >= 0; i--)
   fixHeap(i, n);
```

Note that the loop ends with index 0. When working with a given array, we don't have the luxury of skipping the 0 entry. We consider the 0 entry the root and adjust the formulas for computing the child and parent index values.

After the array has been turned into a heap, we repeatedly remove the root element. Recall from the preceding section that removing the root element is achieved by placing the last element of the tree in the root and calling the `fixHeap` method. In the sorting algorithm, we will *swap* the root element with the last element of the tree and then reduce the tree length. As a result, the largest array value ends up in the last position of the array, the next-largest value in the preceding position, and so on (see Figure 11).

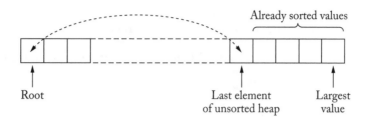

Already sorted values

Root

Last element
of unsorted heap

Largest
value

Figure 11

Using Heapsort to Sort an Array

The following class implements the heapsort algorithm.

File HeapSorter.java

```
1   /**
2       This class applies the heapsort algorithm to sort an array.
3   */
4   public class HeapSorter
5   {
6       /**
7           Constructs a heap sorter that sorts a given array.
8           @param anArray  an array of integers
9       */
10      public HeapSorter(int[] anArray)
11      {
12          a = anArray;
13      }
14
15      /**
16          Sorts the array managed by this heap sorter.
17      */
18      public void sort()
19      {
20          int n = a.length - 1;
21          for (int i = (n - 1) / 2; i >= 0; i--)
22              fixHeap(i, n);
23          while (n > 0)
24          {
25              swap(0, n);
26              n--;
27              fixHeap(0, n);
28          }
29      }
30
31      /**
32          Ensures the heap property for a subtree, provided its
33          children already fulfill the heap property.
34          @param rootIndex  the index of the subtree to be fixed
35          @param lastIndex  the last valid index of the tree that
36          contains the subtree to be fixed.
37      */
38      private void fixHeap(int rootIndex, int lastIndex)
39      {
```

```
40          // remove root
41          int rootValue = a[rootIndex];
42
43          // promote children while they are larger than the root
44
45          int index = rootIndex;
46          boolean more = true;
47          while (more)
48          {
49             int childIndex = getLeftChildIndex(index);
50             if (childIndex <= lastIndex)
51             {
52                // use right child instead if it is larger
53                int rightChildIndex = getRightChildIndex(index);
54                if (rightChildIndex <= lastIndex
55                   && a[rightChildIndex] > a[childIndex])
56                {
57                   childIndex = rightChildIndex;
58                }
59
60                if (a[childIndex] > rootValue)
61                {
62                   // promote child
63                   a[index] = a[childIndex];
64                   index = childIndex;
65                }
66                else
67                {
68                   // root value is larger than both children
69                   more = false;
70                }
71             }
72             else
73             {
74                // no children
75                more = false;
76             }
77          }
78
79          // store root value in vacant slot
80          a[index] = rootValue;
81       }
82
83       /**
84          Swaps two entries of the array.
85          @param i the first position to swap
86          @param j the second position to swap
87       */
88       private void swap(int i, int j)
89       {
90          int temp = a[i];
91          a[i] = a[j];
92          a[j] = temp;
93       }
94
95       /**
96          Returns the index of the left child.
97          @param index the index of a node in this heap
```

```
 98          @return  the index of the left child of the given node
 99     */
100     private static int getLeftChildIndex(int index)
101     {
102         return 2 * index + 1;
103     }
104
105     /**
106         Returns the index of the right child.
107         @param index  the index of a node in this heap
108         @return  the index of the right child of the given node
109     */
110     private static int getRightChildIndex(int index)
111     {
112         return 2 * index + 2;
113     }
114
115     private int[] a;
116 }
```

CHAPTER SUMMARY

1. The insertion sort algorithm sorts a sequence by repeatedly inserting elements into a sequence that is kept sorted.

2. Insertion sort is an $O(n^2)$ algorithm.

3. When removing a node with only one child from a binary search tree, the child replaces the node to be removed.

4. When removing a node with two children from a binary search tree, replace it with the smallest node of the right subtree.

5. Tree traversal schemes include preorder traversal, inorder traversal, and postorder traversal.

6. Postorder traversal of an expression tree yields the instructions for evaluating the expression on a stack-based calculator.

7. When removing an element from a priority queue, the element with the highest priority is retrieved.

8. A heap is an almost complete tree in which the values of all nodes are at least as large as those of their children.

9. Inserting or removing a heap element is an $O(\log(n))$ operation.

10. The regular layout of a heap makes it possible to store heap nodes efficiently in an array.

11. The heapsort algorithm is based on inserting elements into a heap and removing them in sorted order.

12. Heapsort is an $O(n \log(n))$ algorithm.

REVIEW EXERCISES

Exercise R20A.1. Simulate the insertion sort algorithm manually to sort the array

    11 27 8 14 45 6 24 81 29 33

Show all steps.

Exercise R20A.2. How many visits does the insertion sort algorithm carry out on an array that is already sorted?

Exercise R20A.3. On what kind of array does the insertion sort algorithm carry out the minimum number of visits?

Exercise R20A.4. The software that controls the events in a user interface keeps the events in a data structure. Whenever an event such as a mouse move or repaint request occurs, the event is added. Events are retrieved according to their importance. What abstract data type is appropriate for this application?

Exercise R20A.5. Could a priority queue be implemented efficiently as a binary search tree? Give a detailed argument for your answer.

Exercise R20A.6. Will preorder, inorder, or postorder traversal print a heap in sorted order? Why or why not?

Exercise R20A.7. Prove that a heap of height h contains at least 2^{h-1} elements but less than 2^h elements.

Exercise R20A.8. Suppose the heap nodes are stored in an array, starting with index 1. Prove that the child nodes of the heap node with index i have index $2 \cdot i$ and $2 \cdot i + 1$, and the parent heap node of the node with index i has index $i/2$.

Exercise R20A.9. Simulate the heapsort algorithm manually to sort the array

    11 27 8 14 45 6 24 81 29 33

Show all steps.

Exercise R20A.10. What principal advantage does the heapsort algorithm have over merge sort?

PROGRAMMING EXERCISES

Exercise P20A.1. Modify the insertion sort algorithm to sort a linked list.

Exercise P20A.2. In the `Tree` class, modify the `remove` method so that a node with two children is replaced by the largest child of the left subtree.

Exercise P20A.3. Implement methods that use preorder and postorder traversal to print the elements in a binary search tree.

Exercise P20A.4. Suppose an interface `Visitor` has a single method

```
void visit(Object obj)
```

Supply methods

```
void inOrder(Visitor v)
void preOrder(Visitor v)
void postOrder(Visitor v)
```

to the `Tree` class. These methods should visit the tree nodes in the specified traversal order and apply the `visit` method to the data of the visited node.

Exercise P20A.5. Apply the preceding exercise to compute the average value of the elements in a binary search tree. That is, supply an object of an appropriate class that implements the `Visitor` interface.

Exercise P20A.6. Modify the expression parser of Chapter 17 to parse an arithmetic expression into an expression tree. Then use postorder traversal of the expression tree to determine its value.

Exercise P20A.7. Modify the implementation of the `Heap` class so that the parent and child index positions are computed directly, without calling helper methods.

Exercise P20A.8. Modify the implementation of the `Heap` class so that the 0 element of the array is not wasted.

Exercise P20A.9. Program an algorithm animation of the heapsort algorithm, displaying the tree graphically and stopping after each call to `fixHeap`.

Exercise P20A.10. Time the results of heapsort and merge sort. Which algorithm behaves better in practice? For best timing results, you should eliminate the helper methods that compute parent and child index values.

APPENDIX **B**

Exercise Solutions

■ Chapter 2

Answers to Multiple Choice Questions

1. a
2. b
3. a

4. e
5. e

Answers to Free Response

1a.
```java
public class Basics
{
    public static void main(String[] args)
    {
        System.out.println("The secret to success is in
            C:\\Temp\\Success.txt.");
    }
}
```

1b.
```java
public class Basics
{
    public static void main(String[] args)
    {
        System.out.println("The\nsecret\nto\nsuccess\nis\nin\n
            C:\\Temp\\Success.txt.");
    }
}
```

■ Chapter 3

Answers to Multiple Choice Questions

1.	b	6.	d
2.	c	7.	d
3.	a	8.	a
4.	b	9.	e
5.	a	10.	e

Answers to Free Response

1a.
```java
public Employee(String firstName, String lastName, double
        moneyEarned)
{
    fName = firstName;
    lName = lastName;
    salary = moneyEarned;
}
```

1b.
```java
public void raiseSalary(double byPercent)
{
    double amountOfRaise = byPercent / 100 * salary;
    salary = salary + amountOfRaise;
}
```

2a.
```java
public Book(String name, String writer, double cost)
{
    title = name;
    author = writer;
    price = cost;
}
```

2b.
```java
public void giveDiscount(double byPercent)
{
    double amountOfDiscount = byPercent / 100 * price;
    double newPrice = price - amountOfDiscount;
    price = newPrice;
}
```

■ Chapter 4

Answers to Multiple Choice Questions

1.	c	6.	b
2.	c	7.	a
3.	c	8.	e
4.	d	9.	e
5.	a	10.	d

Answers to Free Response

1a.
```
public double findGasUsed(double numMiles)
{
    return numMiles / mpg;
}
```

1b.
```
public void drive(double numMiles)
{
    mileage += numMiles;
    double gas = findGasUsed(numMiles);
    gasInTank -= gas;
}
```

2a.
```
public int totalInPennies()
{
    return (int)(PENNIES_PER_DOLLAR * getTotal())
}
```

2b.
```
public int getDollars()
{
    int amount = totalInPennies();
    return amount / PENNIES_PER_DOLLAR;
}
```

2c.
```
public int getCents()
{
    int amount = totalInPennies();
    return amount % PENNIES_PER_DOLLAR;
}
```

■ Chapter 5

Answers to Multiple Choice Questions

1. d
2. b
3. e
4. a
5. d

6. d
7. e
8. c
9. d
10. c

Answers to Free Response

1a.
```
public void fillTank()
{
    if (gasInTank < 0.5 * tankCapacity)
        gasInTank = tankCapacity;
}
```

1b.
```
public void drive(double numMiles)
{
    if (mpg * gasInTank >= numMiles)
    {
        mileage += numMiles;
        gasInTank -= gasUsed(numMiles);
    }
    else
    {
        mileage += mpg * gasInTank;
        gasInTank = 0;
    }
}
```

2a.
```
public double getDistanceFromOrigin()
{
    double d = Math.sqrt(x * x + y * y);
    return d;
}
```

2b.
```
public static Point findFarPoint(Point p1, Point p2, Point p3)
{
    double d1 = p1.getDistanceFromOrigin();
    double d2 = p2.getDistanceFromOrigin();
    double d3 = p3.getDistanceFromOrigin();

    double longest = d1;
    Point far = p1;
    if (d2 > longest)
    {
        longest = d2;
        far = p2;
    }
    if (d3 > longest)
    {
        longest = d3;
        far = p3;
    }
    return far;
}
```

2c.
```
public boolean equals(Point p2)
{
    return (x == p2.getX()) && (y == p2.getY());
}
```

■ Chapter 6

Answers to Multiple Choice Questions

1. c
2. e
3. d
4. e
5. c
6. a
7. c
8. c

9. e
10. d
11. c
12. c
13. c
14. b
15. c

Answers to Free Response

1a.
```
public void waitForYears(int y)
{
    for (int i = 1; i <= y; i++)
    {
        double interest = balance * rate / 100;
        balance += interest;
    }
}
```

1b.
```
public void compoundTheInterest(int y, int n)
{
    for (int i = 1; i <= y; i++)
    {
        for (int q = 1; q <= n; q++)
        {
            double interest = balance * rate / 100 / n;
            balance += interest;
        }
    }
}
```

2a.
```
public Game(Purse myPurse)
{
    myWheel = new Spinner(4);
}
```

2b.
```
public int spinTheWheel()
{
    int number = myWheel.spin();
    if (number >= 2)
        return number;
    else return 0;
}
```

2c.
```
public double playRoulette(Purse myPurse)
{
    double myMoney = myPurse.getTotal();
    double myEndMoney = 2 * myMoney;
    Coin aCoin;

    while (myPurse.coinCount() > 0 && myPurse.getTotal() <
        myEndMoney)
    {
        aCoin = myPurse.removeCoin();
        int r = spinTheWheel();
        for (int i = 1; i <= r; i++)
        {
            myPurse.add(new Coin(aCoin.getValue(), aCoin.getName()));
        }
    }
    return myPurse.getTotal();
}
```

■ Chapter 7

Answers to Multiple Choice Questions

1. c	6. c
2. c	7. a
3. d	8. e
4. e	9. c
5. d	10. c

Answers to Free Response

1a.
```
public class Book
{
    // Constructor
    // Precondition: cost > 0
    // Postcondition: Book object created
    public Book(String name, String writer, double cost) {...}

    // Postcondition: Returns the identification number of the book
    public double getIdentificationNumber(); {...}
```

```
        // Postcondition: Returns author's name
        public String getAuthor() {...}

        // Precondition: newPrice > 0
        // Postcondition: Book price is updated and now equals newPrice
        public void setPrice(double newPrice) {...}

        // Postcondition: Returns price of book
        public double getPrice() {...}
    }
```

1b.
```
    private String title;
    private String author;
    private double price;
    private int idNum;

    private static int identification = 0;
```

1c.
```
    // Precondition: cost > 0
    // Postcondition: Book object created
    public Book(String name, String writer, double cost)
    {
        if (cost <= 0)
            throw new IllegalArgumentException();    // AB only
        title = name;
        author = writer;
        price = cost;
        identification++;
        idNum = identification;
    }
```

1d. Alternative 1: Throw an exception if the precondition is not met. The advantage is that control will be transferred to the exception handler and if there isn't an exception handler, the program stops. There will be no data corruption. The disadvantage is that the program may stop prematurely.

Alternative 2: Assume the precondition is always satisfied. The advantage is that there is no extra work on programmer's part. It is the responsibility of the calling method to check the precondition, not the method's responsibility. The disadvantage is that there may be data corruption or other failures that occur that will be the result of the caller's failure to satisfy the precondition.

2a.
```
    public class Client
    {
        // Constructor
        public Client(String who, int inches, int lbs, String
            gender) {...}

        // Postcondition: returns client name
        public String getName() {...}
```

```
        // Postcondition: returns client height
        public int getHeight() {...}

        // Postcondition: returns client weight
        public int getWeight() {...}

        // setCalories omitted

        // Postcondition: returns suggested calorie intake per day
        public int getCalories() {...}
    }
```

2d.
```
    private String name;
    private int weight;
    private int height;
    private String sex;
    private int caloriesPerDay;
```

2c.
```
    public void setCalories(WeightCalculator plan)
    {
        final int CALORIES_TO_CUT = 500;

        int idealWeight = plan.getIdealWeight(sex, height);
        int calories = plan.getCalorieIntake(height, sex);
        if (idealWeight < weight)
        {
            calories -= CALORIES_TO_CUT;
        }
        caloriesPerDay = calories;
    }
```

■ Chapter 8

Answers to Multiple Choice Questions

1.	b	6.	e
2.	a	7.	c
3.	d	8.	c
4.	c	9.	d
5.	a	10.	a

Answers to Free Response

1a.
```
public void withdraw(double amount)
{
    if (amount > balance    // (AB students)
    {
        throw new IllegalArgumentException();
    }
    double newBalance = balance - amount;
    balance = newBalance;
}
```

1b.   `// Precondition: 0 < amount and amount <= balance`

1c. Test cases would include typical values, boundary values, and degenerate values. For the specific example given, test values would include:
- typical test values: 1, 499
- boundary values: 0, 500
- degenerate test values : −1, 501

Specific numerical answers may vary.

■ Chapter 9

Answers to Multiple Choice Questions

1.	d	6.	c
2.	b	7.	a
3.	c	8.	d
4.	e	9.	b
5.	c	10.	c

Answers to Free Response

1a.   `public class SkiJumper implements Flier, Athlete, Comparable`

1b.
```
public int compareTo(Object obj)
{
    SkiJumper temp = (SkiJumper)obj;
    if (numberOfJumps < temp.numberOfJumps)
        return -1;
    if (numberOfJumps == temp.numberOfJumps)
        return 0;
    return -1;
}
```

```java
2.      public int compareTo(Object obj)
        {
            Purse temp = (Purse)obj;
            if (getTotal() < temp.getTotal())
                return -1;
            if (getTotal() > temp.getTotal())
                return 1;
            return 0;
        }
```

■ Chapter 10

Answers to Multiple Choice Questions

1.	c	6. a
2.	d	7. e
3.	d	8. e
4.	d	9. b
5.	e	10. e

Answers to Free Response

```java
1a.     public Person(String fName, String lName)
        {
            firstName = fName;
            lastName = lName;
            emailAddress = firstName.substring(0, 1);
            if (lastName.length() >= 5)
            {
                emailAddress += lastName.substring(0, 5);
                // Substring expression would throw a
                // StringIndexOutOfBoundsException if the
                // length of lastName is less than 5.
            }
            else
            {
                emailAddress += lastName.substring(0, lastName.length());
                // for short last names
            }
            emailAddress += "@ccj.com";
        }
```

1b.
```java
public class Student extends Person
{
    private static int lastIDAssigned = 20030;

    public Student(String fName, String lName)
    {
        super(fName,lName);
        gpa = 0;
        numberOfCredits = 0;
        lastIDAssigned++;
        studentID = lastIDAssigned;
        System.out.println(getName() + " " + getEmailAddress() + " "
            + studentID);
    }

    private double gpa;
    private double numberOfCredits;
    private int studentID;
}
```

1c.
```java
public String toString()
{
    return ("name = " + firstName()+ " " + lastName +
        "\nemail address = " + emailAddress);
}
```

1d.
```java
public String toString()
{
    String s = super.toString();
    return s + "\ngpa = " + gpa +
        "\nnumberOfCredits = " + numberOfCredits +
        "\nid = " + studentID;
}
```

1e.   `public class Student extends Person implements Comparable`

1f.
```java
public int compareTo (Object other)
{
    Student temp = (Student)other;
    if (gpa < temp.gpa) return -1;
    if (gpa > temp.gpa) return 1;
    return 0;
}
```

2.
```java
public class Marathoner extends Runner
{
    public Marathoner(String fName, String lName)
    {
        super(fName, lName);
    }
```

```
public void race(double raceLength)
{
    if (raceLength > 10)
    {
        super.race(raceLength);
    }
    else
    {
        double trainingTime = 8.5 * raceLength / 60;
        train(trainingTime);
    }
}
}
```

3. Hierarchy Diagram

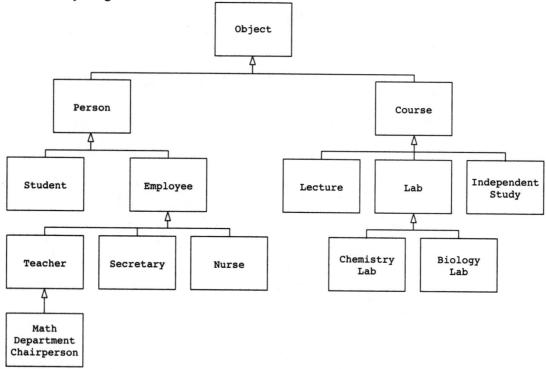

Note: MathDepartmentChairperson may be subclass of Employee. Nurse may be subclass of Teacher.

■ Chapter 11

Answers to Multiple Choice Questions

1. d
2. d
3. e
4. b
5. b
6. a
7. b
8. e
9. b

10. d
11. b
12. d
13. d
14. b
15. d
16. d
17. c

Answers to Free Response

1a.
```
// Constructor
// Precondition: numLetters > 0; numLetters is the length
// of the strings to be added to availableFoos.
public FooList(int numLetters)
{
    fooLength = numLetters;
    availableFoos = new ArrayList();
}
```

1b.
```
// Returns true if key is in FooList's list of strings, false
// otherwise
public boolean found(String key)
{
    for (int i = 0; i < availableFoos.size(); i++)
    {
        String temp = (String)availableFoos.get(i);
        if (temp.equals(key))
            return true;
    }
    return false;
}
```

Alternate Iterator Solution (AB only)

```
public boolean found(String key)
{
    Iterator iter = possibleFoos.iterator();
    while (iter.hasNext())
    {
        String temp = (String)iter.next();
        if (temp.equals(key))
            return true;
    }
    return false;
}
```

1c.
```java
// Adds the string, entry, to FooList's list if it is the correct
// length and not already in the list. If the string is already
// in the list or if the string is not the correct length, it is
// not added.
public void addFoo(String entry)
{
    if (entry.length() == fooLength && !found(entry))
    {
        availableFoos.add(entry);
    }
}
```

1d.
```java
// Removes and returns a random entry from FooList's list of
// strings.
public String removeRandomFoo()
{
    Random generator = new Random();
    int choice = generator.nextInt(availableFoos.size());
    String temp = (String)availableFoos.remove(choice);
    return temp;
}
```

2a.
```java
// Randomly fills this concentration board with tiles. The
// number of distinct tiles used on the board is size / 2.
// Any one tile image appears exactly twice.
// Precondition: number of positions on board is even,
// possibleTileValues contains at least size / 2
// elements
private void fillBoard()
{
    Random generator = new Random();
    for (int i = 0; i < size / 2; i++)
    {
        String word =
            (String)(possibleTileValues.removeRandomFoo());
        for (int j = 0; j < 2; j++)
        {
            int place = generator.nextInt(size);
            while (gameBoard[place] != null)
            {
                place = generator.nextInt(size);
            }
            gameBoard[place] = new Tile(word);
        }
    }
}
```

2b.
```
// Precondition: Tile in position p is face-down.
// Postcondition: Tile in position p is face-up.
public void lookAtTile(int p)
{
    gameBoard[p].turnFaceUp();
}
```

2c.
```
// Checks if the Tiles is pos1 and pos2 have the same image.
// If they do, the Tiles are turned face-up. If not, the Tiles are
// turned face-down.
// Precondition: gameBoard[pos1] is face-up,
// gameBoard[pos2] is face-up.
public void checkMatch(int pos1, int pos2)
{
    if (gameBoard[pos1].equals(gameBoard[pos2]))
    {
        numberOfTilesFaceUp += 2;
    }
    else
    {
        gameBoard[pos1].turnFaceDown();
        gameBoard[pos2].turnFaceDown();
    }
}
```

2d.
```
// Board is printed for the player. If the Tile is turned face-up,
// the image is printed. If the Tile is turned face-down, the Tile
// position is printed.
public void printBoard()
{
    final int PADDING = 3;   // spacing of tiles
    int spacing = possibleTileValues.getFooLength() + PADDING;
    for (int i = 0; i < size; i++)
    {
        if (gameBoard[i].isFaceUp())
        {
            String temp = gameBoard[i].showFace();
            System.out.print(format(temp, spacing));
        }
        else
        {
            System.out.print(format(i, spacing));
        }
        if (i % rowLength == rowLength - 1)
            System.out.println("\n");
    }
}
```

3a.
```
// Randomly fills this concentration board with tiles. The
// number of distinct tiles used on the board is size / 2.
// Any one tile image appears exactly twice.
// Precondition : number of positions on board is even,
// possibleTileValues contains at least size / 2 elements
private void fillBoard()
{
    Random generator = new Random();
    for (int i = 0; i < size / 2; i++)
    {
        String word =
            (String) (possibleTileValues.removeRandomFoo());
        for (int j = 0; j < 2; j++)
        {
            int row = generator.nextInt(rowLength);
            int col = generator.nextInt(rowLength);
            while (gameBoard[row][col] != null)
            {
                row = generator.nextInt(rowLength);
                col = generator.nextInt(rowLength);
            }
            gameBoard[row][col] = new Tile(word);
        }
    }
}
```

3b.
```
// Board is printed for the player. If the Tile is turned face-up,
// the image is printed. If the Tile is turned face-down, the Tile
// position is printed.
public void printBoard()
{
    final int PADDING = 8;    // for proper spacing of tiles
    int spaces = possibleTileValues.getFooLength() + PADDING;
    for (int row = 0; row < rowLength; row++)
    {
        for (int col = 0; col < rowLength; col++)
        {
            if (gameBoard[row][col].isFaceUp())
            {
                String temp = gameBoard[row][col].showFace();
                System.out.print(format(temp, spaces));
            }
            else
            {
                String temp = "[" + row + "][" + col + "]";
                System.out.print(format(temp, spaces));
            }
        }
        System.out.println();
    }
}
```

■ Chapter 12

Answers to Multiple Choice Questions

1.	b	6.	e
2.	a	7.	b
3.	d	8.	c
4.	c	9.	a
5.	d	10.	b

Answers to Free Response

1.
```java
public class Teacher extends Person
{
    public Teacher(String first, String last, double money)
    {
        super(first,last);
        if (money <= 0)
        {
            throw new IllegalStateException("Salary must be a
                positive number.");
        }
        salary = money;
    }

    public void getRaise(double more)
    {
        if (more <= 0)
        {
            throw new IllegalArgumentException("Raise must be a
                positive number.");
        }
        salary += more;
    }

    private double salary;
}
```

2a.
```java
public CoinTosser()
{
    generator = new Random();
    tossesRemaining = generator.nextInt(21);
}
```

2b.
```java
private int tossesRemaining;
private Random generator;
```

2c.
```java
public boolean hasMoreTosses()
{
    return (tossesRemaining > 0);
}
```

2d.
```java
public String nextToss()
{
    if (hasMoreTosses())
    {
        tossesRemaining--;
        int toss = generator.nextInt(2);
        if (toss == 1)
            return "HEADS";
        else
            return "TAILS";
    }
    else    // (AB only)
        throw new NoSuchElementException("No tosses remaining.");
}
```

■ Chapter 13

Multiple Choice Questions

1. a   6. e
2. c   7. a
3. a   8. d
4. d   9. b
5. e   10. a

Answers to Free Response

1a.
```java
public class Car
{
    public Car(String carMake, int yearMade, double howMuch,
            double miles)
    {
        make = carMake;
        year = yearMade;
        mileage = miles;
        price = 0;
    }

    public void setPrice(double howMuch)
    {
        price = howMuch;
    {

    public void addMiles(double milesDriven)
    {
        mileage += milesDriven;
    }
```

```
   public double getPrice()
   {
      return price;
   }

   public String getMake()
   {
      return make;
   }

   public int getYear()
   {
      return year;
   }

   public double getMiles()
   {
      return mileage;
   }

   public void printCarInfo()
   {
      System.out.println(getYear() + " " + getMake()
            + " with " + getMiles() + " miles"
            + " costs $" + getPrice());

   private String make;
   private int year;
   private double price;
   private double mileage;
}
```

1b.
```
   public void addCar(Car aNewCar)
   {
      if (numberOfCars < MAX_CARS)
      {
         lot[numberOfCars] = aNewCar;
         numberOfCars++;
      }
      else   // AB students
      {
         throw new IllegalStateException("No room in lot.");
      }
   }
```

1c.
```
   public void printCarsInLot()
   {
      for (int i = 0; i < numberOfCars; i++)
      {
         lot[i].printCarInfo();
      }
   }
```

2a. (Note: Variable and method names may be different but should be descriptive.)

```
Class name: Employee
Methods:
    public Employee(String fName, String lName)    // Constructor
    public String getName()    // needed to return name of employee
            with highest total sales
    public double getCommission()
    public double getTotalSales()    // needed to find employee with
            highest total sales
    public int getId()    // needed to remove employee from company
    public void addSale(double money)

Instance fields:
    private String firstName;
    private String lastName;
    private int idNumber;
    private double totalSales;

Static variables:
    int nextAvailableId;
```

```
Class name: Company
Methods:
    public Company()    // Constructor
    public void addEmployee(Employee worker)
    public void removeEmployee(int idNum)
    public Employee getHigh()

Instance fields:
    private ArrayList realEstateCompany;

// No static variables needed
```

2b. (Note: Variable names may be different but should be descriptive and consistent with part a.)

```
public class Employee
{
    private static int nextAvailableId = 0;

    Employee(String fName, String lName)
    {
        firstName = fName;
        lastName = lName;
        nextAvailableId++;
        idNumber = nextAvailableId;
        totalSales = 0;
    }
}
```

2c. (Note: Variable names may be different but should be descriptive and consistent with part a.)

```
public class Company
{
   public Company()
   {
      realEstateCompany = new ArrayList();
   }

   private ArrayList realEstateCompany;
}
```

3a. ComputerPlayer *is-a* Player
HumanPlayer *is-a* Player
NimGame *has-a* HumanPlayer
NimGame *has-a* ComputerPlayer
NimGame *has-a* NimPile

3b. NimGame class

```
public class NimGame
{
   // Constructs game. Creates players and pile of marbles.
   public NimGame(int low, int high) {...}

   // Plays game.
   public void playNim() {...}

   private HumanPlayer human;
   private NimPile pile;
   private Player computer;
}
```

NimPile class

```
public class NimPile
{
   // Constructs marble pile for Nim with a random number of
   // marbles between a (inclusive) and b (exclusive).
   public NimPile(int a, int b) {...}

   // Returns number of marbles in pile.
   public int getMarbles() {...}

   // n <= numMarblesInPile
   public void takeMarbles(int n){...}

   private int numMarblesInPile;
}
```

Player class

```
public class Player
{
    // Constructor.
    public Player(String aName) {...}

    // Generic turn ... stupid player's strategy.
    public int takeTurn(NimPile pile) {...}

    // Returns name
    public String getName() {...}

    private String name;
}
```

SmartPlayer class

```
public class SmartPlayer extends Player
{
    public SmartPlayer(String n) {...}

    // Takes marbles using "smart" algorithm.
    public int takeTurn(NimPile pile) {...}
}
```

HumanPlayer class

```
public class HumanPlayer extends Player
{
    public HumanPlayer(String n) {...}

    // Human decides the number of marbles to take.
    public int takeTurn(NimPile pile) {...}
}
```

3c. NimGame class

```
public class NimGame
{
    // Constructs game. Creates players and pile of marbles.
    public NimGame(int low, int high)
    {
        System.out.print("What is the human player's name?");
        String nm = Utilities.readWord();
        human = new HumanPlayer(nm);
        boolean isStupid = (Utilities.getRandNumber(0, 2) == 1);
        String computerName = "ROBO COMPUTER";
        if (isStupid)
            computer = new Player(computerName);
        else
            computer = new SmartPlayer(computerName);
        pile = new NimPile(low, high);
    }
```

```java
    // Plays game.
    public void playNim()
    {
        boolean computerHasTurn =
                (Utilities.getRandNumber(0, 2) == 1);
        if (computerHasTurn)
            System.out.println(computer.getName() + " goes first!");
        else
            System.out.println(human.getName() + " goes first!");

        while (pile.getMarbles() > 1)
        {
            System.out.println("\nMarbles in pile: " +
                    pile.getMarbles());
            if (computerHasTurn)
            {
                int n = computer.takeTurn(pile);
                System.out.println(computer.getName() + " takes " + n
                    + " marbles");
            }
            else
            {
                human.takeTurn(pile);
            }
            computerHasTurn = !computerHasTurn;

        }
        if (computerHasTurn)
            System.out.println("Congratulations! You won!");
        else
            System.out.println("Sorry, you lost.");

    }
    private HumanPlayer human;
    private NimPile pile;
    private Player computer;
}
```

NimPile class

```java
public class NimPile
{
    // Constructs marble pile for Nim.
    public NimPile(int a, int b)
    {
        numMarblesInPile = Utilities.getRandNumber(a, b);
    }

    // Returns number of marbles in pile.
    public int getMarbles()
    {
        return numMarblesInPile;
    }
```

```
      // n <= numMarblesInPile
      public void takeMarbles(int n)
      {
         numMarblesInPile -= n;
      }

      private int numMarblesInPile;
   }
```

Player class

```
   public class Player
   {
      // Constructor.
      public Player(String aName)
      {
         name = aName;
       }

      // Generic turn...stupid player's strategy.
      public int takeTurn(NimPile pile)
      {
         int n = Utilities.getRandNumber(1, pile.getMarbles() / 2);
         pile.takeMarbles(n);
         return n;
      }

      // Returns name.
      public String getName()
      {
         return name;
      }

      private String name;
   }
```

SmartPlayer class

```
   import java.util.Random;
   public class SmartPlayer extends Player
   {
      public SmartPlayer(String n)
      {
         super(n);
      }

      // Takes marbles using "smart" algorithm.
      public int takeTurn(NimPile pile)
      {
         int marbles = pile.getMarbles();
         int p = Utilities.largestPowerOfTwoMinusOneBelow(marbles);
         int n = marbles - p;
         pile.takeMarbles(n);
```

```
                return n;
            }
        }
```

HumanPlayer class

```
    public class HumanPlayer extends Player
    {
        public HumanPlayer(String n)
        {
            super(n);
        }

        public int takeTurn(NimPile pile)
        {
            int n;
            do
            {
                System.out.println("How many marbles do you take?");
                n = Utilities.readInt();
            }
            while (n <= 0 || n > pile.getMarbles() / 2);
            pile.takeMarbles(n);
            return n;
        }
    }
```

■ Chapter 14

Answers to Multiple Choice Questions

1. e
2. b
3. c
4. b
5. c

6. d
7. c
8. d
9. a
10. d

Answers to Free Response

```
1.   public static int gcd(int num1, int  num2)
     {
         if (num2 == 0)
             return num1;
         else
             return gcd(num2, num1 % num2);
     }
```

2a.
```
public double triangleArea(Point p1, Point p2, Point p3)
{
    double x1 = p1.getX();
    double y1 = p1.getY();
    double x2 = p2.getX();
    double y2 = p2.getY();
    double x3 = p3.getX();
    double y3 = p3.getY();

    double area = Math.abs((x1 * y2)
            + (x2 * y3)
            + (x3 * y1)
            - (y1 * x2)
            - (y2 * x3)
            - (y3 * x1))
            / 2;
    return area;
}
```

2b.
```
public double getArea()
{
    if (corners.size() < 3) return 0;

    Point p1 = (Point)corners.get(0);
    Point p2 = (Point)corners.get(1);
    Point p3 = (Point)corners.get(2);
    double area = triangleArea(p1, p2, p3);

    Polygon remainder = new Polygon();
    remainder.add(p1);
    for (int i = 3; i < corners.size(); i++)
        remainder.add((Point)corners.get(i));
    remainder.add(p2);
    return area + remainder.getArea();
}
```

Chapter 15

Answers to Multiple Choice Questions

1. e
2. d
3. b
4. d
5. a

6. e
7. d
8. d
9. b
10. c

Answers to Free Response

1a.
```java
private String sortWord()
{
    String s = "";
    for (int i = 0; i < originalWord.length(); i++)
    {
        int pos = i - 1;
        String wordLetter = originalWord.substring(i, i + 1);
        while (pos >= 0
                && wordLetter.compareTo(s.substring(pos, pos + 1))
                < 0)
        {
            pos--;
        }
        s = s.substring(0, pos + 1)
                + wordLetter + s.substring(pos + 1);
    }
    return s;
}
```

1b.
```java
public boolean checkAnagram(Word aWord, Word anotherWord)
{
    return
        (anotherWord.getSorted().equals(aWord.getSorted()));
}
```

1c.
```java
public void printAnagrams(String key)
{
    Word newWord = new Word(key);
    for (int i = 0; i < wordList.size(); i++)
    {
        Word temp = (Word)wordList.get(i);
        if (checkAnagram(newWord, temp))
        {
            System.out.println(temp.getWord());
        }
    }
}
```

2a.
```java
public int compareTo(Object obj)
{
    String fullName = getName();
    Person other = (Person)obj;
    String otherFullName = other.getName();
    if(fullName.compareTo(otherFullName) < 0) return -1;
    if(fullName.compareTo(otherFullName) == 0) return 0;
    return 1;
}
```

2b.
```
    private int minimumPosition(int from)
    {
        int minPos = from;
        for (int i = from + 1; i < list.size(); i++)
        {
            Person ithPerson = (Person)(list.get(i));
            Person minPerson = (Person)(list.get(minPos));
            if (ithPerson.compareTo(minPerson) < 0)
                minPos = i;
        }
        return minPos;
    }
```

2c.
```
    private int minimumEmailPosition(int from)
    {
        int minPos = from;
        Comparator comp = new PersonComparator();
        for (int i = from + 1; i < list.size(); i++)
        {
            Person ithPerson = (Person)(list.get(i));
            Person minPerson = (Person)(list.get(minPos));
            if (comp.compare(ithPerson, minPerson) < 0)
                minPos = i;
        }
        return minPos;
    }
```

■ Chapter 16

Answers to Multiple Choice Questions

1. b	11. a
2. d	12. d
3. d	13. e
4. e	14. c
5. e	15. d
6. e	16. d
7. d	17. b
8. b	18. a
9. b	19. d
10. a	20. c

Answers to Free Response

1a. The constructor.

1b.
```
    public ListNode getPrevious();
    public void setPrevious(DLListNode theNewPrevious);
```

1c.
```
public DLListNode(Object initValue, ListNode initNext, ListNode
      initPrev)
{
   super(initValue, initNext);
   previous = initPrev;
}
```

1d.

Operation	Doubly Linked List
`addFirst`	$O(1)$
`addLast`	$O(1)$
`removeLast`	$O(1)$
`removeFirst`	$O(1)$
`isEmpty`	$O(1)$
Linear Traversal	$O(n)$
Random Access	$O(n)$

1e.
```
public DLListNode search(Object key)
{
   DLListNode temp = first;
   while (temp != null && !temp.getValue()).equals(key))
   {
      temp = (DLListNode)temp.getNext();
   }
   return temp;
}
```

1f.
```
public void removeOne(Object key)
{
   DLListNode temp = search(key);
   if (temp == null)   // Key isn't in list.
      return;
   if (temp == first)   // Is it the first node?
   {
      if (temp == last)   // Is it the only node?
         last = null;
      first = (DLListNode)first.getNext();
      if (first != null)
         first.setPrevious(null);
      return;
   }

   if (temp.getNext() == null)   // Deleting last node.
   {
      DLListNode hold = temp.getPrevious();
      hold.setNext(null);
      return;
   }
```

```
        // Deleting a middle node.
        DLListNode hold = temp.getPrevious();
        hold.setNext(temp.getNext());
        hold = (DLListNode)temp.getNext();
        hold.setPrevious(temp.getPrevious());
        return;
    }
```

1g.
```
    public void removeAll(Object key)
    {
        while (search(key) != null)
        {
            removeOne(key);
        }
    }
```

2a.
```
    public static void displayBinary(int decimalNum)
    {
        final int BASE = 2;
        IntStack stck = new IntStack();

        while (decimalNum != 0)
        {
            int remainder = decimalNum % BASE;
            stck.push(new Integer(remainder));
            decimalNum /= BASE;
        }
        while (!stck.isEmpty())
        {
            Integer num = (Integer)stck.pop();
            System.out.print(num);
        }
    }
```

2b.
```
    public static void getOtherBase(int num, int base)
    {
        IntStack stck = new IntStack();

        while (num != 0)
        {
            int remainder = num % base;
            stck.push(new Integer(remainder));
            num /= base;
        }

        while (!stck.isEmpty())
        {
            Integer number = (Integer)stck.pop();
            int numValue = number.intValue();
            String alpha = "ABCDEF";
            if (numValue = 10)
            {
```

```
            int converted = numValue % 10;
            System.out.print(alpha.substring(converted, converted +
                1));
        }
        else
        {
            System.out.print(numValue);
        }
    }
}
```

3a. The appropriate data structure is a linked list. Arrays are not a good choice because the actual number of windows is not known. Array lists are inefficient because of the insertions and deletions to the top. Quite a bit of shifting would necessary. Stacks add and delete from one end so `cycle` would not be an appropriate operation for a stack. Queues add to one end and delete from the other end. The `windowManager` operation of `add` and `remove` both refer to the same end. Therefore a queue is not an appropriate choice.

3b.
```
public void add(Window w)
{
    windows.addFirst(w);
}
```

3c.
```
public void remove()
{
    windows.removeFirst();
}
```

3d.
```
public void cycle()
{
    if (windows.size() == 0) return;
    Window w = (Window)windows.removeFirst();
    windows.addLast(w);
}
```

3e.
```
public void print()
{
    Iterator iter = windows.iterator();
    while (iter.hasNext())
        System.out.println(iter.next());
    System.out.println();
}
```

Note: Knowledge of `java.util.awt.Rectangle` is not tested on the AP Exam.

■ Chapter 17

Answers to Multiple Choice Questions

1.	e	11.	c
2.	d	12.	a
3.	e	13.	d
4.	c	14.	a
5.	a	15.	c
6.	c	16.	d
7.	e	17.	b
8.	e	18.	b
9.	c	19.	e
10.	c	20.	b

Answers to Free Response

1a.
```java
public Set setIntersection(Set set2)
{
    Set set3 = new TreeSet();
    Iterator iter =  iterator();
    while (iter.hasNext())
    {
        Object temp =  iter.next();
        if (set2.contains(temp))
        {
            set3.add(temp);
        }
    }
    return set3;
}
```

1b.
```java
public Set setUnion(Set set2)
{
    Set set3 = new TreeSet();
    Iterator iter = iterator();
    while (iter.hasNext())
    {
        set3.add(iter.next());
    }
    iter = set2.iterator();
    while (iter.hasNext())
    {
        set3.add(iter.next());
    }
    return set3;
}
```

1c.
```
public Set setDifference(Set set2)
{
    Set set3 = new TreeSet();
    Iterator iter = iterator();
    while (iter.hasNext())
    {
        Object temp = iter.next();
        if (!(set2.contains(temp)))
            set3.add(temp);
    }
    return set3;
}
```

1d.
```
public boolean isSubset(Set set2)
{
    Iterator iter = set2.iterator();
    while (iter.hasNext())
    {
        if (!(contains(iter.next())))
            return false;
    }
    return true;
}
```

1e.
```
public boolean isProperSubset(Set set2)
{
    if (!(isSubset(set2)))
        return false;
    else if (size() != set2.size())
        return true;
    else
        return false;
}
```

2a.
```
public void createConcordance(String fileName)
{
    // open infile (fileName) for reading
    while ( !(inFile.eof()))
    {
        String word = inFile.readWord();   // Reads word from file

        if (!(word == null))
        {
            Integer temp = (Integer)concord.get(word);
            if (temp == null)
            {
                concord.put(word, new Integer(1));
            }
            else
```

```
        {
            int value = temp.intValue();
            value++;
            concord.put(word, new Integer(value));
        }
      }
    }
  }
```

2b.   public void printConcordance()
```
        {
            Set concordSet = concord.keySet();
            Iterator iter = concordSet.iterator();
            while (iter.hasNext())
            {
                Object word = iter.next();
                System.out.print(word + " ");
                System.out.println("occurs " +  concord.get(word) +
                    " time(s).");
            }
        }
```

2c. A method similar to `printConcordance` would have the iterator traverse the set created by the `TreeMap`'s `keySet` method to obtain the word and its frequency. A `WordFreq` class would be defined to have instance fields that hold word-frequency pairs. With each move of the iterator, a new `WordFreq` object would be instantiated and its two instance fields would be set. The `WordFreq` objects would then be inserted into one of the following data structures.

- A binary search tree implemented so that duplicates are possible according to the frequency. An inorder traversal would give the required results. Insertion of n `WordFrequency` objects is $O(n \log(n))$. Traversal is $O(n)$.
- A priority queue implemented so that duplicates are possible and where the priority is the frequency. Executing `removeMin` repeatedly would give the desired results. Insertion is $O(n \log(n))$. Traversal is $O(n)$.
- An ordered linked list of nodes whose information field is the `WordFreq` object. Nodes would be inserted in order according to the frequency. A linear traversal of the linked list would give the required results. Insertion is $O(n^2)$ ($O(n)$ for each of n elements). Traversal is $O(n)$.
- An ordered `ArrayList` of `WordFreq` objects ordered by frequency. Insertion is $O(n^2)$. Traversal is $O(n)$.

The ones that won't work:
- A stack cannot maintain frequency order.
- A queue cannot maintain frequency order.
- A hash set and hash map do not maintain order.
- A tree set and tree map cannot have duplicate keys.